STUDY GUIDE

to accompany

essential foundations of
ECONOMICS
Fourth Edition

ROBIN BADE ▪ MICHAEL PARKIN

MARK RUSH
University of Florida

Boston San Francisco New York
London Toronto Sydney Tokyo Singapore Madrid
Mexico City Munich Paris Cape Town Hong Kong Montreal

ISBN-13   978-0-321-53062-2
ISBN-10   0-321-53062-4

3 4 5 6 OPM 11 10 09 08

Table of Contents

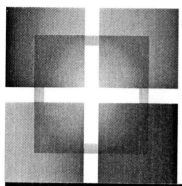

Your Complete Learning Package

■ The Complete Package

Your *Foundations of Economics* package consists of:

- Textbook
- Study Guide
- MyEconLab Access Kit

MyEconLab is a powerful and tightly integrated homework and tutorial system that puts you in control of your own learning. MyEconLab includes

- Practice Tests that let you test your understanding and identify where you need to concentrate your studying
- A personalized Study Plan that evaluates your test results and provides further practice
- Tutorial instruction that will guide you through the areas you have difficulty with
- eText—the entire textbook in Flash format with animated figures accompanied by audio explanations prepared by us and with hyperlinks to all the other components of the Web site
- Economics in the News updated daily during the school year
- Online "Office Hours"—ask a question via e-mail, and one of us will respond within 24 hours!
- Economic links—links to sites that keep you up to date with what's going on in the economy and that enable you to work end-of-chapter Web Exercises

Each new textbook arrives with a MyEconLab Student Access Card that unlocks protected areas of the Web site.

■ Checklist and Checkpoints: The Glue That Holds Your Tools Together

Each chapter of your textbook opens with a Chapter Checklist that tells you what you'll be able to do when you've completed the chapter. The number of tasks varies from two to five and most often is three or four. Begin by reviewing this list thoughtfully and get a good sense of what you are about to learn.

Each part of a chapter in the textbook, Study Guide, and MyEconLab Web site is linked directly to a Checklist item to enable you to know exactly what you're studying and how it will enable you to accomplish your learning objective.

Each part of a chapter in the textbook ends with a Checkpoint—a page that offers you a Practice Problem to test your understanding of the key ideas of the part, a worked and illustrated solution to the Practice Problem, and a further (parallel) exercise. The Checkpoints enable you to review material when it's fresh in your mind—the most effective and productive time to do so. The Checkpoints guide you through the material in a step-by-step approach that takes the guesswork out of learning. The Study Guide reinforces each Checkpoint by providing Additional Practice Problems. Use these if you're still not sure you understand the material or if you want to review before an exam.

The self-test questions in the Study Guide, the Study Plan Exercises on the MyEconLab Web site, and the chapter resources on the MyEconLab Web site are organized by Checkpoint so that you can maintain your focus as you work through the material.

■ Practice Makes Perfect

As you study, distinguish between *practice* and *self-test*. Practice is part of the learning process, learning by doing. Self-test is a check. It shows you where you need to go back and reinforce your understanding, and it helps you build confidence in your knowledge of the material.

The Checkpoint Practice Problems and Exercises, the end-of-chapter Exercises, and the Checkpoint Exercises in MyEconLab are designed for practice. The self-test questions in the Study Guide, the pre- and post-tests, and Study Plan Exercises in MyEconLab are designed to reveal your gaps in understanding and to target your final examination of the material.

■ Learn Your Learning Style

It is unlikely that you'll need to use all the tools that we've created all of the time. Try to discover how you learn best. Then exploit what you discover.

If you learn best by reading with a marker or pencil in your hand, you'll use the textbook and Study Guide more often than the other items. If you learn best by seeing the action, you'll often use the eText and MyEconLab tutorials. If you learn best by hearing, you'll use the eText audio explanations of the action in key figures. If you learn best by participating and acting, you'll often use the Study Plan Exercises.

■ Tell Us What Works for *You*

Please tell us the tools that you find most helpful. And tell us what you think we can improve. You can email us at robin@econ100.com or michael.parkin@uwo.ca, or use the Office Hours in your MyEconLab Web site.

Robin Bade
Michael Parkin
Ontario, Canada
December, 2007

Your Course and Your Study Guide

■ Introduction

My experience has taught me that what students want most from a study guide is help in mastering course material in order to do well on examinations. This Study Guide has been created to respond specifically to that demand. Using this Study Guide alone, however, is not enough to guarantee that you will earn an A or do well in your course. In order to help you overcome the problems and difficulties that most students encounter, I have some general advice on how to study, as well as some specific advice on how best to use this Study Guide.

Economics requires a different style of thinking than what you may encounter in other courses. Economists make extensive use of assumptions to break down complex problems into simple, analytically manageable parts. This analytical style, while ultimately not more demanding than the styles of thinking in other disciplines, feels unfamiliar to most students and requires practice. As a result, it is not as easy to do well in economics on the basis of your raw intelligence and high school knowledge as it is in many other courses. Many students who come to my office are frustrated and puzzled by the fact that they are getting A's and B's in their other courses but only a C or worse in economics. They have not recognized that economics is different and requires practice. In order to avoid a frustrating visit to your instructor after your first test, I suggest you do the following.

■ Don't rely solely on your high school economics.

If you took high school economics, you have seen the material on supply and demand which your instructor will lecture on in the first few weeks. Don't be lulled into feeling that the course will be easy. Your high school knowledge of economic concepts will be very useful, but it will not be enough to guarantee high scores on exams. Your college or university instructors will demand much more detailed knowledge of concepts and ask you to apply them in new circumstances.

■ Keep up with the course material on a weekly basis.

Skim or read the appropriate chapter in the textbook before your instructor lectures on it. In this initial reading, don't worry about details or arguments you can't quite follow — try to get a general understanding of the basic concepts and issues. You may be amazed at how your instructor's ability to teach improves when you come to class prepared. After the lecture, return to the book and read the material more thoroughly and completely. As soon as your instructor has finished covering a chapter, complete the corresponding Study Guide chapter. Avoid cramming the day before or even just the week before an exam. Because economics requires practice, cramming is an almost certain recipe for failure.

■ Keep a good set of lecture notes.

Good lecture notes are vital for focusing your studying. Your instructor will only lecture on a subset of topics from the textbook. The topics your instructor covers in a lecture should usually be given priority when studying. Also give priority to studying the figures and graphs covered in the lecture.

Instructors differ in their emphasis on lecture notes and the textbook, so ask early on in the course which is more important in reviewing for exams — lecture notes or the textbook. If your instructor answers that both are important, then ask the following, typical economic question: which will be more beneficial — spending an extra hour re-reading your lecture notes or an extra hour re-reading the textbook? This question assumes that you have read each textbook chapter twice (once before lecture for a general understanding, and then later for a thorough understanding); that you have prepared a good set of lecture notes; and that you have worked through all of the problems in the appropriate Study Guide chapters. By applying this style of analysis to the problem of efficiently allocating your study time, you are already beginning to think like an economist!

■ Use your instructor and/or teaching assistants for help.

When you have questions or problems with course material, come to the office to ask questions. Remember, you are paying for your education and instructors are there to help you learn. Don't be shy. The personal contact that comes from one-on-one tutoring is professionally gratifying for instructors as well as (hopefully) beneficial for you.

■ Form a study group.

A very useful way to motivate your studying and to learn economics is to discuss the course material and problems with other students. Explaining the answer to a question out loud is a very effective way of discovering how well you understand the question. When you answer a question only in your head, you often skip steps in the chain of reasoning without realizing it. When you are forced to explain your reasoning aloud, gaps and mistakes quickly appear, and you (with your fellow group members) can quickly correct your reasoning. The Exercises at the end of each textbook chapter are extremely good study group material. You might also get together after having worked the Study Guide problems, but before looking at the answers, and help each other solve unsolved problems.

■ Work old exams.

One of the most effective ways of studying is to work through exams your instructor has given in previous years. Old exams give you a feel for the style of question your instructor might ask, and give you the opportunity to get used to time pressure if you force yourself to do the exam in the allotted time. Studying from old exams is not cheating, as long as you have obtained a copy of the exam legally. Some institutions keep old exams in the library, others in the department. If there is a class web page, check there—many instructors now post old exams on their class web pages. Students who have previously taken the course are usually a good source as well. Remember, though, that old exams are a useful study aid only if you use them to understand the reasoning behind each question. If you simply memorize answers in the hopes that your instructor will repeat the identical question, you are likely to fail. From year to year, instructors routinely change the questions or change the numerical values for similar questions.

■ Use All Your Tools

The authors of your book, Robin Bade and Michael Parkin, have created a rich array of learning tools that they describe in the preceding section, "Your Complete Learning Package." Make sure that you read this section because it makes sense to use *all* your tools!

USING THE STUDY GUIDE

You should only attempt to complete a chapter in the Study Guide after you have read the corresponding textbook chapter and listened to your instructor lecture on the material. Each Study Guide chapter contains the following sections.

Chapter Checklist

This first section is a short summary of the key material. It is designed to focus you quickly and precisely on the core material that you must master. It is an excellent study aid for the night before an exam. Think of it as crib notes that will serve as a final check of the key concepts you have studied.

Additional Practice Problems

In each checkpoint in the textbook is at least one and generally more than one practice problem. These problems are extremely valuable because they help you grasp what you have just studied. In the Study Guide are additional Practice Problems. These Practice Problems either extend the Practice Problem in the text or cover another important topic from the Checkpoint. Although the answer is given to the additional Practice Problem, try to solve it on your own before reading the answer.

Following the additional Practice Problem is the Self Test section of the Study Guide. This section has fill in the blank, true or false, multiple choice, complete the graph, and short answer and numeric questions. The questions are designed to give you practice and to test skills and techniques you must master to do well on exams. Before I describe the parts of the Self Test section, here are some general tips that apply to all parts.

First, use a pencil to write your answers in the Study Guide so you have neat, complete pages from which to study and recall how you answered a question when the test approaches. Draw graphs wherever they are applicable. Some questions will ask explicitly for graphs; many others will not but will require a chain of reasoning that involves shifts

of curves on a graph. Always draw the graph. Don't try to work through the reasoning in your head — you are much more likely to make mistakes that way. Whenever you draw a graph, even in the margins of the Study Guide, label the axes. You might think that you can keep the labels in your head, but you will be confronting many different graphs with many different variables on the axes. Also, be sure to understand what the axes are measuring. After finishing Chapter 4, some students think that the vertical axis always shows the price. That belief is simply not so. Hence you must be careful with the axes. In other words, avoid confusion and label. As an added incentive, remember that on exams where graphs are required, instructors often will deduct points for unlabelled axes.

Do the Self Test questions as if they were real exam questions, which means do them without looking at the answers. This is the single most important tip I can give you about effectively using the Study Guide to improve your exam performance. Struggling for the answers to questions that you find difficult is one of the most effective ways to learn. The adage — no pain, no gain — applies well to studying. You will learn the most from right answers you had to struggle for and from your wrong answers and mistakes. Only after you have attempted all the questions should you look at the answers. When you finally do check the answers, be sure to understand where you went wrong and why the right answer is correct.

Fill in the Blanks

This section covers the material in the checkpoint and has blanks for you to complete. Often suggested phrases are given but sometimes there are no hints—in that case you are on your own! Well, not really, because the answers are given at the end of each Study Guide chapter. This section also can help you review for a test because, once completed, they serve as a *very* brief statement of the important points within the important points within the checkpoint.

True or False

Next are true or false questions. Some instructors use true or false questions on exams or quizzes, so these questions might prove very valuable. The answers to the questions are given at the end of the chapter. The answer also has a page reference to the textbook. If you missed the question or did not completely understand the answer, definitely turn to the textbook and study the topic so that you will not miss similar questions on your exams.

Multiple Choice

Many instructors use multiple choice questions on exams, so pay particular attention to these questions. Similar to the true or false questions, the answers are given at the end of the Study Guide chapter and each answer references the relevant page in the text. If you had any difficulty with a question, use this page reference to look up the topic and then study it to remove this potential weakness.

Complete the Graph

The complete the graph questions allow you to practice using one of economists' major tools, graphs. If you will have essay questions on your exams, it is an extremely safe bet that you will be expected to use graphs on at least some of the questions. This section is designed to ensure that you are well prepared to handle these questions. Use the graph in the Study Guide to answer the questions. Although the answer is given at the end of the Study Guide chapter, do *not* look at the answer before you attempt to solve the problem. It is much too easy to deceive yourself into thinking you understand the answer when you simply look at the question and then read the answer. Involve yourself in the material by answering the question and then looking at the answer. If you cannot answer the question or if you got the answer wrong, the Study Guide again has a reference to the relevant page number in the text. Use the text and study the material!

Short Answer and Numeric Questions

The last set of questions are short answer and numeric questions. Short answer and numeric questions are classic exam questions, so pay attention to these questions. Approach them similarly to how you approach all the other questions: Answer them before you look at the answers in the back of the Study Guide. These questions are also excellent for use in a study group. If you and several friends are studying for an exam, you can use these questions to quiz your understanding. If you have disagreements about the correct answers, once again there are page references to the text so that you can settle these disagreements and be sure that everyone has a solid grasp of the point!

FINAL COMMENTS

This Study Guide combines the efforts of many talented individuals. For Chapters 1 through 13, the author of the Chapter Checklists and many of the additional Practice Problems and answers is Tom Meyer, from Rochester Community and Technical College. It was a pleasure to work with Tom; I always looked forward to his emails and the resulting conversations. For the remaining chapters, the authors of the Chapter Checklists and many of the additional Practice Problems and answers are Neil Garston, from California State University, at Los Angeles, and Tom Larson, also from California State University, at Los Angeles. It was a pleasure to work with these fine scholars.

For the multiple choice questions, we assembled a team of truly outstanding teachers:

- Ali Ataiifar, Delaware County Community College
- Diego Mendez-Carbajo, Illinois Wesleyan University
- William Mosher, Assumption College
- Cynthia Tori, Valdosta State University
- Nora Underwood, University of California, Davis

- Seemi Ahmad, Dutchess Community College
- Susan Bartlett, University of South Florida
- Jack Chambless, Valencia Community College
- Paul Harris, Camden County Community College
- William Mosher, Assumption College
- Terry Sutton, Southeast Missouri State University

I added a few multiple choice questions and wrote the fill in the blank, true or false, complete the graph, and short answer and numeric questions. I also served as an editor to assemble the material into the book before you.

The Study Guide and other supplements were checked for accuracy by a team of instructors. For a previous edition, the team included:

- David Bivin, Indiana University-Purdue University
- Geoffrey Black, Boise State University
- Jeffrey Davis, ITT Technical Institute
- Ken Long, New River Community College
- Barbara Wiens-Tuers, Penn State University, Altoona
- Joachim Zietz, Middle Tennessee State University
- Armand Zottola, Central CT State University
- Carol Conrad, Cerro Coso Community College
- Marie Duggan, Keene State University
- Steven Hickerson, Mankato State University
- Douglas Kinnear, Colorado State University
- Tony Lima, California State University, at Eastbay (Tony, I believe you were one of my instructors when I was an undergraduate—thanks for helping excite me about economics!)
- Michael Milligan, Front Range Community College

- Barbara Ross-Pfeiffer, Kapiolani Community College

Jeannie Shearer-Gillmore, University of Western Ontario, checked every word, every sentence, every paragraph, and every page of the first edition of this book and many of the words, sentences, paragraphs, and pages of the third edition. She made a huge number of corrections and comments. The easiest way to distinguish her work and mine is to determine if there is an error in a passage. If there is, it's my work; if there is not, it's her work.

Students who have used this book in earlier editions also have found errors that I did not catch. I think we owe these students a special thanks for their conscientious work and generous initiative to report the errors:

- Lisa Salazar-Rich, at Cal Poly Pomona
- Professor Tom McCaleb's class at Florida State University

Robin Bade and Michael Parkin, the authors of your book, also need thanks. Not only have they written such a superior book that it was easy to be enthusiastic about writing the Study Guide to accompany it, both Robin and Michael played a very hands-on role in creating this Study Guide. They corrected errors and made suggestions that vastly improved the Study Guide.

I want to thank my family: Susan, Tommy, Bobby, and Katie, who, respectively: allowed me to work all hours on this book; helped me master the intricacies of FTPing computer files; let me postpone working on our trains with him until after the book was concluded; and would run into my typing room to share her new discoveries. Thanks a lot!

Finally, I want to thank Butterscotch, Mik, Lucky, (and the late, beloved Snowball) and Pearl, who sometimes sat on my lap and sometimes sat next to the computer in a box peering out the window (and occasionally meowed) while I typed.

We (well, all of us except the cats) have tried to make the Study Guide as helpful and useful as possible. Undoubtedly I have made some mistakes; mistakes that you may see. If you find any, I, and following generations of students, would be grateful if you could point them out to me. At the end of my class at the University of Florida, when I ask my students for their advice, I point out to them that this advice won't help them at all because they have just completed the class. But comments they make will influence how future students are taught. Thus just as they owe a debt of gratitude for the comments and suggestions that I received from students before them, so too will students after them owe them an (unpaid and unpayable) debt. You are in the same situation. If you have questions, suggestions, or simply comments, let me know. My address follows, or you can reach me via e-mail at MARK.RUSH@CBA.UFL.EDU. Your input probably won't benefit you directly, but it will benefit following generations. And if you give me permission, I will note your name and school in following editions so that any younger siblings (or, years down the road, maybe even your children!) will see your name and offer up thanks.

Mark Rush
Economics Department
University of Florida
Gainesville, Florida 32611
December, 2007.

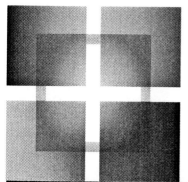

Getting Started

Chapter

1

CHAPTER CHECKLIST

Chapter 1 defines economics, discusses the three major questions of *what, how,* and *for whom*, covers the five core economic ideas that shape how economists think about issues, defines the differences between microeconomics and macroeconomics, and examines methods used by economists to study the economic world.

1 Define economics and explain the kinds of questions that economist try to answer.

Economic questions exist because of scarcity, the point that wants exceed the ability of resources to satisfy them. Economics is the social science that studies the choices that individuals, businesses, government, and entire societies make as they cope with scarcity and the incentives that influence these choices. Economics studies how choices wind up determining: *what* goods and services get produced?; *how* are goods and services produced?; and *for whom* are goods and services produced? Economics also studies when choices made in someone's self-interest also serve the social interest. For instance, are the self-interested choices made about globalization and international outsourcing, use of tropical rain forests, and social security also promote the social interest about these issues?

2 Explain the core ideas that define the economic way of thinking.

The five ideas that are the core of the economic approach: people make rational choices by comparing benefits and costs; cost is what you must give up to get something; benefit is what you gain when you get something and is measured by what you are willing to give up to get it; a rational choice is made on the margin; and choices respond to incentives. A rational choice uses the available resources to most effectively satisfy the wants of the person making the choice. The opportunity cost of an activity is the highest-valued alternative forgone. The benefit of a good or service is the gain or pleasure it brings and is measured by what someone is willing to give up to get the good or service. Making choices on the margin means comparing all the relevant alternatives systematically and incrementally to determine which is the best choice. A choice on the margin is one that adjusts a plan. The marginal cost is the cost of a one-unit increase in an activity; the marginal benefit is the gain from a one-unit increase in an activity. Rational choices compare the marginal benefit of an activity to its marginal cost. Microeconomics studies choices made by individuals and businesses. Macroeconomics studies the national economy and global economy. Statements about "what is" are positive statements; statements about "what should be" are normative statements. Economists are interested in positive statements about cause and effect but determining causality can be difficult because usually many things change simultaneously. So economists often use the idea of *ceteris paribus,* a Latin term that means "other things equal" and is used to sort out the effect of individual influence. Correlation is the tendency for the values of two variables to move together in a predictable way. Economics can be used by individuals, business, and governments as a policy tool to help them make better decisions.

CHECKPOINT 1.1

■ **Define economics and explain the kinds of questions that economist try to answer.**

Quick Review

- *Self-interest* The choices that people make that they think are the best for them.
- *Social interest* The choices that are best for society as a whole.

Additional Practice Problems 1.1

1. Which of the following headlines deals with *what, how,* and *for whom* questions?:
   a. A new government program is designed to provide high-quality school lunches for children from poorer families.
   b. Intel researchers discover a new chip-making technology.
   c. Regis Hairstyling sets a record for hairstylings in month of July

2. Which of the following headlines concern social interest and self interest?
   a. A new government program is designed to provide high-quality school lunches for children from poorer families.
   b. Intel researchers discover a new chip-making technology.
   c. Regis Hairstyling sets a record for hairstylings in month of July.

Solutions to Additional Practice Problems 1.1

1a. "More lunches" is a *what* question and "for children from poorer families" is a *for whom* question.

1b. "New chip-making technology" is a *how* question because it deals with how computer chips will be manufactured.

1c. "Record for hairstylings" is a *what* question because it notes that a record number of hairstylings have taken place in July.

2a. The decision to implement a new government program is a decision that is most likely made in the social interest. The self-interest of the government bureaucrat who

made the decision might also be involved, particularly if the bureaucrat also will help manage the program.

2b. Intel's decision to research new chip-making technology is made in Intel's self-interest.

2c. Regis's decision to offer hairstylings is made in its self-interest as are the decisions of the people who had their hair styled by Regis.

■ Self Test 1.1

Fill in the blanks

Economic questions arise because ____ (human wants; resources) exceed the ____ (human wants; resources) available to satisfy them. Faced with ____, people must make choices. Choices that are the best for the person who makes them are choices made in ____ (self-interest; social interest). Choices that are best for everyone as a whole are choices made in ____ (self-interest; social interest).

True or false

1. Faced with scarcity, we must make choices.
2. The question of *what* refers to what production method should a firm use?
3. The answers to the *what, how* and *for whom* questions depend on the interactions of the choices people, businesses, and governments make.
4. If Sam buys a pizza because she is hungry, her choice is made in the social interest.
5. Because everyone is a member of society, all choices made in self-interest are also in the social interest.

Multiple choice

1. The characteristic from which all economic problems arise is
   a. political decisions.
   b. providing a minimal standard of living for every person.
   c. how to make a profit.
   d. hunger.
   e. scarcity.

2. Scarcity results from the fact that
    a. people's wants exceed the resources available to satisfy them.
    b. not all goals are desirable.
    c. we cannot answer the major economic questions.
    d. choices made in self-interest are not always in the social interest.
    e. the population keeps growing.

3. To economists, scarcity means that
    a. limited wants cannot be satisfied by the unlimited resources.
    b. a person looking for work is not able to find work.
    c. the number of people without jobs rises when economic times are bad.
    d. there can never be answers to the *what, how* or *for whom* questions.
    e. unlimited wants cannot be satisfied by the limited resources.

4. The question "Should we produce video tapes or DVD discs?" is an example of a ____ question.
    a. what
    b. how
    c. for whom
    d. where
    e. why

5. The question "Should we produce houses using bricks or wood?" is an example of a ____ question.
    a. what
    b. how
    c. for whom
    d. where
    e. why

6. The question "Should economics majors or sociology majors earn more after they graduate?" is an example of a ____ question.
    a. what
    b. how
    c. for whom
    d. where
    e. why

7. If a decision is made and it is the best choice for society, the decision is said to be
    a. a valid economic choice.
    b. made in self-interest.
    c. made in social interest.
    d. consistent with scarcity.
    e. a want-maximizing choice.

Short answer and numeric questions
1. Will there ever come a time without scarcity?
2. If there was no scarcity, would there be a need for economics?
3. What are the three major questions answered by people's economic choices?
4. Why is the distinction between choices made in self-interest and choices made in social interest important?

CHECKPOINT 1.2

■ **Explain the core ideas that define the economic way of thinking.**

Quick Review

- *Opportunity cost* The opportunity cost of something is the best thing you must give up to get it.
- *Marginal cost* The opportunity cost that arises from a one-unit increase in an activity.
- *Marginal benefit* The benefit that arises from a one-unit increase in an activity.
- *Rational choice* A choice that uses the available resources to most effectively satisfy the wants of the person making the choice.
- *Positive statement* A positive statement tells what is currently understood about the way the world operates. We can test a positive statement.
- *Normative statement* A normative statement tells what ought to be. It depends on values. We cannot test a normative statement.

Practice Problems 1.2

1. What are the opportunity costs of using this *Study Guide*?

2. Kate usually plays tennis for two hours a week and her grade on each math test is usually 70 percent. Last week, after playing two hours of tennis, Kate thought long and hard about playing for another hour. She decided to play another hour of tennis and cut her study time by one additional hour. But the grade on last week's math test was 60 percent.
   a. What was Kate's opportunity cost of the third hour of tennis?
   b. Given that Kate made the decision to play the third hour of tennis, what can you conclude about the comparison of her marginal benefit and marginal cost of the second hour of tennis?
   c. Was Kate's decision to play the third hour of tennis rational?

3. Classify each of the following statements as positive or normative:
   a. There is too much poverty in the United States.
   b. An increase in the gas tax will cut pollution.
   c. Cuts to social security in the United States have been too deep.

Solutions to Additional Practice Problems 1.2

1. The opportunity cost is mainly the time spent using the *Study Guide* because that time could be devoted to other activities. The highest-valued activity forgone, be it studying for another class, or sleeping, or some other activity, which is forgone because of the time spent using the *Study Guide* is the opportunity cost. Once you have purchased this *Study Guide*, its price is *not* an opportunity cost of using the *Study Guide* because you have already paid the price. The price is, instead, a sunk cost.

2a. The opportunity cost of the third hour of tennis was the 10 percentage point drop on her math test grade because she cut her studying time by one hour to play an additional hour of tennis. If Kate had not played tennis for the third hour, she would have studied and her grade would not have dropped.

2b. Kate chose to play the third hour of tennis, so the marginal benefit of the third hour of tennis was greater than the marginal cost of the third hour. If the marginal benefit of the third hour of tennis was less than the marginal cost of the third hour, Kate would have chosen to study rather than play tennis.

2c. Even though her grade fell, Kate's choice used the available time to most effectively satisfy her wants because the marginal benefit of the third hour of playing tennis exceeded the marginal cost of the third hour. This was a choice made in her self-interest.

3a. A normative statement because it depends on the speaker's values and cannot be tested.

3b. A positive statement because it can be tested by increasing the gas tax and then measuring the change in pollution.

3c. A normative statement because it depends on the speaker's values (someone else might propose still deeper cuts) and cannot be tested.

■ Self Test 1.2

Fill in the blanks

A _____ choice uses the available resources to most effectively satisfy the wants of the person making the choice. The opportunity cost of an activity is _____ (all of the activities forgone; the highest-valued alternative forgone). The benefit of an activity is measured by what you _____ (are willing to; must) give up. We make a rational choice to do an activity if the marginal benefit of the activity _____ the marginal cost. (Macroeconomics; Microeconomics) _____ is the study of the choices of individuals and businesses, the interaction of these choices, and the influences that governments exert on these classes. A statement that tells "what is" is a _____ (positive; normative) statement. A statement that tells "what ought to be" is a _____ (positive; normative) statement. The term meaning "other things being equal" is _____ (*ceteris paribus; sunk cost*).

True or false

1. Instead of attending his microeconomics class for two hours, Jim can play a game of tennis or watch a movie. For Jim the opportunity cost of attending class is forgoing the game of tennis *and* watching the movie.

2. Marginal cost is what you gain when you get one more unit of something.

3. A rational choice involves comparing the marginal benefit of an action to its marginal cost.

4. A change in marginal benefit or a change in marginal cost brings a change in the incentives that we face and leads us to change our actions.

5. The subject of economics divides into two main parts, which are macroeconomics and microeconomics.

6. The statement, "When more people volunteer in their communities, crime rates decrease" is a positive statement.

Multiple choice

1. Jamie has enough money to buy either a Mountain Dew, or a Pepsi, or a bag of chips. He chooses to buy the Mountain Dew. The opportunity cost of the Mountain Dew is
   a. the Pepsi and the bag of chips.
   b. the Pepsi or the bag of chips, whichever the highest-valued alternative forgone.
   c. the Mountain Dew.
   d. the Pepsi because it is a drink, as is the Mountain Dew.
   e. zero because he enjoys the Mountain Dew.

2. The benefit of an activity is
   a. purely objective and measured in dollars.
   b. the gain or pleasure that it brings.
   c. the value of its sunk cost.
   d. measured by what must be given up to get one more unit of the activity.
   e. not measurable on the margin.

3. The cost of a one-unit increase in an activity
   a. is the total one-unit cost.
   b. is called the marginal cost.
   c. decreases as you do more of the activity.
   d. is called the marginal benefit/cost.
   e. is called the sunk cost.

4. The marginal benefit of an activity is
   i. the benefit from a one-unit increase in the activity.
   ii. the benefit of a small, unimportant activity.
   iii. measured by what the person is willing to give up to get one additional unit of the activity.
   a. i only.
   b. ii only.
   c. iii only.
   d. i and iii.
   e. ii and iii.

5. If the marginal benefit of the next slice of pizza exceeds the marginal cost, you will
   a. eat the slice of pizza.
   b. not eat the slice of pizza.
   c. be unable to choose between eating or not eating.
   d. eat half the slice.
   e. More information is needed about how much the marginal benefit exceeds the marginal cost to determine if you will or will not eat the slice.

6. When people make rational choices, they
   a. behave selfishly.
   b. do not consider their emotions.
   c. weigh the costs and benefits of their options and act to satisfy their wants.
   d. necessarily make a decision in the social interest.
   e. are necessarily making the best decision.

7. Which of the following is a microeconomic issue?
   a. Why has unemployment risen nation-wide?
   b. Why has economic growth been rapid in China?
   c. What is the impact on the quantity of Pepsi purchased if consumers' tastes change in favor of non-carbonated drinks?
   d. Why is the average income lower in Africa than in Latin America?
   e. Why did overall production within the United States increase last year?

8. A positive statement
   a. must always be right.
   b. cannot be tested.
   c. can be tested against the facts.
   d. depends on someone's value judgment.
   e. cannot be negative.

9. Which of the following is an example of a normative statement?
   a. If cars become more expensive, fewer people will buy them.
   b. Car prices should be affordable.
   c. If wages increase, firms will fire some workers.
   d. Fewer people die in larger cars than in smaller cars.
   e. Cars emit pollution.

10. The Latin term *ceteris paribus* means
    a. after this, therefore because of this.
    b. other things being equal.
    c. what is correct for the part is not correct for the whole.
    d. on the margin.
    e. when one variable increases, the other variable decreases.

Short answer and numeric questions

1. What is an opportunity cost?

2. You have $12 and can buy a pizza, a movie on a DVD, or a package of CD-Rs. You decide to buy the pizza and think that if you hadn't been so hungry, you would have purchased the DVD. What is the opportunity cost of your pizza?

3. What is a sunk cost?

4. What is benefit and how is it measured?

5. What is a marginal cost? A marginal benefit? How do they relate to rational choice?

6. Explain the difference between microeconomics and macroeconomics.

7. Becky is writing an essay about the law that requires all passengers in a car to use a seat belt and its effectiveness. What might be a positive statement and a normative statement that she will include in her essay?

SELF TEST ANSWERS

■ CHECKPOINT 1.1

Fill in the blanks

Economic questions arise because <u>human wants</u> exceed the <u>resources</u> available to satisfy them. Faced with <u>scarcity</u>, people must make choices. Choices that are the best for the person who makes them are choices made in <u>self-interest</u>. Choices that are best for everyone as a whole are choices made in <u>social interest</u>.

True or false

1. True; page 2
2. False; page 3
3. True; page 4
4. False; page 4
5. False; page 5

Multiple choice

1. e; page 2
2. a; page 2
3. e; page 2
4. a; page 3
5. b; page 3
6. c; page 4
7. c; page 4

Short answer and numeric questions

1. There will never be a time without scarcity because human wants are unlimited; page 2.

2. If there was no scarcity, then there likely would be no need for economics. Economics studies the choices that people make to cope with scarcity, so if there was no scarcity, then people's choices would not be limited by scarcity; page 3.

3. The questions are "*What* goods and services get produced and in what quantities?", "*How* are goods and services produced?", and "*For whom* are the goods and services produced?" page 3.

4. In general economists believe that people make choices according to their self-interest. These choices might or might not be in the social interest. Part of what economists study is when choices made in people's self-interest also further the social interest; page 5.

■ CHECKPOINT 1.2

Fill in the blanks

A <u>rational</u> choice uses the available resources to most effectively satisfy the wants of the person making the choice. The opportunity cost of an activity is <u>the highest-valued alternative forgone</u>. The benefit of an activity is measured by what you <u>are willing to</u> give up. We make a rational choice to do an activity if the marginal benefit of the activity <u>exceeds</u> the marginal cost. <u>Microeconomics</u> is the study of the choices of individuals and businesses, the interaction of these choices, and the influences that governments exert on these classes. A statement that tells "what is" is a <u>positive</u> statement. A statement that tells "what ought to be" is a <u>normative</u> statement. The term meaning "other things being equal" is <u>*ceteris paribus*</u>.

True or false

1. False; page 11
2. False; page 12
3. True; page 13
4. True; page 13
5. True; page 14
6. True; page 15

Multiple choice

1. b; page 11
2. b; page 11
3. b; page 12
4. d; page 12
5. a; page 13
6. c; page 13
7. c; page 14
8. c; page 15
9. b; page 15
10. b; page 15

Short answer and numeric questions

1. The opportunity cost of something is the highest-valued other thing that must be given up. The opportunity cost is only the single highest-valued alternative forgone, *not* all alternatives forgone; page 11.

2. The opportunity cost of the pizza is the highest-valued alternative forgone, which in this case is the DVD. The opportunity cost is *not* the DVD and the CD-Rs because you would not have been able to purchase both of them with your $12; page 11.

3. A sunk cost is a previously occurred and irreversible cost; page 11.

4. The benefit of something is the gain or pleasure that it brings. Economists measure the benefit of something by what a person is willing to give up to get it; pages 11, 12.

5. Marginal cost is the cost of a one-unit increase in an activity. Marginal benefit is the benefit of a one-unit increase in an activity. A rational choice is made by comparing the marginal cost and marginal benefit, so that if the marginal benefit of an activity exceeds or equals the marginal cost, the activity is undertaken; pages 12-13.

6. Microeconomics studies individual units within the economy, such as a consumer, a firm, a market, and so forth. Macroeconomics studies the overall, or aggregate, economy, such as the overall unemployment rate, or overall economic growth rate; page 14.

7. A positive statement is "People who wear seat belts are involved in fewer road deaths." This statement can be tested. A normative statement is "People should be free to choose whether to wear a seat belt or not." This statement cannot be tested; page 15.

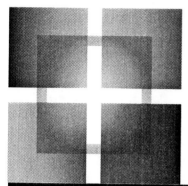

Chapter

1

APPENDIX CHECKLIST

After you have completed the appendix, you will have thoroughly reviewed the graphs used in your economics course.

▐ Making and using graphs.

Graphs represent quantities as distances. The vertical axis is the y-axis and the horizontal axis is the x-axis. A scatter diagram plots a graph of one variable against the value of another variable. A time-series graph measures time along the x-axis and the variable (or variables) of interest along the y-axis. A cross-section graph shows the values of an economic variable for different groups in the population at a point in time. Graphs can show the relationship between two variables in an economic model. Variables that move in the same direction have a positive, or direct, relationship. Variables that move in the opposite direction have a negative, or inverse, relationship. Some relationships have minimum or maximum points. The slope of a relationship is the change in the value of the variable measured on the y-axis divided by the change in the value of the variable measured on the x-axis. To graph a relationship among more than two variables, we use the *ceteris paribus* assumption and graph the relationship between two of the variables, holding the other variables constant.

CHECKPOINT I

■ Making and using graphs.

Additional Practice Problems

1. You have data on the average monthly rainfall and the monthly expenditure on umbrellas in Seattle, Washington. What sort of graph would be the best to reveal if any relationship exists between these variables?

2. In Figure A1.1, draw a straight line showing a positive relationship and another straight line showing a negative relationship.

■ FIGURE A1.1

Year	Price (dollars per gallon)
1997	1.29
1998	1.12
1999	1.22
2000	1.56
2001	1.53
2002	1.44
2003	1.64
2004	1.92
2005	2.34
2006	2.64

3. The table has the average price of a gallon of gasoline, including taxes, for ten years. In Figure A1.2, label the axes and then plot these data. What type of graph are you creating? What is the general trend of gas prices during this decade?

■ **FIGURE A1.2**

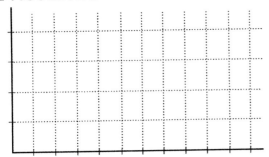

4. Figure A1.3 shows the relationship between the price of a paperback book and the quantity of paperback books a publisher is willing to sell. What is the slope of the line in Figure A1.3?

■ **FIGURE A1.3**

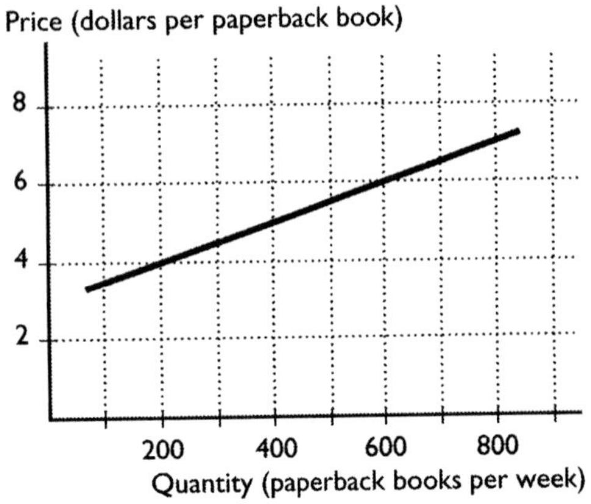

Price (dollars per paperback book)

8

6

4

2

200   400   600   800

Quantity (paperback books per week)

Solution to Additional Practice Problems 1

1. A scatter diagram would be the best graph to use. A scatter diagram would plot the monthly value of, say, rainfall along the vertical axis (the y-axis) and the monthly value of umbrella expenditure along the horizontal axis (the x-axis).

■ **FIGURE A1.4**

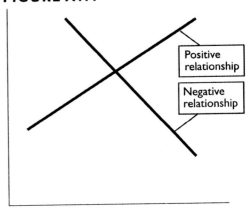

Positive relationship

Negative relationship

2. Figure A1.4 has two lines, one showing a positive relationship and the other showing a negative relationship. Your figure does not need to have identical lines. The key point your figure needs is that the line for the positive relationship slopes up as you move rightward along it and the line for the negative relationship slopes down as you move rightward along it.

■ **FIGURE A1.5**

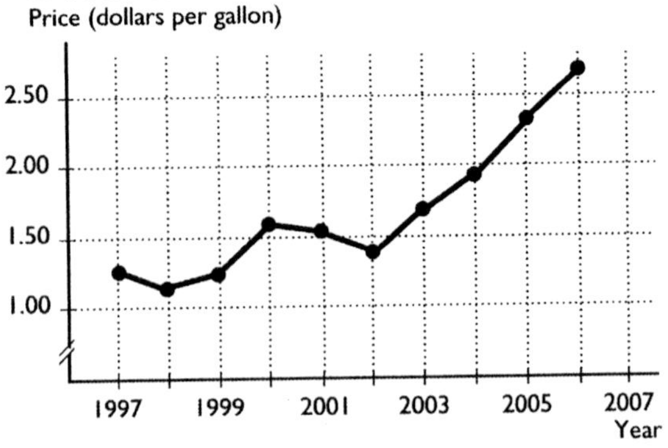

Price (dollars per gallon)

2.50

2.00

1.50

1.00

1997   1999   2001   2003   2005   2007

Year

3. Figure A1.5 labels the axes and plots the data in the table. The graph is a time-series graph. The trend is positive because gas prices generally increased during these years.

■ **FIGURE A1.6**

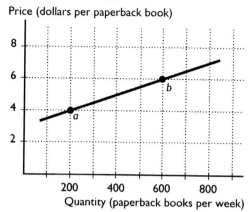

Price (dollars per paperback book)

Quantity (paperback books per week)

4. The slope of a line is the change the variable measured on the *y*-axis divided by the change in the variable measured on the *x*-axis. To calculate the slope of the line in the figure, use points *a* and *b* in Figure A1.6. Between *a* and *b*, *y* rises by 2, from 4 to 6. And *x* increases by 400, from 200 to 600. The slope equals $2/400 = 0.005$.

■ **Self Test I**

Fill in the blanks

In a graph, the vertical line is called the ____ (*x*-axis; *y*-axis) and the horizontal line is called the ____ (*x*-axis; *y*-axis). A ____ (scatter diagram; time-series graph; cross-section graph) is a graph of the value of one variable against the value of another variable. A ____ (scatter diagram; time-series graph; cross-section graph) measures time along the *x*-axis and the variable along the *y*-axis. A ____ (scatter diagram; time-series graph; cross-section graph) shows the values of an economic variable for different groups in the population at a point in time. If the graph of a relationship between two variables slopes up to the right, the two variables have a ____ (positive; negative) relationship. If the graph between two variables is a vertical line, the two variables ____ (are; are not) related. The slope of a relationship is the change in the value of the variable measured along the ____ (*x*-axis; *y*-axis) divided by the change in the value of the variable measured along the ____ (*x*-axis; *y*-axis). By using the *ceteris paribus*

assumption, it ____ (is; is not) possible to graph a relationship that involves more than two variables.

True or false

1. A point that is above and to the right of another point will have a larger value of the *x*-axis variable and a larger value of the *y*-axis variable.

2. A scatter diagram shows the values of an economic variable for different groups in a population at a point in time.

3. A time-series graph compares values of a variable for different groups at a single point in time.

4. A trend is a measure of the closeness of the points on a graph.

5. A positive relationship is always a linear relationship.

6. A relationship that starts out sloping upward and then slopes downward has a maximum.

7. A graph that shows a horizontal line indicates variables that are unrelated.

8. The slope at a point on a curve can be found by calculating the slope of the line that touches the point and no other point on the curve.

Multiple choice

1. Demonstrating how an economic variable changes from one year to the next is best illustrated by a
   a. scatter diagram.
   b. time-series graph.
   c. linear graph.
   d. cross-section graph.
   e. trend-line

2. To show the values of an economic variable for different groups in a population at a point in time, it is best to use a
   a. scatter diagram.
   b. time-series graph.
   c. linear graph.
   d. cross-section graph.
   e. trend diagram.

3. If whenever one variable increases, another variable also increases, these variables are
   a. positively related.
   b. negatively related.
   c. inversely related.
   d. cross-sectionally related.
   e. not related.

4. A graph of the relationship between two variables is a line that slopes down to the right. These two variables are ____ related.
   a. positively
   b. directly
   c. negatively
   d. not
   e. trend-line

5. Two variables are unrelated if their graph is
   i. a vertical line.
   ii. a 45 degree line.
   iii. a horizontal line.
   a. i only.
   b. ii only
   c. iii only
   d. i and iii.
   e. i, ii, and iii.

■ FIGURE A1.7

Price (dollars per pound of rutabagas)

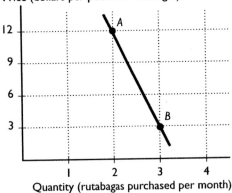

Quantity (rutabagas purchased per month)

6. In figure A1.7, between points A and B, what is the slope of the line?
   a. 12
   b. 3
   c. 9
   d. –9
   e. 0

■ FIGURE A1.8

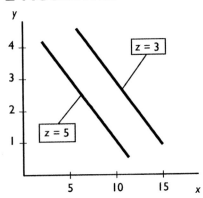

7. In Figure A1.8, an increase in z leads to a
   a. movement up along one of the lines showing the relationship between x and y.
   b. movement down along one of the lines showing the relationship between x and y.
   c. rightward shift of the line showing the relationship between x and y.
   d. leftward shift of the line showing the relationship between x and y.
   e. trend change in both x and y.

8. In Figure A1.8, *ceteris paribus*, an increase in x is associated with
   a. an increase in y.
   b. a decrease in y.
   c. an increase in z.
   d. a random change in z.
   e. no change in either y or z.

Complete the graph

Year	Workers (millions)
1990	6.5
1991	6.5
1992	6.6
1993	6.8
1994	7.1
1995	7.4
1996	7.5
1997	7.6
1998	7.8
1999	7.9

1. The table above gives the number of people working in restaurants and bars in the United States during the decade of the 1990s.

■ FIGURE A1.9

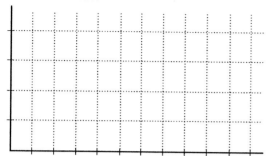

In Figure A1.9, measure time on the horizontal axis and the number of workers on the vertical axis, and then plot these data.

a. What type of graph are you creating?
b. Using your figure, what was the trend in the number of people working in restaurants and bars during the 1990s?

Year	Revenue (billions of dollars)	Workers (millions)
1990	190	6.5
1991	194	6.5
1992	200	6.6
1993	213	6.8
1994	222	7.1
1995	230	7.4
1996	239	7.5
1997	254	7.6
1998	267	7.8
1999	285	7.9

2. The table above gives the annual revenue for restaurants and bars and the number of people employed in restaurants and bars in the United States during the decade of the 1990s. In Figure A1.10, measure the revenue along the horizontal axis and the number of workers along the vertical axis and plot the data.

a. What type of graph are you creating?
b. What relationship do you see in your figure between the revenue and the number of workers?

■ FIGURE A1.10

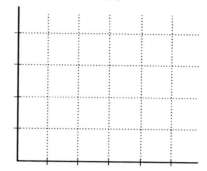

Price (dollars per sack of cat food)	Quantity (sacks of cat food per month)
1	10,000
2	8,000
3	7,000
4	4,000

3. The number of sacks of premium cat food that cat lovers will buy depends on the price of a sack of cat food. The relationship is given in the table above. In Figure A1.11, plot this relationship, putting the price on the vertical axis and the quantity on the horizontal axis.

■ FIGURE A1.11

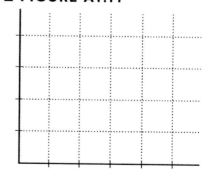

a. If the price of a sack of cat food is $2, how many sacks will be purchased?
b. If the price of a sack of cat food is $3, how many sacks will be purchased?
c. Is the relationship between the price and the quantity positive or negative?

4. In Figure A1.12, label the maximum and minimum points.

■ **FIGURE A1.12**

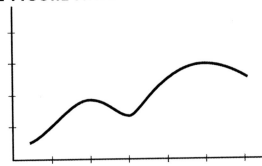

5. In Figure A1.13, draw a line through point *A* with a slope of 2. Label the line "1." Draw another line through point *A* with a slope of –2. Label this line "2."

■ **FIGURE A1.13**

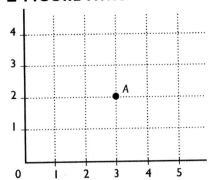

Price (dollars per DVD)	Quantity of DVDs purchased, low income	Quantity of DVDs purchased, high income
11	4	5
12	3	4
13	1	3
14	0	2

6. Bobby says that he buys fewer DVDs when the price of a DVD is higher. Bobby also says that he will buy more DVDs after he graduates and his income is higher. The table above shows the number of DVDs Bobby buys in a month at different prices when his income is low and when his income is high.

■ **FIGURE A1.14**

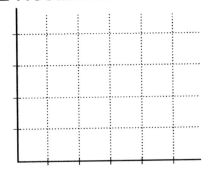

a. In Figure A1.14, put the price on the vertical axis and the quantity purchased on the horizontal axis. Show the relationship between the number of DVDs purchased and the price when Bobby's income is low.

b. On the same figure, draw the relationship between the number of DVDs purchased and the price when his income is high.

c. Does an increase in Bobby's income shift the relationship between the price of a DVD and the number of DVDs purchased rightward or leftward?

Short answer and numeric questions

1. What are the three types of graphs?

2. If two variables are positively related, will the slope of a graph of the two variables be positive or negative? If two variables are negatively related, will the slope of a graph of the two variables be positive or negative?

3. If a line slopes upward to the right, is its slope positive or negative? If a line slopes downward to the right, is its slope positive or negative?

■ **FIGURE A1.15**

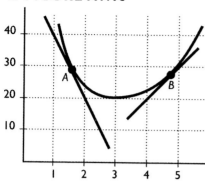

4. In Figure A1.15, what is the slope of the curved line at point *A*? At point *B*?

SELF TEST ANSWERS

■ CHECKPOINT I

Fill in the blanks

In a graph, the vertical line is called the y-axis and the horizontal line is called the x-axis. A scatter diagram is a graph of the value of one variable against the value of another variable. A time-series graph measures time along the x-axis and the variable along the y-axis. A cross-section graph shows the values of an economic variable for different groups in the population at a point in time. If the graph of a relationship between two variables slopes up to the right, the two variables have a positive relationship. If the graph between two variables is a vertical line, the two variables are not related. The slope of a relationship is the change in the value of the variable measured along the y-axis divided by the change in the value of the variable measured along the x-axis. By using the *ceteris paribus* assumption, it is possible to graph a relationship that involves more than two variables.

True or false

1. True; page 23
2. False; page 24
3. False; page 24
4. False; page 24
5. False; page 26
6. True; page 28
7. True; page 28
8. True; page 29

Multiple choice

1. b; page 24
2. d; page 24
3. a; page 26
4. c; page 27
5. d; page 28
6. d; page 29
7. d; page 30
8. b; page 30

Complete the graph

■ **FIGURE A1.16**

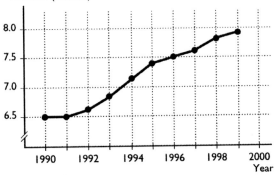

Workers (millions)

1. Figure A1.16 plots the data.
   a. This is a time-series graph; page 24.
   b. The trend is positive. During the 1990s there is an increase in the number of people working in restaurants and bars; page 24.

■ **FIGURE A1.17**

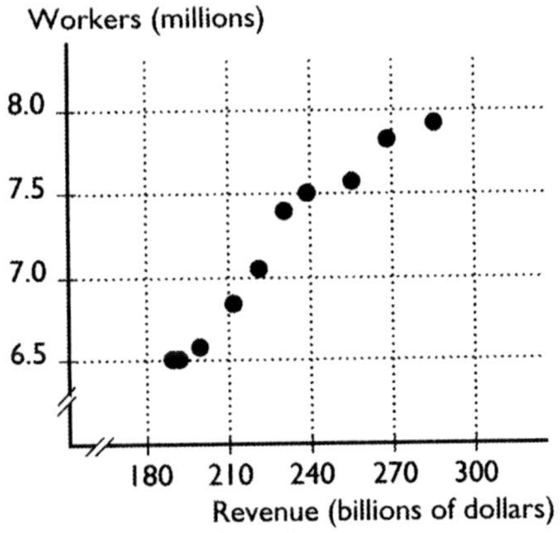

Workers (millions)

2. Figure A1.17 plots the data.
   a. The figure is a scatter diagram; page 24.
   b. The relationship between the revenue and the number of workers is positive; page 26.

■ **FIGURE A1.18**

Price (dollars per sack)

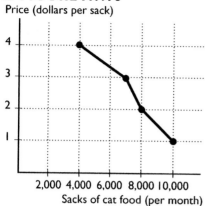

Sacks of cat food (per month)

3. Figure A1.18 plots the relationship.
   a. If the price is $2 per sack, 8,000 sacks are purchased; page 23.
   b. If the price is $3 per sack, 7,000 sacks are purchased; page 23.
   c. The relationship between the price and quantity of sacks is negative; page 27.

■ **FIGURE A1.19**

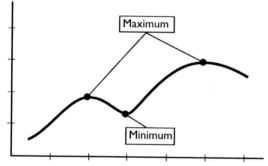

4. Figure A1.19 labels the two maximum points and one minimum point; page 28.

■ **FIGURE A1.20**

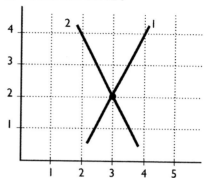

5. Figure A1.20 shows the two lines; page 29.

■ **FIGURE A1.21**

Price (dollars per DVD)

DVDs purchased

6. a. Figure A1.21 plots the relationship; page 30.
   b. Figure A1.21 plots the relationship; page 30.
   c. An increase in Bobby's income shifts the relationship rightward; page 30.

Short answer and numeric questions

1. The three types of graphs are scatter diagram, time-series graph, and cross-section graph; page 24.

2. If two variables are positively related, a graph of the relationship will have a positive slope. If two variables are negatively related, a graph of the relationship will have a negative slope; pages 26, 27, 29.

3. If a line slopes upward to the right, its slope is positive. If a line slopes downward to the right, its slope is negative; page 29.

4. The slope of a curved line at a point equals the slope of a straight line that touches that point and no other point on the curve. The slope of the curved line at point A is -20 and the slope of the curved line at point B is 10; page 29.

The U.S. and Global Economies

Chapter 2

Chapter 2 introduces fundamental concepts about how households, firms, markets, and government are linked together. A circular flow model is presented to show how goods and services and expenditures flow from and to households, firms, and the government.

1 **Describe what, how, and for whom goods and services are produced in the United States.**

The production of goods and services, the "what" question, is divided into four broad categories defined in terms of the ultimate buyer: individuals (consumption goods and services), businesses (capital goods), governments (government goods and services), and other countries (export goods and services). The "how" of production involves the factors of production: land, labor, capital, and entrepreneurship. Goods and services are sold to those who have income, so the personal distribution of income is one way of showing who ends up with our national output. The functional distribution of income shows how much is paid to the owners of each type of productive resource. The largest share of national income goes to labor, so workers get the largest share of our nation's goods and services.

2 **Use the circular flow model to provide a picture of how households, firms, and government interact.**

The circular flow model shows that households provide the services from the factors of production, and firms hire these services in factor markets. The circular flow also shows that households purchase goods and services, and firms sell goods and services in goods markets. The decisions made by households and firms (and the government) in these markets determine the answers to the "what," "how," and "for whom" questions. The federal government provides public goods and services, and makes social security and other benefit payments. In the circular flow, the government purchases goods and services in goods markets. It makes transfers to firms and households and also taxes them. The federal government's largest expenditure is Social Security benefits and its largest source of tax revenue is personal income taxes.

3 **Describe what, how, and for whom goods and services are produced in the global economy.**

Countries are divided into advanced economies, the richest 29 countries, and emerging market and developing economies. The advanced economies produce 51 percent of the world's total output, with 20 percent produced in the United States. Two third's of the world's oil reserves and two fifths of the natural gas reserves are in the Middle East. The share of agriculture in the advanced economies is much smaller than in the other countries but the advanced economies still produce one third of the world's food. The advanced economies have much more human capital and physical capital than the developing countries. Inequality of incomes across the entire world has decreased during the past twenty years, primarily because incomes in China and India have grown rapidly.

CHECKPOINT 2.1

■ **Describe what, how, and for whom goods and services are produced in the United States.**

Quick Review

- *Consumption goods and services* Goods and services that are bought by individuals and used to provide personal enjoyment and contribute to a person's standard of living.
- *Capital goods* Goods that are bought by businesses to increase their productive resources.
- *Government goods and services* Goods and services that are bought by governments.
- *Exports* Goods and services produced in the United States and sold in other countries.

Additional Practice Problems 2.1

1. Tell whether the following goods and services are consumption goods and services, capital goods, government goods and services, or exports.
   a. A taco at Taco Bell purchased for lunch by Shaniq.
   b. An HP printer manufactured in Idaho purchased by Maria in Peru.
   c. A new grill purchased by Taco Bell.
   d. A tour down the Colorado river from Rimrock Adventures purchased by the Miller family.
   e. CamelBak drinking packs purchased by the U.S. Marine Corp.
   f. CamelBak drinking packs purchased by Rimrock Adventures for use by their customers during tours.
   g. A CamelBak drinking pack purchased by Anne for use while mountain biking.
   h. A CamelBak drinking pack purchased by Sebastian, a German racing in the Tour de France.

2. How much labor is there in the United States? What determines the quantity of labor?

Solutions to Additional Practice Problems 2.1

1a. Shaniq's taco is a consumption good.
1b. Maria's printer is an export good.
1c. The new grill is a capital good.
1d. The tour is a consumption service.
1e. The drinking pack purchased by the Marines is a government good because it is purchased by the government.
1f. The drinking pack purchased by Rimrock Adventures is a capital good because it is purchased by a business.
1g. The drinking pack purchased by Anne is a consumption good.
1h. The drinking pack purchased by Sebastian is an export good.

2. In the United States, in 2007 about 152 million people had jobs or were available for work and they provided about 270 billion hours of labor a year. The quantity of labor depends on the size of the population, the percentage of the population that takes jobs, and on social relationships that influence things such as how many women take paid work. An increase in the proportion of women who have taken paid work has increased the quantity of labor in the United States over the past 50 years.

■ **Self Test 2.1**

Fill in the blanks

Goods and services that are bought by individuals and used to provide personal enjoyment and to contribute to a person's standard of living are ____ (consumption; capital; export) goods. Goods that are bought by businesses to increase their productive resources are ____ (consumption; capital; export) goods. Goods that are produced in the United States and sold in other countries are ____ (consumption; capital; export) goods. Of the four large groups of goods and services in the United States, ____ (consumption goods and services; capital goods; government goods and services; export goods and services) have the largest share of total production. Productive resources are called ____ and are grouped into four categories: ____,

____, ____, and ____. In 2006, ____ (labor; capital) received 64 percent of total income. The distribution of income among households is called the ____ (functional; personal) distribution of income.

True or false

1. Consumption goods and services include a slice of pizza purchased to eat at home.

2. A gold mine is included in the "land" category of productive resources.

3. Michael Dell, the person who founded and manages Dell computers, is an example of an entrepreneur.

4. In the United States, the factor of production that earns the most income is labor.

5. In the United States, the richest 20 percent of individuals earn approximately 30 percent of total income.

Multiple choice

1. When the total U.S. production of goods and services is divided into consumption goods and services, capital goods, government goods and services, and export goods and services, the largest component is
   a. consumption goods and services.
   b. capital goods.
   c. government goods and services.
   d. export goods and services.
   e. capital goods and government goods and services tie for the largest component.

2. An example of a capital good is
   a. a fiber optic cable TV system.
   b. an insurance policy.
   c. a hair cut.
   d. an iPod.
   e. a slice of pizza.

3. Goods and services produced in the United States and sold in other countries are called
   a. consumption goods and services.
   b. capital goods.
   c. government goods and services.
   d. export goods and services.
   e. import goods and services.

4. Which of the following correctly lists the categories of factors of production?
   a. machines, buildings, land, and money
   b. hardware, software, land, and money
   c. capital, money, and labor
   d. owners, workers, and consumers.
   e. land, labor, capital, and entrepreneurship

5. Human capital is
   a. solely the innate ability we are born with.
   b. the money humans have saved.
   c. the knowledge humans accumulate through education and experience.
   d. machinery that needs human supervision.
   e. any type of machinery.

6. Wages are paid to ____ and interest is paid to ____.
   a. entrepreneurs; capital
   b. labor; capital
   c. labor; land
   d. entrepreneurs; land
   e. labor; entrepreneurs

7. Dividing the nation's income among the factors of production, the largest percentage is paid to
   a. labor.
   b. land.
   c. capital.
   d. entrepreneurship.
   e. labor and capital, with each receiving about 41 percent of the total income.

8. The personal distribution of income shows
   a. that labor receives the largest percentage of total income.
   b. how profit accounts for the largest fraction of total income.
   c. that the richest 20 percent of people earn 23 percent of total income.
   d. that interest accounts for most of the income of the richest 20 percent of people.
   e. that the poorest 20 percent of people earn less than 4 percent of total income.

Short answer and numeric questions

1. Is an automobile a consumption good or a capital good?

2. Compare the incomes earned by the poorest and richest 20 percent of individuals.

CHECKPOINT 2.2

■ **Use the circular flow model to provide a picture of how households, firms, and governments interact.**

Quick Review

- *Circular flow model* A model of the economy, illustrated in Figure 2.1, that shows the circular flow of expenditures and incomes that result from firms', households', and governments' choices.

■ **FIGURE 2.1**

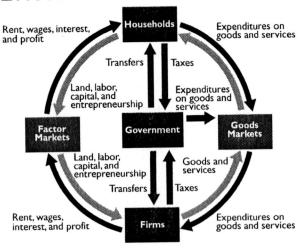

Additional Practice Problem 2.2

1. Describe where the following money flows fit in the circular flow.
   a. Shaniq pays for a taco at Taco Bell.
   b. Sam receives his monthly Social Security payment.
   c. Jennifer gets a $10,000 end of the year bonus from Bank of America, where she works.
   d. Exxon pays landowners in Texas $20,000 for the oil under their land.
   e. Bill pays property tax of $6,000.

2. In the circular flow, what is the relationship between the flow of expenditures into the goods markets (from households and the government) and the flow of revenues out of the goods markets to firms?

Solutions to Additional Practice Problems 2.2

1a. Shaniq's payment is an expenditure on a good that flows from households through the goods market to Taco Bell, a firm.

1b. Sam's check is a transfer payment from the government to households.

1c. Jennifer's payment is wages flowing from a firm, Bank of America, through the factor market to households.

1d. Exxon's payment is rent flowing from a firm, Exxon, through the factor market to households.

1e. Bill's payment is a tax flowing from households to government.

2. The flow of expenditures into the goods markets–the funds that households and the government spend on the goods and services they purchase–equals the flow of revenue out of the goods markets.

■ **Self Test 2.2**

Fill in the blanks

The ____ model shows the flows of expenditure and incomes. An arrangement that brings buyers and sellers together is a ____ (firm; household; market). A market in which goods and services are bought and sold is a ____ (goods; factor) market and a market in which the services of the factors of production are bought and sold is a ____ (goods; factor) market. In 2006, as a percentage of the total value of the goods and services produced in the United States, the federal government spent about ____ (20; 13) percent while state and local governments spent about ____ (20; 13) percent. A large part of what the federal government spends is ____ (social security payments; personal income taxes). The two components that account for most of the federal government's tax revenue are ____. The largest part of the expenditures of state and local governments is spending on ____ (education; highways).

True or false

1. Firms own the factors of production.

2. A market is any arrangement where buyers and sellers meet face-to-face.

3. Factors of production flow from households to firms through goods markets.

4. Rent, wages, interest, and profit are the payments made by firms to households through factor markets.

5. Social security payments are made by state and local governments.

6. The largest part of the expenditures of state and local government is on education.

Multiple choice

1. Within the circular flow model, economists define households as
   a. families with at least 2 children.
   b. families living in their own houses.
   c. individuals or groups living together.
   d. married or engaged couples.
   e. individuals or groups within the same legally defined family.

2. A market is defined as
   a. the physical place where goods are sold.
   b. the physical place where goods and services are sold.
   c. any arrangement that brings buyers and sellers together.
   d. a place where money is exchanged for goods.
   e. another name for a store such as a grocery store.

3. In the circular flow model,
   a. only firms sell in markets.
   b. only households buy from markets.
   c. some firms only sell and some firms only buy.
   d. the money used to buy goods and the goods themselves travel in the same direction.
   e. both firms and households buy or sell in different markets.

4. ____ choose the quantities of goods and services to produce, while ____ choose the quantities of goods and services to buy.
   a. Households; firms
   b. Firms; households and the government
   c. The government; firms
   d. Firms; only households
   e. Households; the government

5. A circular flow model shows the interrelationship between the ____ market and the ____ markets.
   a. household; goods
   b. household; factor
   c. business; household
   d. expenditure; income
   e. goods; factor

6. In the circular flow model, the expenditures on goods and services flow in the
   a. same direction as goods and services in all cases.
   b. same direction as goods and services *only if* they both flow through the goods market.
   c. same direction as goods and services *only if* they both flow through the factor market.
   d. opposite direction as goods and services.
   e. same direction as factor markets.

7. Of the following, the smallest expenditure category of the federal government is
   a. national defense and homeland security.
   b. Social Security.
   c. Social Security benefits.
   d. Medicare and Medicaid.
   e. interest on the national debt.

8. Of the following, the largest source of revenue for the federal government is
   a. personal income taxes.
   b. sales taxes.
   c. corporate income taxes.
   d. property taxes.
   e. lottery revenue.

Complete the graph

■ FIGURE 2.2

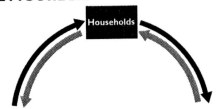

1. Figure 2.2 ignores the government and shows the flows into and out of households. Label the flows and identify who they come from and who they go to.

■ FIGURE 2.3

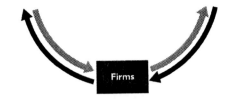

2. Figure 2.3 ignores the government and shows the flows into and out of firms. Label the flows and identify who they come from and who they go to.

■ FIGURE 2.4

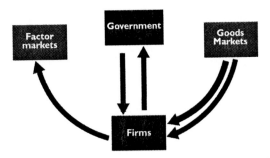

3. Figure 2.4 now includes the government and shows the money flows into and out of firms. Label the money flows.

Short answer and numeric questions

1. Ignoring taxes and transfer payments, what funds flow into firms and what funds flow out of them?

2. In the circular flow model, what are the sources of expenditures on goods and services?

3. Is it possible for something to affect households and not firms? To affect firms and not households? Explain your answers.

4. The circular flow reveals that which two groups interact to determine what will be the payments to the factors of production?

5. In 2006, which spent more, the federal government or state and local governments?

CHECKPOINT 2.3

■ **Describe what, how, and for whom goods and services are produced in the global economy.**

Quick Review

- *Advanced economies* The 29 countries (or areas) that have the highest living standards.

- *Emerging markets and Developing economies* Emerging markets are the 28 countries in Europe and Asia that were until the early 1990s part of the Soviet Union or its satellites and are changing the way they organize their economies. Developing economies are the 118 countries in Africa, the Middle East, Europe, and Central and South America that have not yet achieved a high standard of living for their people.

Additional Practice Problems 2.3

1. What percentage of the world's population live in developing economies? In places such as China, India, and Africa, what was the average income per day?

2. What percentage of the world's population live in advanced economies? In countries such as the United States, Canada, and Japan, what was the average income per day?

3. How does production within the advanced economies, the emerging market economies, and the developing economies compare?

4. How is it possible that income inequality within most countries has increased in recent years yet income inequality across the whole world has decreased in recent years?

Solutions to Additional Practice Problems 2.3

1. The world's population is about 6.6 billion. More than 5 billion of the people live in developing economies. So, approximately 80 percent of the world's population lives in developing economies. Average daily income in China is $24, in India is $10, and in Africa is $8. Because these are the average, many people live on less than these amounts.

2. About 1 billion people, or 15 percent of the world's population live in the 28 advanced economies. The average income per day in the United States was $124, in Canada was $102, and in Japan was $90.

3. Of the world's total production, the advanced economies produce 51 percent (20 percent is produced in the United States). The emerging market economies produce 7 percent of the world's production and the developing economies produce the remainder, 42 percent.

4. While income inequality within nations has been increasing, the difference in incomes among different nations has been decreasing. In particular, both China and India have seen rapid growth in income. The growth in income for these two poor but populous nations has decreased income inequality in the world as a whole.

■ Self Test 2.3

Fill in the blanks

Most of the world's population lives in the ____ (advanced economies; emerging market economies; developing economies). The lowest average income is in the ____ (advanced economies; emerging market economies; developing economies). Advanced economies produce about ____ (24; 51; 72) percent of the world's total production and the United States, alone, produces about ____ (6; 20; 33) percent of the world's total production. About ____ (33; 50; 67) percent of the world's proven oil reserves are located in ____ (North America; the Middle East). As a fraction of total output, agricultural is a ____ (larger; smaller) part of the economy in developing economies than in advanced economies. Factories in advanced economies are much ____ (less; more) capital intensive than in developing economies. During the past 20 years, the distribution of income in the world economy has become ____ (more; less) equal.

True or false

1. About 50 percent of the world's population lives in the advanced economies.

2. Mexico is an emerging market economy.

3. Taken as a group, the 118 developing economy nations produce a larger percentage of total world production than do the 29 advanced economy nations.

4. Most of the world's energy reserves are in North America.

5. Workers in the advanced economies have much more human capital than workers in the developing economies.

6. Income inequality within most nations has increased over the past years.

Multiple choice

1. The world population is approximately ____ people.
   a. 6.6 million
   b. 2 trillion
   c. 6.6 billion
   d. 1.4 trillion
   e. 660 million

2. The percentage of the world's population that lives in the advanced economies is
   a. more than 51 percent.
   b. between 41 percent and 50 percent.
   c. between 31 percent and 40 percent.
   d. between 20 percent and 30 percent.
   e. less than 20 percent.

3. Which of following groups of countries are *all* advanced economies?
   a. Australia, Brazil, and the United States
   b. Hong Kong, Japan, France, and the United Kingdom
   c. Italy, the United States, China, and Russia
   d. Singapore, Russia, France, and Chad
   e. Mexico, Canada, Germany, and Egypt

4. The emerging market economies are
   a. the largest grouping including the nations of China and India.
   b. in transition from state-owned production to free markets.
   c. most of the nations of Western Europe.
   d. the nations that are currently agricultural in nature.
   e. the nations with the highest standards of living.

5. As a percentage of total world production, production in the 29 advanced economies is about ____ percent of total world production and in the 118 developing economies is about ____ percent of total world production.
   a. 51; 42
   b. 23; 62
   c. 59; 12
   d. 30; 46
   e. 19; 73

6. Agricultural is about ____ percent of total production within advanced economies and the advanced economies produce about ____ percent of the world's food.
   a. 2; 33
   b. 12; 12
   c. 28; 63
   d. 4; 12
   e. 8; 20

7. Compared to the developing economies, the advanced economies have ____ human capital and ____ physical capital.
   a. more; more
   b. more; less
   c. the same; the same
   d. less; more
   e. less; less

8. Among the United States, Canada, Russia, India, and the United Kingdom, the country with the highest average income per person and the highest living standard is
   a. the United States.
   b. Russia.
   c. India.
   d. Canada.
   e. the United Kingdom.

Short answer and numeric questions

1. What are the groups the International Monetary Fund uses to classify countries? Describe each group. Which group has the largest number of countries? The largest number of people?

2. As a fraction of total production, how does agricultural production within the advanced economies compare to agricultural production within the developing economies? Why are the advanced economies able to produce about one third of the world's food?

3. How does the amount of human capital in the advanced economies compare to that in the developing economies?

4. How does the distribution of income within the United States compare to the distribution of income in the world economy?

SELF TEST ANSWERS

■ CHECKPOINT 2.1

Fill in the blanks

Goods and services that are bought by individuals and used to provide personal enjoyment and to contribute to a person's standard of living are <u>consumption</u> goods. Goods that are bought by businesses to increase their productive resources are <u>capital</u> goods. Goods that are produced in the United States and sold in other countries are <u>export</u> goods. Of the four large groups of goods and services in the United States, <u>consumption goods and services</u> have the largest share of total production. Productive resources are called <u>factors of production</u> and are grouped into four categories: <u>labor</u>, <u>land</u>, <u>capital</u>, and <u>entrepreneurship</u>. In 2006, <u>labor</u> received 64 percent of total income. The distribution of income among households is called the <u>personal</u> distribution of income.

True or false

1. True; page 34
2. True; page 36
3. True; page 39
4. True; page 40
5. False; page 40

Multiple choice

1. a; page 34
2. a; page 34
3. d; page 34
4. e; page 36
5. c; page 37
6. b; page 39
7. a; page 40
8. e; page 40

Short answer and numeric questions

1. An automobile might be either a consumption or a capital good. It is a consumption good if it is purchased by a household. It is a capital good if it is purchased by a business for use within the business; page 34.

2. The richest 20 percent of households earn about 50 percent of the total U.S. income. The poorest 20 percent of individuals have an average income of about $11,000 and earn about 3 percent of the total U.S. income; page 40.

■ CHECKPOINT 2.2

Fill in the blanks

The <u>circular flow</u> model shows the flows of expenditures and incomes. An arrangement that brings buyers and sellers together is a <u>market</u>. A market in which goods and services are bought and sold is a <u>goods</u> market and a market in which the services of the factors of production are bought and sold is a <u>factor</u> market. In 2006, as a percentage of the total value of the goods and services produced in the United States, the federal government spent about <u>20</u> percent while state and local governments spent about <u>13</u> percent. A large part of what the federal government spends is <u>social security payments</u>. The two components that account for most of the federal government's tax revenue are <u>personal income taxes and Social Security taxes</u>. The largest part of the expenditures of state and local governments is spending on <u>education</u>.

True or false

1. False; page 42
2. False; pages 42-43
3. False; pages 42-43
4. True; pages 42-43
5. False; page 44
6. True; page 47

Multiple choice

1. c; page 42
2. c; page 42
3. e; pages 42-43
4. b; pages 42-43
5. e; pages 42-43
6. d; page 43
7. e; page 46
8. a; page 46

Complete the graph
■ FIGURE 2.5

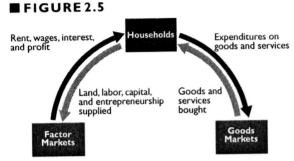

1. Figure 2.5 labels the flows. Rent, wages, interest, and profits (or losses) flow from the factor markets while the services from land, labor, capital, and entrepreneurship flow to the factor markets. In addition, expenditures on goods and services flow to the goods market, and goods and services flow from the goods market; page 43.

■ FIGURE 2.6

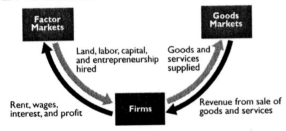

2. Figure 2.6 labels the flows. Revenue from the sale of goods and services, which are the expenditures on goods and services, flow to firms from the goods market and payments of rent, wages, interest, and profit (or loss) flow from firms into the factor market. The services from land, labor, capital, and entrepreneurship flow to firms from the factor markets, and goods and services flow from firms into the goods markets; page 43.

3. Figure 2.7 labels the money flows into and out of firms. The difference between this figure and Figure 2.6 is the addition of transfers and taxes; page 45.

■ FIGURE 2.7

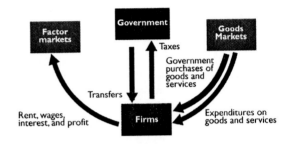

Short answer and numeric questions

1. Funds that flow into firms are households' expenditures and government purchases of goods and services. Funds that flow out of firms are payments for rent, wages, interest, and profit (or loss) to households in exchange for the factors of production; pages 43, 45.

2. The circular flow identifies two sources of expenditures on goods and services, expenditures by households and expenditures by the government; page 45.

3. The circular flow shows that at the macroeconomic level it is impossible for something to influence only firms or only households. An influence that changes households' buying behavior in goods markets affects firms because they sell to households in goods markets; page 43.

4. Payments to the factors of production are determined by the interaction of households, who own and provide the services from the factors of production, and firms, who employ the services from these factors; page 43.

5. In 2006, the federal government spent $2.9 trillion and state and local governments spent $1.6 trillion. The federal government spent significantly more than state and local governments; page 46.

■ CHECKPOINT 2.3

Fill in the blanks

Most of the world's population lives in the <u>developing economies</u>. The lowest average income is in the <u>developing economies</u>. Advanced economies produce about <u>51</u> percent of the world's total production and the United States, alone, produces about <u>20</u> percent of the world's total production. About <u>67</u> percent of the world's proven oil reserves are located in <u>the Middle East</u>. As a fraction of total output, agricultural is a <u>larger</u> part of the economy in developing economies than in advanced economies. Factories in advanced economies are much <u>more</u> capital intensive than in developing economies. During the past 20 years, the distribution of income in the world economy has become <u>more</u> equal.

True or false
1. False; page 49
2. False; page 49
3. False; page 50
4. False; page 51
5. True; page 53
6. True; page 55

Multiple choice
1. c; page 49
2. e; page 49
3. b; page 49
4. b; page 49
5. a; page 50
6. a; page 52
7. a; page 53
8. a; page 55

Short answer and numeric questions
1. The groups are the advanced economies and the emerging market and developing economies. Advanced economies have the highest standard of living. Emerging market and developing economies have yet to achieve a high standard of living. The emerging market economies are changing their economies from government management and state-ownership of capital to market-based economies similar to that in the United States. There are more nations, 118, and more people, almost 5 billion, in developing economies; page 49.

2. Agriculture accounts for about 1.8 percent of total production in advanced economies and about 14 percent of total production within developing economies. Even though advanced economies have a much smaller fraction of their total production devoted to food, because the farms within these nations are large, efficient, and well-equipped with capital and because farmers within these nations are paid by their governments to produce food, the advanced economies produce about one third of world's food; page 52.

3. The human capital possessed by workers in the advanced economies is *much* larger than that in the developing economies. People in the advanced economies have vastly more education, more on-the-job training and, in general, better health than in the developing economies; page 53.

4. The distribution of income within the United States is more equal than the distribution of income in the world economy. In the United States, the poorest 20 percent of households receive about 3 percent of the total income and the richest 20 percent of households receive about 50 percent of total income. In the world economy, the poorest 20 percent of households receive about 2 percent of total income and the richest 20 percent receive about 70 percent of total income; page 54.

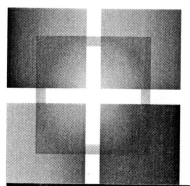

Chapter

3

The Economic Problem

Chapter 3 develops an economic model, the production possibilities frontier, or *PPF*, model. The *PPF* shows how the opportunity cost of a good or service increases as more of the good or service is produced. It can be used to illustrate economic growth and to demonstrate societies and individuals gain by specializing according to comparative advantage.

1   Explain and illustrate the concepts of scarcity, production efficiency, and tradeoff using the production possibilities frontier.

The production possibilities frontier, *PPF*, is the boundary between the combinations of goods and services that can be produced and those that cannot be produced, given the available factors of production and technology. Production points outside the *PPF* are unattainable. Points on and inside the *PPF* are attainable. Production points on the *PPF* are production efficient while production points within the *PPF* are inefficient. Moving along the *PPF* producing more of one good, less of another good is produced—a tradeoff. Moving from inside the *PPF* to a point on the *PPF*, more of some goods and services can be produced without producing less of others—a free lunch.

2   Calculate opportunity cost.

Along the *PPF* all choices involve a tradeoff. Along the *PPF*, the opportunity cost of the good on the *x*-axis is the loss of the good measured along the *y*-axis and is equal to the decrease in the good on the *y*-axis divided by the increase in the good on the *x*-axis. As more of a good is produced, its opportunity cost increases, so the *PPF* is bowed outward. The opportunity cost increases because resources are not equally productive in all activities. In the real world, most activities have increasing opportunity cost.

3   Explain what makes production possibilities expand.

Economic growth is the sustained expansion of production possibilities. If more capital is accumulated production possibilities increase and the *PPF* shifts outward. The (opportunity) cost of economic growth is that resources used to increase capital cannot be used to produce current consumption goods and services.

4   Explain how people gain from specialization and trade.

A person has a comparative advantage in an activity if he or she can perform the activity at lower opportunity cost than someone else. People can gain from specializing in production according to comparative advantage and then trading with others. In this situation people (and nations) can consume combinations of goods and services that lie beyond their production possibilities frontiers. An absolute advantage occurs when one person is more productive than another person in several or even all activities. A person can have an absolute advantage in all activities but cannot have a comparative advantage in all activities.

CHECKPOINT 3.1

■ **Explain and illustrate the concepts of scarcity, production efficiency, and tradeoff using the production possibilities frontier.**

Quick Review

- *Production possibilities frontier* The boundary between combinations of goods and services that can be produced and combinations that cannot be produced, given the available factors of production and the state of technology.

- *Unattainable points* Production points outside the *PPF* are unattainable.

- *Tradeoff* A constraint or limit to what is possible that forces an exchange or a substitution of one thing for something else.

Additional Practice Problem 3.1

Possibility	Fish (pounds)		Fruit (pounds)
A	0.0	and	36.0
B	4.0	and	35.0
C	7.5	and	33.0
D	10.5	and	30.0
E	13.0	and	26.0
F	15.0	and	21.0
G	16.5	and	15.0
H	17.5	and	8.0
I	18.0	and	0.0

1. The table above shows Crusoe's *PPF*. Can Crusoe gather 21 pounds of fruit and catch 30 pounds of fish? Explain your answer. Suppose that Crusoe discovers another fishing pond with more fish, so that he can catch twice as many fish as before. Now can Crusoe gather 21 pounds of fruit and catch 30 pounds of fish? Explain your answer.

Solution to Additional Practice Problem 3.1

1. Initially, Crusoe cannot gather 21 pounds of fruit and catch 30 pounds of fish. This production point lies outside his *PPF* and so is unattainable. Once Crusoe discovers the new pond, however, he can gather 21 pounds of fruit and catch 30 pounds of fish. (In Row *F*, double the

amount of Crusoe's fish.) The *PPF* depends on the available factors of production and when the factors of production increase, Crusoe's production possibilities change.

■ **Self Test 3.1**

Fill in the blanks

The ____ is the boundary between the combinations of goods and services that can and that cannot be produced given the available ____ (goods; factors of production) and ____ (number of services; state of technology). Production points outside the *PPF* ____ (are unattainable; are attainable; represent a free lunch). Production points ____ (on; beyond; within) the *PPF* are production efficient. Society has the possibility of a free lunch if production occurs ____ (inside; on; outside) the *PPF*. When resources are fully employed we face a ____ (free lunch; tradeoff).

True or false

1. A point outside the production possibilities frontier is unattainable.

2. If all the factors of production are fully employed, the economy will produce at a point on the production possibilities frontier.

3. Moving from one point on the *PPF* to another point on the *PPF* illustrates a free lunch.

4. All production points on the *PPF* are production efficient.

Multiple choice

1. The production possibilities frontier is a graph showing the
   a. exact point of greatest efficiency for producing goods and services.
   b. tradeoff between free lunches.
   c. maximum combinations of goods and services that can be produced.
   d. minimum combinations of goods and services that can be produced.
   e. resources available for the economy's use.

2. The production possibilities frontier is a boundary that separates
   a. the combinations of goods that can be produced from the combinations of services.
   b. attainable combinations of goods and services that can be produced from unattainable combinations.
   c. equitable combinations of goods that can be produced from inequitable combinations.
   d. reasonable combinations of goods that can be consumed from unreasonable combinations.
   e. affordable production points from unaffordable points.

3. Points inside the *PPF* are all
   a. unattainable and have fully employed resources.
   b. attainable and have fully employed resources.
   c. unattainable and have some unemployed resources.
   d. attainable and have some unemployed resources.
   e. unaffordable.

4. Points on the *PPF* are all
   a. unattainable and have fully employed resources.
   b. free lunches.
   c. inefficient.
   d. attainable and have some unemployed resources.
   e. production efficient.

5. During a time with high unemployment, a country can increase the production of one good or service
   a. without decreasing the production of something else.
   b. but must decrease the production of something else.
   c. and must increase the production of something else.
   d. by using resources in the production process twice.
   e. but the opportunity cost is infinite.

6. Moving along the production possibilities frontier itself illustrates
   a. the existence of tradeoffs.
   b. the existence of unemployment of productive resources.
   c. the benefits of free lunches.
   d. how free lunches can be exploited through trade.
   e. how tradeoffs need not occur if the economy is efficient.

Complete the graph

■ **FIGURE 3.1**

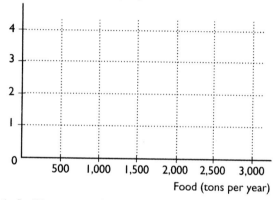

1. In Figure 3.1, draw a production possibilities frontier showing combinations of computers and food. Label the points that are attainable and unattainable. Label the points that have full employment and the points that have unemployment.

Short answer and numeric questions
1. What factors limit the amount of our production?
2. What points are production efficient? Moving between these points, is there a tradeoff or a free lunch?
3. What is the relationship between unemployment and a free lunch? Between full employment and a tradeoff?

CHECKPOINT 3.2

■ Calculate opportunity cost.

Quick Review

- *Opportunity cost is a ratio* Along a *PPF*, the opportunity cost of one good equals the quantity of the other good forgone divided by the increase in the good.

Additional Practice Problem 3.2

Possibility	Fish (pounds)		Fruit (pounds)
A	0.0	and	36.0
B	4.0	and	35.0
C	7.5	and	33.0
D	10.5	and	30.0
E	13.0	and	26.0
F	15.0	and	21.0
G	16.5	and	15.0
H	17.5	and	8.0
I	18.0	and	0.0

1. The table above shows Robinson Crusoe's production possibilities. How does Crusoe's opportunity cost of a pound of fish change as he catches more fish?

Solution to Additional Practice Problem 3.2

Move from	Increase in fish (pounds)	Decrease in fruit (pounds)	Opportunity cost of fish (pounds of fruit)
A to B	4.0	1.0	0.25
B to C	3.5	2.0	0.57
C to D	3.0	3.0	1.00
D to E	2.5	4.0	1.60
E to F	2.0	5.0	2.50
F to G	1.5	6.0	4.00
G to H	1.0	7.0	7.00
H to I	0.5	8.0	16.00

1. The table above shows Crusoe's opportunity cost of a pound of fish. His opportunity cost of a pound of fish increases as he catches more fish. As he moves from point *A* to point *B* and catches his first fish, the opportunity cost is only 0.25 pounds of fruit per pound of fish. But as he moves from point *H* to point *I* and catches only fish, the opportunity cost has increased to 16.0 pounds of fruit per pound of fish.

■ Self Test 3.2

Fill in the blanks

Along a production possibilities frontier, the opportunity cost of obtaining one more unit of a good is the amount of another good that is _____ (gained; forgone). The opportunity cost is equal to the quantity of the good forgone _____ (plus; divided by) the increase in the quantity of the other good. As more of a good is produced, its opportunity cost _____.

True or false

1. Moving from one point on the *PPF* to another point on the *PPF* has no opportunity cost.

2. When moving along the *PPF*, the quantity of CDs increases by 2 and the quantity of DVDs decreases by 1, so the opportunity cost is 2 CDs minus 1 DVD.

3. Increasing opportunity costs are common.

Multiple choice

1. The opportunity cost of one more slice of pizza in terms of sodas is the
   a. number of pizza slices we have to give up to get one extra soda.
   b. number of sodas we have to give up to get one extra slice of pizza.
   c. total number of sodas that we have divided by the total number of pizza slices that we have.
   d. total number of pizza slices that we have divided by the total number of sodas that we have.
   e. price of pizza minus the price of the soda.

2. Moving between two points on a *PPF*, a country gains 6 automobiles and forgoes 3 trucks. The opportunity cost of 1 automobile is
   a. 3 trucks.
   b. 6 automobiles – 3 trucks.
   c. 2 trucks.
   d. 1/2 of a truck.
   e. 1 automobile.

3. Moving between two points on a *PPF*, a country gains 8 desktop computers and forgoes 4 laptop computers. The opportunity cost of 1 desktop computer is
   a. 4 laptops.
   b. 8 desktops.
   c. 1 desktop.
   d. 2 laptops.
   e. 1/2 of a laptop.

4. A country produces only cans of soup and pens. If the country produces on its *PPF* and increases the production of cans of soup, the opportunity cost of additional
   a. cans of soup is increasing.
   b. cans of soup is decreasing.
   c. cans of soup remain unchanged.
   d. ink pens is increasing.
   e. More information is needed to determine what happens to the opportunity cost.

5. Moving along a country's *PPF*, a reason opportunity costs increase is that
   a. unemployment decreases as a country produces more and more of one good.
   b. unemployment increases as a country produces more and more of one good.
   c. technology declines as a country produces more and more of one good.
   d. some resources are better suited for producing one good rather than the other.
   e. technology must advance in order to produce more and more of one good.

6. Increasing opportunity costs exist
   a. in the real world.
   b. as long as there is high unemployment.
   c. only in theory but not in real life.
   d. for a country but not for an individual.
   e. inside the *PPF* but not on the *PPF*.

Complete the graph

1. The table at the top of the next column shows the production possibilities for a nation.
   a. Placing MP3 players on the vertical axis, label the axes in Figure 3.2 and graph the production possibilities frontier.

Production point	MP3 players (millions per year)		DVD players (millions per year)
A	4.0	and	0.0
B	3.0	and	3.0
C	2.0	and	4.0
D	1.0	and	4.7
E	0.0	and	5.0

■ **FIGURE 3.2**

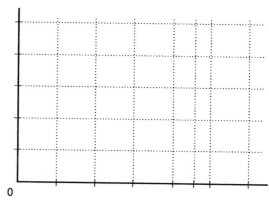

b. What is the opportunity cost per DVD player of moving from point *A* to point *B*? *B* to *C*? *C* to *D*? *D* to *E*? How does the opportunity cost change as more DVD players are produced?

Short answer and numeric questions

Production point	Cans of soda (millions per year)		Candy bars (millions per year)
A	8.0	and	0.0
B	6.0	and	4.0
C	4.0	and	6.0
D	2.0	and	7.0
E	0.0	and	7.5

1. The table above shows the production possibilities for Sweetland.
   a. What is the opportunity cost per candy bar player of moving from point *A* to point *B*? *B* to *C*? *C* to *D*? *D* to *E*?
   b. What is the opportunity cost per can of soda of moving from point *E* to point *D*? *D* to *C*? *C* to *B*? *B* to *A*?
   c. How does the opportunity cost of a candy bar change as more candy bars are produced? How does the opportunity cost of

a soda change as more sodas are produced?

2. What is the opportunity cost of increasing the production of a good while moving along a *PPF*? Why does this opportunity cost increase?

3. What does it mean for the opportunity cost to be a ratio?

CHECKPOINT 3.3

■ **Explain what makes production possibilities expand.**

Quick Review

• *Opportunity cost of growth* The opportunity cost of economic growth is the current consumption goods and services forgone.

Additional Practice Problem 3.3

1. Does economic growth eliminate scarcity?

Solution to Additional Practice Problem 3.3

1. Economic growth does not eliminate scarcity. Scarcity exists as long as people's wants exceed what can be produced. Economic growth increases the goods and services that can be produced but people's wants will continue to outstrip the ability to produce. While economic growth means that additional wants can be satisfied, people's wants are infinite and so scarcity will continue to be present even with economic growth.

■ **Self Test 3.3**

Fill in the blanks

A sustained expansion of production possibilities is called ____. Economic growth shifts the *PPF* ____ (inward; outward). The *PPF* shows that economic growth requires ____ (a decrease; an increase) in the current production of consumption goods. The opportunity cost of increasing economic growth is the loss of the ____ (current; future) goods that can be consumed.

True or false

1. Economic growth abolishes scarcity.

2. The opportunity cost of economic growth is less consumption goods in the future.

3. Production possibilities per person in the United States have remained constant during the last 30 years.

Multiple choice

1. To increase its economic growth, a nation should
   a. limit the number of people in college because they produce nothing.
   b. encourage spending on goods and services.
   c. encourage education because that increases the quality of labor.
   d. increase current consumption.
   e. eliminate expenditure on capital goods.

2. If Mexico devotes more resources to train its population than Spain,
   a. Mexico will be able to eliminate opportunity cost faster than Spain.
   b. Mexico will be able to eliminate scarcity faster than Spain.
   c. Spain will grow faster than Mexico.
   d. Mexico will grow faster than Spain.
   e. Mexico will have more current consumption than Spain.

3. If a nation devotes a larger share of its current production to consumption goods, then
   a. its economic growth will slow down.
   b. the *PPF* will shift outward.
   c. the *PPF* will shift inward.
   d. some productive factors will become unemployed.
   e. it must produce at a point within its PPF.

4. Which of the following is correct?
   i. As an economy grows, the opportunity costs of economic growth decrease.
   ii. Economic growth has no opportunity cost.
   iii. The opportunity cost of economic growth is current consumption forgone.
   a. i only.
   b. ii only.
   c. iii only.
   d. i and iii.
   e. i and ii.

5. When a country's production possibilities frontier shifts outward over time, the country is experiencing
   a. no opportunity cost.
   b. economic growth.
   c. higher unemployment of resources.
   d. a decrease in unemployment of resources.
   e. an end to opportunity cost.

6. The opportunity cost of economic growth is _____ and the benefit of economic growth is _____.
   a. increased current consumption; increased future consumption
   b. increased current consumption; decreased future consumption
   c. decreased current consumption; increased future consumption
   d. decreased current consumption; decreased future consumption.
   e. nothing; increased future consumption.

Complete the graph

■ **FIGURE 3.3**
Automobiles (millions per year)

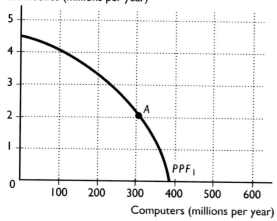

1. In the above figure, illustrate what happens if there is a technological breakthrough in the production of computers but not in the production of automobiles.
   a. Suppose the economy was initially producing at point *A*. After the breakthrough, is it possible for the economy to produce more computers *and* more automobiles?

Short answer and numeric questions
1. What is the opportunity cost of economic growth?
2. What is the benefit of economic growth?

CHECKPOINT 3.4

■ **Explain how people gain from specialization and trade.**

Quick Review
- *Comparative advantage* The ability of a person to perform an activity or produce a good or service at a lower opportunity cost than someone else.

Additional Practice Problem 3.4

1. Tony and Patty produce scooters and snowboards. The figure shows their production possibilities per day. With these production possibilities, the opportunity cost of a snowboard for

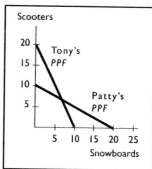

Patty is 1/2 a scooter and for Tony is 2 scooters. Patty has a lower opportunity cost and therefore she has the comparative advantage in snowboards. The opportunity cost of a scooter for Patty is 2 snowboards and for Tony is 1/2 of a snowboard. Tony has a lower opportunity cost and so he has the comparative advantage in scooters.

Suppose Patty acquires new equipment for scooter production that lets her produce a maximum of 60 rather than 10 scooters a day, should Patty and Tony specialize and trade?

Solution to Additional Practice Problem 3.4

1. Once Patty can produce 60 scooters a day, her opportunity costs change. Her opportunity cost of a scooter falls to 1/3 of a snowboard per scooter and her opportunity cost of a snowboard rises to 3 scooters per snowboard. With these opportunity costs, the comparative ad-

vantages have switched: Patty now has a comparative advantage in scooters and Tony in snowboards. Patty and Tony should still specialize and trade, only now Patty will specialize in scooters and Tony will specialize in snowboards. Comparative advantage can switch as the production possibilities frontier shifts outward.

■ Self Test 3.4

Fill in the blanks

A person has ____ (a comparative; an absolute) advantage in an activity if that person can perform the activity at a lower opportunity cost than someone else. If people specialize according to ____ (comparative; absolute) advantage and then trade, they can get ____ (outside; inside) their production possibilities frontiers. A person has ____ (a comparative; an absolute) advantage if they are more productive than someone else in all activities. It ____ (is; is not) possible for someone to have a comparative advantage in all activities. It ____ (is; is not) possible for someone to have an absolute advantage in all activities.

True or false

1. A person has an absolute advantage in an activity if the person can perform the activity at lower opportunity cost than someone else.

2. To achieve the gains from trade, a producer specializes in the product in which he or she has a comparative advantage and then trades with others.

3. Specialization and trade can make both producers better off even if one of them has an absolute advantage in producing all goods.

Multiple choice

1. "Comparative advantage" is defined as a situation in which one person can produce
   a. more of all goods than another person.
   b. more of a good than another person.
   c. a good for a lower dollar cost than another person.
   d. a good for a lower opportunity cost than another person.
   e. all goods for lower opportunity costs than another person.

For the next three questions, use the following information: Scott and Cindy both produce only pizza and tacos. In one hour, Scott can produce 20 pizzas or 40 tacos. In one hour, Cindy can produce 30 pizzas or 40 tacos.

2. Scott's opportunity cost of producing 1 taco is
   a. 1/2 of a pizza.
   b. 1 pizza.
   c. 2 pizzas.
   d. 20 pizzas.
   e. 2 tacos

3. Cindy's opportunity cost of producing 1 taco is
   a. 3/4 of a pizza.
   b. 1 pizza.
   c. 30 pizzas.
   d. 40 pizzas.
   e. 1 taco.

4. Based on the data given,
   a. Cindy has a comparative advantage in producing tacos.
   b. Scott has a comparative advantage in producing tacos.
   c. Cindy and Scott have the same comparative advantage when producing tacos.
   d. neither Cindy nor Scott has a comparative advantage when producing tacos.
   e. Cindy and Scott have the same comparative advantage when producing pizzas.

5. In one hour John can produce 20 loaves of bread or 8 cakes. In one hour Phyllis can produce 30 loaves of bread or 15 cakes. Which of the following statements is true?
   a. Phyllis has a comparative advantage when producing bread.
   b. John has a comparative advantage when producing cakes.
   c. Phyllis has an absolute advantage in both goods.
   d. John has an absolute advantage in both goods.
   e. Phyllis has a comparative advantage in producing both cakes and bread.

6. In one hour John can produce 20 loaves of bread or 16 cakes. In one hour Phyllis can produce 30 loaves of bread or 15 cakes. Which of the following statements is true?
   a. Phyllis has a comparative advantage when producing cakes.
   b. John has a comparative advantage when producing cakes.
   c. Phyllis has an absolute advantage in both goods.
   d. John has an absolute advantage in both goods.
   e. Phyllis has a comparative advantage in producing both cakes and bread.

Complete the graph

■ **FIGURE 3.4**

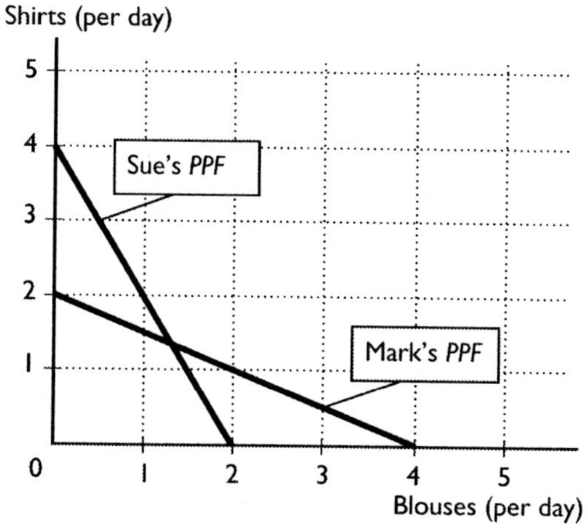

Shirts (per day)

1. Figure 3.4 shows Mark and Sue's *PPF*s.
   a. What is Sue's opportunity cost of produc-

   ing a shirt? What is Mark's opportunity cost of producing a shirt?
   b. Who has the comparative advantage in producing shirts?
   c. What is Sue's opportunity cost of producing a blouse? What is Mark's opportunity cost of producing a blouse?
   d. Who has the comparative advantage in producing blouses?
   e. Who should specialize in producing blouses and who should specialize in producing shirts?
   f. If Mark and Sue specialize according to their comparative advantage, indicate the total production of shirts and blouses by putting a point in Figure 3.4 showing the total production. Label the point *A*.
   g. How does point *A* show the gains from trade?

Short answer and numeric questions
1. Why should people specialize according to their comparative advantage?
2. To achieve gains from trade, the opportunity costs of the trading partners must diverge. Why?
3. When it comes to trading one good for another, why is comparative advantage crucial and absolute advantage unimportant?

■ CHECKPOINT 3.1

Fill in the blanks

The <u>production possibilities frontier or *PPF*</u> is the boundary between the combinations of goods and services that can and that cannot be produced given the available <u>factors of production</u> and <u>state of technology</u>. Production points outside the *PPF* <u>are unattainable</u>. Production points <u>on</u> the *PPF* are production efficient. Society has the possibility of a free lunch if production occurs <u>inside</u> the *PPF*. When resources are fully employed we face a <u>tradeoff</u>.

True or false

1. True; page 64
2. True; page 64
3. False; page 65
4. True; pages 64-65

Multiple choice

1. c; page 62
2. b; page 64
3. d; page 64
4. e; pages 64-65
5. a; page 65
6. a; page 65

Complete the graph

■ FIGURE 3.5

Computers (millions per year)

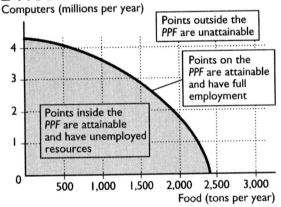

1. Figure 3.5 shows a *PPF* between computers and food; pages 63-64.

Short answer and numeric questions

1. The factors that limit the amount of our production are the available resources and the state of technology; page 62.
2. All points *on* the production possibilities frontier are production efficient. Moving from one point to another incurs an opportunity cost so there is tradeoff; pages 64-66
3. When the nation is producing at a point with unemployment, there are free lunches available because the production of some goods and services can be increased without decreasing the production of anything else. When the nation is producing at full employment, it is on the *PPF* and so only tradeoffs are available: If the production of one good or service is increased, the production of something else must be decreased; pages 65-66.

■ CHECKPOINT 3.2

Fill in the blanks

Along a production possibilities frontier, the opportunity cost of obtaining one more unit of a good is the amount of another good that is <u>forgone</u>. The opportunity cost is equal to the quantity of the good forgone <u>divided by</u> the increase in the quantity of the other good. As more of a good is produced, its opportunity cost <u>increases</u>.

True or false

1. False; page 68
2. False; page 69
3. True; page 70

Multiple choice

1. b; page 68
2. d; page 68
3. e; page 68
4. a; page 69
5. d; page 70
6. a; page 70

Complete the graph

■ FIGURE 3.6

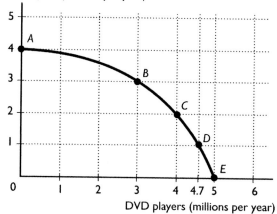

1. a. Figure 3.6 illustrates the production possibilities frontier; page 68.

   b. The opportunity cost of moving from point *A* to point *B* to is 0.33 MP3 players per DVD player; from *B* to *C* is 1.00 MP3 player per DVD player; from *C* to *D* is 1.43 MP3 players per DVD player; and, from *D* to *E* is 3.33 MP3 players per DVD player. The opportunity cost increases; page 68

Short answer and numeric questions

1. a. The opportunity cost of moving from point *A* to point *B* to is 0.5 cans of soda per candy bar; from *B* to *C* is 1.0 can of soda per candy bar; from *C* to *D* is 2.0 cans of soda per candy bar; and, from *D* to *E* is 4.0 cans of soda per candy bar; page 68.

   b. The opportunity cost of moving from point *E* to point *D* to is 0.25 candy bars per can of soda; from *D* to *C* is 0.50 candy bars per can of soda; from *C* to *B* is 1.00 candy bar per can of soda; and, from *B* to *A* is 2.00 candy bars per can of soda; page 68.

   c. As more candy bars are produced, the opportunity cost increases. As more cans of soda are produced, the opportunity cost increases; page 69.

2. The opportunity cost of increasing production of one good is the production of some other good forgone. The opportunity cost increases, so that increasingly large amounts of the other good are forgone, because resources are not equally productive in all activities. When initially increasing the production of one good, resources that are well suited for its production are used. When still more of the good is produced, resources that are less well suited must be used. Because the resources are ill suited, more are necessary to increase the production of the first good, and the forgone amount of the other good increases; page 70.

3. The opportunity cost is the amount of a good forgone to gain an additional unit another good. We divide the quantity of the good forgone by the increase in the other good. So opportunity cost is a ratio—the change in the quantity of one good divided by the change in the quantity of another good; page 70.

■ CHECKPOINT 3.3

Fill in the blanks

A sustained expansion of production possibilities is called <u>economic growth</u>. Economic growth shifts the *PPF* <u>outward</u>. The *PPF* shows that economic growth requires <u>a decrease</u> in the current production of consumption goods. The opportunity cost of increasing economic growth is the loss of the <u>current</u> goods that can be consumed.

True or false

1. False; page 73
2. False; pages 73-74
3. False; page 74

Multiple choice

1. c; page 73
2. d; pages 73-74
3. a; page 73
4. d; page 73
5. b; page 73
6. c; pages 73-79

Complete the graph

■ FIGURE 3.7
Automobiles (millions per year)

Computers (millions per year)

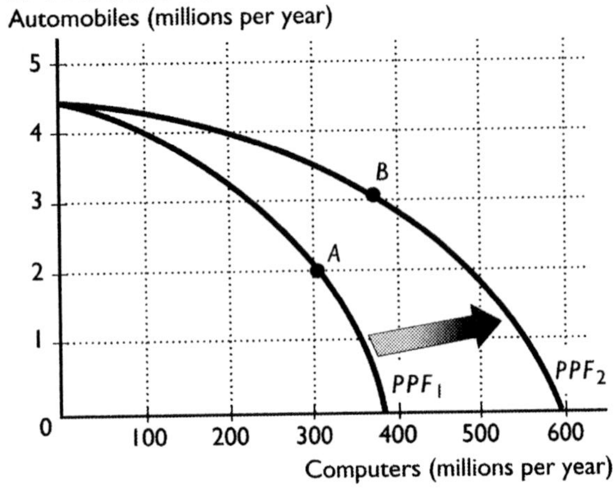

1. Figure 3.7 illustrates the new production possibilities frontier. Because the technological breakthrough did not affect automobile production, the maximum amount of automobiles that can be produced on the vertical axis does not change; pages 73-74.

1. a. Figure 3.7 shows that it is possible for the production of *both* automobiles and computers to increase, as a movement from the initial point A to a possible new point B illustrates; page 73.

Short answer and numeric questions

1. Economic growth requires either developing new technologies, accumulating more human capital, or accumulating more capital. All of these avenues require resources, so the opportunity cost of economic growth is the decrease in the current production of goods and services; page 73.

2. The benefit from economic growth is increased consumption per person in the future after the production possibilities frontier has expanded; page 73.

■ CHECKPOINT 3.4

Fill in the blanks

A person has <u>a comparative</u> advantage in an activity if that person can perform the activity at a lower opportunity cost than someone else. If people specialize according to <u>comparative</u> advantage and then trade, they can get <u>outside</u> their production possibilities frontiers. A person has <u>an absolute</u> advantage if they are more productive than someone else in all activities. It <u>is not</u> possible for someone to have a comparative advantage in all activities. It <u>is</u> possible for someone to have an absolute advantage in all activities.

True or false

1. False; pages 75-76
2. True; page 76
3. True; pages 76-77

Multiple choice

1. d; page 75
2. a; page 75
3. a; page 75
4. b; pages 75-76
5. c; page 76
6. b; page 76

Complete the graph

1. a. Sue's opportunity cost of a shirt is 1/2 of a blouse because, when moving along her *PPF* to produce 1 more shirt she forgoes 1/2 of a blouse. Mark's opportunity cost of a shirt is 2 blouses; page 75

   b. Sue has the comparative advantage in producing shirts because her opportunity cost is lower; page 75.

   c. Sue's opportunity cost of a blouse is 2 shirts because, when moving along her *PPF*, to produce 1 more blouse she forgoes 2 shirts. Mark's opportunity cost of a blouse is 1/2 of a shirt; page 75.

   d. Mark has the comparative advantage in producing blouses because his opportunity cost is lower; page 76.

   e. Mark should specialize in producing blouses and Sue should specialize in producing shirts; page 76.

■ **FIGURE 3.8**

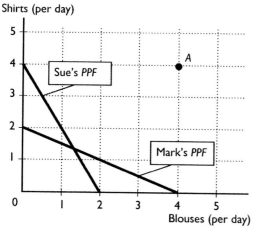

Shirts (per day)

f. Mark produces 4 blouses and Sue produces 4 shirts, so a total of 4 shirts and 4 blouses are produced. Figure 3.8 shows this production as point *A*; pages 76-77.

g. If the total production at point *A* is divided evenly, both Mark and Sue will receive 2 shirts and 2 blouses. When both were producing only for themselves, they could not produce 2 shirts and 2 blouses because this point is beyond both their *PPFs*. By specializing and trading, Mark and Sue get outside their *PPFs*; page 77.

Short answer and numeric questions

1. A person's comparative advantage is the good that the person can produce at a lower opportunity cost than other people. When this person specializes in the production of the good, it is produced at the lowest cost; page 76.

2. If the trading partners' opportunity costs are the same, there is no incentive for them to trade. For instance, if two people produce either gum or soda and both have the same opportunity cost of 5 gums for 1 soda, neither is willing to buy or sell to the other. Only when opportunity costs diverge will one person be willing to buy (the person with the higher opportunity cost) and the other willing to sell (the person with the lower opportunity cost); page 75-76.

3. People are willing to trade if they can obtain a good at lower opportunity cost than what it costs them to produce the good. Comparative advantage tells which person has a lower opportunity cost. Even if a person has an absolute advantage in all goods, he or she does not have a comparative advantage in all goods. So comparative advantage determines who produces a product and who buys it; page 76.

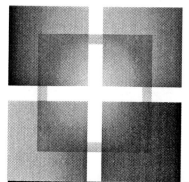

Demand and Supply

Chapter

4

The tools of demand and supply explain how competitive markets work. We use the demand and supply tools to determine the quantities and prices of the goods and services produced and consumed.

1 Distinguish between quantity demanded and demand, and explain what determines demand.

The quantity demanded is the amount of any good, service, or resource that people are willing and able to buy during a specified period at a specified price. Demand is the relationship between the quantity demanded and the price of a good when all other influences on buying plans remain the same. The law of demand states that other things remaining the same, if the price of a good rises, the quantity demanded of that good decreases; and if the price of a good falls, the quantity demanded of that good increases. A demand curve is a graph of the relationship between the quantity demanded of a good and its price when all other influences on buying plans remain the same. The market demand is the sum of the demands of all the buyers in a market. A change in price leads to a *change in the quantity demanded* and a movement along the demand curve. Factors that *change demand* and shift the demand curve are: prices of related goods; income; expectations; number of buyers; and preferences.

2 Distinguish between quantity supplied and supply, and explain what determines supply.

The quantity supplied is the amount of any good, service, or resource that people are willing and able to sell during a specified period at a specified price. Supply is the relationship between the quantity supplied and the price of a good when all other influences on selling plans remain the same. The law of supply states that other things remaining the same, if the price of a good rises, the quantity supplied of that good increases; and if the price of a good falls, the quantity supplied of that good decreases. A supply curve is a graph of the relationship between the quantity supplied of a good and its price when all other influences on selling plans remain the same. A change in price leads to a *change in the quantity supplied* and a movement along the supply curve. Factors that *change supply* and shift the supply curve are: prices of related goods; prices of resources and other inputs; expectations; number of sellers; and productivity. If supply increases (decreases), the supply curve shifts rightward (leftward).

3 Explain how demand and supply determine price and quantity in a market and explain the effects of changes in demand and supply.

The equilibrium price and equilibrium quantity occur when the quantity demanded equals the quantity supplied. An increase in demand raises the price and increases the quantity. An increase in supply lowers the price and increases the quantity. An increase in both demand and supply increases the quantity and the price might rise, fall, or not change. An increase in demand and a decrease in supply raises the price and the quantity might increase, decrease, or not change. Changes in demand and supply in the opposite direction to those given above lead to reverse changes in price and quantity.

CHECKPOINT 4.1

■ **Distinguish between quantity demanded and demand, and explain what determines demand.**

Quick Review

- *Change in the quantity demanded* A change in the quantity of a good that people plan to buy that results from a change in the price of the good.
- *Law of demand* If the price of a good rises, the quantity demanded of that good decreases; and if the price of a good falls, the quantity demanded of that good decreases.
- *Change in demand* A change in the quantity that people plan to buy when any influence on buying plans, other than the price of the good, changes. These other influences include: prices of related goods, income, expectations, number of buyers, and preferences.

Additional Practice Problems 4.1

1. In the market for motor scooters, several events occur, one at a time. Explain the influence of each event on the quantity demanded of scooters and on the demand for scooters. Illustrate the effects of each event either by a movement along the demand curve or a shift in the demand curve for scooters and say which event (or events) illustrates the law of demand in action. These events are:
   a. The price of a scooter falls.
   b. The price of a car falls.
   c. Citing rising injury rates, cities and towns ban scooters from busy streets.
   d. Scooters are a normal good and income increases.
   e. Scooters become unfashionable and the number of buyers decreases.

2. Suppose that each year Anna, Ben, Carol, and Dana are willing and able to buy scooters as shown in the table.

Price (dollars per scooter)	Quantity demanded			
	Anna	Ben	Carol	Dana
100	0	0	0	0
75	1	0	0	0
50	2	1	1	0
25	2	1	2	1

■ FIGURE 4.1

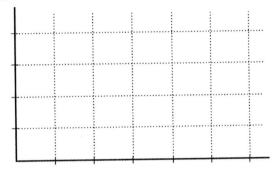

Using the information in the table:
   a. Label the axes in Figure 4.1 above.
   b. Graph the market demand curve.

Solutions to Additional Practice Problems 4.1

1a. This problem emphasizes the distinction between a change in the quantity demanded and a change in demand. A fall in the price of a scooter brings an increase in the quantity demanded of scooters, which is illustrated by a movement down along the demand curve for scooters as shown in the figure. This event illustrates the law of demand in action.

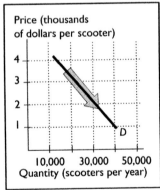

1b. A car is a substitute for a scooter. With the lower price of a car, some people who previously would have bought a scooter will now buy a car instead. So a fall in the price of cars decreases the demand for scooters. The demand curve for scooters shifts leftward as shown in the figure below.

1c. Rising injury rates and banning scooters from streets changes preferences and makes scooters less desirable. The demand for scooters decreases and the demand curve for the scooters

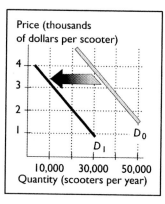

shifts leftward as shown in the figure leftward as shown in the figure by the shift from demand curve D_0 to demand curve D_1.

1d. A scooter is a normal good, so people will buy more scooters when their income increases. The demand for scooters increases and the demand curve shifts right-

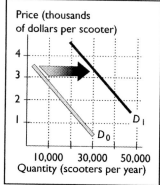

ward as illustrated in the figure.

1e. A decrease in the number of buyers decreases the demand for scooters. The demand curve shifts leftward.

■ FIGURE 4.2

Price (dollars per scooter)

![Figure 4.2 graph showing demand curve D with points at (0,100), (1,75), (4,50), (6,25); x-axis Quantity (scooters per year) from 0 to 6, y-axis Price 25,50,75,100]

Quantity (scooters per year)

2a. Figure 4.2 labels the axes.

2b. The market demand curve is derived by adding the quantities demanded by Anna, Ben, Carol, and Dana at each price. The market demand curve is illustrated in Figure 4.2.

■ Self Test 4.1

Fill in the blanks

The _____ (demand schedule; law of demand) states that other things remaining the same, if the price of a good rises, the _____ (quantity demanded of; demand for) that good decreases. A _____ is a graph of the relationship between the quantity demanded of a good and its price. Demand curves are _____ (downward; upward) sloping. An increase in demand shifts the demand curve _____. Factors that change demand lead to a _____ (shift of; movement along) the demand curve. Factors that change demand are _____, _____, _____, _____, and _____.

True or false

1. The law of demand states that other things remaining the same, if the price of a good rises, the quantity demanded of that good increases.

2. If the quantity of ice cream demanded at each price increases, there is a movement along the demand curve for ice cream.

3. When Sue's income increases, her demand for movies increases. For Sue, movies are a normal good.

4. A rise in the price of a computer increases the demand for computers because a computer is a normal good.

5. If people's incomes fall and all other influences on buying plans remain the same, the demand for computers will decrease and there will be a movement along the demand curve.

Multiple choice

1. The "law of demand" indicates that if the University of Maine increases the tuition, all other things remaining the same,
   a. the demand for classes will decrease at the University of Maine.
   b. the demand for classes will increase at the University of Maine.
   c. the quantity of classes demanded will increase at the University of Maine.
   d. the quantity of classes demanded will decrease at the University of Maine.
   e. both the demand for and the quantity of classes demanded will decrease at the University of Maine.

2. Other things remaining the same, the quantity of a good or service demanded will increase if the price of the good or service
   a. rises.
   b. falls.
   c. does not change.
   d. rises or does not change.
   e. rises or falls.

3. Teenagers demand more soda than other age groups. If the number of teenagers increases, everything else remaining the same,
   a. market demand for soda increases.
   b. market demand for soda decreases.
   c. market demand for soda does not change.
   d. there is a movement along the market demand curve for soda.
   e. None of the above answers is correct because the effect on the demand depends whether the supply curve shifts.

4. One reason the demand for laptop computers might increase is a
   a. fall in the price of a laptop computers.
   b. fall in the price of a desktop computer.
   c. a change in preferences as laptops have become more portable, with faster processors and larger hard drives.
   d. poor quality performance record for laptop computers.
   e. a decrease in income if laptops are a normal good.

5. The number of buyers of sport utility vehicles, SUVs, decreases sharply. So
   a. the demand curve for SUVs shifts leftward.
   b. the demand curve for SUVs shifts rightward.
   c. there is neither a shift nor a movement along the demand curve for SUVs.
   d. there is a movement down along the demand curve for SUVs.
   e. the supply curve for SUVs shifts rightward.

■ FIGURE 4.3
Price (dollars per pizza)

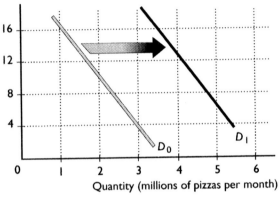

Quantity (millions of pizzas per month)

6. The shift of the demand curve for pizza illustrated in Figure 4.3 could be the result of
   a. a rise in income if pizza is a normal good.
   b. a fall in the price of fried chicken, a substitute for pizza.
   c. consumers coming to believe that pizza is unhealthy.
   d. the belief that pizza will fall in price next month.
   e. a fall in the price of a pizza.

7. The shift of the demand curve for pizza illustrated in Figure 4.3 could be the result of
   a. a rise in income if pizza is an inferior good.
   b. a fall in the price of soda, a complement for pizza.
   c. a decrease in the number of college students if college students eat more pizza than other age groups.
   d. a rise in the price of a pizza.
   e. a fall in the price of a pizza.

8. When moving along a demand curve, which of the following changes?
   a. the consumers' incomes
   b. the prices of other goods
   c. the number of buyers
   d. the price of the good
   e. the consumers' preferences

9. If the price of a CD falls,
   i. the demand curve for CDs shifts rightward.
   ii. the demand curve for CDs will not shift.
   iii. there is a movement along the demand curve for CDs.
   a. i only.
   b. ii only.
   c. iii only.
   d. ii and iii.
   e. i and iii.

10. Pizza and tacos are substitutes and the price of a pizza increases. Which of the following correctly indicates what happens?
    a. The demand for pizzas decreases and the demand for tacos increases.
    b. The demand for both goods decreases.
    c. The quantity of tacos demanded increases and the quantity of pizza demanded decreases.
    d. The quantity of pizza demanded decreases and the demand for tacos increases.
    e. The demand for each decreases because both are normal goods.

Complete the graph

Price (dollars per bundle of cotton candy)	Quantity (bundles of cotton candy per month)
1	10,000
2	8,000
3	7,000
4	4,000

1. The demand schedule for cotton candy is given in the following table. In Figure 4.4, draw the demand curve. Label the axes.
   a. If the price of cotton candy is $2 a bundle, what is the quantity demanded?

■ **FIGURE 4.4**

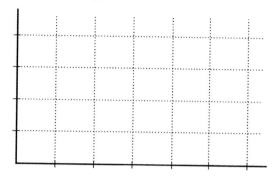

   b. If the price of cotton candy is $3 a bundle, what is the quantity demanded?
   c. Does the demand curve you drew slope upward or downward?

■ **FIGURE 4.5**

Price (dollars per pound of butter)

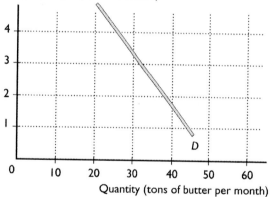

Quantity (tons of butter per month)

2. Butter is a normal good and margarine is substitute for butter. Figure 4.5 shows the demand curve for butter.
   a. In Figure 4.5, show how the demand curve shifts if incomes rise. Label this demand curve D_1.
   b. In Figure 4.5, show how the demand curve shifts if margarine falls in price. Label this demand curve D_2.
   c. If the price of butter falls from $4 a pound to $3 a pound, does the demand curve shift toward demand curve D_1, D_2, or neither? Explain your answer.

Short answer and numeric questions

Price (dollars per gallon)	Quantity demanded (gallons per week)
3.10	320
3.20	316
3.30	310
3.40	300
3.50	205

1. The table above gives the demand schedule for gasoline for a group of students. If the price of gasoline falls from $3.30 to $3.20 per gallon, how much gas will the students buy?

2. Explain the difference between a change in quantity demanded and a change in demand.

3. What is the difference between a movement along a demand curve and a shift in a demand curve?

CHECKPOINT 4.2

■ **Distinguish between quantity supplied and supply and explain what determines supply.**

Quick Review

- *Change in quantity supplied* A change in the quantity of a good that suppliers plan to sell that results from a change in the price of the good.

- *Change in supply* A change in the quantity that suppliers plan to sell when any influence on selling plans, other than the price of the good, changes. These other influences include: prices of related goods, prices of inputs, expectations, number of sellers, and productivity.

Additional Practice Problems 4.2

1. In the market for motor scooters, several events occur, one at a time. Explain the influence of each event on the quantity supplied of scooters and on the supply of scooters. Illustrate the effects of each event either by a movement along the supply curve or a shift in the supply curve and say which event (or events) illustrates the law of supply in action. These events are:

   a. The price of a scooter rises.

   b. The price of the steel used to make scooters rises.

   c. The number of firms making scooters decreases.

   d. Technological change increases the productivity of the factories making scooters.

Price (dollars per ton of plywood)	Quantity supplied (tons of plywood per month)			
	Eddy	Franco	George	Helen
100	2	2	1	1
75	2	1	1	1
50	1	1	1	0
25	0	0	1	0

■ **FIGURE 4.6**

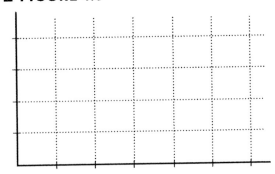

2. Each month Eddy, Franco, George, and Helen are willing and able to sell plywood as shown in the table above.

   a. Label the axes in Figure 4.6.

   b. Graph the market supply curve.

Solutions to Additional Practice Problems 4.2

1a. This problem emphasizes the distinction between a change in the quantity supplied and a change in supply. A rise in the price of a motor scooter brings an increase in the

quantity supplied of scooters, which is illustrated by a movement up along the supply curve for scooters as shown in the figure. There is no change in the supply and the supply curve does not shift. This event illustrates the law of supply in action.

1b. When the price of the steel used to make scooters rises, the cost to produce scooters increases. As a result, the supply of scooters decreases. The supply curve shifts leftward as illustrated.

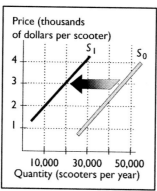

1c. A decrease in the number of firms producing scooters decreases the supply of scooters. The supply curve shifts leftward, as illustrated in the figure above.

1d. An increase in the productivity of the factories making scooters lowers the costs of producing scooters. The supply of scooters increases and the supply curve shifts rightward, as illustrated in the figure.

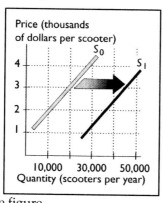

2a. The axes are labeled in Figure 4.7.

Price (dollars per ton of plywood)	Quantity supplied (tons per month)
100	6
75	5
50	3
25	1

2b. The market supply curve is derived by adding the quantities supplied by Eddy, Franco, George, and Helen at each price. The table above gives the resulting sum and the market supply curve is illustrated in Figure 4.7.

■ **FIGURE 4.7**

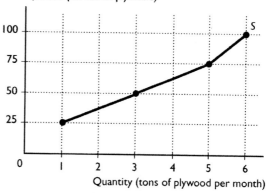

■ **Self Test 4.2**

Fill in the blanks

The ____ (quantity supplied; supply) of a good is the amount people are willing and able to sell during a specified period at a specified price. The law of supply states that other things remaining the same, if the price of a good rises, the quantity supplied ____. A supply curve is ____ (upward; downward) sloping. A change in the price of a good changes ____ (supply; the quantity supplied) and is illustrated by a ____ the supply curve. Factors that change supply are ____, ____, ____, ____, and ____.

True or false

1. The law of supply states that other things remaining the same, if the price of a good rises, the supply of the good increases.

2. When new technology for producing computers is used by manufacturers, the supply of computers increases.

3. If the wage rate paid to chefs rises and all other influences on selling plans remain the same, the supply of restaurant meals will increase.

4. If the price of coffee is expected to rise next month, the supply of coffee this month will decrease.

5. The supply of a good will increase and there will be a movement up along the supply curve of the good if the price of one of its substitutes in production falls.

Multiple choice

1. The quantity supplied of a good, service, or resource is ____ during a specified period and at a specified price.
   a. the amount that people are able to sell
   b. the amount that people are willing to sell
   c. the amount that people are able and willing to sell
   d. the amount that people are willing and able to buy
   e. the amount sold

2. One reason supply curves have an upward slope is because
   a. increased supply will require increased technology.
   b. people will pay a higher price when less is supplied.
   c. a higher price brings a greater profit, so firms want to sell more of that good.
   d. to have more of the good supplied requires more firms to open.
   e. None of the above answers is correct because supply curves have a downward slope.

3. Which of the following indicates that the law of supply applies to makers of soda?
   a. An increase in the price of a soda leads to an increase in the demand for soda.
   b. An increase in the price of a soda leads to an increase in the supply of soda.
   c. An increase in the price of a soda leads to an increase in the quantity of soda supplied.
   d. A decrease in the price of a soda leads to an increase in the quantity of soda demanded.
   e. A decrease in the price of a soda leads to an increase in the supply of soda.

4. The market supply curve is the ____ of the ____.
   a. horizontal sum; individual supply curves
   b. vertical sum; individual supply curves
   c. horizontal sum; individual supply curves minus the market demand
   d. vertical sum; individual supply curves minus the market demand
   e. vertical average; individual supply curves

5. If the costs to produce pizza increase, which will occur?
   a. The supply of pizza will decrease.
   b. The quantity of pizzas supplied will increase as sellers try to cover their costs.
   c. Pizza will cease to be produced and sold.
   d. The demand curve for pizza will shift leftward when the price of a pizza increases.
   e. The demand curve for pizza will shift rightward when the price of a pizza increases.

6. A rise in the price of a substitute in production for a good leads to
   a. an increase in the supply of that good.
   b. a decrease in the supply of that good.
   c. no change in the supply of that good.
   d. a decrease in the quantity of that good supplied.
   e. no change in either the supply or the quantity supplied of the good.

7. An increase in the productivity of producing jeans results in
   a. the quantity of jeans supplied increasing.
   b. the supply of jeans increasing.
   c. buyers demanding more jeans because they are now more efficiently produced.
   d. buyers demanding fewer jeans because their price will fall, which signals lower quality.
   e. some change but the impact on the supply of jeans is impossible to predict.

■ **FIGURE 4.8**
Price (dollars per pizza)

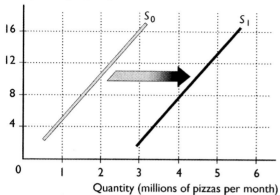

8. The shift of the supply curve of pizza illustrated in Figure 4.8 could be the result of
   a. a rise in the price of cheese used to produce pizza.
   b. a decrease in the number of firms producing pizza.
   c. an increase in the productivity of the firms producing pizza.
   d. a rise in the price of a substitute in production.
   e. a rise in the price of a pizza.

9. The shift of the supply curve of pizza illustrated in Figure 4.8 could be the result of
   a. a rise in income if pizza is a normal good.
   b. a fall in the price of soda, a consumer complement for pizza.
   c. an increase in the number of firms producing pizza.
   d. a rise in the price of a pizza.
   e. a rise in the wage paid the workers who make pizza.

10. Suppose the price of leather used to produce shoes increases. As a result, there is ____ in the supply of shoes and the supply curve of shoes ____.
   a. an increase; shifts rightward
   b. an increase; shifts leftward
   c. a decrease; shifts rightward
   d. a decrease; shifts leftward
   e. no change; does not shift

Complete the graph

Price (dollars per bundle of cotton candy)	Quantity (bundles of cotton candy per month)
1	4,000
2	8,000
3	10,000
4	12,000

1. The supply schedule for cotton candy is given in the table above. In Figure 4.4, you previously drew a demand curve for cotton candy. Now use the supply schedule to draw the supply curve in Figure 4.4.
   a. If the price of cotton candy is $2 a bundle, what is the quantity supplied?
   b. If the price of cotton candy is $3 a bundle, what is the quantity supplied?
   c. Does the supply curve you drew slope upward or downward?

■ **FIGURE 4.9**
Price (dollars per ton of rubber bands)

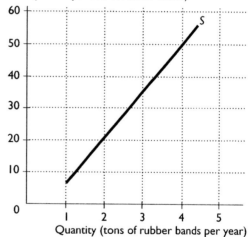

2. Figure 4.9 shows a supply curve for rubber bands. Suppose the productivity of producing rubber bands increases. In Figure 4.9, illustrate the effect of this event.

■ **FIGURE 4.10**

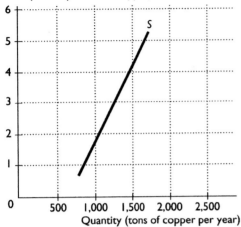

Price (dollars per ton of copper)

3. Figure 4.10 shows the supply curve for copper. The cost of the natural gas used to refine copper ore into copper rises. In Figure 4.10, show the effect of this event.

Short answer and numeric questions

1. What is the law of supply?

Price	Quantity supplied (pizza per day)			
(dollars per pizza)	Tom	Bob	Kate	Market supply
14	20	12	15	____
12	16	10	10	____
10	12	8	5	____
8	8	6	0	____

2. The table gives the supply schedules for the three pizza producers in a small town. Calculate the market supply schedule.

3. What influence(s) lead to a change in the quantity supplied?

4. What influences lead to a change in supply?

CHECKPOINT 4.3

■ **Explain how demand and supply determine the price and quantity in a market and explain the effects of changes in demand and supply.**

Quick Review

• *Market equilibrium* When the quantity demanded equals the quantity supplied.

Additional Practice Problems 4.3

1. Hot dogs are an inferior good and people's incomes rise. What happens to the equilibrium price and quantity of hot dogs?

2. Hot dog producers develop new technology that increases their productivity. What happens to the price and quantity of hot dogs?

3. The price of a hot dog bun falls and, simultaneously, the number of hot dog producers increases. The effect of the fall in the price of a hot dog bun is less than the effect of the increase in the number of producers. What happens to the equilibrium price and quantity of hot dogs?

Solutions to Additional Practice Problems 4.3

1. When income increases, the demand for an inferior good decreases and the demand curve shifts leftward. The supply does not change and the supply curve does not shift. The equilibrium price of a hot dog falls and the equilibrium quantity decreases, as illustrated in the figure.

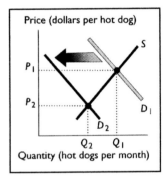

2. When the productivity of producing a good increases, the supply of the good increases and the supply curve shifts rightward. So the supply curve of hot dogs shifts rightward. The demand does not change and so the demand curve does not shift. As illustrated, the price of a hot dog falls and the quantity increases.

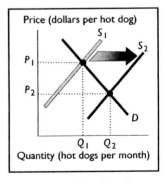

3. The fall in the price of a complement, hot dog buns, increases the demand for hot dogs and the demand curve for hot dogs shifts rightward. The

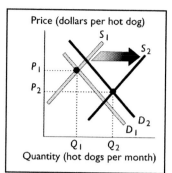

increase in the number of producers increases the supply of hot dogs and the supply curve shifts rightward. Because the increase in supply exceeds the increase in demand, the price of a hot dog falls and the quantity increases, as shown in the figure.

■ Self Test 4.3

Fill in the blanks

The price at which the quantity demanded equals the quantity supplied is the _____. In a diagram, the _____ is determined where the supply and demand curves intersect. If the price exceeds the equilibrium price, the price _____ (rises; falls). An increase in demand _____ (raises; lowers) the equilibrium price and _____ (increases; decreases) the equilibrium quantity. An increase in supply _____ (raises; lowers) the equilibrium price and _____ (increases; decreases) the equilibrium quantity. If both the demand and supply increase, definitely the equilibrium _____ increases but the effect on the equilibrium _____ is ambiguous.

True or false

1. If the price of asparagus is below the equilibrium price, there is a shortage of asparagus and the price of asparagus will rise until the shortage disappears.

2. When the demand for skateboards decreases and the supply of skateboards remains unchanged, the quantity supplied of skateboards decreases as the price rises.

3. Gasoline refiners expect the price of oil will fall next month. If the supply of oil does not change, the equilibrium price of oil today falls and the equilibrium quantity today decreases.

4. As summer comes to an end and winter sets in, the demand for and supply of hamburger buns decrease. The price of a hamburger bun definitely remains the same.

5. The number of buyers of grapefruit juice increases and at the same time severe frost decreases the supply of grapefruit juice. The price of grapefruit juice will rise.

Multiple choice

1. The equilibrium price of a good occurs if the
   a. quantity of the good demanded equals the quantity of the good supplied.
   b. quantity of the good demanded is greater than the quantity of the good supplied.
   c. quantity of the good demanded is less than the quantity of the good supplied.
   d. demand for the good is equal to the supply of the good.
   e. price of the good seems reasonable to most buyers.

2. Which of the following is correct?
   i. A surplus puts downward pressure on the price of a good.
   ii. A shortage puts upward pressure on the price of a good
   iii. There is no surplus or shortage at equilibrium.
   a. i and ii..
   b. i and iii.
   c. ii and iii.
   d. i, ii, and iii.
   e. only iii.

3. The number of buyers of ceiling fans increases, so there is an increase in the
   a. quantity of ceiling fans demanded and a surplus of ceiling fans.
   b. demand for ceiling fans and a rise in the price of a ceiling fan.
   c. demand for ceiling fans and a surplus of ceiling fans.
   d. supply of ceiling fans and no change in the price of a ceiling fan.
   e. demand for ceiling fans and in the supply of ceiling fans.

4. Which of the following is the best explanation for why the price of gasoline increases during the summer months?
   a. Oil producers have higher costs of production in the summer.
   b. Sellers have to earn profits during the summer to cover losses in the winter.
   c. There is increased driving by families going on vacation.
   d. There is less competition among oil refineries in the summer.
   e. The number of gas stations open 24 hours a day rises in the summer months and so the price must rise to cover the higher costs.

5. Suppose that the price of lettuce used to produce tacos increases. As a result, the equilibrium price of a taco ____ and the equilibrium quantity ____.
   a. rises; increases
   b. rises; decreases
   c. falls; increases
   d. falls; decreases
   e. does not change; decreases

6. The technology associated with manufacturing computers has advanced enormously. This change has led to the price of a computer ____ and the quantity ____.
   a. rising; increasing
   b. rising; decreasing
   c. falling; increasing
   d. falling; decreasing
   e. falling; not changing

7. Candy makers accurately anticipate the increase in demand for candy for Halloween so that the supply of candy and the demand for candy increase the same amount. As a result, the price of candy ____ and the quantity of candy ____.
   a. rises; does not change
   b. falls; increases
   c. does not change; increases
   d. does not change; does not change
   e. rises; rises

8. During 2007 the supply of petroleum decreased while at the same time the demand for petroleum increased. If the magnitude of the increase in demand was greater than the magnitude of the decrease in supply, then the equilibrium price of gasoline ____ and the equilibrium quantity ____.
   a. increased; increased
   b. increased; decreased
   c. increased; did not change
   d. decreased; did not change
   e. did not change; increased

Complete the graph

1. In Checkpoint 4.1 you drew a demand curve in Figure 4.4; in Checkpoint 4.2, you drew a supply curve in that figure. Return to Figure 4.4 and answer the following questions.
   a. If the price of cotton candy is $1, what is the situation in the market?
   b. If the price of cotton candy is $3, what is the situation in the market?
   c. What is the equilibrium price and equilibrium quantity of cotton candy?

Price (dollars per sweatshirt)	Quantity demanded (sweatshirts per season) Hockey team	Soccer team	Quantity supplied (sweatshirts per season)
35	5	8	32
30	6	9	25
25	8	11	19
20	12	15	12
15	17	20	8

2. The table gives the demand and supply schedules for sweatshirts. What is the market demand schedule? At what price will the quantity demanded be equal to the quantity supplied? What is the equilibrium quantity?

■ **FIGURE 4.11**
Price (dollars per piece of gold jewelry)

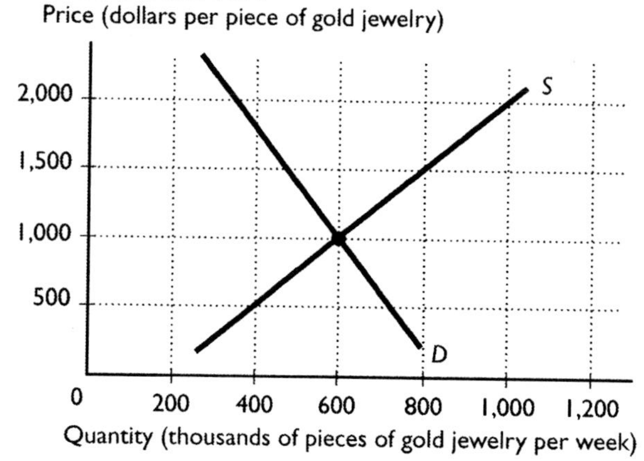

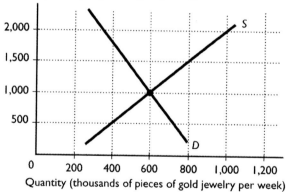

3. Figure 4.11 shows the supply and demand for gold jewelry. In the figure, show what happens to the price and quantity if gold jewelry is a normal good and people's incomes rise.

■ **FIGURE 4.12**
Price (dollars per piece of gold jewelry)

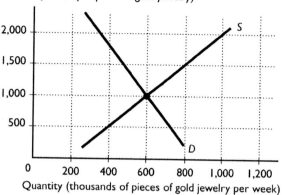

4. Figure 4.12 shows the supply and demand for gold jewelry. Suppose that consumers think that silver jewelry is a substitute for gold jewelry. In Figure 4.12, show what happens to the price and quantity if the price of silver jewelry falls.

■ **FIGURE 4.13**
Price (dollars per piece of gold jewelry)

5. Figure 4.13 shows the supply and demand for gold jewelry. Suppose the price of the gold that is used to produce gold jewelry rises. In the figure, show what happens to the price and quantity of gold jewelry.

Short answer and numeric questions

1. How is a shortage different from a surplus?

2. People read that drinking orange juice helps prevent heart disease. What is the effect on the equilibrium price and quantity of orange juice?

3. The cost of memory chips used in computers falls. What is the effect on the equilibrium price and quantity of computers?

4. New cars are a normal good and people's incomes increase. Simultaneously, auto manufacturers must pay more for their workers' health insurance. What is the effect on the price and quantity of new cars?

5. The Eye on Your Life on page 105 points out that supply and demand will be a big part of your life. How can you use the model to make day-to-day decisions, such as when to buy gasoline?

SELF TEST ANSWERS

■ CHECKPOINT 4.1

Fill in the blanks

The <u>law of demand</u> states that other things remaining the same, if the price of a good rises,
the <u>quantity demanded of</u> that good decreases.
A <u>demand curve</u> is a graph of the relationship
between the quantity demanded of a good and
its price. Demand curves are <u>downward</u> sloping. An increase in demand shifts the demand
curve <u>rightward</u>. Factors that change demand
lead to a <u>shift of</u> the demand curve. Factors that
change demand are <u>prices of related goods</u>, <u>in-
come</u>, <u>expectations</u>, <u>number of buyers</u>, and
<u>preferences</u>.

True or false

1. False; page 85
2. False; page 84
3. True; page 89
4. False; page 89
5. False; page 90

Multiple choice

1. d; page 85
2. b; page 85
3. a; page 89
4. c; page 89
5. a; page 89
6. a; page 89
7. b; page 89
8. d; page 90
9. d; page 90
10. d; page 89-90

Complete the graph

1. a. Figure 4.14 illustrates the demand curve,
   labeled *D* in the diagram. (The supply
   curve is from the first "Complete the
   Graph" question in Checkpoint 4.2.)
   a. 8,000 bundles per month
   b. 7,000 bundles per month
   c. The demand curve slopes downward;
      pages 90.

■ FIGURE 4.14

Price (dollars per bundle of cotton candy)

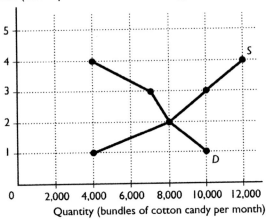

■ FIGURE 4.15

Price (dollars per pound of butter)

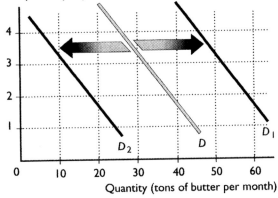

2. a. The demand increases and the demand
   curve shifts rightward, as shown in Figure
   4.15 by the shift to *D*₁; page 90
   b. The demand decreases and the demand
   curve shifts leftward, as shown in Figure
   4.15 by the shift to *D*₂; page 90
   c. The demand curve does not shift. The fall
   in the price of butter leads to an increase
   in the quantity demanded and a movement along the demand curve, not a shift
   of the demand curve; page 90.

Short answer and numeric questions

1. When the price falls from $3.30 a gallon to
   $3.20 a gallon, the quantity of gasoline de-

manded increases from 310 gallons to 316 gallons; page 86.

2. A change in the quantity demanded occurs when the price of the good changes. A change in demand occurs when any other influence on buying plans other than the price of the good changes; page 88.

3. A movement along a demand curve reflects a change in the quantity demanded and is the result of a change in the price of the product. A shift in a demand curve reflects a change in demand and is the result of a change in any factor, other than the price, that affects demand; page 90.

■ CHECKPOINT 4.2

Fill in the blanks

The quantity supplied of a good is the amount people are willing and able to sell during a specified period at a specified price. The law of supply states that other things remaining the same, if the price of a good rises, the quantity supplied increases. A supply curve is upward sloping. A change in the price of a good changes the quantity supplied and is illustrated by a movement along the supply curve. Factors that change supply are prices of related goods, prices of resources and other inputs, expectations, number of sellers, and productivity.

True or false

1. False; page 92
2. True; page 96
3. False; page 96
4. True; page 96
5. False; page 96

Multiple choice

1. c; page 92
2. c; page 92
3. c; page 92
4. a; page 94
5. a; page 96
6. b; page 96
7. b; page 96
8. c; page 96
9. c; page 96
10. d; page 97

Complete the graph

1. The supply curve is illustrated in Figure 4.14, labeled S in the diagram.
   a. 8,000 bundles per month.
   b. 10,000 bundles per month.
   c. The supply curve slopes upward; page 93.

■ FIGURE 4.16

Price (dollars per box of rubber bands)

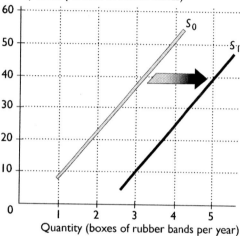

2. Figure 4.16 illustrates the shift; pages 96-97.

■ FIGURE 4.17

Price (dollars per ton of copper)

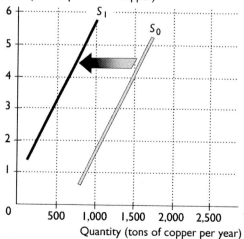

3. Figure 4.17 illustrates the shift; pages 96-97.

Short answer and numeric questions

1. If other things remain the same, when the price of a good or service falls (rises), sellers decrease (increase) the quantity they supply. page 92.

Price (dollars per pizza)	Market supply (pizzas per day)
14	47
12	36
10	25
8	14

2. The market supply schedule is in the last column in the table above; page 94.

3. Change in the price of the product; page 97.

4. Changes in: prices of related goods; prices of resources and other inputs; expectations; number of sellers; and productivity; page 97.

■ CHECKPOINT 4.3

Fill in the blanks

The price at which the quantity demanded equals the quantity supplied is the <u>equilibrium</u> <u>price</u>. In a diagram, the <u>equilibrium</u> <u>price</u> is determined where the supply and demand curves intersect. If the price exceeds the equilibrium price, the price <u>falls</u>. An increase in demand <u>raises</u> the equilibrium price and <u>increases</u> the equilibrium quantity. An increase in supply <u>lowers</u> the equilibrium price and <u>increases</u> the equilibrium quantity. If both the demand and supply increase, definitely the equilibrium <u>quantity</u> increases but the effect on the equilibrium <u>price</u> is ambiguous.

True or false

1. True; page 99
2. False; page 101
3. True; page 102
4. False; page 104
5. True; page 104

Multiple choice

1. a; page 99
2. d; page 100
3. b; page 101
4. c; page 101
5. b; page 102
6. c; page 102
7. c; page 104
8. a; page 104

Complete the graph

1. a. A shortage of 6,000 bundles a month; page 100.
   b. A surplus of 3,000 bundles a month; page 100.
   c. The equilibrium price is $2 a bundle of cotton candy and the equilibrium quantity is 8,000 bundles a month; page 100.

Price (dollars per sweatshirt)	Quantity demanded (sweatshirts per season)
35	13
30	15
25	19
20	27
15	37

2. The market demand schedule is obtained by summing the Hockey team's demand and the Soccer team's demand and is in the table above. The price that equates the quantity demanded to the quantity supplied is $25 and the equilibrium quantity is 19 sweatshirts; page 100.

■ FIGURE 4.18

Price (dollars per piece of gold jewelry)

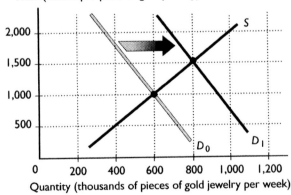

Quantity (thousands of pieces of gold jewelry per week)

3. Figure 4.18 shows the effect of the increase in income. The increase in income increases the demand for normal goods, such as gold jew-

elry. The demand curve shifts rightward and the supply curve does not shift. The price of gold jewelry rises, to $1,500 in the figure, and the quantity increases, to 800 pieces per week in the figure; page 101.

■ **FIGURE 4.19**

Price (dollars per piece of gold jewelry)

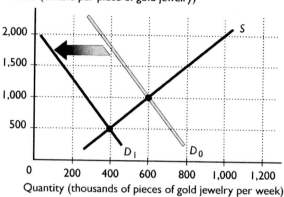

Quantity (thousands of pieces of gold jewelry per week)

4. Figure 4.19 shows the effect of the fall in price of silver jewelry. A fall in the price of a substitute decreases the demand gold jewelry. The demand curve shifts leftward and the supply curve does not shift. The price of gold jewelry falls, to $500 in the figure, and the quantity decreases, to 400 pieces per week in the figure; page 101.

■ **FIGURE 4.20**

Price (dollars per piece of gold jewelry)

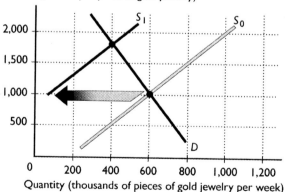

Quantity (thousands of pieces of gold jewelry per week)

5. Figure 4.20 shows the effect of the fall in the price of gold. The price of gold is a cost to the producers of gold jewelry. A rise in the cost decreases the supply of the good. The supply

curve shifts leftward and the demand curve does not shift. The price of gold jewelry rises, to $1,750 in the figure, and the quantity decreases, to 400 pieces per week in the figure; page 102.

Short answer and numeric questions

1. When a shortage exists, the price of the good is below the equilibrium price. The quantity demanded is greater than the quantity supplied. When a surplus exists, the price of the good is above the equilibrium price. The quantity demanded is less than the quantity supplied; page 100.

2. The increase in preferences increases the demand for orange juice and the demand curve shifts rightward. The price of orange juice rises and the quantity increases; page 101.

3. The fall in cost increases the supply of computers. The supply curve of computers shifts rightward. The price falls and the quantity increases; page 102.

4. The increase in income increases the demand for normal goods and shifts the demand curve for new cars rightward. The increase in health insurance premiums decreases the supply of new cars and shifts the supply curve of new cars leftward. The price of a new car definitely rises. The effect on the quantity is ambiguous: it rises if the demand effect is larger, falls if the supply effect is larger, and does not change if the two effects are the same size; page 104.

5. You can use supply and demand to determine if you want to buy gasoline immediately or perhaps hold off for a few days. For instance, if you read that a hurricane threatens oil derricks in the Gulf of Mexico, you can reason that if the hurricane actually strikes, the supply of oil will decrease and price of oil will soar. In this case, you ought to fill up your car today to beat the potential of paying a higher price next week.

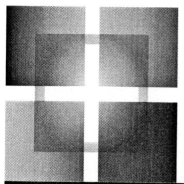

Elasticities of Demand and Supply

Chapter

5

In Chapter 5 we study the price elasticity of demand, the price elasticity of supply, the cross elasticity of demand, and the income elasticity of demand.

1 Define, explain the factors that influence, and calculate the price elasticity of demand.

The price elasticity of demand is a measure of the extent to which the quantity demanded of a good changes when the price of the good changes and all other influences on buyers' plans remain the same. The price elasticity of demand equals the percentage change in the quantity demanded divided by the percentage change in price, with the negative sign ignored. Demand is elastic if the percentage change in the quantity demanded exceeds the percentage change in price. Demand is unit elastic if the percentage change in the quantity demanded equals the percentage change in price. Demand is inelastic if the percentage change in the quantity demanded is less than the percentage change in price. Elasticity is a *units-free* measure. Along a linear demand curve demand is unit elastic at the midpoint of the curve, demand is elastic at all points above the midpoint of the curve, and demand is inelastic at all points below the midpoint of the curve. The total revenue from the sale of a good equals the price of the good multiplied by the quantity sold. If a price change changes total revenue in the opposite direction, demand is elastic. If a price change leaves total revenue unchanged, demand is unit elastic. If a price change changes total revenue in the same direction, demand is inelastic.

2 Define, explain the factors that influence, and calculate the price elasticity of supply.

The price elasticity of supply is a measure of the extent to which the quantity supplied of a good changes when the price of the good changes and all other influences on sellers' plans remain the same. The two main influences on the price elasticity of supply are production possibilities and storage possibilities. If the good can be stored, supply is more elastic. The price elasticity of supply equals the percentage change in the quantity supplied divided by the percentage change in the price. If the price elasticity of supply is greater than 1, supply is elastic. If the price elasticity of supply equals 1, supply is unit elastic. If the price elasticity of supply is less than 1, supply is inelastic.

3 Define and explain the factors that influence the cross elasticity of demand and the income elasticity of demand.

The cross elasticity of demand is a measure of the responsiveness of the demand for a good to a change in the price of a substitute or complement, other things remaining the same. The cross elasticity of demand is positive for substitutes and negative for complements. The income elasticity of demand is a measure of the responsiveness of the demand for a good to a change in income changes, other things remaining the same. The income elasticity of demand is positive for a normal good and negative for an inferior good.

CHECKPOINT 5.1

■ **Define, explain the factors that influence, and calculate the price elasticity of demand.**

Quick Review

- *Price elasticity of demand* The price elasticity of demand equals the magnitude of the percentage change in the quantity demanded divided by the percentage change in the price.
- *Elastic demand* When the percentage change in the quantity demanded exceeds the percentage change in price. The elasticity of demand is greater than 1 in value.
- *Inelastic demand* When the percentage change in the quantity demanded is less than the percentage change in price. The elasticity of demand is less than 1 in value.
- *Factors affecting elasticity* The demand for a good is more elastic if a substitute is easy to find. The factors that influence the ability to find a substitute for a good are whether the good is a luxury or a necessity, how narrowly it is defined, and the amount of time available to find a substitute for it.

Additional Practice Problems 5.1

1. For each of the following price changes, calculate the price elasticity of demand. Is the demand elastic, unit elastic, or inelastic?
   a. A 10 percent increase in price results in a 5 percent decrease in the quantity demanded.
   b. A 6 percent increase in price results in a 12 percent decrease in the quantity demanded.
   c. A 4 percent increase in price results in a 4 percent decrease in the quantity demanded.

Price (dollars per bag of cat food)	Quantity (bags of cat food per year)	Total revenue (dollars)
5	4	____
4	8	____
3	12	____
2	16	____
1	20	____

2. The table above gives the demand schedule for bags of cat food. A graph of this demand schedule gives a linear demand curve.
   a. Finish the table by calculating the total revenue for each row.
   b. When is the demand elastic? inelastic? unit elastic?
   c. Explain your answers to part (b).

Solutions to Additional Practice Problems 5.1

1a. The price elasticity of demand equals the magnitude of the percentage change in the quantity demanded divided by the percentage change in the price. So the elasticity of demand equals (5 percent) ÷ (10 percent) = 0.5. Because the elasticity of demand is less than 1, demand is inelastic.

1b. The price elasticity of demand equals (12 percent) ÷ (6 percent) =2.0. Because the elasticity of demand is greater than 1, demand is elastic.

1c. The price elasticity of demand equals (4 percent) ÷ (4 percent) = 1.0. Because the elasticity of demand equals 1, demand is unit elastic.

Price (dollars per bag of cat food)	Quantity (bags of cat food per year)	Total revenue (dollars)
5	4	20
4	8	32
3	12	36
2	16	32
1	20	20

2a. The completed table is above. Total revenue equals the price times the quantity sold.

2b. The demand is elastic at prices greater than $3 a bag. The demand is inelastic at prices less than $3 a bag. The demand is unit elastic at a price of $3 a bag.

2c. Demand is unit elastic at the midpoint of the demand curve. When demand is unit elastic, a price change leaves total revenue unchanged. The midpoint of the curve occurs when the price is $3 a bag, so demand is unit elastic at a price of $3 a bag.

Demand is elastic at all points above the midpoint of the demand curve. So when the price is greater than $3 a bag, demand is elastic. When demand is elastic, price and total revenue change in opposite directions. For example, when the price *rises* from $4 to $5, total revenue *decreases* from $32 to $20.

Demand is inelastic at all points below the midpoint of the demand curve. So when the price is less than $3 a bag, demand is inelastic. When demand is inelastic, price and total revenue change in the same direction. For example, when the price *rises* from $1 to $2, total revenue *increases* from $20 to $32.

■ Self Test 5.1

Fill in the blanks

To calculate the percentage change in price, the midpoint formula divides the change in price by the _____ (initial price; new price; average of the initial and the new price) and then multiplies by 100. If the percentage change in the quantity demanded exceeds the percentage change in the price, demand is _____ (elastic; inelastic). The demand for a product is more elastic if there are _____ (more; fewer) substitutes for it. The demand for a necessity is generally _____ (elastic; inelastic). The price elasticity of demand equals the percentage change in the _____ (price; quantity demanded) divided by the percentage change in the _____ (price; quantity demanded). Moving along a straight-line demand curve, the slope _____ (is constant; varies) and the elasticity _____ (is constant; varies). If demand is elastic, an increase in price _____ (increases; decreases) total revenue.

True or false

1. The price elasticity of demand equals the magnitude of the slope of the demand curve.

2. If the price increases by 10 percent and the quantity demanded decreases by 8 percent, the price elasticity of demand equals 1.25.

3. As the price of a good increases, if the quantity demanded of it remains the same, then demand for the good is perfectly inelastic.

4. Above the midpoint of a straight-line demand curve, demand is elastic.

5. When the price of a service increases by 5 percent and the quantity demanded decreases by 5 percent, total revenue remains unchanged.

6. If the price of tuna increases by 5 percent and the total revenue of tuna producers increases, then the demand for tuna is inelastic.

Multiple choice

1. The price elasticity of demand is a measure of the extent to which the quantity demanded of a good changes when _____ changes and all other influences on buyers' plans remain the same.
   a. income
   b. the price of a related good
   c. the price of the good
   d. the demand alone
   e. both the demand and supply simultaneously

2. Suppose the price of a movie falls from $9 to $7. Using the midpoint method, what is the percentage change in price?
   a. 33 percent
   b. −33 percent
   c. 25 percent
   d. −25 percent
   e. −97 percent

3. Suppose the price of a tie rises from $45 to $55. Using the midpoint method, what is the percentage change in price?
   a. 10 percent
   b. −10 percent
   c. 20 percent
   d. −20 percent
   e. 100 percent

4. Demand is elastic if
   a. consumers respond strongly to changes in the product's price.
   b. a large percentage change in price brings about a small percentage change in quantity demanded.
   c. a small percentage change in price brings about a small percentage change in quantity demanded.
   d. the quantity demanded is not responsive to price changes.
   e. the demand curve is vertical.

5. During the winter of 2000–2001, the price of electric power increased enormously in California but the quantity demanded decreased only a little. This response indicates that the demand for electric power in California was
   a. inelastic.
   b. elastic.
   c. unit elastic.
   d. perfectly elastic.
   e. perfectly inelastic.

6. If substitutes for a good are readily available, the demand for that good
   a. does not change substantially if the price rises.
   b. does not change substantially if the price falls.
   c. is inelastic.
   d. is elastic.
   e. Both answers (a) and (b) are correct.

7. If the price of a product increases by 5 percent and the quantity demanded decreases by 5 percent, then the elasticity of demand is
   a. 0.
   b. 1.
   c. indeterminate.
   d. 5.
   e. 25.

8. The price of a bag of pretzels rises from $2 to $3 and the quantity demanded decreases from 100 to 60. What is the price elasticity of demand?
   a. 1.0
   b. 1.25
   c. 40.0
   d. 20.0
   e. 0.80

9. When a firm raises the price of its product, what happens to total revenue?
   a. If demand is elastic, total revenue decreases.
   b. If demand is unit elastic, total revenue increases.
   c. If demand is inelastic, total revenue decreases.
   d. If demand is elastic, total revenue increases.
   e. If demand is unit elastic, total revenue decreases.

Complete the graph

■ **FIGURE 5.1**

1. In Figure 5.1, label the axes and then draw a demand curve for a good that has a perfectly elastic demand.

■ **FIGURE 5.2**

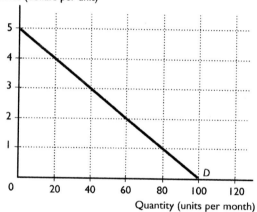

2. In Figure 5.2, label the axes and then draw a demand curve for a good that has a perfectly inelastic demand.

■ **FIGURE 5.3**

Price (dollars per unit)

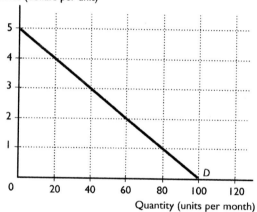

Quantity (units per month)

3. In Figure 5.3, darken the part of the demand curve along which demand is elastic. Label the point on the demand curve at which demand is unit elastic.

Short answer and numeric questions

	Percentage change in price	Percentage change in quantity demanded	Price elasticity of demand
A	5	10	____
B	8	4	____
C	3	0	____
D	6	6	____
E	1	8	____

1. Complete the table above by calculating the price elasticity of demand.
   a. Which row has the most elastic demand?
   b. Which row has the least elastic demand?

2. Suppose the price elasticity of demand for oil is 0.3. If the quantity of oil decreases by 6 percent, what is the effect on the price of oil?

3. What does it mean when the demand for a good is inelastic?

4. What is the relationship between how narrowly a good is defined and the number of substitutes it has?

5. The Eye on Your Life explains how you can use elasticity in your personal life. You can also use it in your business life. Suppose you are a brand manager for Crest toothpaste and you are thinking about raising its price. How will this price hike affect the total revenue from sales of Crest?

CHECKPOINT 5.2

■ **Define, explain the factors that influence, and calculate the price elasticity of supply.**

Quick Review

- *Price elasticity of supply* A measure of the extent to which the quantity supplied of a good changes when the price of the good changes and all other influences on sellers' plans remain the same.

Additional Practice Problems 5.2

1. For each of the following price changes, calculate the price elasticity of supply.
   a. A 10 percent increase in price results in a 15 percent increase in the quantity supplied.
   b. A 6 percent increase in price results in a 3 percent increase in the quantity supplied.
   c. A 7 percent increase in price results in a 7 percent increase in the quantity supplied.

2. Over one month the elasticity of supply of avocados is 0.1 and over 5 years the elasticity of supply of avocados is 2.0. If the price of avocados rises 10 percent, what is the increase in quantity supplied in one month and in 5 years? Why is there a difference in the quantities?

Solutions to Additional Practice Problems 5.2

1a. The elasticity of supply equals the percentage change in the quantity supplied divided by the percentage change in price, which is (15 percent) ÷ (10 percent) = 1.5.

1b. The elasticity of supply equals (3 percent) ÷ (6 percent) = 0.5.

1c. The elasticity of supply equals (7 percent) ÷ (7 percent) = 1.0.

2. The increase in the quantity supplied equals the percentage change in the price times the elasticity of supply. In one month the quantity supplied increases by (10 percent) × (0.1), which is 1 percent. In 5 years the quantity supplied increases by (10 percent) × (2.0), which is 20 percent. The increase in the quantity supplied is much greater after 5 years because more changes can be made as more time passes. Existing avocado trees can be more carefully cultivated and additional fertilizer used. Eventually additional avocado trees can be planted, mature, and then be harvested. The supply of avocados increases as time passes, making the supply more elastic.

■ Self Test 5.2

Fill in the blanks

When supply has a vertical supply curve, then the supply of the good is perfectly _____ (elastic; inelastic). Goods that can be produced at an almost constant opportunity cost have an _____ (elastic; inelastic) supply. As time passes, the elasticity of supply _____ (increases; decreases). The price elasticity of supply equals the percentage change in the _____ (price; quantity supplied) divided by the percentage change in the _____ (price; quantity supplied). If the elasticity of supply is greater than 1, supply is _____ (elastic; inelastic).

True or false

1. If the percentage change in the quantity supplied is zero when the price changes, supply is perfectly elastic.

2. Goods that can be produced at a constant (or very gently rising) opportunity cost have an elastic supply.

3. The supply of apples is perfectly elastic on the day of a price change.

4. The supply of a storable good is perfectly inelastic.

5. When the price of a pizza is $20, 10 pizzas are supplied and when the price rises to $30 a pizza, 14 pizzas are supplied. The price elasticity of supply of pizzas is 0.83.

6. If a 5 percent increase in price increases the quantity supplied by 10 percent, the elasticity of supply equals 2.0.

Multiple choice

1. The price elasticity of supply is a measure of the extent to which the quantity supplied of a good changes when only the
   a. cost of producing the product increases.
   b. quantity of the good demanded increases.
   c. supply increases.
   d. price of the good changes.
   e. number of firms changes.

2. When the percentage change in the quantity supplied exceeds the percentage change in price, then supply is
   a. elastic.
   b. inelastic.
   c. unit elastic.
   d. perfectly inelastic.
   e. perfectly elastic.

3. The supply of beachfront property on St. Simon's Island is
   a. elastic.
   b. unit elastic.
   c. negative.
   d. inelastic.
   e. perfectly elastic.

4. For a product with a rapidly increasing opportunity cost of producing additional units,
   a. demand is price elastic.
   b. supply is price elastic.
   c. demand is price inelastic.
   d. supply is price inelastic.
   e. the demand curve is vertical.

5. The greater the amount of time that passes after a price change, the
   a. less elastic supply becomes.
   b. more elastic supply becomes.
   c. more negative supply becomes.
   d. steeper the supply curve becomes.
   e. more vertical the supply curve becomes.

6. The price elasticity of supply equals the percentage change in the
   a. quantity demanded divided by the percentage change in the price of a substitute or complement.
   b. quantity supplied divided by the percentage change in price.
   c. quantity demanded divided by the percentage change in price.
   d. supply divided by the percentage change in the demand.
   e. quantity supplied divided by the percentage change in income.

7. If a firm supplies 200 units at a price of $50 and 100 units at a price of $40, using the midpoint formula what is the price elasticity of supply?
   a. 0.33
   b. 1.00
   c. 3.00
   d. 5.00
   e. 8.50

8. If the quantity supplied increases by 8 percent when the price rises by 2 percent, the price elasticity of supply is ____ percent.
   a. 10.0
   b. 6.0
   c. 0.25
   d. 16.0
   e. 4.0

9 If the price of a good increases by 10 percent and the quantity supplied increases by 5 percent, then the elasticity of supply is
   a. greater than one and supply is elastic.
   b. negative and supply is inelastic.
   c. less than one and supply is elastic.
   d. less than one and supply is inelastic.
   e. greater than one and supply is inelastic.

Complete the graph

■ FIGURE 5.4

1. In Figure 5.4, label the axes and then draw a supply curve for a good that has a perfectly inelastic supply.

Short answer and numeric questions

1. Suppose the elasticity of supply of wheat is 0.3 and the elasticity of supply of magazines is 1.3. If the price of wheat rises 10 percent, what is the increase in the quantity of wheat supplied? If the price of a magazine rises 10 percent, what is the increase in the quantity of magazines supplied?

	Price (dollars)	Quantity supplied (units per week)
A	5	10
B	15	30
C	25	50
D	35	90

2. The table above gives a supply schedule. Calculate the price elasticity of supply between points A and B; between points B and C; and between points C and D.

	Percentage change in price	Percentage change in quantity supplied	Price elasticity of supply
A	6	8	___
B	8	4	___
C	4	8	___

3. Complete the table above by calculating the price elasticity of supply.

4. Describe the elasticity of supply of a good that can be stored.

5. Why does the elasticity of supply increase as time passes after a price change?

CHECKPOINT 5.3

■ **Define and explain the factors that influence the cross elasticity of demand and the income elasticity of demand.**

Quick Review

- *Cross elasticity of demand* A measure of the extent to which the demand for a good changes when the price of a substitute or complement changes, other things remaining the same.
- *Income elasticity of demand* A measure of the extent to which the demand for a good changes when income changes, other things remaining the same.

Additional Practice Problems 5.3

1. For each of the following, calculate the cross elasticity of demand. Are the goods substitutes or complements?
   a. A 10 percent increase in the price of lettuce results in a 15 percent increase in the quantity of spinach demanded.
   b. A 5 percent increase in the price of beef results in a 10 percent increase in the quantity of pork demanded.
   c. A 4 percent increase in the price of a golf club results in a 2 percent decrease in the quantity of golf balls demanded.

2. For each of the following, calculate the income elasticity of demand. Are the goods normal or inferior goods?
   a. A 3 percent increase in income results in a 1 percent increase in the quantity demanded.
   b. A 6 percent increase in income results in a 3 percent decrease in the quantity demanded.
   c. A 2 percent increase in income results in a 4 percent increase in the quantity demanded.

3. Pepsi and Coke are substitutes. Pepsi and Tropicana orange juice also are substitutes. But quite likely the two cross elasticities of demand differ in size. Which cross elasticity do you think is larger and why?

Solutions to Additional Practice Problems 5.3

1a. The cross elasticity of demand equals the percentage change in the quantity demanded of one good divided by the percentage change in the price of the other good, which is (15 percent) ÷ (10 percent) = 1.5. The cross elasticity of supply is positive for substitute and negative for complements, so lettuce and spinach are substitutes.

1b. The cross elasticity of demand equals (10 percent) ÷ (5 percent) = 2.0. Beef and pork are substitutes.

1c. The cross elasticity of demand equals (–2 percent) ÷ (4 percent) = –0.5. Golf clubs and golf balls are complements.

2a. The income elasticity of demand equals the percentage change in the quantity demanded divided by the percentage change in income, which is (1 percent) ÷ (3 percent) = 0.33. The income elasticity is positive for a normal good and negative for an inferior good, so this good is a normal good.

2b. The income elasticity of demand equals (–3 percent) ÷ (6 percent) = –0.5. The good is an inferior good.

2c. The income elasticity of demand equals (4 percent) ÷ (2 percent) = 2.0. The good is a normal good.

3. The cross elasticity between Pepsi and Coke is likely much larger than the cross elasticity between Pepsi and Tropicana orange juice. For many people, Pepsi and Coke are close to indistinguishable. Even a slight rise in the price of a Coke will increase the quantity of Pepsi demanded significantly, so their cross elasticity is large. Pepsi and Tropicana orange juice are less close substitutes. So, although an increase in the price of Tropicana orange juice will increase the demand for Pepsi, the increase will be relatively slight and the cross elasticity will be small.

■ Self Test 5.3

Fill in the blanks

The ____ (price; cross; income) elasticity of demand is a measure of the extent to which the demand for a good changes when the price of a substitute or complement changes, other things remaining the same. The cross elasticity of demand is ____ (positive; negative) for a substitute and ____ (positive; negative) for a complement. The income elasticity of demand equals the percentage change in ____ (the quantity demanded; income) divided by the percentage change in ____ (quantity demanded; income). The income elasticity of demand is ____ (positive; negative) for a normal good and ____ (positive; negative) for an inferior good.

True or false

1. If the cross elasticity of demand is negative, the two goods are substitutes.

2. If the cross elasticity between hamburgers and hot dogs is positive, then hamburgers and hot dogs are substitutes.

3. An inferior good has a negative income elasticity of demand.

4. When the income elasticity of demand is positive, the good is a normal good.

5. A normal good is a good that has a positive cross elasticity of demand.

Multiple choice

1. The measure used to determine whether two goods are complements or substitutes is called the
   a. price elasticity of supply.
   b. cross elasticity of demand.
   c. price elasticity of demand.
   d. income elasticity.
   e. substitute elasticity of demand.

2. If beef and pork are substitutes, the cross elasticity of demand between the two goods is
   a. negative.
   b. positive.
   c. indeterminate.
   d. elastic.
   e. greater than one.

3. When the price of a pizza is $10, the quantity of soda demanded is 300 drinks. When the price of pizza is $15, the quantity of soda demanded is 100 drinks. The cross elasticity of demand equals
   a. –0.25.
   b. –0.40.
   c. –2.50.
   d. –25.00.
   e. 4.0.

4. When the price of going to a movie rises 5 percent, the quantity of DVDs demanded increases 10 percent. The cross elasticity of demand equals
   a. 10.0.
   b. 0.50.
   c. –0.50.
   d. –2.0.
   e. 2.0.

5. If two goods have a cross elasticity of demand of –2, then when the price of the one increases, the demand curve of the other good
   a. shifts rightward.
   b. shifts leftward.
   c. remains unchanged.
   d. may shift rightward, leftward, or remain unchanged.
   e. remains unchanged but the supply curve shifts leftward.

6. The income elasticity of demand is the percentage change in the _____ divided by the percentage change in _____.
   a. quantity demanded; the price of a substitute or complement
   b. quantity supplied; price
   c. quantity demanded; price
   d. quantity demanded; income
   e. quantity demanded when income changes; the quantity supplied

7. When income increases from $20,000 to $30,000 the number of home-delivered pizzas per year increases from 22 to 40. The income elasticity of demand for home-delivered pizza equals
   a. 1.45.
   b 0.69.
   c. 0.58.
   d. 0.40.
   e. 2.86.

8. When income increases by 6 percent, the demand for potatoes decreases by 2 percent. The income elasticity of demand for potatoes equals
   a. −2.00.
   b. 3.00.
   c. −3.00.
   d. 0.33.
   e. −0.33.

9. If a product is a normal good, then its income elasticity of demand is
   a. zero.
   b. positive.
   c. negative.
   d. indeterminate.
   e. greater than one.

10. The income elasticity of demand for used cars is less than zero. So, used cars are
   a. an inferior good.
   b. a normal good.
   c. an inelastic good.
   d. a perfectly inelastic good.
   e. substitute goods.

Complete the graph

■ FIGURE 5.5

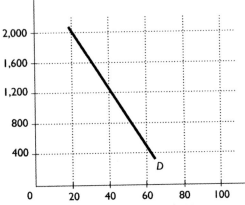

Price (dollars per large screen television)

1. The income elasticity of demand for large screen televisions is positive. In Figure 5.5, show the change when income increases.

Short answer and numeric questions

1. Do you think the cross elasticity of demand between Pepsi and Coke is positive or negative, large or small? Why?

	Percentage change in price of good A	Percentage change in quantity demanded of good B	Cross elasticity of demand
A	3	6	_____
B	5	−10	_____
C	−4	−8	_____
D	8	4	_____

2. Complete the table above. Which row has substitutes and which row has complements?

3. The income elasticity of demand for inter-city bus trips is negative. What does this fact tell you about inter-city bus trips?

	Percentage change in income	Percentage change in quantity demanded	Income elasticity of demand
A	5	10	_____
B	5	−10	_____
C	5	2	_____
D	6	6	_____

4. Complete the table above. Which row indicates an inferior good and which row indicates a good that is income elastic?

SELF TEST ANSWERS

■ CHECKPOINT 5.1

Fill in the blanks

To calculate the percentage change in price, the midpoint formula divides the change in price by the <u>average of the initial and the new price</u> and then multiplies by 100. If the percentage change in the quantity demanded exceeds the percentage change in the price, demand is <u>elastic</u>. The demand for a product is more elastic if there are <u>more</u> substitutes for it. The demand for a necessity is generally <u>inelastic</u>. The price elasticity of demand equals the percentage change in the <u>quantity demanded</u> divided by the percentage change in the <u>price</u>. Moving along a straight-line demand curve, the slope <u>is constant</u> and the elasticity <u>varies</u>. If demand is elastic, an increase in price <u>decreases</u> total revenue.

True or false

1. False; page 116
2. False; page 116
3. True; page 114
4. True; page 118
5. True; page 120
6. True; page 120

Multiple choice

1. c; page 112
2. d; page 112
3. c; page 113
4. a; page 114
5. a; page 114
6. d; page 114
7. b; page 116
8. b; page 116
9. a; page 120

Complete the graph

1. Figure 5.6 labels the axes and illustrates a demand curve for a good with a perfectly elastic demand; page 115.

2. Figure 5.7 labels the axes and illustrates a demand curve for a good with a perfectly inelastic demand; page 115.

■ FIGURE 5.6

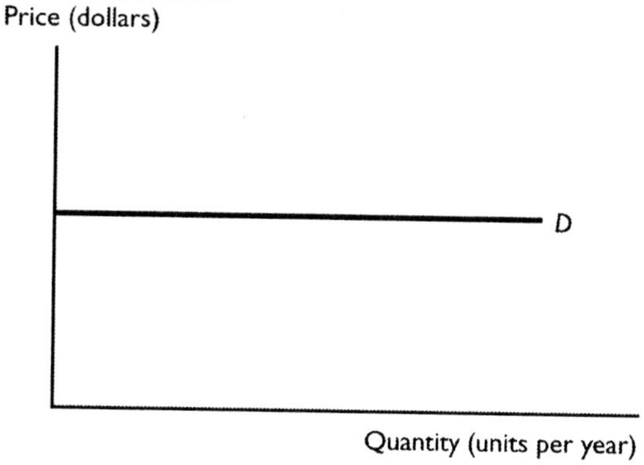

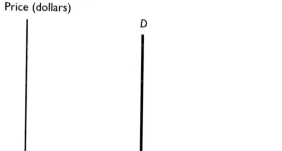

■ FIGURE 5.7

Price (dollars)

■ FIGURE 5.8

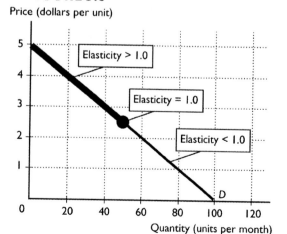

2. In Figure 5.8, demand is elastic along the dark portion of the demand curve. Demand

is unit elastic at the midpoint of curve. Demand is inelastic along the demand curve below the midpoint; page 118.

Short answer and numeric questions

	Percentage change in price	Percentage change in quantity demanded	Price elasticity of demand
A	5	10	2.0
B	8	4	0.5
C	3	0	0.0
D	6	6	1.0
E	1	8	8.0

1. The complete table is above; page 116.
   a. The most elastic demand is in row E; page 116.
   b. The least elastic demand is in row C (the demand is perfectly inelastic); page 116.

2. The price rises by 20 percent; page 116.

3. Demand is inelastic if the percentage change in the quantity demanded is less than the percentage change in the price; page 114.

4. The more narrow the definition of the good, the more substitutes exist. For example, there are more substitutes for a slice of Pizza Hut pizza than for pizza in general; page 116.

5. When the price of a good rises, total revenue increases if demand is inelastic, does not change if demand is unit elastic, and decreases if demand is elastic. As brand manager, you can use this relationship to predict whether the total revenue from Crest will rise, fall, or stay the same if you boost its price; page 120.

■ CHECKPOINT 5.2

Fill in the blanks

When supply has a vertical supply curve, then the supply of the good is perfectly inelastic. Goods that can be produced at an almost constant opportunity cost have an elastic supply. As time passes, the elasticity of supply increases. The price elasticity of supply equals the percentage change in the quantity supplied divided by the percentage change in the price. If the elasticity of supply is greater than 1, supply is elastic.

True or false

1. False; page 124
2. True; page 124
3. False; page 126
4. False; page 126
5. True; page 126
6. True; page 126

Multiple choice

1. d; page 126
2. a; page 126
3. d; page 126
4. d; page 126
5. b; page 126
6. b; page 126
7. c; page 126
8. e; page 126
9. d; page 126

Complete the graph

■ FIGURE 5.9

Price (dollars)

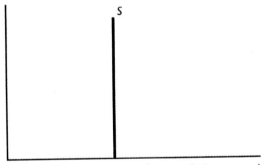

Quantity (units per year)

1. Figure 5.9 labels the axes and illustrates a supply curve for a good with a perfectly inelastic supply; page 125.

Short answer and numeric questions

1. If the price of wheat rises 10 percent, the increase in the quantity supplied equals (10 percent) × (0.3), which is 3 percent. If the price of a magazine rises 10 percent, the increase in the quantity supplied equals (10 percent) × (1.3), which is 13 percent; pages 124 and 126.

2. The price elasticity of supply between points A and B is 1.00; between points B and C is 1.00; and between points C and D is 1.71; page 126.

	Percentage change in price	Percentage change in quantity supplied	Price elasticity of supply
A	6	8	1.33
B	8	4	0.50
C	4	8	2.00

3. The completed table is above; page 126.

4. The elasticity of supply of a good that can be stored depends on the decision to keep the good in storage or offer it for sale. A small price change can make a big difference to this decision, so the supply of a storable good is highly elastic; page 126.

5. As time passes after a price change, it becomes easier to change production plans and supply becomes more elastic. For example, many manufactured goods have an inelastic supply if production plans have had only a short period in which to change. But after all the technologically possible ways of adjusting production have been exploited, supply is extremely elastic for most manufactured items; page 126.

■ CHECKPOINT 5.3

Fill in the blanks

The <u>cross</u> elasticity of demand is a measure of the extent to which the demand for a good changes when the price of a substitute or complement changes, other things remaining the same. The cross elasticity of demand is <u>positive</u> for a substitute and <u>negative</u> for a complement. The income elasticity of demand equals the percentage change in <u>quantity demanded</u> divided by the percentage change in <u>income</u>. The income elasticity of demand is <u>positive</u> for a normal good and <u>negative</u> for an inferior good.

True or false

1. False; page 129
2. True; page 129
3. True; page 130

4. True; page 130
5. False; page 130

Multiple choice

1. b; page 129
2. b; page 129
3. c; page 129
4. e; page 129
5. b; page 130
6. d; page 130
7. a; page 130
8. e; page 130
9. b; page 130

Complete the graph

■ **FIGURE 5.10**

Price (dollars per large screen television)

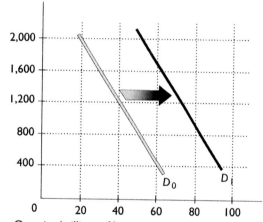

Quantity (millions of large screen televisions per year)

1. Because the income elasticity of demand is positive, we know that large screen televisions are a normal good. In Figure 5.10 an increase in income shifts the demand curve rightward from D_0 to D_1; page 130.

Short answer and numeric questions

1. The cross elasticity of demand between Pepsi and Coke is most likely positive and large. Pepsi and Coke are substitutes for most people, so their cross elasticity of demand is positive. They are close substitutes for many people, so their cross elasticity of demand is large; page 129.

	Percentage change in price of good A	Percentage change in quantity demanded of good B	Cross elasticity of demand
A	3	6	2.0
B	5	−10	−2.0
C	−4	−8	2.0
D	8	4	0.5

2. The completed table is above. The goods in row B are complements; the goods in rows A, C, and D are substitutes; page 129.

3. The fact that the income elasticity of demand for inter-city bus trips is negative indicates that an inter-city bus trip is an inferior good. When people's incomes increase, they take fewer inter-city bus trips and instead fly, drive, or take the train; page 130.

	Percentage change in income	Percentage change in quantity demanded	Income elasticity of demand
A	5	10	2.0
B	5	−10	−2.0
C	5	2	0.4
D	6	6	1.0

4. The completed table is above. The good in Row B is an inferior good. The good in row A is income elastic; page 130.

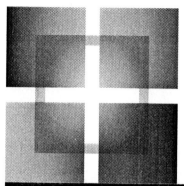

Efficiency and Fairness of Markets

Chapter 6

1 Describe the alternative methods of allocating scarce resources and define and explain the features of an efficient allocation.

Ways of allocating resources include: market price; command; majority rule; contest; first-come, first-served; sharing equally; lottery; personal characteristics; and force. Allocative efficiency occurs when we produce the quantities of goods and services on the *PPF* that people value most highly. Marginal benefit is the benefit that people receive from consuming one more unit of the product; marginal cost is the opportunity cost of producing one more unit of the product. The marginal benefit curve is downward sloping and the marginal cost curve is upward sloping. Allocative efficiency requires producing where the curves intersect, at the quantity that makes the marginal benefit equal the marginal cost.

2 Distinguish between value and price and define consumer surplus.

Value is what buyers get and price is what buyers pay. The value is the *marginal benefit*, which is the maximum price that buyers are willing to pay for another unit of the good. The demand curve is the marginal benefit curve. Consumer surplus is the marginal benefit from a good minus the price paid for it, summed over the quantity consumed.

3 Distinguish between cost and price and define producer surplus.

Cost is what a seller gives up to produce a good and price is what a seller receives when the good is sold. The cost of producing one more unit of a good or service is its *marginal cost*. The supply curve is the marginal cost curve. Producer surplus is the price of a good minus the marginal cost of producing it, summed over the quantity produced.

4 Evaluate the efficiency of the alternative methods of allocating scarce resources.

When marginal benefit equals the marginal cost, the efficient quantity is produced. The sum of consumer surplus and producer surplus is maximized at a competitive equilibrium. According to Adam Smith, each participant in a competitive market is "led by an invisible hand" to promote the efficient use of resources. Underproduction and overproduction create a deadweight loss. Government imposed price and quantity regulations, taxes and subsidies, externalities, public goods, common resources, monopoly, and high transactions costs are obstacles to efficiency. Other means of allocation are sometimes but not necessarily efficient.

5 Explain the main ideas about fairness and evaluate the fairness of the alternative methods of allocating scarce resources.

Two views of fairness are: it's not fair if the *rules* aren't fair and it's not fair if the *result* isn't fair. When private property and property rights are protected and exchanges are voluntary, competitive markets are fair according to the rules view of fairness. The fair results idea of income equality ignores the cost of making income transfers, which leads to the big tradeoff between efficiency and fairness.

CHECKPOINT 6.1

■ **Describe the alternative methods of allocating scarce resources and define and explain the features of an efficient allocation.**

Quick Review

- *Allocation methods* Resources can be allocated by: using the market price; command; majority rule; a contest, first-come, first served; sharing equally; lottery; personal characteristics; and force.
- *Allocation methods* Resources can be allocated by: using the market price; command; majority rule; a contest, first-come, first served; sharing equally; lottery; personal characteristics; and force.
- *Marginal benefit* The benefit that a person receives from consuming one more unit of a good or service.
- *Marginal cost* The opportunity cost of producing one more unit of a good or service.

Additional Practice Problems 6.1

1. Why is it necessary to allocate resources?
2. What is the command method of allocating resources?
3. Explain the relationship between production efficiency and allocative efficiency.

Solutions to Additional Practice Problems 6.1

1. Resources are scarce, so not everyone's wants can be fulfilled. As a result, some method must be used to determine whether or not resources are to be allocated to fulfilling each specific want.

2. The command method of allocating resources relies upon someone in authority to order how resources shall be allocated. The former Soviet Union and currently North Korea and Cuba are examples of entire economies in which command was (and is for North Korea and Cuba) the major allocation method.

3. Production efficiency is a situation in it is impossible to produce more of one good or service without producing less of some other good or service—production is at a point on the *PPF*. Allocative efficiency is the most highly valued combination of goods and services on the *PPF*.

■ Self Test 6.1

Fill in the blanks

Because only one person can become chair of General Electric and collect a salary of tens of millions of dollars, this position is allocated in a type of _____ (first-come, first-served; contest; command) allocation scheme. _____ (Production; Allocative) efficiency occurs at each combination of goods and services on the *PPF*. _____ (Production; Allocative) efficiency occurs when the economy produces the most highly valued combination of goods and services on the *PPF*. As more of a good is consumed, its marginal benefit _____ (increases; decreases), and as more of a good is produced, its marginal cost _____ (increases; decreases). Allocative efficiency occurs when the marginal benefit of a good is _____ (greater than; equal to; less than) the marginal cost of the good.

True or false

1. When market prices are used to allocate resources, only the people who are able and willing to pay get the resources.

2. All combinations of goods and services on the production possibilities frontier are combinations of allocative efficiency.

3. The marginal benefit of a good increases as more of the good is consumed.

4. A production point can be allocative efficient but not production efficient.

Multiple choice

1. If a person will rent an apartment only to married couples over 30 years old, that person is allocating resources using a ____ allocation method.
   a. first-come, first-served
   b. market price
   c. contest
   d. personal characteristics
   e. command

2. Allocative efficiency occurs when
   a. the most highly valued goods and services are produced.
   b. all citizens have equal access to goods and services.
   c. the environment is protected at all cost.
   d. goods and services are free.
   e. production takes place at any point on the PPF.

3. Marginal benefit equals the
   a. benefit that a person receives from consuming another unit of a good.
   b. additional efficiency from producing another unit of a good.
   c. increase in profit from producing another unit of a good.
   d. cost of producing another unit of a good.
   e. total benefit from consuming all the units of the good or service.

4. In general, the marginal cost curve
   a. has a positive slope.
   b. has a negative slope.
   c. is horizontal.
   d. is vertical.
   e. is U-shaped.

5. Allocative efficiency is achieved when the marginal benefit of a good
   a. exceeds marginal cost by as much as possible.
   b. exceeds marginal cost but not by as much as possible.
   c. is less than its marginal cost.
   d. equals the marginal cost.
   e. equals zero.

Complete the graph

■ FIGURE 6.1

Marginal benefit and marginal cost (trucks per tractor)

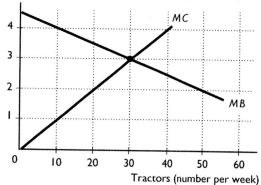

1. An economy produces only trucks and tractors and Figure 6.1 shows the marginal benefit and marginal cost of tractors. How many tractors are produced at the point of allocative efficiency?

Short answer and numeric questions

1. Suppose the price of a new BMW is $50,000. Which two kinds of people decide not to buy these BMWs? Is it true that when resources are allocated by market price, the rich always consume everything?

2. Only one person can become President of Sony, yet many of Sony's top executives would like that job. What allocation method is typically used to determine who becomes President? How does this allocation method benefit Sony?

3. Along a production possibilities frontier, to produce the first skateboard, 1 pair of roller blades must be forgone. To produce the second skateboard, 2 more pairs of roller blades must be forgone. Is the marginal cost of the second skate board 2 or 3 pairs of roller blades?

4. Why does allocative efficiency require producing where marginal benefit equals marginal cost rather than where marginal benefit exceeds marginal cost?

CHECKPOINT 6.2

■ **Distinguish between value and price and define consumer surplus.**

Quick Review

- *Value* In economics the idea of value is called marginal benefit, which we measure as the maximum price that people are willing to pay for another unit of a good or service.
- *Consumer surplus* Consumer surplus is the marginal benefit from a good or service minus the price paid for it, summed over the quantity consumed.

Additional Practice Problem 6.2

1. The figure shows the demand curve for magazines and the market price of a magazine. Use the figure to answer the following questions.

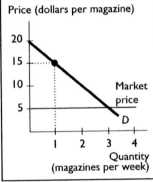

a. What is the value of the 1st magazine? What is the marginal benefit of the 1st magazine? What is the consumer surplus of the 1st magazine?

b. What is the marginal benefit of the 2nd magazine? What is the consumer surplus of the 2nd magazine?

c. What is the total quantity of magazines bought and the consumer surplus?

d. If the price of a magazine rises to $10, what is the quantity bought and what is the consumer surplus?

2. Your friend paid a lawyer $50 for the hour it took the lawyer to write a letter to settle a rent dispute. Your friend wonders if the concepts of value, marginal benefit, and consumer surplus apply not only to goods but also to services, such as the lawyer's letter. What do you tell your friend?

Solutions to Additional Practice Problems 6.2

1a. The value of the 1st magazine equals the maximum price a consumer is willing to pay for the magazine. The figure shows that the maximum price for the 1st magazine is $15, so the value of the magazine equals $15. The marginal benefit of the magazine is equal to the maximum price the consumer will pay, which is $15. The consumer surplus is equal to the marginal benefit of the 1st magazine ($15) minus the price of the magazine ($5) so the consumer surplus is $10.

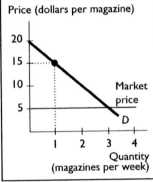

1b. The marginal benefit of the magazine is equal to the maximum price the consumer will pay. The figure shows that the maximum price for the 2nd magazine is $10, so the marginal benefit of the magazine equals $5. The consumer surplus is equal to $5.

1c. The quantity bought is 3 magazines because the demand curve shows that the quantity demanded at the price of $5 is 3 magazines. The consumer surplus equals the area of the darkened triangle in the figure. Calculating the area of the con-

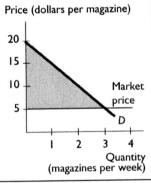

sumer surplus triangle, which is equal to one half the base of the triangle multiplied by the height or $1/2 \times (3 - 0) \times (\$20 - \$5)$, which is $22.50.

1d. If the price of a magazine rises to $10, the quantity bought is 2 magazines. The consumer surplus now equals $1/2 \times (2 - 0) \times (\$20 - \$10)$, which is $10.00.

2. All the concepts of value, marginal benefit, and consumer surplus apply to services as well as to goods. In your friend's case, there was some maximum amount your friend was willing to pay the attorney to write the letter. This maximum amount was the value to your friend of the letter. It is also the marginal benefit of the letter. Presumably your friend got the letter for some amount less than the maximum your friend was willing to pay. The difference between the marginal benefit of the letter and the price paid it is the consumer surplus your friend enjoyed from the letter.

■ Self Test 6.2

Fill in the blanks

The benefit a person receives from consuming one more unit of a good is its ____. The opportunity cost of producing one more unit of a good is its ____. Allocative efficiency is at the quantity where the marginal benefit is ____ (greater than; equal to; less than) marginal cost. The demand curve ____ (is; is not) the marginal benefit curve. The consumer surplus equals the marginal benefit of a good ____ (plus; multiplied by; minus) the price paid for it.

True or false

1. In economics, value and price refer to the same thing.

2. A demand curve is a marginal benefit curve.

3. The consumer surplus from one unit of a good is the marginal benefit from the good minus the price paid for it.

4. Consumer surplus always equals zero because consumers always pay for the goods and services they consume.

Multiple choice

1. Value is
   a. the price we pay for a good.
   b. the cost of resources used to produce a good.
   c. objective so that it is determined by market forces, not preferences.
   d. the marginal benefit we get from consuming another unit of a good or service.
   e. the difference between the price paid for a good and the marginal cost of producing that unit of the good.

2. A marginal benefit curve
   a. is the same as a demand curve.
   b. is the same as a supply curve.
   c. slopes upwards.
   d. is a vertical line at the efficient quantity.
   e. is U-shaped.

3. In general, as the consumption of a good or service increases, the marginal benefit from consuming that good or service
   a. increases.
   b. decreases.
   c. stays the same.
   d. at first increases and then decreases.
   e. at first decreases and then increases.

4. The difference between the marginal benefit from a new pair of shoes and the price of the new pair of shoes is
   a. the consumer surplus from that pair of shoes.
   b. what we get.
   c. what we have to pay.
   d. the price when the marginal benefit is maximized.
   e. the consumer's expenditure on the shoes.

5. Suppose the price of a scooter is $200 and Cora Lee is willing to pay $250. Cora Lee's
   a. consumer surplus from that scooter is $200.
   b. consumer surplus from that scooter is $50.
   c. marginal benefit from that scooter is $200.
   d. consumer surplus from that scooter is $200.
   e. consumer surplus from that scooter is $250.

6. If the price of a pizza is $10 per pizza, the consumer surplus from the first pizza consumed _____ the consumer surplus from the second pizza consumed.
   a. is greater than
   b. equals
   c. is less than
   d. cannot be compared to
   e. None of the above answers is correct because more information is needed about the marginal cost of producing the pizzas to answer the question.

Complete the graph

■ **FIGURE 6.2**

Price (dollars per pair of roller blades)

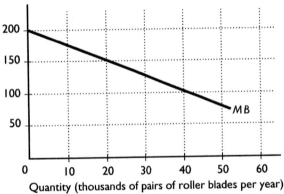

1. Figure 6.2 shows the demand curve for roller blades.
   a. What is the marginal benefit of the 20,000th pair of roller blades?
   b. What is the marginal benefit of the 40,000th pair of roller blades?
   c. If the price of a pair of roller blades is $100, what is the consumer surplus on the 20,000th pair of roller blades?
   d. If the price of a pair of roller blades is $100, what is the consumer surplus on the 40,000th pair of roller blades?
   e. If the price of a pair of roller blades is $100, what is the quantity of roller blades purchased? What is the amount of the consumer surplus?

■ **FIGURE 6.3**

Price (dollars per bag of potato chips)

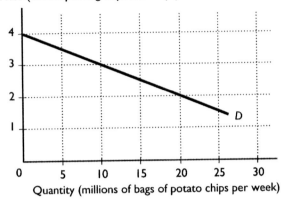

Quantity (millions of bags of potato chips per week)

2. Figure 6.3 shows the demand curve for bags of potato chips.
   a. What is the maximum price a consumer is willing to pay for the 10 millionth bag of chips?
   b. What is the marginal benefit from the 10 millionth bag of chips? What is the relationship between your answer to part (a) and your answer to this part?
   c. If the price of a bag of chips equals $2, in Figure 6.3 shade the area that equals the amount of the consumer surplus.
   d. If the price of a bag of chips equals $2, what is the amount of consumer surplus?

Short answer and numeric questions

Price (dollars per MP3 player)	Quantity (millions of MP3 players per year)	Consumer surplus (dollars)
500	4	_____
400	8	_____
300	12	_____
200	16	_____
100	20	_____

1. The table above gives the demand schedule for MP3 players. Suppose the price of an MP3 player is $200.
   a. Complete the table by calculating the consumer surplus. In the first row, calculate the consumer surplus for the 4 millionth MP3 player; in the second row, calculate the consumer surplus for the 8 millionth MP3 player; and so on.

b. As more MP3 players are purchased, what happens to the consumer surplus of the last unit purchased? Why?

2. What is the relationship between the value of a good, the maximum price a consumer is willing to pay for the good, and the marginal benefit from the good?

3. What is the relationship between the marginal benefit of a slice of pizza, the price paid for the slice, and its consumer surplus?

CHECKPOINT 6.3

■ **Distinguish between cost and price and define producer surplus.**

Quick Review

- *Cost* Cost is what the seller must give up to produce a good.
- *Producer surplus* The producer surplus of a good equals the price of a good minus the marginal cost of producing it.

Additional Practice Problems 6.3

1. The figure shows the supply curve of magazines and the market price of a magazine. Use the figure to answer the following questions.

a. What is the marginal cost of the 10 millionth magazine?

b. What is the minimum supply price of the 10 millionth magazine?

c. What is the producer surplus on the 10 millionth magazine?

d. What are the quantity of magazines sold and the total producer surplus?

2. Why is the minimum price for which a seller will produce a product equal to the product's marginal cost?

Solutions to Additional Practice Problems 6.3

1a. The marginal cost of the 10 millionth magazine is equal to the minimum supply price of the 10 millionth magazine. The supply curve, which is also the marginal cost curve, shows this price. In the figure, the supply curve shows that the marginal cost of 10 millionth magazine is $2.50.

1b. The minimum supply price of the 10 millionth magazine equals its marginal cost, $2.50.

1c. The producer surplus on the 10 millionth magazine is equal to its market price minus its marginal cost, which is $5 – $2.50 = $2.50.

1d. At the market price of $5, 20 million magazines are sold. The producer surplus equals the area of the grey triangle in the figure. Calculating the area of the triangle as one half the base multiplied by the height, or $1/2 \times (20 \text{ million} - 0) \times (\$5 - 0)$, the producer surplus equals $50 million.

2. A seller is willing to produce a good as long as the price the seller receives covers all the costs of producing the good. So the minimum price for which a seller is willing to produce a unit of the good must be the amount that just equals the cost of the producing that unit. But the cost of producing any unit of a good is its marginal cost, so the minimum supply price equals the good's marginal cost.

■ Self Test 6.3

Fill in the blanks

_____ (Price; Cost) is what a seller must give up to produce a good and _____ (price; cost) is what a seller receives when the good is sold. A _____ (demand; supply) curve is a marginal cost curve. A firm receives a producer surplus when price is _____ (greater; less) than marginal cost.

True or false

1. In economics, cost and price are the same thing.
2. The minimum price for which Bobby will grow another pound of rice is 20¢, so the marginal cost of an additional pound of rice is 20¢.
3. A supply curve is a marginal benefit curve.
4. Producer surplus equals the marginal benefit of a good minus the cost of producing it.

Multiple choice

1. Cost
   a. is what the buyer pays to get the good.
   b. is always equal to the marginal benefit for every unit of a good produced.
   c. is what the seller must give up to produce the good.
   d. is greater than market price, which results in a profit for firms.
   e. means the same thing as price.

2. If a firm is willing to supply the 1,000th unit of a good at a price of $23 or more, we know that $23 is the
   a. highest price the seller hopes to realize for this output.
   b. minimum price the seller must receive to produce this unit.
   c. average price of all the prices the seller could charge.
   d. price that sets the marginal benefit equal to the marginal cost.
   e. only price for which the seller is willing to sell this unit of the good.

3. A supply curve shows the _____ of producing one more unit of a good or service.
   a. producer surplus
   b. consumer surplus
   c. total benefit
   d. marginal cost
   e. marginal benefit to the producer

4. Producer surplus is
   a. equal to the marginal benefit from a good minus its price.
   b. equal to the price of a good minus the marginal cost of producing it.
   c. always equal to consumer surplus.
   d. Both answers (a) and (c) are correct.
   e. Both answers (b) and (c) are correct.

5. Suppose you're willing to tutor a student for $10 an hour. The student pays you $15 an hour. What is your producer surplus?
   a. $5 an hour
   b. $10 an hour
   c. $15 an hour
   d. $25 an hour
   e. more than $25 an hour

6. In a figure that shows a supply curve and a demand curve, producer surplus is the area
   a. below the demand curve and above the market price.
   b. below the supply curve and above the market price.
   c. above the demand curve and below the market price.
   d. above the supply curve and below the market price.
   e. between the demand curve and the supply curve.

Complete the graph

1. Figure 6.4 (on the next page) shows the supply curve for bags of potato chips.
   a. What is the minimum price for which a supplier is willing to produce the 10 millionth bag of chips?
   b. What is the marginal cost of the 10 millionth bag of chips? What is the relationship between your answer to part (a) and your answer to this part?

■ **FIGURE 6.4**

Price (dollars per bag of potato chips)

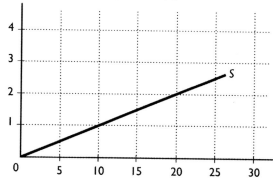

Quantity (millions of bags of potato chips per week)

c. If the price of a bag of chips equals $2, in Figure 6.4 shade the area that equals the amount of the producer surplus.

d. If the price of a bag of chips equals $2, calculate the producer surplus.

Short answer and numeric questions

1. What is the relationship between the minimum price a supplier must receive to produce a slice of pizza and the marginal cost of the slice of pizza? What is the relationship between the marginal cost curve and the supply curve?

2. What is producer surplus? As the price of a good or service rises and the supply curve does not shift, what happens to the amount of the producer surplus?

CHECKPOINT 6.4

■ **Evaluate the efficiency of the alternative methods of allocating scarce resources.**

Quick Review

• *Efficiency of competitive equilibrium* The condition that marginal benefit equals marginal cost delivers an efficient use of resources. It allocates resources to the activities that create the greatest possible value. Marginal benefit equals marginal cost at a competitive equilibrium, so a competitive equilibrium is efficient.

• *Deadweight loss* The decrease in consumer surplus and producer surplus that results from an inefficient level of production.

Additional Practice Problems 6.4

1. The figure shows the market for paper. Use the figure to answer the following questions.

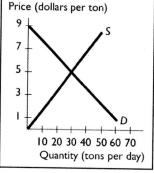

Price (dollars per ton)

Quantity (tons per day)

a. What are the equilibrium price and the equilibrium quantity of paper? What is the efficient quantity of paper?

b. In the market equilibrium, use the figure above to shade the consumer surplus and the producer surplus.

c. What does the consumer surplus equal? What does the producer surplus equal? What does the total surplus equal?

d. Is the market for paper efficient? Why or why not? Can the total surplus be any larger at any other level of production?

2. Who benefits from a deadweight loss?

Solutions to Additional Practice Problems 6.4

1a. The equilibrium is shown in the figure and is where the supply and demand curves intersect. The equilibrium price is $5 a ton and the equilibrium quantity is 30 tons a day. The efficient quantity is where the marginal benefit and marginal cost curves intersect. Because the demand curve is the marginal benefit curve and the supply curve is the marginal cost curve, the efficient quantity is 30 tons a day.

1b. The consumer surplus is illustrated in the figure on the next page as the area of the top, dark triangle. The producer surplus equals the area of the lower, lighter triangle.

1c. The consumer surplus equals the area of the darker triangle, or 1/2 × (30 tons) × ($4 per ton) = $60, where $4 a ton is the height of the triangle, $9 a ton – $5 a ton. The producer surplus equals the area of the lighter triangle, or 1/2 × (30 tons) × ($5 per ton) = $75, where $5 a ton is the height of the triangle, $5 a ton – $0 a ton.

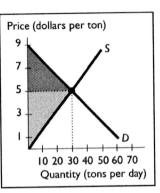

Price (dollars per ton)

The total surplus equals the sum of the consumer surplus plus the producer surplus, which is $135.

1d. The efficient use of resources occurs when marginal benefit equals marginal cost. The market equilibrium is efficient because the marginal benefit of a ton of paper equals its marginal cost. The sum of the consumer surplus and producer surplus, which equals the total surplus, is at its maximum at the efficient level of production so the total surplus cannot be larger at any other amount of production.

2. No one gains from a deadweight loss. Deadweight loss is a decrease in consumer surplus and producer surplus that results from an inefficient level of production. The deadweight loss is borne by the entire society. It is not a loss for the consumers and a gain for the producer. It is a social loss.

■ Self Test 6.4

Fill in the blanks

Equilibrium in a competitive market _____ (is; is not) efficient. Adam Smith believed that each participant in a competitive market is "led by _____ (an invisible hand; government actions)." A price _____ (ceiling; floor) is a regulation that makes it illegal to charge a price higher than a specified level. _____ (An externality; A public good) is a good or service that is consumed simultaneously by everyone, even if they don't pay for it. Deadweight loss is the decrease in _____ (only consumer surplus; consumer surplus

and producer surplus; only producer surplus) that results from an inefficient level of production.

True or false

1. When the demand curve is the marginal benefit curve and the supply curve is the marginal cost curve, the competitive equilibrium is efficient.

2. When the efficient quantity of a good is produced, the consumer surplus is always zero.

3. According to Adam Smith, the invisible hand suggests that competitive markets require government action to ensure that resources are allocated efficiently.

4. Producing less than the efficient quantity of a good results in a deadweight loss but producing more than the efficient quantity does not result in a deadweight loss.

Multiple choice

■ **FIGURE 6.5**

Price (dollars per computer)

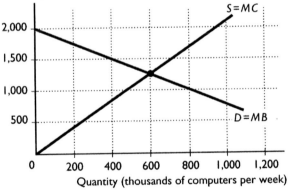

Quantity (thousands of computers per week)

1. Figure 6.5 shows the market for computers. What is the equilibrium quantity of computers?
   a. 0 computers per week
   b. 200,000 computers per week
   c. 400,000 computers per week
   d. 600,000 computers per week
   e. more than 600,000 computers per week

2. Figure 6.5 shows the market for computers. What is the efficient quantity of computers?
   a. 0 computers per week
   b. 200,000 computers per week
   c. 400,000 computers per week
   d. 600,000 computers per week
   e. more than 600,000 computers per week

3. When a market is efficient the
   a. sum of consumer surplus and producer surplus is maximized.
   b. deadweight gain is maximized.
   c. quantity produced is maximized.
   d. marginal benefit of the last unit produced exceeds the marginal cost by as much as possible.
   e. total benefit equals the total cost.

4. Which of the following occurs when a market is efficient?
   a. producers earn the highest income possible
   b. production costs equal total benefit
   c. consumer surplus equals producer surplus
   d. scarce resources are used to produce the goods and services that people value most highly
   e. every consumer has all of the good or service he or she wants.

5. The concept of "the invisible hand" suggests that markets
   a. do not produce the efficient quantity.
   b. are always fair.
   c. produce the efficient quantity.
   d. are unfair though they might be efficient.
   e. allocate resources unfairly and inefficiently.

6. When underproduction occurs,
   a. producers gain more surplus at the expense of consumers.
   b. marginal cost is greater than marginal benefit.
   c. consumer surplus increases to a harmful amount.
   d. there is a deadweight loss that is borne by the entire society.
   e. the deadweight loss harms only consumers.

7. When production moves from the efficient quantity to a point of overproduction,
   a. consumer surplus definitely increases.
   b. the sum of producer surplus and consumer surplus increases.
   c. there is a deadweight loss.
   d. consumers definitely lose and producers definitely gain.
   e. consumers definitely gain and producers definitely lose.

8. Which of the following can result in a market producing an inefficient quantity of a good?
   i.   competition
   ii. an external cost or an external benefit
   iii. a tax
   a. i only.
   b. ii only.
   c. iii only.
   d. ii and iii.
   e. i and iii.

Complete the graph

■ FIGURE 6.6

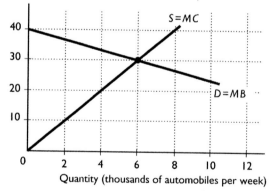

Price (thousands of dollars per automobile)

1. In Figure 6.6, what is the equilibrium quantity of automobiles? What is the efficient quantity of automobiles? Shade the consumer surplus and the producer surplus and calculate their amounts.

2. Figure 6.7 (on the next page) is identical to Figure 6.6.
   a. Suppose that 8,000 automobiles are produced. Shade the deadweight loss light grey and calculate its amount.

■ **FIGURE 6.7**
Price (thousands of dollars per automobile)

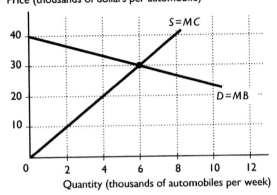

b. Suppose that 4,000 automobiles are produced. Shade the deadweight loss dark grey and calculate its amount.

Short answer and numeric questions

1. What is the relationship between a competitive market, efficiency, and the invisible hand?

2. Suppose the demand for cotton clothing increases. What effect does the increase in demand have on the equilibrium quantity and on the efficient quantity?

3. What factors might lead a market to produce an inefficient amount of a product?

CHECKPOINT 6.5

■ **Explain the main ideas about fairness and evaluate the fairness of alternative methods of allocating scarce resources.**

Quick Review

- *Big tradeoff* The big tradeoff is the tradeoff between efficiency and fairness that results when income transfers are made.

Additional Practice Problem 6.5

1. If Bill Gates gives $1,000 to a homeless person, would the transaction be fair? If Mr. Gates is taxed $1,000 by the government and the government gives the $1,000 to the same homeless person, would the transaction be fair? Comment on your answers.

Solution to Additional Practice Problem 6.5

1. If Mr. Gates gives $1,000 to a homeless person, the action is considered fair. The exchange is fair according to the fair rules principle because the exchange is voluntary. And the outcome is fair according to the fair results principle because there is more equality of income. If Mr. Gates is taxed by the government, the outcome is fair according to the fair results principle because there is more equality of income. But the transaction is not fair according to the fair rules principle because the exchange does not occur voluntarily.

■ Self Test 6.5

Fill in the blanks

Two views of fairness are that "it's not fair if the _____ (result; income distribution) isn't fair;" and "it's not fair if the _____ (rules; tradeoffs) aren't fair." According to Robert Nozick, fair-rules ideas require _____ (government intervention; property rights and voluntary exchange).

True or false

1. The principle that "it's not fair if the result isn't fair" can conflict with the principle that "it's not fair if the rules aren't fair."

2. The big tradeoff is the tradeoff between efficiency and happiness.

3. According to the "fair-rules" view of fairness, in times of natural disasters it is fair to force people to make available necessary goods and services at lower than usual prices.

Multiple choice

1. The "fair-rules" view of fairness is based on
   a. income transfers from the rich to the poor.
   b. property rights and voluntary exchange.
   c. efficiency.
   d. the big tradeoff.
   e. allocating resources using majority rule.

2. The idea that unequal incomes is unfair generally uses the _____ principle of fairness.
   a. big tradeoff
   b. involuntary exchange
   c. voluntary exchange
   d. it's not fair if the result isn't fair
   e. it's not fair if the rules aren't fair

3. Which of the following is an example in which "the big tradeoff" can occur?
   a. the government redistributes income from the rich to the poor
   b. Ford increases the price of a pickup truck
   c. a basketball player signs a $5 million contract
   d. a college lowers tuition
   e. the price of personal computers falls year after year

4. Suppose a hurricane is poised to strike Miami and the price of plywood jumps from $15 a board to $28. If the government buys all the plywood at $28 and offers it to consumers for $15, which of the following is true?
   a. There will be enough plywood for everyone at the $15 government price.
   b. There will be a surplus of plywood at the $15 government price.
   c. Some people who buy plywood at the $15 government price will resell the plywood to consumers who are willing to pay $28, earning a producer surplus of $13.
   d. Because the government is both buying and selling the plywood, there is no need to impose a tax to pay for the government intervention.
   e. The big tradeoff means that more plywood will be purchased with the government intervention than would be the case without the government intervention.

Short answer and numeric questions

1. In the United States, richer people generally pay a larger fraction of their income as taxes than do poorer people. Is this arrangement fair? Answer from a fair-results view and from a fair-rules view.

2. Suppose that during their working lifetimes, Matt and Pat have earned identical incomes as computer programmers. The only difference between the two is that Matt spent all of his income while Pat saved a large portion of hers. Now that they are retired, Pat's income is substantially higher than Matt's because of Pat's saving. Is it fair for Pat's income to be higher than Matt's? Answer from a fair results and from a fair rules perspective.

3. What is the effect of the big tradeoff in transferring income from people with high incomes to people with low incomes?

4. Is it fair for the government to limit the prices sellers charge for bottled water after a flood destroys a town's water supply? Why or why not?

SELF TEST ANSWERS

■ CHECKPOINT 6.1

Fill in the blanks

Because only one person can become chair of General Electric and collect a salary of tens of millions of dollars, this position is allocated in a type of <u>contest</u> allocation scheme. <u>Production</u> efficiency occurs at each combination of goods and services on the *PPF*. <u>Allocative</u> efficiency occurs when the economy produces the most highly valued combination of goods and services on the *PPF*. As more of a good is consumed, its marginal benefit <u>decreases</u>, and as more of a good is produced, its marginal cost <u>increases</u>. Allocative efficiency occurs when the marginal benefit of a good is <u>equal to</u> the marginal cost of the good.

True or false

1. True; page 138
2. False; page 141
3. False; page 142
4. False; page 138

Multiple choice

1. d; page 140
2. a; page 141
3. a; page 142
4. a; page 143
5. d; pages 143-144

Complete the graph

1. Allocative efficiency is the most highly valued combination of goods and services on the *PPF*. It is the combination where marginal cost equals marginal benefit. In Figure 6.1, allocative efficiency is achieved when 30 tractors a week are produced; page 144.

Short answer and numeric questions

1. The people who do not buy these BMWs are the people cannot afford to pay $50,000 for the new BMW and the people who can afford to pay but choose not to pay it. The fact that people can decide not to buy a particular good or service shows that the rich do not necessary consume everything; they buy and consume only the goods and services for which they choose to pay the market price; page 138.

2. Sony is using a contest allocation method. Sony benefits from this allocation scheme because all the top executives who want to be President will work extremely hard for Sony in an effort to win the contest; page 139.

3. The marginal cost of the second skate board is 2 pairs roller blades. Marginal cost is the opportunity cost of producing one more unit of a good or service. It is not the cost of all the units produced; pages 142-143.

4. As long as the marginal benefit from an additional good or service exceeds the marginal cost, the unit should be produced because its production benefits society more than it costs society to produce. Producing where marginal benefit equals marginal cost insures that *all* units that have a net benefit for society are produced, so this level of production is the point of allocative efficiency; page 144.

■ CHECKPOINT 6.2

Fill in the blanks

The benefit a person receives from consuming one more unit of a good is its <u>marginal benefit</u>. The opportunity cost of producing one more unit of a good is its <u>marginal cost</u>. Allocative efficiency is at the quantity where the marginal benefit is <u>equal to</u> marginal cost. The demand curve <u>is</u> the marginal benefit curve. The consumer surplus equals the marginal benefit of a good <u>minus</u> the price paid for it.

True or false

1. False; page 146
2. True; page 146
3. True; page 147
4. False; page 147

Multiple choice

1. d; page 146
2. a; page 146
3. b; page 146

4. a; page 147

5. b; page 147

6. a; page 147

Complete the graph

1. a. The marginal benefit of the 20,000th pair of roller blades is the maximum price a consumer is willing to pay for that pair, which is $150; page 146.

   b. The marginal benefit of the 40,000th pair of roller blades is the maximum price a consumer is willing to pay for that pair, which is $100; page 146.

   c. The consumer surplus is the difference between the marginal benefit, $150, minus the price paid, $100, or $50; page 147.

   d. The consumer surplus is the difference between the marginal benefit, $100, minus the price paid, $100, or $0; page 147.

   e. If the price is $100, then 40,000 pairs of roller blades will be purchased. The consumer surplus equals $1/2 \times (\$200 - \$100) \times (40,000 - 0)$, or $40,000,000; page 147.

2. a. The maximum price is $3; page 146.

   b. The marginal benefit is $3. The marginal benefit is the maximum price a consumer is willing to pay for another bag of potato chips; page 146.

■ **FIGURE 6.8**

Price (dollars per bag of potato chips)

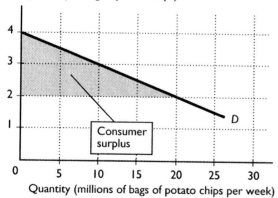

Quantity (millions of bags of potato chips per week)

   c. Figure 6.8 shades the area of the consumer surplus; page 147.

   d. The consumer surplus equals the area of the shaded triangle in Figure 6.8, which is

$1/2 \times (\$4 - \$2) \times 20$ million $= \$20$ million; page 147.

Short answer and numeric questions

Price (dollars per MP3 player)	Quantity (millions of MP3 players per year)	Consumer surplus (dollars)
500	4	300
400	8	200
300	12	100
200	16	0
100	20	0

1. a. The table above has the consumer surpluses. The consumer surplus is zero for the 20 millionth MP3 player because when the price is $200, the 20 millionth MP3 player is not purchased. For the remaining quantities, the consumer surplus is the marginal benefit, which equals the maximum price consumers are willing to pay minus the price; page 147.

   b. The consumer surplus decreases as more MP3 players are purchased because the value of an additional MP3 player decreases as more are purchased; page 147.

2. The value of a good is equal to the maximum price a buyer is willing to pay, which also equals the marginal benefit; page 146.

3. The marginal benefit of the slice of pizza equals the price paid plus the consumer surplus on that slice; page 147.

■ **CHECKPOINT 6.3**

Fill in the blanks

<u>Cost</u> is what a seller must give up to produce a good and <u>price</u> is what a seller receives when the good is sold. A <u>supply</u> curve is a marginal cost curve. A firm receives a producer surplus when price is <u>greater</u> than marginal cost.

True or false

1. False; page 149

2. True; page 149

3. False; page 149

4. False; page 150

Multiple choice

1. c; page 149

2. b; page 149

3. d; page 149

4. b; page 150

5. a; page 150

6. d; page 150

Complete the graph

1. a. The minimum price is $1; page 149.

   b. The marginal cost is $1. The marginal cost of the 10 millionth bag is the minimum price for which a supplier is willing to produce that bag of chips; page 149.

■ **FIGURE 6.9**

Price (dollars per bag of potato chips)

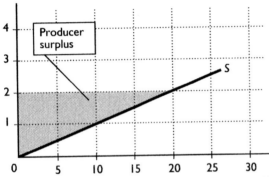

   c. Figure 6.9 shades the area of the producer surplus; page 150.

   d. The producer surplus equals the area of the shaded triangle in Figure 6.9, so producer surplus is 1/2 × ($2 – $0) × 20 million, which equals $20 million; page 150.

Short answer and numeric questions

1. The minimum price for which a firm will produce a slice of pizza equals the marginal cost of producing that slice. It is just worth producing one more slice of pizza if the price for which it can be sold equals its marginal cost. The supply curve tells us this price. So the supply curve is the same as the marginal cost curve; page 149.

2. Producer surplus equals the price of a good or service minus the marginal cost of producing it. As the price of a good or service rises and the supply curve does not shift, the producer surplus increases; page 150.

■ CHECKPOINT 6.4

Fill in the blanks

Equilibrium in a competitive market <u>is</u> efficient. Adam Smith believed that each participant in a competitive market is "led by <u>an invisible hand</u>." A price <u>ceiling</u> is a regulation that makes it illegal to charge a price higher than a specified level. <u>A public good</u> is a good or service that is consumed simultaneously by everyone, even if they don't pay for it. Deadweight loss is the decrease in <u>consumer surplus and producer surplus</u> that results from an inefficient level of production.

True or false

1. True; page 152

2. False; page 152

3. False; page 153

4. False; page 155

Multiple choice

1. d; page 152

2. d; page 152

3. a; page 153

4. d; page 152

5. c; page 153

6. d; page 155

7. c; page 155

8. d; page 156

Complete the graph

■ **FIGURE 6.10**

Price (thousands of dollars per automobile)

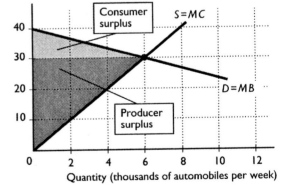

1. In Figure 6.10 the equilibrium quantity of

automobiles is 6,000 a week. The efficient quantity of automobiles is also 6,000 a week because that is the quantity at which the marginal benefit equals the marginal cost. The consumer surplus and producer surplus are the shown in the figure. The consumer surplus is the area of the light grey triangle, which is 1/2 × ($40.00 − $30.00) × (6,000) = $60,000. The producer surplus is the area of the dark grey triangle, which is 1/2 × ($30.00 − $0.00) × (60,000) = $90,000; page 152.

■ FIGURE 6.11

Price (thousands of dollars per automobile)

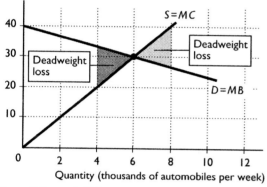

2. a. When 8,000 automobiles are produced, there is a deadweight loss from overproduction because for the last 2,000 automobiles, the marginal cost exceeds the marginal benefit. The deadweight loss is the area of the light grey triangle in Figure 6.11, which is 1/2 × ($40.00 − $26.67) × (8,000 − 6,000) = $1,330; page 155.

   b. If 4,000 automobiles are produced, there again is a deadweight loss, this time from underproduction, because automobiles for which the marginal benefit exceeds the marginal cost are not produced. The amount of the deadweight loss is the area of dark grey triangle in Figure 6.11, which is 1/2 × ($33.33 − $20.00) × (6,000 − 4,000) = $1,330; page 155.

Short answer and numeric questions

1. Adam Smith was the first to suggest that competitive markets send resources to the uses in which they have the highest value so that competitive markets are efficient. Smith

said that each participant in a competitive market is "led by an invisible hand to promote an end [the efficient use of resources] which is no part of his intention;" page 153.

2. If the demand for cotton clothing increases, the demand curve for cotton clothing shifts rightward and the equilibrium quantity increases. The demand curve is the marginal benefit curve, so when the demand curve shifts rightward, the marginal benefit curve also shifts rightward. The efficient quantity also increases; page 152.

3. Governments influence markets by setting price and quantity regulations as well as taxes and subsidies, all of which can create inefficiency. Other obstacles to achieving an efficient allocation of resources are externalities, public goods, common resources, monopoly, and high transactions costs; pages 156-157.

■ CHECKPOINT 6.5

Fill in the blanks

Two views of fairness are that "it's not fair if the result isn't fair;" and "it's not fair if the rules aren't fair." According to Robert Nozick, fair-rules ideas require property rights and voluntary exchange.

True or false

   1. True; page 159
   2. False; page 160
   3. False; page 161

Multiple choice

   1. b; page 159
   2. b; page 160
   3. a; page 160
   4. c; page 161

Short answer and numeric questions

1. The tax arrangement is fair from a fair-results view because it leads to a greater equality of income. The tax arrangement is not fair from a fair-results view because the tax is not a voluntary exchange; pages 159-160.

2. From a fair-results view, it is not fair for Pat's income to be substantially higher than Matt's. From a fair-rules view, it is fair because Pat and Matt had the same opportunities; pages 159-160.

3. Income can be transferred from people with high incomes to people with low incomes only by taxing incomes, which discourages work. This tax results in the quantity of labor being less than the efficient quantity. Similarly, taxing income from capital discourages saving, which results in the quantity of capital being less than the efficient quantity. With less labor and less capital than the efficient amounts, the total amount of production is less than the efficient amount. So the greater the amount of income redistribution through income taxes, the greater is the inefficiency and the smaller is the economic pie; page 160.

4. Limiting the price that can be charged is unfair because it compels the seller to help and such compulsion is unfair; page 161.

Government Influences on Markets

Chapter 7

CHAPTER CHECKLIST

1 **Explain how taxes change prices and quantities, are shared by buyers and sellers, and create inefficiency.**

Taxes raise the price and decrease the quantity of the good that is taxed. Tax incidence is the division of the burden of a tax between the buyers and the sellers and depends on the elasticities of demand and supply. The excess burden of a tax is the deadweight loss from a tax. For a given elasticity of supply, the buyers pay a larger share of the tax the more inelastic is the demand for the good. Similarly, for a given elasticity of demand, the sellers pay a larger share of the tax the more inelastic is the supply of the good. The more inelastic the demand or supply, the smaller is the excess burden of the tax.

2 **Explain how a price ceiling works and show how a rent ceiling creates a housing shortage, inefficiency, and unfairness.**

A price ceiling makes it illegal to charge more than a specified price. A rent ceiling is a price ceiling. A rent ceiling set *below* the equilibrium rent leads to a housing shortage because the quantity of housing demanded exceeds the quantity of housing supplied. A black market is an illegal market that operates alongside a government regulated market. When a rent ceiling creates a shortage of housing, search activity, which is the time spent looking for someone with whom to do business, increases. A rent ceiling creates a deadweight loss. Rent ceilings violate the fair-rules view of fairness because they block voluntary exchange. Rent ceilings exist because of political support from current renters.

3 **Explain how a price floor works and show how the minimum wage creates unemployment, inefficiency, and unfairness.**

A minimum wage law is a government regulation that makes hiring labor for less than a specified wage illegal. A minimum wage law is a price floor. A minimum wage set *above* the equilibrium wage rate leads to unemployment because the quantity of labor supplied exceeds the quantity of labor demanded. A minimum wage increases job search activity. The minimum wage creates a deadweight loss. The minimum wage is unfair because it delivers an unfair result and imposes unfair rules.

4 **Explain how a price support in the market for an agricultural product creates a surplus, inefficiency, and unfairness.**

When governments intervene in agricultural markets, they isolate the domestic market from global competition by limiting imports and then introduce a price floor, called a price support. The price support leads to a surplus, so the government pays the farmers a subsidy by purchasing the surplus to keep the price at the support level. Consumers are harmed because the price rises and the quantity they purchase decreases. Farmers are helped because the price is higher. A deadweight loss is created. Farmers in other countries are harmed because their exports to the nation are limited and because the government sells the surplus it has purchased in the rest of the world, thereby lowering the price.

CHECKPOINT 7.1

■ **Explain how taxes change prices and quantities, are shared by buyers and sellers, and create inefficiency..**

Quick Review

- *Effect of a sales tax on the supply curve* A sales tax decreases the supply of the good and the supply curve shifts leftward. The vertical distance between the supply curve without the tax and the supply curve with the tax equals the amount of the tax.

- *Tax incidence and elasticities of demand and supply* For a given elasticity of supply, the more inelastic the demand, the larger the share of a tax paid by the buyer. And, for a given elasticity of demand, the more inelastic the supply, the larger the share of a tax paid by the seller.

Additional Practice Problem 7.1

1. The figure illustrates the initial equilibrium in the markets for Coke and Pepsi. The price of a 2 liter bottle of a Coke and a Pepsi are the same, $1.50, and the quantity of each are the same, 12 million bottles a week. The supply of Coke is identical to the supply of Pepsi and both are given by supply curve *S* in the figure. However, as shown in the figure with the demand curve *Dc* for Coke and *Dp* for Pepsi, the demand for Coke is more elastic than the demand for Pepsi. The government now imposes a $1 per bottle sales tax on Coke and Pepsi.

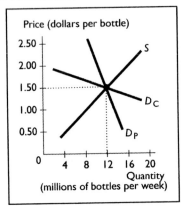

   a. Does the price paid by consumers for a Coke rise by more than, less than, or the same amount as the price paid for a Pepsi?

   b. Do the consumers of Coke pay more of their tax than do consumers of Pepsi? Do the producers of Coke pay more of their tax than do the producers of Pepsi?

   c. Does the quantity of Coke decrease by more than, less than, or the same amount as the quantity of Pepsi?

   d. Does the government collect more than, less than, or the same amount of tax revenue from the tax on Coke as it does from the tax on Pepsi?

   e. Is the deadweight loss from the tax on Coke larger than, less than, or the same amount as the deadweight loss from the tax on Pepsi?

Solution to Additional Practice Problem 7.1

1a. A tax is like an increase in the suppliers' costs, so a tax decreases the supply and shifts the supply curve leftward. The vertical dis-

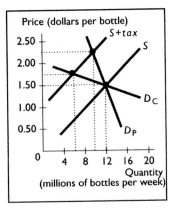

tance between the supply curve with the tax and the supply curve without the tax is equal to the amount of the tax, $1 per bottle in this problem. The figure shows this effect, with the supply curves for Coke and Pepsi both shifting to the curve labeled *S+tax*. The demand for Coke is more elastic, so the price paid by consumers for a Coke rises only to $1.75, a 25¢ increase. The demand for Pepsi is less elastic, so the price paid for a Pepsi rises to $2.25, a 75¢ increase.

1b. The demand for Coke is more elastic, so consumers play less of the tax imposed on Coke. The price paid by consumers for a Coke rises 25¢, so consumers pay 25¢ of this tax and producers pay the remaining 75¢. The demand for Pepsi is more inelastic, so consumers pay more of a tax imposed on Pepsi. The price paid by consumers for a Pepsi rises 75¢, so consumers pay 75¢ of this tax and producers pay 25¢.

1c. The quantity of Coke decreases by more than the quantity of Pepsi because the demand for Coke is more elastic than the demand for Pepsi. In the figure, the equilibrium quantity of Coke decreases to 6 million bottles per week and the equilibrium quantity of Pepsi decreases only to 10 million bottles per week.

1d. The total amount of tax revenue equals the tax multiplied by the quantity sold. Because the decrease in the quantity of Coke is greater than the decrease in the quantity of Pepsi, less Coke than Pepsi is sold after the tax is imposed, and the government collects less tax revenue from the tax on Coke.

1e. Because the decrease in the quantity of Coke is greater than the decrease in the quantity of Pepsi, the deadweight loss of the tax is greater for Coke than for Pepsi.

■ Self Test 7.1

Fill in the blanks

The tax ____ (elasticity; incidence) is the division of the burden of a tax between the buyer and the seller. A tax is like ____ (a decrease; an increase) in suppliers' costs. For a given elasticity of supply, the buyer pays a larger share of the tax the more ____ (elastic; inelastic) is the demand for the good. If the supply is perfectly ____ (elastic; inelastic), the seller pays the entire tax. Taxes ____ (create; do not create) a deadweight loss. The excess burden of a tax is the ____ (deadweight loss; surplus) from the tax and is larger the ____ (more; less) elastic the demand for the good being taxed.

True or false

1. When the government imposes a tax on the sale of a good, the burden of the tax falls entirely on the buyer.

2. A tax on fast-food meals does not create a deadweight loss because the elasticity of supply of fast-food meals equals 1.0.

3. The excess burden of a tax is the deadweight loss from the tax.

4. For a given elasticity of supply, the more inelastic the demand for a good, the smaller the share of the tax paid by the buyer.

5. When the government taxes a good that has a perfectly elastic supply, the buyer pays the entire tax.

Multiple choice

1. Tax incidence refers to
   a. how government taxes are spent by the government.
   b. the incidences of tax revolts by the tax payers.
   c. the amount of a tax minus its burden.
   d. the division of the burden of a tax between the buyers and the sellers.
   e. tax revenue minus excess burden.

2. Neither the supply of nor demand for a good is perfectly elastic or perfectly inelastic. So imposing a tax on the good results in a ____ in the price paid by buyers and ____ in the equilibrium quantity.
   a. rise; an increase
   b. rise; a decrease
   c. fall; an increase
   d. fall; a decrease
   e. rise; no change

3. Neither the supply of nor demand for a good is perfectly elastic or perfectly inelastic. So imposing a tax on the good results in a ____ in the price received by sellers and a ____ in the price paid by buyers.
   a. rise; rise
   b. rise; fall
   c. fall; rise
   d. fall; fall
   e. no change; rise

4. A sales tax ____ consumer surplus and ____ producer surplus.
   a. increases; increases
   b. increases; decreases
   c. decreases; increases
   d. decreases; decreases
   e. does not change; does not change

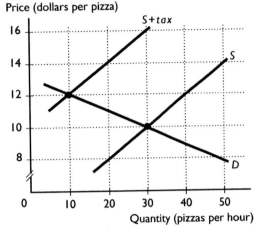

■ **FIGURE 7.1**

Price (dollars per pizza)

5. Figure 7.1 shows the market for delivered pizza. The government has imposed a tax of _____ per pizza.
   a. $6
   b. $8
   c. $10
   d. $12
   e. $16

6. In Figure 7.1, before the tax was imposed consumers paid _____ for a pizza and after the tax is imposed consumers pay _____ for a pizza.
   a. $10: $16
   b. $12; $16
   c. $10; $12
   d. $12; $16
   e. $10; $6

7. In Figure 7.1, the division of the tax is that consumers pay _____ of the tax and suppliers pay _____ of the tax.
   a. $6: $0
   b. $3; $3
   c. $0; $6
   d. $4; $2
   e. $2; $4

8. The deadweight loss from a tax is called the
   a. marginal benefit of the tax.
   b. marginal cost of the tax.
   c. excess burden of the tax.
   d. net gain from taxation.
   e. net loss from taxation.

9. A sales tax creates a deadweight loss because
   a. there is some paperwork opportunity cost of sellers paying the sales tax.
   b. demand and supply both decrease.
   c. less is produced and consumed.
   d. citizens value government goods less than private goods.
   e. the government spends the tax revenue it collects.

10. To determine who bears the greater share of a tax, we compare
    a. the number of buyers to the number of sellers.
    b. the elasticity of supply to the elasticity of demand.
    c. the size of the tax to the price of the good.
    d. government tax revenue to the revenue collected by the suppliers.
    e. the pre-tax quantity to the post-tax quantity.

11. Suppose the demand for barley is perfectly elastic. The supply curve of barley is upward sloping. If a tax is imposed on barley,
    a. barley sellers pay the entire tax.
    b. barley buyers pay the entire tax.
    c. the government pays the entire tax.
    d. the tax is split evenly between barley buyers and sellers.
    e. who pays the tax depends on whether the government imposes the tax on barley sellers or on barley buyers.

Complete the graph

■ **FIGURE 7.2**

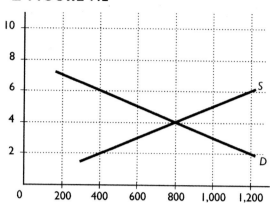

1. The supply curve and the demand curve for pizza slices are shown in Figure 7.2. The price is in dollars per slice and the quantity is pizza slices per day. Label the axes.
   a. What is the equilibrium price and quantity of pizza slices?
   b. Suppose the government imposes a sales tax of $4 a slice of pizza. In Figure 7.2, draw the new supply curve after the tax is imposed.
   c. After the tax is imposed, what is the price paid by buyers for a slice of pizza? What is the price received by sellers for a slice of pizza? What is the incidence of the tax?
   d. In Figure 7.2, darken the area of the deadweight loss from the tax.

2. The supply curve and the demand curve for pizza slices are again shown in Figure 7.3. The price is in dollars per slice and the quantity is pizza slices per day. Once again, label the axes.
   a. Suppose the government imposes a tax on buyers of $4 a slice of pizza. In Figure 7.3, draw the new demand curve after the tax is imposed.
   b. After the tax is imposed, what is the price paid by buyers for a slice of pizza? What is the price received by sellers for a slice of pizza? What is the incidence of the tax?

■ **FIGURE 7.3**

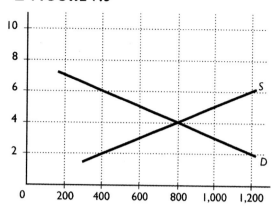

   c. How do the prices paid and the tax incidence in this question compare to those in question 1? What general principle does your answer uncover?

Short answer and numeric questions

Price (dollars per golf ball)	Quantity demanded (golf balls)	Before-tax quantity supplied (golf balls)	After-tax quantity supplied (golf balls)
0.50	1,100	600	0
1.00	1,000	620	0
1.50	900	680	0
2.00	700	700	0
2.50	600	850	___
3.00	300	950	___
3.50	60	1,180	680

1. The above table gives the monthly demand and supply schedules for golf balls at the College Hills Golf Shop. With no tax, what is the equilibrium price and quantity? Suppose a $2 per ball tax is imposed.
   a. Complete the last column of the table.
   b. What is the equilibrium price and quantity after the tax is imposed?
   c. How much of the tax is paid by the buyer? How much is paid by the seller?
   d. How much tax revenue does the government collect?

2. The government decides to tax high blood pressure medicine. The supply by drug companies is elastic; the demand by patients is inelastic. Do the drug companies bear the en-

tire tax burden? Is there much deadweight loss from this tax?

3. What is the relationship between the dead-weight loss from a tax and the excess burden of a tax? Why does a tax create a deadweight loss?

CHECKPOINT 7.2

■ **Explain how a price ceiling works and show how a rent ceiling creates a housing shortage, inefficiency, and unfairness.**

Quick Review

- *Price ceiling* A government regulation that places an *upper* limit on the price at which a particular good, service, or factor of production may be traded.
- *Rent ceiling* A government regulation that makes it illegal to charge more than a specified rent for housing.
- *Effective rent ceiling* When a rent ceiling is set below the equilibrium rent, the quantity of housing demanded is greater than the equilibrium quantity and the quantity of housing supplied is less than the equilibrium quantity. A housing shortage occurs.

Additional Practice Problems 7.2

1. The figure shows the rental market for apartments in Ocala, Florida.
   a. With no government intervention in this market, what is the rent and how many apartments are rented?

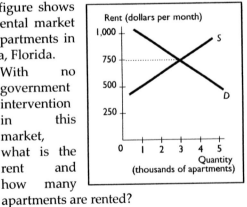

b. If the government imposes a rent ceiling of $500 a month, what is the rent and how many apartments are rented?

c. Tell why with a strictly enforced $500 rent ceiling the housing market is inefficient. What is the amount of the deadweight loss?

d. With a strictly enforced $500 rent ceiling, is there a shortage or surplus of apartments?

Price (dollars per round of golf)	Quantity demanded	Quantity supplied
	(rounds per week)	
50	2,000	2,800
40	2,300	2,700
30	2,600	2,600
20	2,900	2,500
10	3,200	2,400

2. The table above gives the supply and demand schedules for rounds of golf.
   a. What is the equilibrium price and equilibrium quantity of rounds of golf?
   b. Suppose the city government imposes a price ceiling of $40 a round of golf. What will be the price and quantity of rounds of golf? Is there a shortage?
   c. Suppose the city government imposes a price ceiling of $20 a round of golf. What will be the price and quantity of rounds of golf? Is there a shortage?

Solutions to Additional Practice Problems 7.2

1a. In the figure, the equilibrium rent and the equilibrium quantity are determined at the point where the demand curve and the supply curve intersect. The

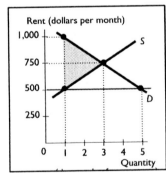

rent is $750 a month and 3,000 apartments are rented.

1b. To answer this practice problem remember that a rent ceiling is effective only when it is set below the equilibrium price. The rent ceiling of $500 per month is below the equilibrium rent, so it has an effect. The quantity of apartments rented decreases to 1,000 and the rent is $500.

1c. The market is inefficient because the marginal benefit of the last apartment rented, the 1,000th apartment, exceeds the marginal cost of the apartment. Because the housing market is inefficient a deadweight loss arises. In the figure the deadweight loss is shown by the gray triangle. The amount of the deadweight loss equals the area of the gray triangle. This area is $1/2 \times (\$1,000 - \$500) \times (3,000 - 1,000) = \$500,000$.

1d. There is a shortage of apartments. At the $500 rent ceiling, the quantity of apartments demanded is 5,000 and the quantity supplied is 1,000. So there is a shortage of 4,000 apartments.

2a. The equilibrium price is $30 a round of golf and the equilibrium quantity is 2,600 rounds a week.

2b. The price ceiling is above the equilibrium price, so the price remains at $30 a round and the quantity remains at 2,600 rounds a week. There is no shortage.

2c. The price ceiling is below the equilibrium price. The price falls to $20 a round. The quantity played equals the quantity supplied at $20, which is 2,500 rounds a week. There is a shortage of 400 rounds a week.

■ Self Test 7.2

Fill in the blanks

A price ceiling is the _____ (highest; lowest) price at which it is legal to trade a particular good, service, or factor of production. A rent ceiling is effective if it is set _____ (above; below) the equilibrium rent. A rent ceiling can create a housing _____ (shortage; surplus), which leads to _____ (increased; decreased) search activity. Rent ceilings _____ (can result in; do not result in) inefficiency. The _____ (less; more) inelastic the demand or the supply of housing, the smaller the deadweight loss created by a rent ceiling. Rent ceilings _____ (are; are not) fair.

True or false

1. A rent ceiling always lowers the rent paid.
2. When a rent ceiling is higher than the equilibrium rent, a black market emerges.
3. The opportunity cost of a dorm room is equal to its rent plus the value of the search time spent finding the dorm room.
4. Rent ceilings are efficient because they lower the cost of housing to low-income families.
5. The total loss from a rent ceiling exceeds the deadweight loss.

Multiple choice

1. A price ceiling is a government regulation that makes it illegal to charge a price
   a. below the equilibrium price.
   b. above the equilibrium price.
   c. for a good or service.
   d. above some specified level.
   e. that is not equal to the equilibrium price.

2. When a price ceiling is set below the equilibrium price, the quantity supplied _____ the quantity demanded and _____ exists.
   a. is less than; a surplus
   b. is less than; a shortage
   c. is greater than; a surplus
   d. is greater than; a shortage
   e. equals; an equilibrium

3. In a housing market with a rent ceiling set below the equilibrium rent,
   a. some people seeking an apartment to rent will not be able to find one.
   b. the total cost of renting an apartment will decrease for all those seeking housing.
   c. some landlords will not be able to find renters to fill available apartments.
   d. search will decrease because renters no longer need to search for less expensive apartments.
   e. None of the above answers are correct because to have an impact the rent ceiling must be set *above* the equilibrium rent.

4. A rent ceiling on housing creates a problem of allocating the available housing units because
   a. the demand for housing decreases and the demand curve shifts leftward.
   b. the supply of housing increases and the supply curve shifts rightward.
   c. a shortage of apartments occurs.
   d. a surplus of apartments occurs.
   e. it eliminates search, which is one of the major ways housing units are allocated.

■ **FIGURE 7.4**

Rent (dollars per month)

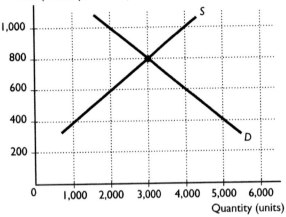

Quantity (units)

5. Figure 7.4 shows a housing market. If the government imposes a rent ceiling of $1,000 per month, there will be a
   a. surplus of 2,000 units.
   b. shortage of 2,000 units.
   c. surplus of 4,000 units.
   d. shortage of 1,000 units.
   e. neither a shortage nor a surplus of units.

6. Figure 7.4 shows a housing market. If the government imposes a rent ceiling of $400 per month, there will be a
   a. shortage of 1,000 units.
   b. shortage of 2,000 units.
   c. shortage of 3,000 units.
   d. shortage of 4,000 units.
   e. neither a shortage nor a surplus of units.

7. Figure 7.4 shows a housing market. Of the rent ceilings listed below, the deadweight loss from a rent ceiling is largest when the rent ceiling equals _____ per month.
   a. $1,000
   b. $800
   c. $600
   d. $400
   e. More information is needed to determine which of the rent ceilings has the largest deadweight loss.

8. Rent ceilings
   a. increase search activity.
   b. result in surpluses.
   c. are efficient.
   d. benefit producers.
   e. have no effect if they are set below the equilibrium rent.

9. Suppose that the government imposes a price ceiling on gasoline that is below the equilibrium price. The black market for gasoline is _____ market in which the price _____ the ceiling price.
   a. a legal; exceeds
   b. an illegal; exceeds
   c. a legal; is less than
   d. an illegal; is less than
   e. an illegal; equals

10. A rent ceiling creates a deadweight loss
   a. if it is set below the equilibrium rent.
   b. if it is set equal to the equilibrium rent.
   c. if it set above the equilibrium rent.
   d. if it decreases the taxes the government collects in the housing market.
   e. never, because if it did create a deadweight loss, the government would not impose it.

11. Rent ceilings
   a. eliminate the problem of scarcity.
   b. allocate resources efficiently.
   c. ensure that housing goes to the poorer people.
   d. benefit renters living in rent-controlled apartments.
   e. benefit all landlords because the landlords know what rent to charge their renters.

Complete the graph

■ FIGURE 7.5

Price (dollars per purse)

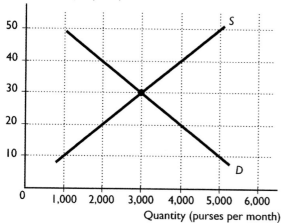

1. Figure 7.5 shows the market for purses.
   a. What is the equilibrium price and quantity of purses?
   b. Suppose the government imposes a $20 price ceiling. With the price ceiling, what is the quantity of purses demanded and the quantity of purses supplied? What is the shortage? Indicate the shortage in the figure.
   c. The price ceiling creates a deadweight loss. Show the deadweight loss in the figure.

Rent	Quantity demanded	Quantity supplied
(dollars per month)	(housing units per month)	
900	200	350
800	300	300
700	400	250
600	500	200
500	600	150

2. The table above gives the demand and supply schedules for housing in a small town. In Figure 7.6, graph the demand and supply curves. Label the axes.
   a. What is the equilibrium rent and quantity of housing?
   b. Suppose the government imposes a $600 a month rent ceiling. With the rent ceiling, what is the quantity of housing demanded and the quantity of housing supplied?

■ FIGURE 7.6

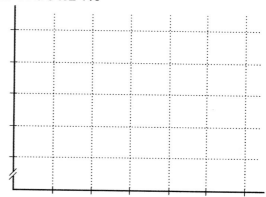

   c. Does the rent ceiling result in a shortage or a surplus of housing? Indicate the shortage or surplus in Figure 7.6.

Short answer and numeric questions

1. What is a price ceiling?

Price (dollars per carton)	Quantity demanded	Quantity supplied
	(cartons per day)	
1.00	200	110
1.25	175	130
1.50	150	150
1.75	125	170
2.00	100	190

2. The table above gives the demand and supply schedules for milk.
   a. What is the market equilibrium in the milk market?
   b. Suppose the government imposes a price ceiling of $1.25 per carton. What is the price of a carton of milk and what quantity is purchased? Is there a shortage or surplus of milk?
   c. Suppose the government imposes a price ceiling of $1.75 per carton. What is the price of a carton of milk and what quantity is purchased? Is there a shortage or surplus of milk?

3. Are rent ceilings efficient?

4. Are rent ceilings fair?

CHECKPOINT 7.3

■ **Explain how a price floor works and show how the minimum wage creates unemployment, inefficiency, and unfairness.**

Quick Review

- *Price floor* A government regulation that places a *lower* limit on the price at which a particular good, service, or factor of production may be traded.
- *Minimum wage law* A government regulation that makes hiring labor for less than a specified wage illegal.
- *Effective minimum wage law* When the minimum wage is set above the equilibrium wage rate, the quantity of labor demanded is less than the equilibrium quantity and the quantity of labor supplied is greater than the equilibrium quantity. Unemployment occurs.

Additional Practice Problems 7.3

1. The figure shows the market for fast food workers in Lake City Florida.
   a. What is the equilibrium wage rate of the workers and what is the equilibrium quantity of workers employed?

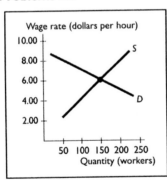

   b. If Lake City introduces a minimum wage for fast food workers of $10 an hour, how many fast food workers are employed?
   c. With the minimum wage, is there a surplus or a shortage of fast food workers? Indicate the amount of any shortage or surplus in the figure.
   d. Is the minimum wage of $10 an hour efficient? Is it fair?

Price (cents per pound)	Quantity demanded	Quantity supplied
	(tons of sugar per year)	
10	300	225
15	275	275
20	250	325
25	225	375
30	200	425

2. The above table gives the supply and demand schedules for sugar.
   a. What is the equilibrium price and quantity of sugar?
   b. Suppose the government imposes a price floor of 25¢ a pound. What is the quantity demanded and the quantity supplied? Is there a shortage or surplus and, if so, how much?

Solutions to Additional Practice Problems 7.3

1a. The equilibrium wage rate and the equilibrium quantity of the workers are determined where the labor demand curve and the labor supply curve intersect. The equilibrium wage rate is $7.50 an hour and the equilibrium quantity of workers is 150.

1b. In the figure, 50 fast food workers are employed. This amount equals the quantity of labor demanded when the wage rate is $10 an hour.

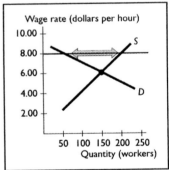

1c. The minimum wage creates a surplus of workers. At the $10 wage rate, 200 workers are willing to work but firms are willing to hire only 50 workers. There is a surplus of 150 workers, that is, there are 150 workers unemployed. In the figure, the length of the arrow shows the 150 unemployed workers.

1d. The minimum wage of $10 an hour is not efficient because the marginal benefit to restaurants who demand workers exceeds the marginal cost borne by the workers who supply work. A deadweight loss is created.

An additional loss arises as unemployed workers search for jobs. The minimum wage is not fair. It violates the "fair-rules" view of fairness because it prevents voluntary exchange. It violates the "fair-results" view of fairness because 100 workers lose their jobs and are made poorer.

2a. The equilibrium price is 15¢ a pound and the equilibrium quantity is 275 tons a year.

2b. The quantity demanded at 25¢ a pound is 225 tons and the quantity supplied is 375 tons. There is a surplus of 150 tons.

■ Self Test 7.3

Fill in the blanks

A minimum wage is a price _____ (ceiling; floor). A price floor is the _____ (highest; lowest) price at which it is legal to trade a particular good, service, or factor of production. If a minimum wage is set above the equilibrium wage rate, the quantity of labor demanded _____ (decreases; increases) and the quantity of labor supplied _____ (decreases; increases). A minimum wage _____ (creates; does not create) unemployment and _____ (decreases; increases) job search activity. An efficient allocation of labor occurs when the marginal _____ (benefit; cost) to firms _____ (equals; is greater than; is less than) the marginal _____ (benefit; cost) borne by workers. The minimum wage is _____ (fair; unfair). Labor unions _____ (do not support; support) the minimum wage.

True or false

1. Firms hire labor, so they determine how much labor to supply in a market.

2. A minimum wage is effective when it is set above the equilibrium wage rate.

3. A minimum wage law can lead to increased job search activity and illegal hiring.

4. When a minimum wage is set above the equilibrium wage rate, the employee's marginal cost of working exceeds the employer's marginal benefit from hiring labor.

5. A minimum wage is fair because low-income workers receive an increase in take-home pay.

Multiple choice

1. A price floor
   a. is the highest price at which it is legal to trade a particular good, service, or factor of production.
   b. is the lowest price at which it is legal to trade a particular good, service, or factor of production.
   c. is an illegal price to charge.
   d. is the equilibrium price when the stock market crashes.
   e. is the lowest price for which the quantity demanded equals the quantity supplied.

2. To be effective in raising people's wages, a minimum wage must be set
   a. above the equilibrium wage rate.
   b. below the equilibrium wage rate.
   c. equal to the equilibrium wage rate.
   d. below $5.
   e. either above or below the equilibrium wage depending on whether the supply curve of labor shifts rightward or leftward in response to the minimum wage.

3. A minimum wage set above the equilibrium wage rate
   a. increases the quantity of labor services supplied.
   b. decreases the quantity of labor services supplied.
   c. has no effect on the quantity of labor services supplied.
   d. shifts the labor supply curve rightward.
   e. shifts the labor supply curve leftward.

4. Suppose the current equilibrium wage rate for lifeguards in Houston is $7.85 an hour. A minimum wage law that creates a price floor of $8.50 an hour leads to
   a. a surplus of lifeguards in Houston.
   b. a shortage of lifeguards in Houston.
   c. no changes in the lifeguard market.
   d. a change in the quantity of lifeguards supplied but no change in the quantity of lifeguards demanded.
   e. an increase in the number of lifeguards employed.

5. An increase in the minimum wage ____ employment and ____ unemployment.
   a. increases; increases
   b. increases; decreases
   c. decreases; increases
   d. decreases; decreases
   e. does not change; increases

■ **FIGURE 7.7**

Wage rate (dollars per hour)

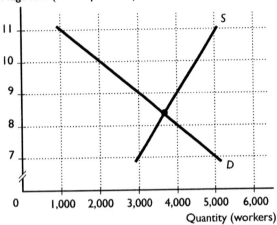

6. Figure 7.7 shows the market for fast food workers in San Francisco. A minimum wage of $11 per hour leads to unemployment of ____ workers.
   a. 1,000
   b. 2,000
   c. 3,000
   d. 4,000
   e. 5,000

7. In Figure 7.7, which of the following minimum wages creates the most unemployment?
   a. $7 an hour
   b. $8 an hour
   c. $9 an hour
   d. $10 an hour
   e. $11 an hour

8. If a minimum wage is introduced that is above the equilibrium wage rate,
   a. the quantity of labor demanded increases.
   b. job search activity increases.
   c. the supply of labor increases and the supply of labor curve shifts rightward.
   d. unemployment decreases because more workers accept jobs at the higher minimum wage rate.
   e. the quantity of labor supplied decreases because of the increase in unemployment.

9. The minimum wage is set above the equilibrium wage rate. Does the minimum wage create inefficiency?
   a. Yes.
   b. No.
   c. Only if the supply of labor is perfectly inelastic.
   d. Only if the supply of labor is perfectly elastic.
   e. Only if employment exceeds the efficient amount.

10. When the minimum wage is raised, the ____ union labor ____.
    a. demand for; increases
    b. demand for; decreases
    c. supply of; increases
    d. supply of; decreases
    e. demand for; does not change

Complete the graph

Wage rate (dollars per hour)	Quantity demanded	Quantity supplied
	(workers per day)	
6	3,500	2,750
7	3,000	3,000
8	2,500	3,250
9	2,000	3,500
10	1,500	3,750

1. The table above gives the demand and supply schedules for labor in a small town.
   a. In Figure 7.8, on the next page, label the axes. Draw the labor demand and labor supply curves. What is the equilibrium wage rate and employment.

■ FIGURE 7.8

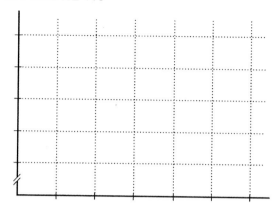

b. Suppose the government imposes a $4 an hour minimum wage. What is the effect on the wage rate and levels of employment and unemployment?

c. Suppose the government raises the minimum wage from $6 an hour to $9 an hour. What is the effect on the wage rate and levels of employment and unemployment? Indicate any unemployment.

■ FIGURE 7.9

Wage rate (dollars per hour)

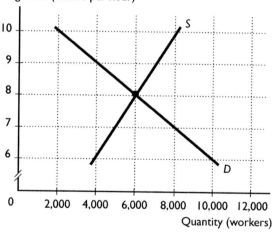

2. Figure 7.9 shows the labor demand and labor supply curves for Rochester, New York. Suppose the city is considering instituting a minimum wage. Indicate the minimum wages that lead to unemployment by dark-

ening the vertical axis for all the minimum wages that create unemployment.

Short answer and numeric questions

1. What is the effect of a minimum wage set below the equilibrium wage rate?

2. How does a minimum wage affect the time needed to find a job?

3. Do all low-wage workers benefit from a minimum wage?

CHECKPOINT 7.4

■ **Explain how a price support in the market for an agricultural product creates a surplus, inefficiency, and unfairness.**

Quick Review

• *Price support* A price support is a price floor in an agricultural market maintained by a government guarantee to buy any surplus output at that price. The price support is the minimum price for which the product may be sold.

Additional Practice Problems 7.4

1. The figure shows the market for sugar.

    a. What are the equilibrium price and quantity of sugar?

    b. Suppose the government puts in place a price support for sugar at $4 per pound. In the figure above, indicate this price support.

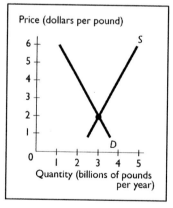

    c. With the price support, how much sugar is produced? How much sugar is purchased by private consumers? How much is purchased by the government?

d. With the price support, what is the subsidy received by sugar producers?

e. Are consumers made better off or worse off with the price support?

f. Without the price support, is the market efficient? With the price support, is the market efficient?

2. With a price support, the government pays a subsidy to farmers by buying part of the crop. Why is this purchase necessary?

Solutions to Additional Practice Problems 7.4

1a. The equilibrium price and the equilibrium quantity of sugar are determined where the demand curve and the supply curve intersect. The figure shows that the equilibrium price is $2 a pound and the equilibrium quantity is 3 billion pounds a year.

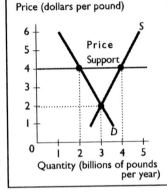

1b. The price support is shown in the figure as the solid line at $4 per pound.

1c. With the price support, the supply curve shows that at $4 per pound, 4 billion pounds of sugar are produced. The demand curve shows that at this price consumers buy 2 billion pounds. The government buys the surplus quantity of sugar, 2 billion pounds.

1d. The government buys 2 billion pounds of sugar at $4 per pound, so the subsidy is 2 billion pounds × $4 per pound, which is $8 billion.

1e. Consumers are worse off with the price support. With the price support the price they must pay for sugar increases, from $2 per pound to $4 per pound. In response consumers decrease the quantity of sugar they consume from 3 billion pounds to 2 billion pounds.

1f. Without the price support, the market is efficient. With the price support, the market is not efficient.

2. The price support leads to a surplus of the crop. If the government did not buy the surplus, the farmers would not be able to cover their costs because there would be part of the crop left unsold.

■ Self Test 7.4

Fill in the blanks

A price support is a _____ (price ceiling; price floor) in an agricultural market. The government maintains the price support by guaranteeing to _____ (buy; sell) the product at the support price. The government gives a _____ to producers to cover part of the costs of production. When the price support is above the equilibrium price, producers _____ (increase; decrease) the quantity supplied and consumers _____ (increase; decrease) the quantity demanded. Farmers _____ (gain; lose) from a price support and consumers _____ (gain; lose) from a price support. A price support _____ (creates; does not create) inefficiency and a deadweight loss.

True or false

1. In order to have an effective price support, the government isolates the domestic market from the world market by restricting imports.

2. A price support sets the maximum price for which farmers may sell their crop.

3. In order to keep the price of a crop above the equilibrium price and equal to the supported price, the government must buy some of the crop.

4. Because they decrease production, price supports decrease farmers' total revenue.

5. Price supports are efficient because they guarantee production of the good.

Multiple choice

1. Price supports are generally used in
   a. labor markets.
   b. industrial markets.
   c. housing markets.
   d. markets for services.
   e. agricultural markets.

2. To have an effective price support program, the government must
   i. isolate the domestic market from the world market
   ii. pay the farmers a subsidy
   iii. introduce a price floor
      a. i only.
      b. ii only.
      c. iii only.
      d. ii and iii.
      e. i, ii, and iii.

3. A price support directly sets the
   a. amount of production.
   b. subsidy the government must receive from producers.
   c. equilibrium quantity.
   d. lowest price for which the good may be sold.
   e. highest price for which the good may be sold.

4. To keep the price at the level set by the price support, the government must
   a. buy some of the good.
   b. sell some of the good.
   c. receive a subsidy from the producers.
   d. insure that imports are readily available.
   e. be careful to always set the price support below the equilibrium price.

5. With a price support program, who receives a subsidy?
   a. only consumers
   b. only producers
   c. the government
   d. importers
   e. both consumers and producers receive a subsidy

6. When a price support is set above the equilibrium price, producers ____ the quantity supplied and consumers ____ the quantity demanded.
   a. increase; increase
   b. increase; decrease
   c. decrease; increase
   d. decrease; decrease
   e. do not change; do not change

■ **FIGURE 7.10**

Price (dollars per ton)

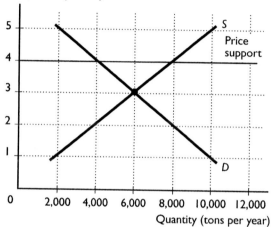

7. Figure 7.10 shows a price support program in an agricultural market. The amount of the subsidy necessary to keep the price at the price support is
   a. $4.
   b. $32,000.
   c. $8,000.
   d. $16,000.
   e. $24,000.

8. A price support ____ producers and ____ a deadweight loss.
   a. has no effect on; does not create
   b. benefits; creates
   c. harms; creates
   d. benefits; does not create
   e. harms; does not create

Complete the graph

Price (dollars per bushel)	Quantity demanded	Quantity supplied
	(millions of bushels per year)	
3	3,500	2,000
4	3,000	3,000
5	2,500	4,000
6	2,000	5,000
7	1,500	6,000

1. The table gives the demand and supply schedules for wheat.
   a. In Figure 7.11 label the axes. Draw the demand curve and supply curve and indicate the equilibrium price and quantity.

■ **FIGURE 7.11**

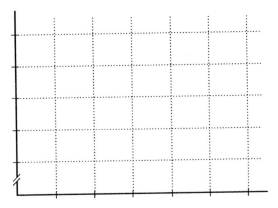

   b. Suppose the government imposes a price support of $5 per bushel. What is the effect on the price of wheat, the quantity of wheat produced and the marginal cost of a bushel of wheat? Is there a deadweight loss?
   c. With the $5 per bushel price support, how much wheat do consumers buy? What is the subsidy the government must pay to producers?

■ **FIGURE 7.12**
Price (dollars per ton)

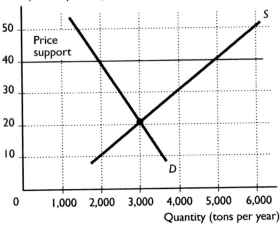

Quantity (tons per year)

2. Figure 7.12 shows the demand and supply curves for peanuts. There is a price support of $40 per ton of peanuts.
   a. At the support price, what is the quantity of peanuts produced? What is the quantity consumers buy? How many tons of peanuts must the government buy? Indicate the amount the government must buy in Figure 7.12.
   b. How much is the subsidy paid by the government to producers?

Short answer and numeric questions

1. Why must a price support be set above the equilibrium price in order to have an effect?
2. "A price support program benefits producers and harms consumers. But there is no overall net effect on society." Comment on the above assertion. Is it correct or incorrect?

SELF TEST ANSWERS

■ CHECKPOINT 7.1

Fill in the blanks

The tax <u>incidence</u> is the division of the burden of a tax between the buyer and the seller. A tax is like <u>an increase</u> in suppliers' costs. For a given elasticity of supply, the buyer pays a larger share of the tax the more <u>inelastic</u> is the demand for the good. If the supply is perfectly <u>inelastic</u>, the seller pays the entire tax. Taxes <u>create</u> a deadweight loss. The excess burden of a tax is the <u>deadweight loss</u> from the tax and is larger the <u>more</u> elastic the demand for the good being taxed.

True or false

1. False; pages 168-169
2. False; page 171
3. True; page 170
4. False; page 171
5. True; page 172

Multiple choice

1. d; page 168
2. b; page 169
3. c; page 169
4. d; page 170
5. a; page 169
6. c; page 169
7. e; page 169
8. c; page 170
9. c; page 170
10. b; page 171
11. b; page 171

Complete the graph

1. The axes are labeled in Figure 7.13.
   a. The price is $4 a slice and the quantity is 800 slices a day; pages 169.
   b. Figure 7.13 shows the supply curve after the tax is imposed; page 169.
   c. Buyers pay $6 a slice; sellers receive $2 a slice. The tax is split equally; page 169.
   d. The deadweight loss is the gray triangle in Figure 7.13; page 170.

■ FIGURE 7.13

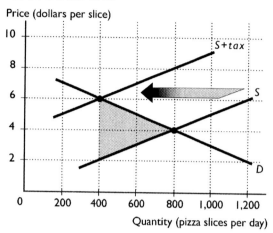

Price (dollars per slice)

■ FIGURE 7.14

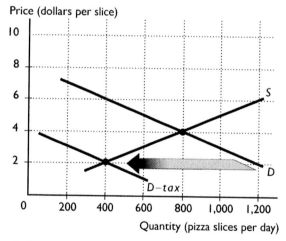

Price (dollars per slice)

2. The axes are labeled in Figure 7.14.
   a. Figure 7.14 shows the demand curve after the tax is imposed; page 169.
   b. Buyers pay $6 a slice; sellers receive $2 a slice. The tax is split equally; page 169.
   c. The price paid and the tax incidence is the same in problem 1, when the tax is imposed on sellers, and in problem 2, when the tax is imposed on buyers. The general principle is that the tax incidence depends on the elasticity of demand and the elasticity of supply, not on who sends the tax to the government; pages 169, 171.

Short answer and numeric questions

1. The equilibrium price is $2.00 a golf ball and the equilibrium quantity is 700 golf balls.

Price (dollars per golf ball)	After-tax quantity supplied (golf balls per month)
2.50	600
3.00	620

a. The completed supply schedule is in the table above; page 168.

b. $2.50 a golf ball and 600 golf balls; page 169.

c. The buyer pays $0.50 of the tax. The seller pays $1.50 of the tax; page 169.

d. The tax revenue is $2 a ball × 600 balls, which is $1,200; page 170.

2. The burden of the tax will fall mainly upon buyers, not the drug companies, because demand is inelastic and supply is elastic. Because the demand is inelastic, the decrease in the quantity will not be large and so the deadweight loss from the tax is small; page 171.

3. The excess burden of a tax is the same as the deadweight loss. The deadweight loss arises because the tax leads to less of the good or service being produced and consumed; page 170.

■ CHECKPOINT 7.2

Fill in the blanks

A price ceiling is the highest price at which it is legal to trade a particular good, service, or factor of production. A rent ceiling is effective if it is set below the equilibrium rent. A rent ceiling can create a housing shortage, which leads to increased search activity. Rent ceilings can result in inefficiency. The more inelastic the demand or the supply of housing, the smaller the deadweight loss created by a rent ceiling. Rent ceilings are not fair.

True or false

1. False; page 174
2. False; pages 174-175
3. True; page 176
4. False; page 178
5. True; page 178

Multiple choice

1. d; page 174
2. b; pages 174-175
3. a; page 175
4. c; page 175
5. e; page 175
6. d; page 175
7. d; page 178
8. a; page 176
9. b; pages 175-176
10. a; page 178
11. d; page 179

Complete the graph

■ FIGURE 7.15

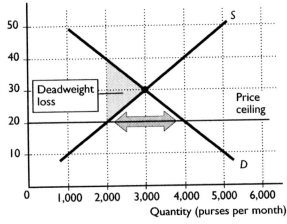

1. a. The equilibrium price is $30 per purse and the equilibrium quantity is 3,000 purses.

b. The quantity of purses demanded is 4,000, the quantity of purses supplied is 2,000, and the shortage equals 2,000 purses. In Figure 7.15, the shortage equals the length of the double-headed arrow; page 175.

c. The deadweight loss is shown in the figure; page 178.

■ FIGURE 7.16

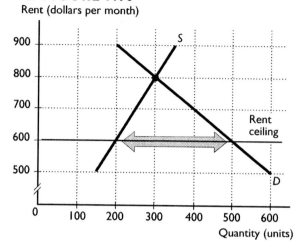

Rent (dollars per month)

2. Figure 7.16 shows the demand curve and supply curve. The equilibrium rent is $800 a month and the quantity is 300 housing units a month.

a. The quantity of housing demanded is 500 units a month; the quantity supplied is 200 units a month; page 175.

b. The shortage of 300 units a month is indicated by the arrow; page 175.

Short answer and numeric questions

1. A price ceiling is the highest price at which it is legal to trade a particular good, service, or factor of production; page 174.

2. a. The equilibrium price is $1.50 a carton and the quantity is 150 cartons a day.

   b. The price is $1.25 a carton and 130 cartons a day are purchased. There is a shortage of 45 cartons a day; page 175.

   c. The price ceiling is above the equilibrium price, and is ineffective. The price is $1.50 a carton, 150 cartons a day are purchased, and there is neither a shortage nor a surplus; page 174.

3. Rent ceilings create a deadweight loss and are not efficient; page 178.

4. Rent ceilings are not fair. They violate both the fair-results view and fair-rules view of fairness; page 179.

■ CHECKPOINT 7.3

Fill in the blanks

A minimum wage is a price <u>floor</u>. A price floor is the <u>lowest</u> price at which it is legal to trade a particular good, service, or factor of production. If a minimum wage is set above the equilibrium wage rate, the quantity of labor demanded <u>decreases</u> and the quantity of labor supplied <u>increases</u>. A minimum wage <u>creates</u> unemployment and <u>increases</u> job search activity. An efficient allocation of labor occurs when the marginal <u>benefit</u> to firms <u>equals</u> the marginal <u>cost</u> borne by workers. The minimum wage is <u>unfair</u>. Labor unions <u>support</u> the minimum wage.

True or false

1. False; page 181
2. True; page 182
3. True; page 183
4. False; page 184
5. False; page 185

Multiple choice

1. b; page 181
2. a; page 182
3. a; page 182
4. a; page 182
5. c; pages 182-183
6. d; page 182
7. e; pages 182-183
8. b; page 183
9. a; page 184
10. a; page 185

Complete the graph

■ FIGURE 7.17

Wage rate (dollars per hour)

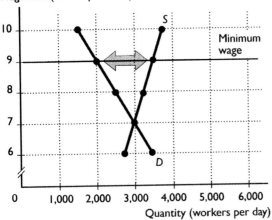

Quantity (workers per day)

1. a. Figure 7.17 shows the demand and supply curves. The equilibrium wage rate is $7.00 an hour and the equilibrium employment is 3,000 workers a day.
   b. The $6 minimum wage is below the equilibrium wage and has no effect; page 182.
   c. The $9 minimum wage raises the wage rate to $9. Employment decreases to 2,000 workers. The number of workers looking for work is 3,500. Unemployment equals 3,500 − 2,000, which is 1,500 people. The amount of unemployment is shown by the arrow in Figure 7.17; page 182.

■ FIGURE 7.18

Wage rate (dollars per hour)

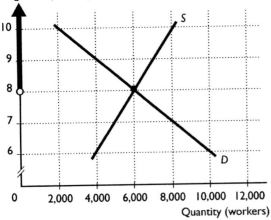

Quantity (workers)

1. In order to have an effect in the market, the minimum wage must be set above the equilibrium wage. As Figure 7.18 shows, any minimum wage above $8 per hour creates unemployment; page 182.

Short answer and numeric questions

1. A minimum wage set below the equilibrium wage rate has no effect on the wage rate or amount of employment; page 182.
2. By decreasing the quantity of labor demanded and creating unemployment, a minimum wage increases the time spent searching for a job; page 183.
3. A minimum wage harms low-wage workers who lose their jobs or cannot find jobs because of the minimum wage; page 185.

■ CHECKPOINT 7.4

Fill in the blanks

A price support is a price floor in an agricultural market. The government maintains the price support by guaranteeing to buy the product at the support price. The government gives a subsidy to producers to cover part of the costs of production. When the price support is above the equilibrium price, producers increase the quantity supplied and consumers decrease the quantity demanded. Farmers gain from a price support and consumers lose from a price support. A price support creates inefficiency and a deadweight loss.

True or false

1. True; page 187
2. False; page 187
3. True; page 188
4. False; page 189
5. False; page 189

Multiple choice

1. e; page 187
2. e; page 187
3. d; page 187
4. a; page 188
5. b; page 188

6. b; page 188

7. d; page 188

8. b; page 189

Complete the graph

■ **FIGURE 7.19**

Price (dollars per bushel)

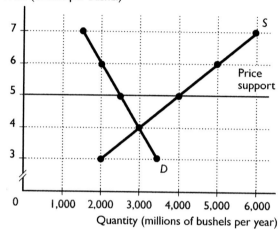

1. a. Figure 7.19 shows the demand and supply curves. The equilibrium price is $4 a bushel and the equilibrium quantity is 3,000 million bushels a year.

   b. The $5 per bushel price support is illustrated in the figure. This price support raises the price of wheat to $5 per bushel. The quantity of wheat produced increases to 4,000 million bushels per year and the marginal cost of the last bushel of wheat produced increases to $5. There is a deadweight loss because the marginal cost exceeds the marginal benefit; pages 188, 189.

   c. With the price support, consumers buy only 2,500 million bushels per year. There is a surplus of 1,500 million bushels (4,000 million bushels produced minus $2,500 million purchased by consumers) that the government must buy. The government pays a subsidy of $5 per bushel × 1,500 million bushels, which is $7.5 billion; page 188.

■ **FIGURE 7.20**

Price (dollars per ton)

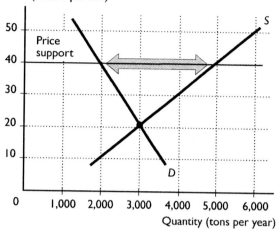

2. a. Figure 7.20 shows that at the support price of $40 per ton, 5,000 tons are produced and consumers buy 2,000 tons. The government must buy the surplus, 3,000 tons. The amount the government must buy is equal to the length of the arrow in Figure 7.20; page 188.

   b. To buy the surplus, the government pays a subsidy to producers of $40 per ton × 3,000 tons, which is $120,000; page 188.

Short answer and numeric questions

1. If a price support is set below the equilibrium price, it does not make the equilibrium price illegal and so is ineffective. If a price support is set above the equilibrium price, it makes the equilibrium price illegal and is effective; page 187.

2. The first assertion is correct: a price support program increases producer surplus (which benefits producers) and decreases consumer surplus (which harms consumers). But the second assertion is incorrect. There is a net effect on society because a deadweight loss is created, which harms society; page 189.

Global Markets in Action

Chapter

8

In Chapter 8 we see that all countries can benefit from free trade but countries nevertheless restrict trade.

1 Explain how markets work with international trade.

The goods and services that we buy from people in other countries are called imports. The goods and services that we sell to people in other countries are called exports. In 2006, the United States accounted for 10 percent of world exports and 15 percent of world imports. Comparative advantage enables countries to gain from trade. A nation has a comparative advantage in producing a good if it can produce that good at a lower opportunity cost than another country. In this case, the domestic no-trade price is lower than the world price. With international trade, the country will export this good.

2 Identify the gains from international trade and its winners and losers.

International trade lowers the prices of the goods and services imported into the country. The lower prices for imported goods mean that consumers gain additional consumer surplus from imports. The lower prices also mean that producers lose producer surplus from imports. The gain to consumers, however, exceeds the loss to producers. International trade raises the prices of the goods and services exported from the country The higher prices for exported goods mean that producers gain additional producer surplus from exports. The higher prices also mean that consumers lose consumer surplus from exports. The gain to producers, however, exceeds the loss to consumers.

3 Explain the effects of international trade barriers.

A tariff is a tax on a good that is imposed by the importing country when an imported good crosses its international boundary. A tariff on a good reduces imports of that good, increases domestic production of the good, yields revenue for the government, and creates a deadweight loss. A quota is a quantitative restriction on the import of a good that limits the maximum quantity of a good that may be imported in a given period of time. Voluntary export restraints are like a quota given to an exporter of a good. Both quotas and voluntary export restraints reduce imports, increase domestic production, and create deadweight losses. A subsidy is a payment by the government to a producer. Some countries subsidize products which are then exported. These export subsidies increase domestic production of the good or service but create deadweight losses.

4 Explain and evaluate arguments used to justify restricting international trade.

The three main arguments for protection and restriction of trade are the national security argument, the infant-industry argument, and the dumping argument. Each of these arguments is flawed. Other flawed arguments for protection are that protection saves jobs, allows us to compete with cheap foreign labor, brings diversity and stability and penalizes lax environmental standards. Tariffs are imposed in some nations to gain revenue for the government. In addition, trade is restricted is because of rent seeking from those who benefit from trade restrictions.

CHECKPOINT 8.1

■ **Explain how markets work with international trade.**

Quick Review

- *Imports* The goods and services that we buy from people in other countries are called imports.
- *Exports* The goods and services that we sell to people in other countries are called exports.
- *Comparative advantage* A nation has a comparative advantage in a good when its opportunity cost of producing the good is lower than another nation's opportunity cost of producing the good.

Additional Practice Problems 8.1

1. The figure shows the market for CPU chips in the United States with no international trade. The world price for a CPU chip is $150.

   Price (dollars per CPU chip)

   | 200 | | | | S |

   150

   100

   50

   D

   5 10 15 20 25

   Quantity (millions per year)

   a. Does the United States have a comparative advantage in producing CPU chips? How can you tell?

   b. If international trade is allowed, will the United States import or export CPU chips?

   c. Will the quantity of CPU chips produced in the United States increase or decrease? By how much?

   d. Will the quantity of CPU chips consumed in the United States increase or decrease? By how much?

   e. How many CPU chips will the United States import or export?

Solutions to Additional Practice Problems 8.1

1a. Because the price of a CPU chip in the United States is lower than the world price, the United States has a comparative advantage in producing CPU chips.

1b. Because the United States has a comparative advantage in producing CPU chips, the United States will export CPU chips.

1c. With international trade, the price of a CPU chip in the United States will be $150. At this price, the supply curve shows that the quantity of chips produced will equal 20 million per year. With no international trade, the equilibrium quantity of CPU chips produced is 15 million, so international trade leads to 5 million more chips being produced.

1d. With international trade, the price of a CPU chip in the United States will be $150. At this price, the demand curve shows that the quantity of chips demanded will equal 10 million per year. With no international trade, the equilibrium quantity of CPU chips consumed is 15 million, so international trade leads to 5 million fewer chips being consumed.

1e. The quantity of CPU chips exported equals the difference between the quantity of CPU chips produced, 20 million per year, and the quantity consumed, 10 million per year. So the United States will export 20 million CPU chips – 10 million CPU chips, which is 10 million CPU chips.

■ **Self Test 8.1**

Fill in the blanks

Global international trade accounts for a bit more than _____ (1/4; 1/2; 2/3) of global production. If a country can produce a good at a lower opportunity cost than any other country, the country has _____ (an export advantage; a comparative advantage) in the production of that good. The United States will export a good if its price in the United States with no international trade is _____ (lower; higher) than its world price. If the United States imports a good, then U.S. production of the good _____ (increases; decreases) and U.S. consumption of the good _____ (increases; decreases).

True or false

1. The United States is the world's largest international trader.

2. If a nation can produce a service at lower opportunity cost than any other nation, the nation has a national comparative advantage in producing that service.

3. If the price of a good in the United States with no international trade is higher than the world price, then with international trade the United States will export that good.

4. As a result of international trade, the U.S. production of goods exported from the Untied States increases and the U.S. production of goods imported into the United States decreases.

Multiple choice

1. Goods and services that we buy from people in other countries are called our
   a. imports.
   b. exports.
   c. inputs.
   d. raw materials.
   e. obligations.

2. If the United States exports planes to Brazil and imports ethanol from Brazil, the price received by U.S. producers of planes ____ and the price received by Brazilian producers of ethanol ____.
   a. does not change; does not change
   b. rises; rises
   c. rises; falls
   d. falls; rises
   e. falls; falls

3. When Italy buys Boeing jets, the price Italy pays is ____ if it produced their own jets and the price Boeing receives is ____ than it could receive from an additional U.S. buyer.
   a. lower than; lower
   b. higher than; higher
   c. lower than; higher
   d. higher than; lower
   e. the same as; higher

4. A nation will import a good if its no-trade, domestic
   a. price is equal to the world price.
   b. price is less than the world price.
   c. price is greater than the world price.
   d. quantity is less than the world quantity.
   e. quantity is greater than the world quantity.

5. When a good is imported, the domestic production ____ and the domestic consumption ____.
   a. increases; increases
   b. increases; decreases
   c. decreases; increases
   d. decreases; decreases
   e. increases; does not change

6. The United States will export a good if its no-trade U.S. price is ____ its world price and with trade, U.S. production of the good will ____ compared to the level of no-trade production.
   a. higher than; not change
   b. higher than; increase
   c. lower than; increase
   d. the same as; increase
   e. the same as; not change

Complete the graph

■ FIGURE 8.1

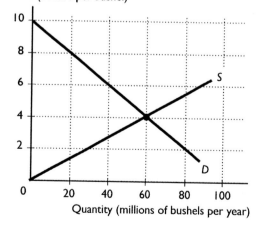

1. Figure 8.1 shows the U.S. demand and sup-

ply curves for wheat.

a. In the absence of international trade, what is the price of a bushel of wheat in the United States?

b. If the world price of a bushel of wheat is $6 a bushel, will the United States import or export wheat? Above what world price for wheat will the United States export wheat? Below what world price for wheat will the United States import wheat?

Short answer and numeric questions

1. French cheese is flown to the United States abroad a United Airlines plane. Classify these transactions from the vantage point of the United States and from the vantage point of France.

Price (dollars per ton)	Quantity supplied (tons per year)	Quantity demanded (tons per year)
400	38	58
500	42	52
600	46	46
700	50	40
800	54	34
900	58	28

2. The table above has the U.S. demand and supply schedules for potatoes.

a. If there is no international trade, what is the equilibrium price and quantity of potatoes?

b. If the world price of potatoes is $800 a ton, what is the quantity supplied and the quantity demanded in the United States? Does the United States import or export potatoes? What quantity?

c. If the world price of potatoes rises to $900 a ton, what are the quantity supplied and the quantity demanded in the United States? Does the United States import or export potatoes? What quantity?

d. Would the United States ever import potatoes?

3. How does international trade affect the domestic production and domestic consumption of goods imported into the country?

CHECKPOINT 8.2

■ **Identify the gains from international trade and its winners and losers.**

Quick Review

* *Consumer surplus* Consumer surplus is the marginal benefit from a good or service minus the price paid for it, summed over the quantity consumed.

* *Producer surplus* The producer surplus of a good equals the price of a good minus the marginal cost of producing it.

Additional Practice Problem 8.2

1. The figure shows the market for CPU chips in the United States with no international trade. The world price for a CPU chip is $150.

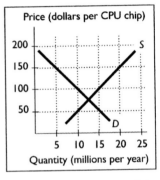

a. Does the United States import or export CPU chips and how many chips are imported or exported?

b. In the United States, tell who gains and who loses from the international trade and explain why they gain or lose. In the figure show the gains, the losses, and the net gain or net loss.

Solution to Additional Practice Problem 8.2

1a. The United States exports 15 million CPU chips per year.

1b. In the United States, producers of CPU chips gains and consumers of CPU chips lose. The gains and loses are in the fig-

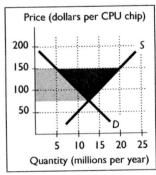

ure. Producers gain producer surplus and consumers lose consumer surplus. Producers gain because the price of a CPU chip with international trade is higher than the price without international trade, which is why the producer surplus increases. The increase in producer surplus is equal to the sum of the area of the dark grey triangle and the light grey trapezoid. Consumers lose for precisely the same reason producers gain: The price of a CPU chip is higher with international trade than without international trade which is why the consumer surplus decreases. The decrease in consumer surplus is equal to the area of the light grey trapezoid. On net, the economy gains from international trade. The increase in producer surplus is larger than the decrease in consumer surplus, as shown in the figure by the area of the dark grey triangle.

■ Self Test 8.2

Fill in the blanks

Imports ____ (decrease; increase) the producer surplus of domestic producers of the product and also ____ (decrease; increase) the consumer surplus of domestic consumers of the product. The consumer surplus from a good that would be exported is larger ____ (with; without) international trade and the consumer surplus from a good that would be imported is larger ____ (with; without) international trade. On net, society ____ (gains; loses) from international trade because the total surplus ____ (increases; decreases) with international trade.

True or false

1. International trade harms the nation.
2. Imports increase consumer surplus and decrease producer surplus.
3. The nation's total surplus increases when goods are exported.
4. Everyone in a nation gains from exports.

Multiple choice

1. International trade is definitely in the social interest if
   a. consumer surplus increases.
   b. producer surplus increases.
   c. consumer surplus does not decrease.
   d. producer surplus does not decrease.
   e. total surplus increases.

2. Imports ____ consumer surplus, ____ producer surplus, and ____ total surplus
   a. decrease; decrease; decrease
   b. increase; increase; increase
   c. increase; decrease; decrease
   d. increase; decrease; increase
   e. decrease; increase; increase

3. When a country imports a good, the ____ in consumer surplus is ____ the ____ in producer surplus.
   a. decrease; larger than; increase
   b. decrease; smaller than; increase
   c. increase; smaller than; decrease
   d. increase; equal to; decrease
   e. increase; larger than; decrease

4. When a country exports a good, the country's producer surplus ____, consumer surplus ____, and the country ____ from the trade.
   a. increases; increases; gains
   b. decreases; increases; gains
   c. increases; decreases; gains
   d. decreases; decreases; loses
   e. increases; decreases; loses

5. Which of the following is correct?
   i.   The U.S. total surplus decreases when the United States exports a good.
   ii. The U.S. total surplus decreases when the United States imports a good.
   iii. The U.S. total surplus increases when the United States imports a good and when it exports a good.
   a. i only.
   b. iii only.
   c. i and ii.
   d. ii only.
   e. None of the above because the U.S. total surplus does not change as a result of trade.

Complete the graph

■ **FIGURE 8.2**

Price (cents per pound)

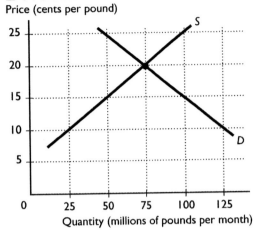

Quantity (millions of pounds per month)

1. Figure 8.2 shows the supply of and demand for sugar in the United States.

   a. If the world price of sugar is 10¢ a pound, draw the world price line in the figure. What is the quantity consumed in the United States, the quantity produced in the United States, and the quantity imported?

   b. Show the changes in consumer surplus, producer surplus, and total surplus once the United States imports sugar.

■ **FIGURE 8.3**

Price (dollars per bushel)

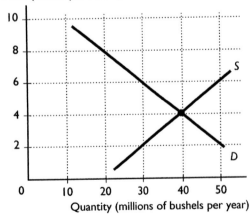

Quantity (millions of bushels per year)

1. Figure 8.3 shows the supply of and demand for wheat in the United States.

   a. If the world price of wheat is $6 a bushel,

draw the world price line in the figure. What is the quantity consumed in the United States, the quantity produced in the United States, and the quantity exported?

   b. Show the changes in consumer surplus, producer surplus, and total surplus once the United States exports wheat.

Short answer and numeric questions

1. How are the gains from international trade measured?

2. Why do consumers gain from imports?

3. Suppose the U.S. price of sugar without any international trade is 30¢ a pound. If the United States then allows international trade, when would the U.S. gain be the largest: when the international price is 20¢ a pound or when the international price is 10¢ a pound? Explain your answer.

4. Why doesn't everyone in a nation gain from exporting a good?

CHECKPOINT 8.3

■ **Explain the effects of international trade barriers.**

Quick Review

- *Tariff* A tariff is a tax on a good that is imposed by the importing country when an imported good crosses its international boundary.

- *Quota* A quota is a quantitative restriction on the import of a good that limits the maximum quantity of a good that may be imported in a given period.

Additional Practice Problems 8.3

Price (dollars per ton of plywood)	U.S. quantity supplied (tons per month)	U.S. quantity demanded (tons per month)
1,000	600	1,400
750	500	1,600
500	300	1,800
250	100	2,000

1. The table above shows the U.S. supply and

demand schedules for plywood. The United States also can buy plywood from Canada at the world price of $500 per ton.

  a. If there are no tariffs or other barriers to trade, what is the price of a ton of plywood in the United States? How much plywood is produced in the United States and how much is consumed? How much plywood is imported from Canada?

  b. Suppose that the United States imposes a $250 per ton tariff on all plywood imported into the country. What now is the price of a ton of plywood in the United States? How much plywood is produced in the United States and how much is consumed? How much plywood is imported from Canada?

  c. Who has gained from the tariff and who has lost?

2. For many years Japan conducted extremely slow, detailed, and costly safety inspections of *all* U.S. cars imported into Japan. In terms of trade, what was the effect of this inspection? How did the inspection affect the price and quantity of cars in Japan?

Solutions to Additional Practice Problems 8.3

1a. With no tariffs or nontariff barriers, the price of a ton of plywood is equal to the world price, $500 per ton. At this price, 300 tons per month are produced in the United States and 1,800 tons per month are consumed. The difference between the quantity consumed and the quantity produced, which is 1,500 tons per month, is imported from Canada.

1b. If a $250 per ton tariff is imposed, the price in the United States rises to $750 per ton. At this price, 500 tons per month are produced in the United States and 1,600 tons per month are consumed. The difference between the quantity consumed and the quantity produced, which is 1,100 tons per month, is imported from Canada.

1c. Gainers from the tariff are U.S. producers of plywood, who have a higher price for plywood and therefore increase their produc-

tion, and the U.S. government, which gains tariff revenue. Losers are U.S. consumers, who consume less plywood with the tariff, and Canadian producers of plywood, who wind up exporting less plywood to the United States.

2. Japan's safety inspection (which has since been eliminated) was an example of a barrier to trade. It served a role similar to tariffs, quotas, and VERs. The safety inspection added to the cost of selling cars in Japan. It raised the price of U.S. produced cars in Japan and decreased the quantity of U.S. cars sold. The Japanese government, however, received no tariff revenue.

■ Self Test 8.3

Fill in the blanks

A tax on a good that is imposed by the importing country when an imported good crosses its international boundary is a ____ (quota; tariff) and a specified maximum amount of a good that may be imported in a given period of time is a ____ (quota; tariff). A tariff ____ (raises; lowers) the price paid by domestic consumers, ____ (increases; decreases) the quantity produced by domestic producers, and ____ (creates; does not create) a deadweight loss. A quota ____ (raises; lowers) the price paid by domestic consumers and ____ (increases; decreases) the quantity produced by domestic producers.

True or false

1. If the United States imposes a tariff, the price paid by U.S. consumers does not change.

2. If a country imposes a tariff on rice imports, domestic production of rice will increase and domestic consumption of rice will decrease.

3. A tariff increases the gains from trade for the exporting country.

4. A quota on imports of a particular good specifies the minimum quantity of that good that can be imported in a given period.

Multiple choice

1. A tax on a good that is imposed by the importing country when an imported good crosses its international boundary is a
   a. quota.
   b. VER.
   c. tariff.
   d. sanction.
   e. border tax.

2. The average U.S. tariff was highest in the
   a. 1930s.
   b. 1940s.
   c. 1970s.
   d. 1980s.
   e. 1990s.

3. Suppose the world price of a shirt is $10. If the United States imposes a tariff of $5 a shirt, then the price of a shirt in the
   a. United States falls to $5.
   b. United States rises to $15.
   c. world falls to $5.
   d. world rises to $5.
   e. world rises to $15.

4. When a tariff is imposed on a good, the _____ increases.
   a. domestic quantity purchased
   b. domestic quantity produced
   c. quantity imported
   d. quantity exported
   e. world price

5. When a tariff is imposed on a good, domestic consumers of the good _____ and domestic producers of the good _____.
   a. win; lose
   b. lose; win
   c. win; win
   d. lose; lose
   e. lose; neither win nor lose

6. Which of the following parties benefits from a quota but not from a tariff?
   a. the domestic government
   b. domestic producers
   c. domestic consumers
   d. the person with the right to import the good
   e. the foreign government

Complete the graph

■ **FIGURE 8.4**

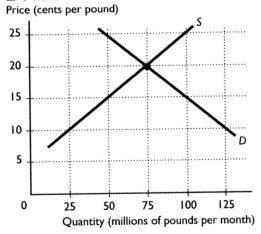
Price (cents per pound)

1. Figure 8.4 shows the supply of and demand for sugar in the United States.
   a. If the world price of sugar is 10¢ a pound, draw the world price line in the figure. What is the quantity consumed in the United States, the quantity produced in the United States, and the quantity imported?
   b. Suppose the government imposes a 5¢ a pound tariff on sugar. Show the effect of the tariff in Figure 8.4. After the tariff, what is the quantity consumed in the United States, the quantity produced in the United States, and the quantity imported?
   c. Who wins and who loses from this tariff?

Short answer and numeric questions

Price (dollars per ton of steel)	U.S. quantity supplied (tons per month)	U.S. quantity demanded (tons per month)
1,000	20,000	20,000
750	17,000	22,000
500	14,000	24,000
250	11,000	26,000

1. The table above gives the U.S. supply and the U.S. demand schedules for steel. Suppose the world price of steel is $500 per ton.
   a. If there are no barriers to trade, what is the price of steel in the United States, the quantity of steel consumed in the United

States, the quantity produced in the United States, and the quantity imported into the United States?

b. If the U.S. government imposes a tariff of $250 per ton of steel, what is the price of steel in the United States, the quantity of steel consumed in the United States, the quantity produced in the United States, and the quantity imported into the United States?

c. Instead of a tariff, if the U.S. government imposes a quota of 5,000 tons of steel per month, what is the price of steel in the United States, the quantity of steel consumed in the United States, the quantity produced in the United States, and the quantity imported into the United States?

d. Comparing your answers to parts (b) and (c), are U.S. consumers better off with the tariff or the quota? Are U.S. producers better off with the tariff or the quota?

2. Suppose the U.S. government imposes a tariff on sugar. How does the tariff affect the price of sugar? How does it affect U.S. sugar consumers? U.S. sugar producers?

3. Suppose the U.S. government imposes a quota on sugar. How does the quota affect the price of sugar? How does it affect U.S. sugar consumers? U.S. sugar producers?

4. Why do consumers lose from a tariff?

CHECKPOINT 8.4

■ **Explain and evaluate arguments used to justify restricting international trade.**

Quick Review

- *Rent seeking* Lobbying and other political activity that seeks to capture the gains from trade.

Additional Practice Problems 8.4

1. Canada has limits on the amount of U.S. television shows that can be broadcast in Canada. What are Canada's arguments for restricting imports of U.S. television shows? Are these arguments correct? Who loses from this restriction of trade?

2. The United States has, from time to time, limited imports of lumber from Canada. What is the argument that the United States has used to justify this quota? Who wins from this restriction? Who loses?

3. In each of the first two additional Practice Problems, identify who is rent seeking.

Solutions to Additional Practice Problems 8.4

1. Canada has used a number of arguments, but they are all incorrect. Canada has argued that Canadian television shows are of a higher quality than U.S. shows, but if Canadian consumers can detect a quality difference, they can watch Canadian shows rather than U.S. shows. Canada also has argued that these limitations are necessary to save Canadian culture, but if Canadian consumers want to protect this part of their heritage, they can watch exclusively Canadian shows rather than U.S. shows. The major losers from the Canadian limitations are Canadian consumers who can watch only a limited number of popular U.S. television shows.

2. In past decades, the United States asserted that the lumber industry was needed because it played a major role in national defense. With the use of more exotic materials in defense armaments, the national defense argument has passed into history. More recently, the United States has set quotas and tariffs allegedly for environmental reasons and allegedly because the Canadian government was subsidizing the production of lumber. Both of these arguments are likely not the true reason for the quotas. The quotas and limitations are the result of political lobbying by lumber producers and lumber workers. The winners from the quotas and tariffs are the lumber producers and lumber workers. The losers are all U.S. lumber consumers.

3. Rent seeking is lobbying and other political activity that seeks to capture the gains from trade. In Practice Problem 1, the Canadian pro-

ducers of television shows are rent seeking. In Practice Problem 2, the U.S. lumber producers and U.S. lumber workers are rent seeking. It is important to keep in mind that free trade promotes prosperity for all countries. Protection reduces the potential gains from trade

■ Self Test 8.4

Fill in the blanks

The assertion that it is necessary to protect a new industry to enable it to grow into a mature industry that can compete in world markets is the ____ (infant-industry; maturing-industry) argument. Dumping occurs when ____ (U.S. jobs are lost to cheap foreign labor; a foreign firm sells its exports at a lower price than its cost of production). Protection ____ (is; is not) necessary to bring diversity and stability to our economy. Protection ____ (is; is not) necessary to penalize countries with lax environmental standards. The major reason why international trade is restricted is because ____ (foreign countries protect their industries; of rent seeking).

True or false

1. The national security argument is the only valid argument for protection.
2. Dumping by a foreign producer is easy to detect.
3. Protection saves U.S. jobs at no cost.
4. International trade is an attractive source for tax collection in developing countries

Multiple choice

1. The national security argument is used by those who assert they want to
   a. increase imports as a way of strengthening their country.
   b. increase exports as a way of earning money to strengthen their country.
   c. limit imports that compete with domestic producers important for national defense.
   d. limit exports to control the flow of technology to third world nations.
   e. limit all imports.

2. The argument that it is necessary to protect a new industry to enable it to grow into a ma-

ture industry that can compete in world markets is the
   a. national security argument.
   b. diversity argument.
   c. infant-industry argument.
   d. environmental protection argument.
   e. national youth protection argument.

3. ____ occurs when a foreign firm sells its exports at a lower price than its cost of production.
   a. Dumping
   b. The trickle-down effect
   c. Rent seeking
   d. Tariff avoidance
   e. Nontariff barrier protection

4. The United States
   a. needs tariffs to allow us to compete with cheap foreign labor.
   b. does not need tariffs to allow us to compete with cheap foreign labor.
   d. should not trade with countries that have cheap labor.
   d. will not benefit from trade with countries that have cheap labor.
   e. avoids trading with countries that have cheap labor.

5. Why do governments in less-developed nations impose tariffs?
   a. The government gains revenue from the tariff.
   b. The government's low-paid workers are protected from high-paid foreign workers.
   c. The nation's total income is increased.
   d. The national security of the country definitely is improved.
   e. The government protects its national culture.

6. What is a major reason international trade is restricted in developed countries?
   a. rent seeking
   b. to allow competition with cheap foreign labor
   c. to save jobs
   d. to prevent dumping
   e. to protect national culture

Short answer and numeric questions

1. What is the dumping argument for protection? What is its flaw?

2. How do you respond to a speaker who says that we need to limit auto imports from Japan in order to save U.S. jobs?

3. Why is it incorrect to assert that trade with countries that have lax environmental standards needs to be restricted?

4. The Eye on Your Life discusses the role international trade plays in your life. Suppose you get a job working for Frito Lay, the maker of corn chips (and other snacks). Frito Lay is a big user of corn. Corn can also be used to produce ethanol and increasingly more ethanol is being used as a replacement (or additive) fuel for gasoline. Currently the U.S. government places a hefty tariff on ethanol imported from Brazil. As a representative of Frito Lay, would you be in favor of this tariff? Explain your answer.

◼ SELF TEST ANSWERS

◼ CHECKPOINT 8.1

Fill in the blanks

Global international trade accounts for a bit more than 1/4 of global production. If a country can produce a good at a lower opportunity cost than any other country, the country has a comparative advantage in the production of that good. The United States will export a good if its price in the United States with no international trade is lower than its world price. If the United States imports a good, then U.S. production of the good decreases and U.S. consumption of the good increases.

True or false

1. True; page 196
2. True; page 196
3. False; pages 198-199
4. True; page 198

Multiple choice

1. b; page 196
2. b; page 196
3. c; page 196
4. c; page 198
5. c; page 198
6. b; page 199

Complete the graph

1. a. In the absence of international trade, the equilibrium price of a bushel of wheat in the United States is $4; pages 198-199.
   b. If the world price of a bushel of wheat is $6 a bushel, the United States will export wheat because the world price exceeds the no-trade price. If the price of wheat exceeds $4 a bushel, the United States will export wheat. If the price of wheat is less than $4 a bushel, the United States will import wheat; pages 198-199.

Short answer and numeric questions

1. From the U.S. vantage, the cheese is an imported good and the air transportation is an exported service. From the French vantage, the cheese is an exported good and the air transportation is an imported service; page 196.

2. a. In the absence of international trade, the equilibrium price is $600 a ton and the equilibrium quantity is 46 tons; pages 198-199.
   b. In the United States, the quantity supplied is 54 tons and the quantity demanded is 34 tons. The United States exports 20 tons of potatoes; pages 199.
   c. In the United States, the quantity supplied is 58 tons and the quantity demanded is 28 tons. The United States exports 30 tons of potatoes; pages 199.
   d. The United States would import potatoes if the world price is less than $600 a ton; pages 198.

3. International trade lowers the domestic price of imported goods. The lower price increases the quantity domestic demanders consume and decreases the quantity domestic suppliers produce; page 198.

◼ CHECKPOINT 8.2

Fill in the blanks

Imports decrease the producer surplus of domestic producers of the product and also increase the consumer surplus of domestic consumers of the product. The consumer surplus from a good that would be exported is larger without international trade and the consumer surplus from a good that would be imported is larger with international trade. On net, society gains from international trade because the total surplus increases with international trade.

True or false

1. False; pages 202-203
2. True; page 202
3. True; page 203
4. False; page 203

Multiple choice

1. e; page 201

2. d; page 202

3. e; page 202

4. c; page 203

5. b; pages 202-203

Complete the graph

■ FIGURE 8.5

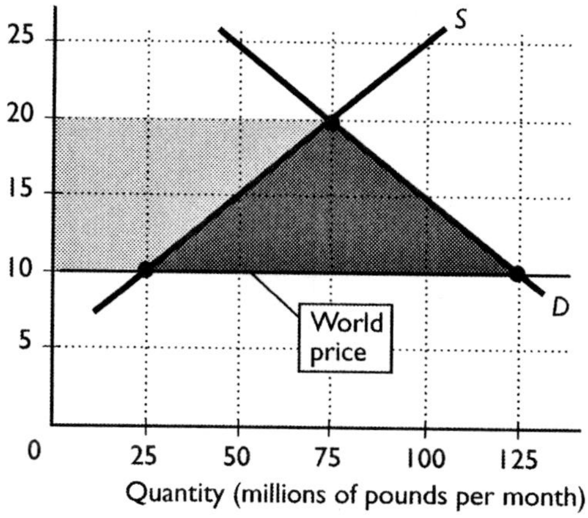

Price (cents per pound)

■ FIGURE 8.6

Price (dollars per bushel)

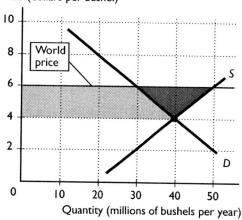

1. a. Figure 8.5 shows the world price line. At this price, 125 million pounds of sugar per month are consumed in the United States and 25 million pounds of sugar are produced in the United States. The difference, 100 million pounds of sugar per month, is imported into the United States; page 202.

   b. Consumer surplus increases. The increase in consumer surplus is equal to the sum of the area of the lighter grey trapezoid plus the area of the dark grey triangle in Figure 8.5. The producer surplus decreases. The decrease is equal to the area of the light grey trapezoid. On net, total surplus increases. The net increase is equal to the area of the dark grey triangle; page 202.

2. a. Figure 8.6 shows the world price line. At this price, 30 million bushels of wheat per year are consumed in the United States and 50 million bushels of wheat are produced in the United States. The difference, 20 million bushels of wheat per year, is exported from the United States; page 203.

   b. Consumer surplus decreases. The decrease in consumer surplus is equal to the area of the lighter grey trapezoid in Figure 8.6. The producer surplus increases. The increase is equal to the sum of the area of the light grey trapezoid plus the area of the dark grey triangle. On net, total surplus increases. The increase is equal to the area of the dark grey triangle; page 203.

Short answer and numeric questions

1. The gains from international trade are measured as increases in consumer surplus or in producer surplus. The net gain from international trade is measured as the gain in the total surplus; page 201.

2. Consumers gain from imports because international trade lowers the prices of imported goods and services. Consumer surplus increases because the price is lower and because The lower price leads consumers to buy more of the good or service; page 202.

3. Consumers are the group in the economy that gain from imports. They gain because international trade lowers the prices of imported goods and services, which then increases their consumer surplus. The increase in consumer surplus will be larger the lower the price. So the United States gains more if the international price of sugar is 10¢ a pound rather than 20¢ a pound; page 202.

4. When a good is exported, its domestic price rises. Producers gain from the higher price but consumers lose. (The gain to the producers, however, is larger than the loss to consumers.) So not everyone gains when a good is exported because consumers of that good lose; page 203.

■ CHECKPOINT 8.3

Fill in the blanks

A tax on a good that is imposed by the importing country when an imported good enters its boundary is called a <u>tariff</u> and a specified maximum amount of a good that may be imported is called a <u>quota</u>. A tariff <u>raises</u> the price paid by domestic consumers, <u>increases</u> the quantity produced by domestic producers, and <u>creates</u> a deadweight loss. A quota <u>raises</u> the price paid by domestic consumers and <u>increases</u> the quantity produced by domestic producers.

True or false

1. False; pages 206
2. True; pages 206
3. False; pages 208
4. False; page 209

Multiple choice

1. c; page 205
2. a; page 205
3. b; page 206
4. b; page 206
5. b; pages 207-208
6. d; page 209

Complete the graph

1. a. The world price line is shown in Figure 8.7. 125 million pounds of sugar are consumed in the United States, 25 million pounds are produced in the United States, and 100 million pounds are imported into the United States; page 206.
   b. The tariff increases the domestic price, as shown in the figure. The quantity con-

■ FIGURE 8.7

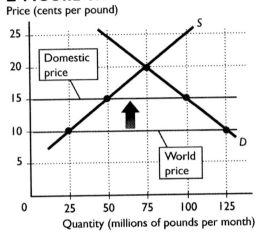

sumed in the United States decreases to 100 million pounds, the quantity produced in the United States increases to 50 million pounds, and the amount imported decreases to 50 million pounds; page 206.
   c. Consumers lose because consumer surplus decreases. Producers win because producer surplus increases. The government also wins because it raises revenue from the tariff; page 208.

Short answer and numeric questions

1. a. The price is the world price, $500 per ton. At this price, the quantity consumed in the United States is 24,000 tons per month, the quantity produced in the United States is 14,000 tons per month, and the quantity imported is the difference, 10,000 tons per month; page 206.
   b. With a $250 per ton tariff, the price is $750 per ton. At this price, the quantity consumed in the United States is 22,000 tons per month, the quantity produced in the United States is 17,000 tons per month, and the quantity imported is the difference, 5,000 tons per month; page 206.
   c. With a quota of 5,000 tons per month, the total supply schedule equals the U.S. supply schedule plus 5,000 tons per month. The price of steel is $750 per ton because this is the price that sets the U.S. quantity demanded (22,000 tons) equal to the U.S.

quantity supplied (17,000 tons) plus the quantity that can be imported (5,000 tons). At this price, the quantity consumed in the United States is 22,000 tons per month and the quantity produced in the United States is 17,000 tons per month; page 209.

d. U.S. consumers are no better off or worse off with the tariff or the quota because both raise the price to $750 per ton and decrease the quantity consumed to 22,000 tons. U.S. producers are no better off or worse off with the tariff or the quota because both raise the price to $750 per ton and increase the quantity produced to 17,000 tons; page 209.

2. The tariff raises the price of sugar. U.S. sugar consumers decrease the quantity they purchase and U.S. sugar producers increase the quantity they produce; pages 206-208.

3. The quota has the same effects as the tariff in the previous question. The quota raises the price of sugar. U.S. sugar consumers decrease the quantity purchased and U.S. sugar producers increase the quantity produced; page 209.

4. Consumers lose from a tariff because the tariff raises the price they pay and the quantity bought decreases. The tariff makes people pay more than the opportunity cost of the good. Society also loses because the tariff creates a deadweight loss; page 208.

■ CHECKPOINT 8.4

Fill in the blanks

The assertion that it is necessary to protect a new industry to enable it to grow into a mature industry that can compete in world markets is the infant-industry argument. Dumping occurs when a foreign firm sells its exports at a lower price than its cost of production. Protection is not necessary to bring diversity and stability to our economy. Protection is not necessary to penalize countries with lax environmental standards. The major reason why international trade is restricted is because of rent seeking.

True or false

1. False; page 213
2. False; page 214
3. False; page 215
4. True; page 216

Multiple choice

1. c; page 213
2. c; page 213
3. a; page 214
4. b; page 215
5. a; page 216
6. a; page 217

Short answer and numeric questions

1. Dumping occurs when a foreign firm sells its exports at a lower price than its cost of production. The dumping argument is flawed for the following reasons. First, it is virtually impossible to detect dumping because it is hard to determine a firm's costs and the fair market price. Second, it is hard to think of a good that is produced by a global natural monopoly. Third, if a firm truly was a global natural monopoly, the best way to deal with it would be by regulation; page 214.

2. Saving jobs is one of the oldest arguments in favor of protection. It is also incorrect. Protecting a particular industry will likely save jobs in that industry but will cost many other jobs in other industries. The cost to consumers of saving a job is many times the wage rate of the job saved; page 215.

3. The assertion that trade with developing countries that have lax environmental standards should be restricted to "punish" the nation for its lower standards is weak. Everyone wants a clean environment, but not every country can afford to devote resources toward this goal. The rich nations can afford this expenditure of resources, but for many poor nations protecting the environment takes second place to more pressing problems such as feeding their people. These nations must develop and grow economically in order to be able to afford to protect their

environment. One important way to help these nations grow is by trading with them. Through trade these nations' incomes will increase and with this increase will also increase their ability and willingness to protect the environment; page 216.

4. The tariff on ethanol imported from Brazil severely limits the quantity of ethanol that can be imported and so serves to keep the price of ethanol high in the United States. The high price for ethanol increases the demand for U.S. corn to be processed into ethanol. As a result, the tariff on ethanol keeps the price of corn in the United States higher than it would be in the absence of the tariff. As a representative of Frito Lay, your interest lies in lowering the price of corn. So you would be in favor of lowering or eliminating entirely this tariff; page 206.

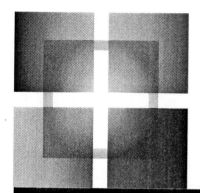

Externalities

Chapter

9

An externality in an unregulated market leads to inefficiency and creates a deadweight loss. Chapter 9 explains the role of the government in markets where an externality is present and how government intervention can result in an efficient level of production.

1 **Explain why negative externalities lead to inefficient overproduction and how property rights, pollution charges, and taxes can achieve a more efficient outcome.**

Marginal private cost is the cost of producing an additional unit of a good or service that is borne by the producer of that good or service. Marginal external cost is the cost of producing an additional unit of a good or service that falls on people other than the producer. And marginal social cost, which is the marginal cost incurred by the entire society, is the sum of marginal private cost and marginal external cost. Producers take account only of marginal private cost and overproduce when there is a marginal external cost. Sometimes it is possible to reduce the inefficiency arising from an externality by establishing a property right where one does not currently exist. The Coase theorem is the proposition that if property rights exist, only a small number of parties are involved, and transactions costs are low, then private transactions are efficient and the outcome is not affected by who is assigned the property right. When property rights cannot be assigned, the three main methods that governments can use to cope with externalities are emission charges (which set a price per unit of pollution that a firm must pay), marketable permits (each firm is issued permits that allow a certain amount of pollution and firms can buy and sell the permits), and taxes (the government imposes a tax equal to the marginal external cost).

2 **Explain why positive externalities lead to inefficient underproduction and how public provision, subsidies, vouchers, and patents can achieve a more efficient outcome.**

Marginal private benefit is the benefit from an additional unit of a good or service that the consumer of that good or service receives. Marginal external benefit is the benefit from an additional unit of a good or service that people other than the consumer of the good or service enjoy. And marginal social benefit, which is the marginal benefit enjoyed by society, is the sum of marginal private benefit and marginal external benefit. External benefits from education arise because better-educated people are better citizens, commit fewer crimes, and support social activities. External benefits from research arise because once someone has worked out a basic idea, others can copy it. When people make decisions about how much schooling to obtain, they neglect its external benefit. The result is that if education were provided only by private schools that charged full-cost tuition, we would produce too few graduates. Four devices that governments can use to overcome the inefficiency created by external benefits are public provision, private subsidies, vouchers, and patents and copyrights.

CHECKPOINT 9.1

■ **Explain why negative externalities lead to inefficient overproduction and how property rights, pollution charges, and taxes can achieve a more efficient outcome.**

Quick Review

- *Marginal external cost* The cost of producing an additional unit of a good or service that falls on people other than the producer.
- *Efficiency* Efficiency is achieved when the marginal social benefit equals the marginal social cost.
- *Coase theorem* If property rights exist, only a small number of parties are involved, and transactions costs are low, then private transactions are efficient and the outcome is not affected by who is assigned the property right.

Additional Practice Problems 9.1

1. The figure illustrates the unregulated market for paper. When the factories produce paper, they also create air pollution. The cost of the pollution is $1,500 per ton. The pollution is a marginal external cost.

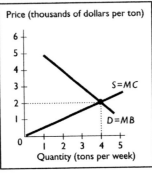

   a. What is the quantity of paper produced in an unregulated market? What is the price of a ton of paper?
   b. Draw the marginal social cost curve in the figure. What is the efficient quantity of paper to produce?
   c. If the government imposed a tax on the firms, what must the tax equal to have the efficient quantity of paper produced? With this tax imposed, what is the equilibrium price of a ton of paper?

2. Two factories each emit 10 tons of the pollutant sulfur dioxide a week. The cost to eliminate a ton of sulfur dioxide to Factory A is $4 and the cost to Factory B is $2. The government wants to eliminate 10 tons of sulfur dioxide a week.
   a. If the government requires that Firm A decrease emissions by 10 tons a week, what is the cost of eliminating the pollution?
   b. If the government requires that Firm B decrease emissions by 10 tons a week, what is the cost of the eliminating the pollution?
   c. If the government gives each firm 5 marketable permits, each good for 1 ton of pollution, what will occur?

Solutions to Additional Practice Problems 9.1

1a. The equilibrium is determined by the intersection of the demand and supply curves. So the equilibrium quantity is 4 tons of paper per week and the equilibrium price is $2,000 per ton.

1b. The figure shows the marginal social cost curve, labeled *MSC*. At 1 ton of paper this curve lies $1,500 above the supply curve; at 2 tons of paper it lies $3,000 above the supply curve;

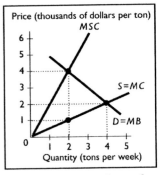

   and so on. The efficient quantity is where the marginal social cost equals the marginal benefit, which the figure shows is 2 tons of paper.

1c. To lead to efficiency, the tax must equal the marginal external cost. So the tax should be $1,500 per ton. At the efficient quantity of 2 tons, the tax is $3,000. With this tax, the equilibrium price is $4,000 per ton of paper.

2a. The cost for Firm A to decrease emissions is $4 a ton multiplied by 10 tons, which is $40 a week.

2b. The cost for Firm B to decrease emissions is $2 a ton multiplied by 10 tons, which is $20 a week.

2c. Firm A is willing to buy permits from Firm B for any price less than $4 per permit; Firm B is willing to sell permits to Firm A for any price greater than $2 per permit. The two companies will settle on a price and Firm A will buy 5 permits from Firm B. Only Firm B will decrease its pollution and incur a cost of $20 a week.

■ Self Test 9.1

Fill in the blanks

Marginal social cost equals marginal private cost _____ (minus; plus) marginal external cost. A pollution externality creates an _____ (efficient; inefficient) equilibrium. According to the Coase theorem, if property rights exist, then private transactions are efficient and the outcome _____ (is; is not) affected by who is assigned the property right. By setting the tax rate equal to the marginal _____ (external; private; social) cost, firms can be made to behave in the same way as they would if they bore the cost of the externality directly.

True or false

1. All externalities are negative.

2. Smoking on a plane creates a negative externality.

3. Marginal social cost equals marginal private cost minus marginal external cost.

4. Copper mining creates land pollution. If the copper mining industry is unregulated, then the quantity of copper mined is less than the efficient quantity.

5. The Coase theorem concludes that if property rights to a polluted river are assigned to the polluter, the quantity of pollution will increase.

6. Emission charges allow the government to set the price for a unit of pollution.

7. By issuing marketable permits, the government sets the price for each unit of pollution produced.

8. If the government imposes a pollution tax on lead mining equal to its marginal external cost, the quantity of lead mined will be the efficient quantity.

Multiple choice

1. Which of the following best describes an externality?
   a. something that is external to the economy
   b. a sales tax on a good in addition to the market price
   c. an effect of a transaction felt by someone other than the consumer or producer
   d. anything produced in other countries
   e. a change from what is normal

2. Pollution is an example of a _____ externality.
   a. negative production
   b. positive production
   c. negative consumption
   d. positive consumption
   e. Coasian

3. The cost of producing one more unit of a good or service that is borne by the producer of that good or service
   a. always equals the benefit the consumer derives from that good or service.
   b. equals the cost borne by people other than the producer.
   c. is the marginal private cost.
   d. is the external cost.
   e. is the marginal social cost.

4. The cost of producing an additional unit of a good or service that falls on people other than the producer is
   a. the marginal cost.
   b. represented by the demand curve.
   c. represented by the supply curve.
   d. the marginal external cost.
   e. the marginal social cost.

5. Which of the following is an example of something that creates an external cost?
   i. second-hand smoke
   ii. sulfur emitting from a smoke stack
   iii. garbage on the roadside
   a. i only.
   b. ii only.
   c. iii only.
   d. ii and iii.
   e. i, ii, and iii.

6. The marginal cost of production that is borne by the entire society is the marginal
   a. private cost.
   b. social cost.
   c. external cost.
   d. public cost.
   e. user cost.

7. If the marginal private cost of producing one kilowatt of power in California is five cents and the marginal social cost of each kilowatt is nine cents, then the marginal external cost equals _____ a kilowatt.
   a. five cents
   b. nine cents
   c. four cents
   d. zero cents
   e. fourteen cents

8. When the production of a good has a marginal external cost, which of the following will occur in an unregulated market?
   i. Overproduction relative to the efficient level will occur
   ii. The market price will be less than the marginal social cost at the equilibrium quantity
   iii. A deadweight loss will occur
   a. i only.
   b. ii only.
   c. iii only.
   d. i and ii.
   e. i, ii, and iii.

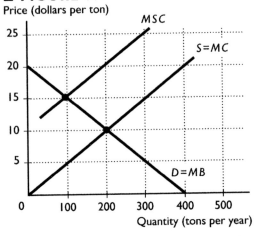

■ FIGURE 9.1

Price (dollars per ton)

9. Figure 9.1 shows the market for a good with an external cost. The external cost equals _____ per ton.
   a. $5
   b. $10
   c. $15
   d. $20
   e. $25

10. Figure 9.1 shows the market for a good with an external cost. If the market is unregulated, the equilibrium quantity is _____ tons per year.
    a. 0
    b. 100
    c. 200
    d. 300
    e. 400

11. Figure 9.1 shows the market for a good with an external cost. The efficient quantity is _____ tons per year.
    a. 0
    b. 100
    c. 200
    d. 300
    e. 400

12. The Coase theorem is the proposition that if property rights exist and are enforced, private transactions are
    a. inefficient.
    b. efficient.
    c. inequitable.
    d. illegal.
    e. unnecessary.

13. A marketable permit
    a. allows firms to pollute all they want without any cost.
    b. allows firms to buy and sell the right to pollute at government controlled prices.
    c. eliminates pollution by setting the price of pollution permits above the marginal cost of polluting.
    d. allows firms to buy and sell the right to pollute.
    e. is the Coase solution to pollution.

14. If we compare air pollution today to air pollution in 1980, we see that
    a. pollution of all forms has increased.
    b. pollution of all forms has been substantially reduced.
    c. pollution of most types has been decreased.
    d. pollution from lead has increased.
    e. pollution of most types has not changed.

15. If a polluting producer is forced to pay an emission charge or a tax on its output, what is the effect on the supply and demand curves for the product?
    a. The quantity supplied along the firm's supply curve will increase.
    b. The firm's demand curve shifts leftward.
    c. The firm's supply curve shifts rightward.
    d. The firm's supply curve shifts leftward.
    e. *Both* the supply curve and the demand curve shift leftward.

Complete the graph

Quantity (megawatts per day)	Marginal private cost (dollars)	Marginal social cost (dollars)	Marginal benefit (dollars)
1	5	10	50
2	10	20	40
3	15	30	30
4	20	40	20

1. The table above shows the marginal private cost, marginal social cost, and marginal benefit schedules for generating electricity.
   a. In Figure 9.2, label the axes and then plot the marginal private cost curve, the marginal social cost curve, and the marginal benefit curve.

■ **FIGURE 9.2**

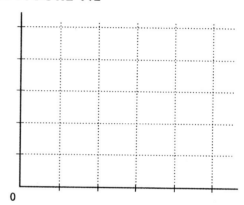

   b. How much electricity will an unregulated market produce? What is the marginal external cost at this amount of production?
   c. What is the efficient amount of electricity? Illustrate the deadweight loss resulting from the market equilibrium.
   d. At the efficient quantity of electricity, what is the marginal external cost? If the government imposes a tax on producing electricity to produce the efficient quantity, what should be the amount of tax? How much electricity is generated and what is its price?

Quantity (tons per day)	Marginal private cost (dollars)	Marginal benefit (dollars)
1	200	600
2	300	500
3	400	400
4	500	300

2. The table above shows the marginal private cost and marginal benefit schedules for producing PBDE, a chemical flame retardant. Suppose that there is an external cost of $100 per ton of PBDE produced.

a. In Figure 9.3, label the axes and then plot the marginal private cost curve, the marginal social cost curve, and the marginal benefit curve.

■ **FIGURE 9.3**

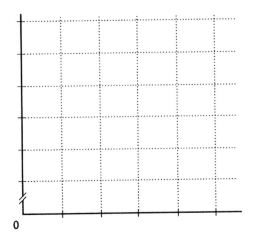

b. How much PBDE will an unregulated market produce? What is the equilibrium price? What is the amount of the marginal external cost at the equilibrium quantity of production?

c. What is the efficient amount of PBDE? At the efficient quantity, what is the amount of the marginal external cost?

d. If the government set an emission charge for producing PBDE, what must the charge equal to lead to the efficient quantity of PBDE?

Short answer and numeric questions

1. If the marginal social cost curve lies above the marginal private cost curve, is there an external cost or benefit from production of the good or service?

Quantity (tons of pesticide per day)	Marginal private cost (dollars per ton)	Marginal external cost (dollars per ton)	Marginal social cost (dollars per ton)
1	100	——	130
2	120	40	
3	——	60	210
4	190	——	280
5	240	120	——

2. The table above shows the costs of producing pesticide. Complete the table.

3. According to the Coase theorem, when are private transactions efficient?

4. What is a marketable permit? What advantage do marketable permits have over the government assigning each firm a limit on how much it can pollute?

5. The production of fertilizer creates water pollution. How do emission charges and taxes result in an efficient quantity of production? What information must the government possess to use emission charges and taxes effectively?

CHECKPOINT 9.2

■ **Explain why positive externalities lead to inefficient underproduction and how public provision, subsidies, vouchers, and patents can achieve a more efficient outcome.**

Quick Review

- *Marginal external benefit* The benefit from an additional unit of a good or service that people other than the consumer of the good or service enjoy.

Additional Practice Problems 9.2

1. The figure shows the marginal private benefit, marginal social benefit, and marginal cost of a college education.

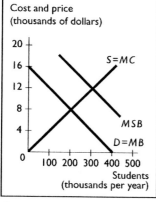

  a. How much does the marginal external benefit equal?

  b. If colleges are private and government has no involvement in college education, how many people will undertake a college education and what will be the tuition?

  c. What is the efficient number of students?

  d. If the government decides to provide public colleges, what tuition will these colleges charge to achieve the efficient number of students? What is the marginal cost of educating this many students? Why is it justified to charge a tuition that is less than the marginal cost?

2. A vaccine for chicken pox was recently developed. The company that developed the vaccine, Merck Incorporated, was required to submit a document comparing the costs and benefits of vaccinating children. The government would approve the drug only if the benefit of vaccination exceeded the cost. The producer reports that the marginal cost of a dose of vaccine is $80. The marginal benefit to the child being vaccinated is estimated to be $30 and an additional marginal benefit to the child's parents is estimated at $60.

  a. How much is the marginal private benefit and the marginal external benefit?

  b. Based on these data, should the government have approved the vaccine?

Solutions to Additional Practice Problems 9.2

1a. The marginal external benefit equals the vertical distance between the marginal social benefit curve, *MSB,* and the marginal private benefit curve, *MB*. In the figure the difference is $8,000, so the marginal external benefit equals $8,000.

1b. If the government has no involvement, the equilibrium tuition and number of students is determined by the equilibrium between supply and demand. The supply curve is the marginal

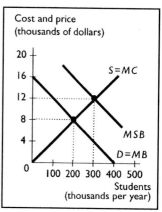

private cost curve, *S* = *MC*, and the demand curve is the marginal private benefit curve, *MB*. The figure shows that the equilibrium tuition equals $8,000 a year and the equilibrium enrollment is 200,000 students a year.

1c. The efficient number of students is 300,000 because this the quantity at which the marginal cost equals the marginal social benefit.

1d. The demand curve, which is the same as the marginal private benefit curve, shows that tuition must be $4,000 in order for 300,000 students to attend college. The marginal cost of educating 300,000 students is $12,000 students per year. It is justified to charge a tuition that is less than the marginal cost because education has external benefits so that society as well as the student benefits from the college education.

2a. The marginal private benefit is the benefit to the child being vaccinated and is $30. The marginal external benefit is the benefit to the child's parents and is $60.

2b. Based on the data that were submitted, the government should have approved the vaccine. The marginal social benefit equals the marginal private benefit to the child of $30 plus the marginal external benefit to the parent of $60, which is $90. The marginal social benefit from the vaccine is greater than the marginal cost.

■ Self Test 9.2

Fill in the blanks

Marginal _____ (social; external) benefit is the benefit enjoyed by society from one more unit of a good or service. If the government leaves education to the private market, _____ (overproduction; underproduction) occurs. A payment that the government makes to private producers that depends on the level of output is _____ (a subsidy; public provision). The property rights of the creators of knowledge and other discoveries are _____ (intellectual property; patent property) rights.

True or false

1. The marginal private benefit from a good or service must exceed the marginal external benefit.

2. The expanded job opportunities from a college degree is a marginal private benefit enjoyed by college graduates.

3. A flu vaccination has an external benefit, so the marginal private benefit curve for flu vaccinations lies above the marginal social benefit curve for flu vaccinations.

4. An unregulated market underproduces products with external benefits, such as education.

5. A public community college is an example of public provision of a good that has an external benefit.

6. To overcome the inefficiency in the market for a good with an external benefit, the government can either tax or subsidize the good.

7. Vouchers can help overcome the inefficiency created by a good with an external cost but not the inefficiency created by a good with an external benefit.

8. A patent protects intellectual property rights by giving the patent holder a monopoly.

Multiple choice

1. The benefit the consumer of a good or service receives is the
   a. social benefit.
   b. external benefit.
   c. private benefit.
   d. public benefit.
   e. consumption benefit.

2. An external benefit is a benefit from a good or service that someone other than the _____ receives.
   a. seller of the good or service
   b. government
   c. foreign sector
   d. consumer
   e. market maker

3. When Ronald takes another economics class, other people in society benefit. The benefit to these other people is called the marginal _____ benefit of the class.
   a. social
   b. private
   c. external
   d. opportunity
   e. extra

4. Marginal social benefit equals
   a. marginal external benefit.
   b. marginal private benefit.
   c. marginal private benefit minus marginal external benefit.
   d. marginal private benefit plus marginal external benefit
   e. marginal external benefit minus marginal private benefit.

5. If an external benefit is present, then the
   a. marginal private benefit curve lies above the marginal private cost curve.
   b. marginal social benefit curve lies above the marginal private benefit curve.
   c. marginal social cost curve lies above the marginal private benefit curve.
   d. marginal social benefit is equal to the marginal social cost.
   e. marginal social benefit curve is the same as the marginal private benefit curve.

6. In an unregulated market with an external benefit, the
   a. quantity produced is greater than the efficient quantity.
   b. price charged is too high for efficiency.
   c. quantity produced is less than the efficient quantity.
   d. producer is causing pollution but not paying for it.
   e. government might impose a tax to help move the market toward the efficient amount of production.

■ **FIGURE 9.4**

Price (hundreds of thousands of dollars per unit)

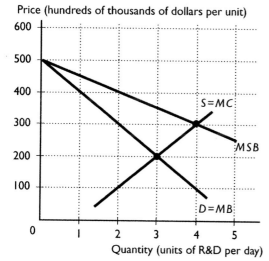

Quantity (units of R&D per day)

7. Figure 9.4 shows the market for research and development, which has ____.
   a. only external costs
   b. only external benefits
   c. both external costs and external benefits
   d. neither external costs nor external benefits
   e. might have external benefits or external costs, but more information is needed

8. Figure 9.4 shows the market for research and development. If the market is unregulated, the equilibrium quantity of R&D is ____ units per day.
   a. 0
   b. 2
   c. 3
   d. 4
   e. 5

9. Figure 9.4 shows the market for research and development. The efficient quantity of R&D is ____ units per day.
   a. 0
   b. 2
   c. 3
   d. 4
   e. 5

10. If all education in the United States were provided by private, tuition-charging schools,
    a. too much education would be consumed.
    b. too little education would be consumed.
    c. the efficient level of education would be provided.
    d. the government would provide *both* students and schools with vouchers.
    e. education would no longer have an external benefit.

11. Which of the following is a method used by government to cope with the situation in which production of a good creates an external benefit?
    a. removing property rights
    b. paying subsidies
    c. issuing marketable permits
    d. running a lottery
    e. imposing a Coasian tax

12. If tuition at a college is $30,000 and the external benefit of graduating from this college is $10,000, then
    i. in the absence of any government intervention, the number of students graduating is less than the efficient number
    ii. the government could increase the number of graduates by giving the college a $10,000 subsidy per student
    iii. the government could increase the number of graduates by giving the students $10,000 vouchers
    a. i only.
    b. i and ii.
    c. i and iii.
    d. ii and iii.
    e. i, ii, and iii.

13. Public universities are a service that is an example of
    a. patent protection.
    b. vouchers.
    c. private subsidies.
    d. public provision.
    e. an emission charge.

14. Which of the following is an example of a voucher?
    a. the postal service
    b. police services
    c. social security
    d. food stamps
    e. a patent on a pharmaceutical drug

15. Which government device is associated with intellectual property rights?
    a. public provision
    b. private subsidies
    c. vouchers
    d. patents and copyrights
    e. taxes

Complete the graph

■ **FIGURE 9.5**

Price (dollars per pound of honey)

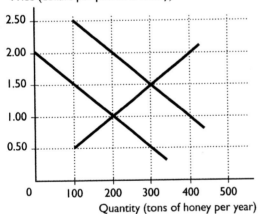

Quantity (tons of honey per year)

1. Figure 9.5 illustrates the market for honey.
   a. Label the curves in the figure.
   b. Based on Figure 9.5, does the production of honey create an external cost? An external benefit?

c. What is the efficient quantity of honey? What is the quantity that will be produced in an unregulated market?
d. Shade the area that equals the deadweight loss in an unregulated market.

Short answer and numeric questions

Quantity (units of R&D per day)	Marginal private cost (dollars per unit of R&D)	Marginal private benefit (dollars per unit of R&D)	Marginal social benefit (dollars per unit of R&D)
100	100	250	340
200	120	200	290
300	150	150	240
400	190	100	190
500	240	50	140

1. The table above shows the benefits and costs of research and development, R&D.
   a. Based on the table, what is the amount of the marginal external benefit?
   b. If the market for R&D was left unregulated, what would be the competitive amount of R&D?
   c. What is the efficient amount of R&D?
   d. Would a subsidy or a tax be the proper government policy to make the market for R&D more efficient?

2. Is efficiency guaranteed when production is such that the marginal private benefit equals the marginal private cost? Or does efficiency require that the marginal social benefit equal the marginal social cost?

3. Most elementary schools require that children be vaccinated before allowing the child to attend school. Can this policy be justified using economic analysis?

4. Is a private subsidy or a tax the correct government policy for a product that has an external benefit?

5. What is a voucher? How do vouchers work? Why is a voucher a proper policy to deal with the inefficiency created by a good or service that has an external benefit?

■ SELF TEST ANSWERS

■ CHECKPOINT 9.1

Fill in the blanks

Marginal social cost equals marginal private cost <u>plus</u> marginal external cost. A pollution externality creates an <u>inefficient</u> equilibrium. According to the Coase theorem, if property rights exist, then private transactions are efficient and the outcome <u>is not</u> affected by who is assigned the property right. By setting the tax rate equal to the marginal <u>external</u> cost, firms can be made to behave in the same way as they would if they bore the cost of the externality directly.

True or false

1. False; page 224
2. True; page 225
3. False; page 226
4. False; page 228
5. False; page 230
6. True; page 232
7. False; page 232
8. True; page 233

Multiple choice

1. c; page 224
2. a; page 224
3. c; page 226
4. d; page 226
5. e; page 226
6. b; page 226
7. c; page 226
8. e; page 228
9. b; page 227
10. c; page 228
11. b; page 228
12. b; page 230
13. d; page 232
14. c; page 231
15. d; page 233

Complete the graph

1. a. Figure 9.6 shows the *MSC*, *MC*, and *MB* curves; page 228.

■ FIGURE 9.6

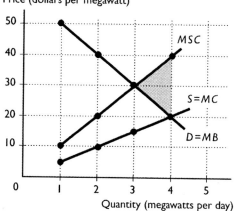

Price (dollars per megawatt)

b. An unregulated market will produce 4 megawatts of electricity a day. The marginal external cost at this production is $20 per megawatt; page 228.
c. The efficient amount of electricity is 3 megawatts a day. The deadweight loss is illustrated in the figure; page 228.
d. At the efficient quantity of electricity, the marginal external cost is $15 a megawatt. The tax is $15 a megawatt. With the tax, 3 megawatts of electricity are produced and the price is $30 per megawatt; page 233.

■ FIGURE 9.7

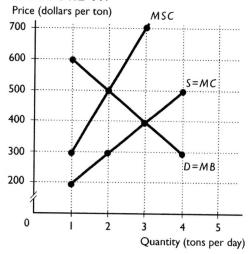

Price (dollars per ton)

2. a. Figure 9.7 shows the *MSC*, *MC*, and *MB* curves; page 228.

b. An unregulated market will produce 3 tons of PBDE a day. At this quantity the marginal external cost is $300; pages 227-228.

c. The efficient quantity of PBDE is 2 tons per day. At this quantity the marginal external cost is $200; pages 227-228.

d. The emission charge will equal $100 per ton of PBDE; page 232.

Short answer and numeric questions

1. If the marginal social cost curve lies above the marginal private cost curve, production of the good creates an external cost; page 227.

Quantity (tons of pesticide per day)	Marginal private cost (dollars per ton)	Marginal external cost (dollars per ton)	Marginal social cost (dollars per ton)
1	100	30	130
2	120	40	160
3	150	60	210
4	190	90	280
5	240	120	360

2. The completed table is above; page 226.

3. According to the Coase theorem, if property rights are assigned, the number of people involved is small, and transactions costs are low, then private transactions are efficient; page 230.

4. A marketable permit is a government-issued permit given to firms that allows the company to pollute up to the limit of the permit. Permits can be bought and sold amongst firms. The advantage marketable permits have over assigning each firm a limit for its pollution is information. In order to assign each firm a limit and achieve efficiency, the government must know each firm's marginal cost schedule. Marketable permits do not require that the government know this information; page 232.

5. Emission charges and taxes are designed to charge polluting firms the cost of their pollution. By forcing a firm to pay this cost, the firm's marginal private cost becomes equal to the marginal social cost. To use emission charges or taxes to overcome the problem of pollution, the government must know the marginal external cost at different levels of output; page 232.

■ CHECKPOINT 9.2

Fill in the blanks

Marginal <u>social</u> benefit is the benefit enjoyed by society from one more unit of a good or service. If the government leaves education to the private market, <u>underproduction</u> occurs. A payment that the government makes to private producers that depends on the level of output is <u>a subsidy</u>. The property rights of the creators of knowledge and other discoveries are <u>intellectual property</u> rights.

True or false

1. False; page 236
2. True; page 236
3. False; page 236
4. True; page 237
5. True; page 238
6. False; page 238
7. False; page 240
8. True; page 241

Multiple choice

1. c; page 236
2. d; page 236
3. c; page 236
4. d; page 236
5. b; page 236
6. c; page 237
7. b; page 236
8. c; page 237
9. d; page 237
10. b; page 237
11. b; page 238
12. e; pages 238-239
13. d; page 238
14. d; page 240
15. d; page 241

Complete the graph

■ FIGURE 9.8

Price (dollars per pound of honey)

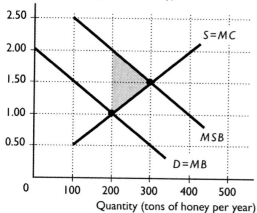

1. a. Figure 9.8 labels the curves; page 237.
   b. The production of honey has an external benefit but no external cost; page 237.
   c. The efficient quantity of honey is 300 tons, a year, at the intersection of the *MSB* curve and the *S* = *MC* curve. In an unregulated market, the equilibrium quantity is 200 tons a year, at the intersection of the *D* = *MB* curve and the *S* = *MC* curve; page 237.
   d. Figure 9.8 shades the deadweight loss; page 237.

Short answer and numeric questions

1. a. The marginal external benefit equals the difference between the marginal social benefit and the marginal social cost, so it is $90 per unit of R&D; page 238.
   b. The competitive equilibrium is where the marginal private cost (which determines the supply) equals the marginal private benefit (which determines the demand), so the equilibrium amount of R&D is 300 units per day; page 239.
   c. The efficient quantity is produced when the marginal social benefit equals the marginal cost, so the efficient amount is 400 units of R&D per day; page 239.
   d. A subsidy would be a proper government policy; page 239.

2. Efficiency is not guaranteed when production sets the marginal private benefit equal to the marginal cost. The efficient quantity is produced when the marginal social benefit equals marginal cost; page 237.

3. Vaccination protects not only the child who is vaccinated, but also makes it less likely for classmates to catch the disease. So a vaccination has an external benefit. Although the marginal cost of a vaccination can be greater than the marginal private benefit of a vaccination, the marginal social benefit exceeds the marginal private benefit. The market might be efficient when vaccination is required; page 237.

3. The correct government action to deal with a good or service that has an external benefit is a private subsidy, not a tax; page 238.

4. A voucher is a token that the government gives to households which they can use to buy specified goods or services. Vouchers increase the demand for the product and shift the demand curve (which is the same as the marginal private benefit curve, or *MB* curve) rightward, closer to the marginal social benefit curve. Vouchers reduce the inefficiency created by a good or service with an external benefit; page 240.

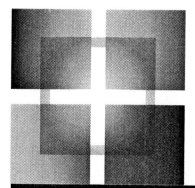

Production and Cost

Chapter 10

In Chapter 10 we study how a firm's costs are determined and how these costs vary as the firm varies its output.

1 Explain how economists measure a firm's cost of production and profit.

The firm's goal is to maximize its profit. The highest-valued alternative forgone is the opportunity cost of a firm's production. A cost paid in money is an explicit cost. A firm incurs an implicit cost when it uses a factor of production but does not make a direct money payment for its use. The return to entrepreneurship is normal profit and is part of the firm's costs because it compensates the entrepreneur for not running another business. A firm's economic profit equals total revenue minus total cost, which is the sum of explicit costs and implicit costs and is the opportunity cost of production.

2 Explain the relationship between a firm's output and labor employed in the short run.

The short run is the time frame in which the quantities of some resources are fixed; the long run is the time frame in which the quantities of all resources can be varied. Marginal product is the change in total product that results from a one-unit increase in the quantity of labor employed. As firms hire labor, initially increasing marginal returns occur but eventually decreasing marginal returns set in. Average product is total product divided by the quantity of an input. When marginal product exceeds the average product, the average product curve slopes upward and average product increases as more labor is employed. And when marginal product is less than average product, the average product curve slopes downward and average product decreases as more labor is employed.

3 Explain the relationship between a firm's output and costs in the short run.

Total cost is the sum of total fixed cost and total variable cost. Marginal cost is the change in total cost that results from a one-unit increase in total product. Average total cost is the sum of average fixed cost and average variable cost. The U-shape of the average total cost curve arises from the influence of two opposing forces: spreading total fixed cost over a larger output and decreasing marginal returns. The marginal cost curve intersects the average variable cost and average total cost curves at their minimum points. The average cost curve and the marginal cost curve shift when technology changes or when the price of a factor of production changes.

4 Derive and explain a firm's long-run average cost curve.

In the long run, all costs are variable. When a firm changes its plant size, it might experience economies of scale, diseconomies of scale, or constant returns to scale. The long-run average cost curve is a curve that shows the lowest average cost at which it is possible to produce each output when the firm has had sufficient time to change both its plant size and labor employed. The long-run average cost curve slopes downward with economies of scale and upward with diseconomies of scale.

CHECKPOINT 10.1

■ **Explain how economists measure a firm's cost of production and profit.**

Quick Review

- *Explicit cost* A cost paid in money.
- *Implicit cost* A cost incurred by using a factor of production but for which no direct money payment is made.
- *Economic profit* Total revenue minus total opportunity cost.

Additional Practice Problem 10.1

1. Gary manufactures toy gliders made of balsa wood. Each week, Gary pays $200 in wages, buys balsa wood for $400, pays $50 to lease saws and sanders, and pays $150 in rent for the workspace. To fund his operations, Gary withdrew his life's savings, $162,500, from his savings account at the bank, which paid interest of $250 a week. The normal profit for a glider company is $250 a week. Gary sells $1,500 worth of gliders a week.

   a. How much are the weekly explicit costs?
   b. How much are the weekly implicit costs?
   c. What does an accountant compute for the weekly profit?
   d. What does an economist compute for the weekly economic profit?

Solution to Additional Practice Problem 10.1

1a. The explicit costs are the wages, the balsa wood, the leased saws and sanders, and rent. The weekly explicit costs are $200 + $400 + $50 + $150, which equals $800.

1b. The implicit costs are the forgone interest and the normal profit. The weekly implicit costs are $250 + $250, which equals $500.

1c. Accountants calculate profit as total revenue minus explicit costs, which is $1,500 − $800 = $700.

1d. Economic profit is total revenue minus total cost. Total cost is the sum of explicit and implicit costs. So Gary's total cost is $800 + $500, which is $1,300. Gary's economic profit equals $1,500 − $1,300, which is $200.

■ Self Test 10.1

Fill in the blanks

The firm's goal is to maximize ____ (growth; market share; profit). A cost paid in money is an ____ (explicit; implicit) cost; a cost incurred when a firm uses a factor of production for which it does not make a direct money payment is an ____ (explicit; implicit) cost. The return to entrepreneurship is ____ (normal; economic) profit and ____ (is; is not) part of the firm's opportunity cost. A firm's total revenue minus total opportunity cost is ____ (normal; economic) profit.

True or false

1. The firm's goal is to maximize profit.
2. An accountant measures profit as total revenue minus opportunity cost.
3. All of a firm's costs must be paid in money.
4. If a firm earns an economic profit, the return to the entrepreneur exceeds normal profit.

Multiple choice

1. The paramount goal of a firm is to
   a. maximize profit.
   b. maximize sales.
   c. maximize total revenue.
   d. minimize its costs.
   e. force its competitors into bankruptcy.

2. For a business, opportunity cost measures
   a. only the cost of labor and materials.
   b. only the implicit costs of the business.
   c. the cost of all the factors of production the firm employs.
   d. only the explicit costs the firm must pay.
   e. all of the firm's costs including its normal profit *and* its economic profit.

3. Costs paid in money to hire a resource is
   a. normal profit.
   b. an implicit cost.
   c. an explicit cost.
   d. an alternative-use cost.
   e. economic profit.

4. Which of the following is an example of an implicit cost?
   a. wages paid to employees
   b. interest paid to a bank on a building loan
   c. the cost of using capital an owner donates to the business
   d. dollars paid to a supplier for materials used in production
   e. liability insurance payments made only once a year

5. The opportunity cost of a firm using its own capital is
   a. economic depreciation.
   b. standard ownership depreciation.
   c. economic loss.
   d. normal loss.
   e. capital loss.

6. The difference between a firm's total revenue and its total cost is its _____ profit.
   a. explicit
   b. normal
   c. economic
   d. accounting
   e. excess

Short answer and numeric questions

1. What is likely to happen to a firm that does not maximize profit?

2. Bobby quits his job as a veterinarian to open a model train store. Bobby made $80,000 a year as a veterinarian. The first year his train store is open, Bobby pays a helper $26,000. He also pays $24,000 in rent, $10,000 in utilities, and buys $200,000 of model trains. Bobby had a good year because he sold all of his model trains for $300,000. Bobby's normal profit is $30,000.
   a. What would an accountant calculate as Bobby's profit?
   b. What is Bobby's total opportunity cost? What is his economic profit?

3. Why are wages a cost to a business? Why is a normal profit a cost to a business?

CHECKPOINT 10.2

■ **Explain the relationship between a firm's output and labor employed in the short run.**

Quick Review

- *Marginal product* The change in total product that results from a one-unit increase in the quantity of labor employed.
- *Formula for the marginal product* The marginal product equals:

Change in total product ÷ change in quantity of labor

Additional Practice Problems 10.2

1. Bobby runs a cat grooming service. Bobby hires students to groom the cats. The table to the right shows how many cats Bobby's service can groom when Bobby changes the number of students he hires.

Labor (students per day)	Total product (cats groomed per day)
0	0
1	5
2	12
3	18
4	22
5	25

Labor (students per day)	Average product (cats groomed per day)	Marginal product (cats groomed per day)
1	____	____
2	____	____
3	____	____
4	____	____
5	____	____

   a. Complete the table above.
   b. Draw Bobby's average product curve and his marginal product curve. When does the marginal product equals the average product?

2. The first five members of the men's basketball squad are each 6 feet tall. A sixth player, whose height is 7 feet, is added. Has the average height increased or decreased with the addi-

tion of this player? A seventh player, whose height is 5 feet, is added. What happens to the team's average height? An eighth player, whose height is 6 feet, is added. What is the effect on the average height? What is the general rule about how the marginal player's height changes the average height of the team?

Solutions to Additional Practice Problems 10.2

Labor (students per day)	Average product (cats groomed per day)	Marginal product (cats groomed per day)
		5.0
1	5.0	
		7.0
2	6.0	
		6.0
3	6.0	
		4.0
4	5.5	
		3.0
5	5.0	

1a. The completed table is above. The average product equals: total product ÷ total labor and the marginal product equals: change in total product ÷ change in quantity of labor.

1b. The figure is to the right. The marginal product equals the average product when the average product is at its maximum. Both equal 6 cats groomed per day.

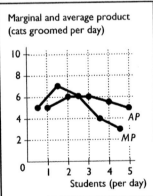

Marginal and average product (cats groomed per day)

AP

MP

Students (per day)

2. The 7-foot player is above the average height, so adding him to the team increases the average height. The 5-foot player is below the average height, so adding him decreases the average height. When the 6-foot player is added, the team's average height equals 6 feet, so his addition has no effect on the average height. The general rule is that when a marginal value lies above the average, the average rises. When the marginal value is below the

average, the average falls. And when the marginal value equals the average, the average does not change.

■ Self Test 10.2

Fill in the blanks

The time frame in which the quantities of some resources are fixed is the ____ (long; market; short) run and the time frame in which the quantities of *all* resources can be varied is the ____ (long; market; short) run. Marginal product equals ____ (total product; the change in total product) divided by the ____ (quantity of labor; increase in the quantity of labor). Average product equals the ____ (total product; change in total product) divided by the ____ (quantity of labor; change in quantity of labor). When the marginal product of an additional worker is less than the marginal product of the previous worker, the firm experiences decreasing ____ (marginal; fixed) returns. The law of decreasing returns states that as a firm uses more of a ____ (fixed; variable) input, with a given quantity of ____ (fixed; variable) inputs, the marginal product of the ____ (fixed; variable) input eventually decreases. If the marginal product exceeds the average product, the average product curve slopes ____ (downward; upward).

True or false

1. In the short run, the firm's fixed inputs cannot be changed.

2. Points on and below the total product curve are efficient.

3. Most production processes initially have decreasing marginal returns followed eventually by increasing marginal returns.

4. When the marginal product of labor exceeds the average product of labor, the average product curve is downward sloping.

Multiple choice

1. The short run is a time period during which
   a. some of the firm's resources are fixed.
   b. all of the firm's resources are fixed.
   c. all of the firm's resources are variable.
   d. the fixed cost equals zero.
   e. the firm cannot increase its output.

2. In the short run, firms can increase output by
   a. only increasing the size of their plant.
   b. only decreasing the size of their plant.
   c. only increasing the amount of labor used.
   d. only decreasing the amount of labor used.
   e. either increasing the amount of labor used or increasing the size of their plant.

3. Which of the following is correct?
   a. The short run for a firm can be longer than the long run for the same firm.
   b. The short run is the same for all firms.
   c. The long run is the time frame in which the quantities of all resources can be varied.
   d. The long run is the time frame in which all resources are fixed.
   e. The long run does not exist for some firms.

4. Marginal product equals
   a. the total product produced by a certain amount of labor.
   b. the change in total product that results from a one-unit increase in the quantity of labor employed.
   c. total product divided by the total quantity of labor.
   d. the amount of labor needed to produce an increase in production.
   e. total product minus the quantity of labor.

5. If 5 workers can wash 30 cars a day and 6 workers can wash 33 cars a day, then the marginal product of the 6th worker equals
   a. 30 cars a day.
   b. 33 cars a day.
   c. 5 cars a day.
   d. 5.5 cars a day.
   e. 3 cars a day.

6. Increasing marginal returns occur when the
   a. average product of an additional worker is less than the average product of the previous worker.
   b. marginal product of an additional worker exceeds the marginal product of the previous worker.
   c. marginal product of labor is less than the average product of labor.
   d. total output of the firm is at its maximum.
   e. total product curve is horizontal.

7. If 25 workers can pick 100 flats of strawberries an hour, then average product is
   a. 100 flats an hour.
   b. 125 flats an hour.
   c. 75 flats an hour.
   d. 4 flats an hour.
   e. More information is needed about how many flats 24 workers can pick.

Complete the graph

Quantity of labor (workers)	Total product (turkeys per day)	Average product (turkeys per worker)	Marginal product (turkeys per worker)
0	0	xx	
			100
1	100	100	
2	300	___	___
3	450	___	___
			30
4	___	___	
5	___	100	___

1. The table gives the total product schedule at Al's Turkey Town Farm.
   a. Complete this table. (The marginal product is entered midway between rows to emphasize that it is the result of changing inputs, that is, moving from one row to the next.)

■ **FIGURE 10.1**

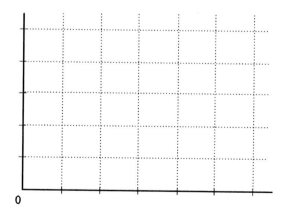

b. In Figure 10.1 label the axes and plot the marginal product (*MP*) and average product (*AP*) curves. (Plot the *MP* curve midway between the quantities of labor.) Where do the two curves intersect?

c. When the *MP* curve is above the *AP* curve, is the *AP* curve rising or falling? When the *MP* curve is below the *AP* curve, is the *AP* curve rising or falling?

Short answer and numeric questions

1. What is the difference between the short run and the long run?

2. Pizza Hut opens a new store nearby. As the owner adds workers, what happens to their marginal product? Why?

3. What is the law of decreasing returns?

4. If the marginal product of a new worker exceeds the average product, what happens to the average product?

CHECKPOINT 10.3

■ Explain the relationship between a firm's output and costs in the short run.

Quick Review

- *Total cost* The cost of all the factors of production used by a firm. Total cost equals the sum of total fixed cost and total variable cost.
- *Marginal cost* The cost that arises from a one-unit increase in output.
- *Average total cost* Total cost per unit of output, which equals average fixed cost plus average variable cost as well as total cost divided by output.

Additional Practice Problems 10.3

1. Pearl owns a company that produces pools. Pearl has total fixed cost of $2,000 a month and pays each of her workers $2,500 a month. The table in the next column shows the number of pools Pearl's company can produce in a month.

   a. Complete the left side of the table.

   b. Suppose that the wage Pearl pays her

Labor	Output	TC	MC	TC	MC
0	0	___	___	___	___
1	1	___	___	___	___
2	5	___	___	___	___
3	9	___	___	___	___
4	12	___	___	___	___
5	14	___	___	___	___
6	15	___	___	___	___

   workers increases to $3,000 a month. Complete the right side of the table.

   c. What was the effect of the wage hike on Pearl's marginal cost?

2. In the figure to the right is an *ATC* curve. In this figure sketch an *AVC* curve and a *MC* curve. Tell what relationships these curves must obey so that they are drawn correctly.

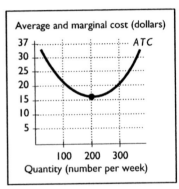

Average and marginal cost (dollars)

Solutions to Additional Practice Problems 10.3

Labor	Output	TC	MC	TC	MC
0	0	2,000	2,500	2,000	3,000
1	1	4,500	625	5,000	750
2	5	7,000	625	8,000	750
3	9	9,500	833	11,000	1,000
4	12	12,000	1,250	14,000	1,500
5	14	14,500	2,500	17,000	3,000
6	15	17,000		20,000	

1a. The completed table is above. Total cost, *TC*, equals the sum of total fixed cost and total variable cost. For example, when Pearl hires 6 workers, total cost is ($2,000) + (6 × $2,500), which is $17,000. Marginal cost equals the change in the total cost divided by the change in output. For example, when output increases from 14 to 15 pools, marginal cost is ($17,000 − $14,500) ÷ (15 − 14), which is $2,500.

1b. The completed table is above.

1c. The increase in the wage rate increased Pearl's marginal cost at every level of output.

2. The completed figure is to the right. To be drawn correctly, there are three requirements: First, the AVC curve must reach its minimum at a lower level of output than does the ATC curve. Second, the vertical distance between the ATC and AVC curves must decrease as output increases. Finally the MC curve must go through the minimum points on both the AVC and ATC curves.

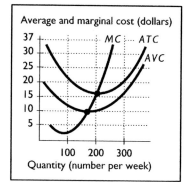

■ Self Test 10.3

Fill in the blanks

Total cost equals total fixed cost _____ (plus; minus; times) total variable cost. _____ (Marginal; Average) cost is the change in total cost that results from a one-unit increase in output. Average total cost equals average fixed cost _____ (plus; minus; times) average variable cost. The average total cost curve is _____ (S-shaped; U-shaped). When the firm hires the quantity of labor so that the marginal product is at its maximum, marginal cost is at its _____ (maximum; minimum).

True or false

1. In the short run, total fixed cost does not change when the firm changes its output.

2. Marginal cost is always less than average total cost.

3. The average total cost curve is U-shaped.

4. An increase in the wage rate shifts the marginal cost curve upward.

Multiple choice

1. Total cost is equal to the sum of
   a. total revenue and total cost.
   b. total variable cost and total product.
   c. total variable cost and total fixed cost.
   d. total fixed cost and total product.
   e. the marginal cost plus the total fixed cost plus the total variable cost.

2. Total fixed cost is the cost of
   a. labor.
   b. production.
   c. a firm's fixed factors of production.
   d. only implicit factors of production.
   e. only explicit factors of production.

3. Jay set up his hot dog stand near the business district. His total variable cost includes the
   a. annual insurance for the hot dog stand.
   b. cost of buying the hot dog stand.
   c. cost of the hot dogs and condiments.
   d. interest he pays on the funds he borrowed to pay for advertising.
   e. revenue he gets when he sells his first hot dog each day.

4. Marginal cost is equal to
   a. the total cost of a firm's production.
   b. the difference between total cost and fixed cost.
   c. a cost that is not related to the quantity produced.
   d. the change in total cost that results from a one-unit increase in output.
   e. the change in fixed cost that results from a one-unit increase in output.

5. To produce 10 shirts, the total cost is $80; to produce 11 shirts, the total cost is $99. The marginal cost of the 11th shirt is equal to
   a. $8.
   b. $9.
   c. $80.
   d. $99.
   e. $19.

6. Average total cost equals
   a. marginal cost divided by output.
   b. average fixed cost plus average variable cost.
   c. total fixed cost plus total variable cost.
   d. marginal cost plus opportunity cost.
   e. marginal cost multiplied by the quantity of output.

7. To produce 10 shirts, the total cost is $80; to produce 11 shirts, the total cost is $99. The average total cost of the 11th shirt is equal to
   a. $8.
   b. $9.
   c. $80.
   d. $99.
   e. $19.

8. One of the major reasons for the U-shaped average total cost curve is the fact that
   a. there are increasing returns from labor regardless of the number of workers employed.
   b. there eventually are decreasing returns from labor as more workers are employed.
   c. prices fall as output increases.
   d. the average fixed cost increases as more output is produced.
   e. the variable cost decreases as more output is produced.

Complete the graph

Labor	Output	TC	ATC	MC
0	0	___	xx	
				___
1	10	___	___	
				___
2	25	___	___	
				___
3	35	___	___	
				___
4	40	___	___	
				___
5	43	___	___	
				___
6	45	___	___	

1. Sue hires workers to produce subs at Sue's Super Supper Sub Shop. Sue pays her workers $10 an hour and has fixed costs of $30 an

■ **FIGURE 10.2**

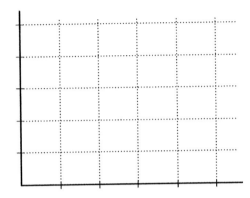

hour. The table shows Sue's total product schedule.
a. Complete the table above the question in the previous column.
b. Using the completed table, plot Sue's *ATC* and *MC* curves in figure 10.2. (Plot the *MC*s midway between the quantities.)

Labor	Output	TC	ATC	MC
0	0	___	xx	
				___
1	10	___	___	
				___
2	25	___	___	
				___
3	35	___	___	
				___
4	40	___	___	
				___
5	43	___	___	
				___
6	45	___	___	

c. Sue's rent increases so her fixed cost rises to $75 an hour. Complete the table above and then plot Sue's new *ATC* and *MC* curves in Figure 10.2.
d. How does the increase in fixed cost change Sue's average total cost curve? Her marginal cost curve?

■ **FIGURE 10.3**

Total cost (dollars per unit)

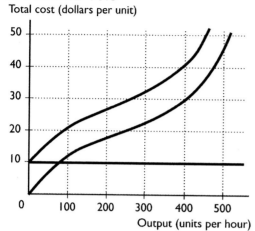

2. Label the cost curves in Figure 10.3.

Short answer and numeric questions

1. If a firm closes and produces nothing, does it still have any costs?

2. What is the difference between marginal cost and average total cost?

3. Why is the average total cost curve U-shaped?

4. Where does the marginal cost curve intersect the average variable cost and average total cost curves?

5. What two factors shift the cost curves?

CHECKPOINT 10.4

■ **Derive and explain a firm's long-run average cost curve.**

Quick Review

• *Long-run average cost curve* The long-run average cost curve shows the lowest average cost at which it is possible to produce each output when the firm has had sufficient time to adjust its labor force and its plant.

Additional Practice Problem 10.4a

1. The figure shows three average total cost curves for A1 Sewing, a company that sells sewing machines. The company can use three different sized stores, which account for the different cost curves.

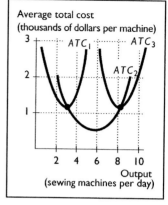

a. Which average cost curve occurs when A-1 uses the smallest store? The largest store?

b. Indicate A1's long-run average cost curve, *LRAC* in the figure.

c. If A1 plans to sell 6 sewing machines per day, what sized store will A1 use?

d. Over what range of output does A1 Sewing have economies of scale? Diseconomies of scale?

2. Describe economies of scale and diseconomies of scale along a long-run average total cost curve.

Solutions to Additional Practice Problems 10.4

1a. When A1 uses the smallest store, its plant size is the smallest and so its average total cost curve is ATC_1 in the figure. When A1 uses the largest store, its plant size is the largest and so its average total cost curve is ATC_2 in the figure.

1b. The long-run average cost curve is the curve that shows the lowest average total cost to produce each output. In the figure to the right, the *LRAC* curve is the darkened parts of the three average total cost curves.

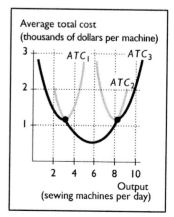

1c. If A1 plans to sell 6 sewing machines, it will use the middle sized store because that is the store that gives it the lowest average total cost when selling 6 sewing machines a day.

1d. A1 has economies of scale when selling from 0 to 6 sewing machines per day. It has diseconomies of scale when it sells more than 6 sewing machines per day.

2. When economies of scale are present, the *LRAC* curve slopes downward. When the *LRAC* curve is horizontal, constant returns to scale are present. And when the *LRAC* curve slopes upward, diseconomies of scale are present.

■ Self Test 10.4

Fill in the blanks

In the long run, a firm _____ (can; cannot) vary its quantity of labor and _____ (can; cannot) vary its quantity of capital. Economies of scale occur if, when a firm increases its plant size and labor employed by the same percentage, the firm's average total cost _____ (increases; decreases). When the firm has _____ (economies; diseconomies) of scale, its long-run average cost curve slopes upward.

True or false

1. All costs are fixed in the long run.

2. When a firm increases its plant size and labor, greater specialization of capital and labor can lead to economies of scale.

3. Constant returns to scale occur when the firm increases its plant size and labor employed by the same percentage and output increases by the same percentage.

4. The long-run average cost curve is derived from the marginal cost curves for different possible plant sizes.

Multiple choice

1. Economies of scale occur whenever
   a. marginal cost decreases as production increases.
   b. total cost increases as production is increased by increasing all inputs by the same percentage.
   c. marginal product increases as labor increases and capital decreases.
   d. a firm increases its plant size and labor employed, and its output increases by a larger percentage.
   e. marginal product decreases as labor increases and capital increases.

2. The main source of economies of scale is
   a. better management.
   b. constant returns to plant size.
   c. specialization.
   d. long-run cost curves eventually sloping downward.
   e. increases in the labor force not matched by increases in the plant size.

3. Diseconomies of scale can occur as a result of which of the following?
   a. increasing marginal returns as the firm increases its size
   b. lower total fixed cost as the firm increases its size
   c. management difficulties as the firm increases its size
   d. greater specialization of labor and capital as the firm increases its size
   e. increases in the labor force not matched by increases in the plant

4. Constant returns to scale occur when an equal percentage increase in plant size and labor
   a. increases total cost.
   b. does not change total cost.
   c. increases average total cost.
   d. does not change average total cost.
   e. does not change production.

5. A firm's long-run average cost curve shows the ____ average cost at which it is possible to produce each output when the firm has had ____ time to change both its labor force and its plant.
   a. highest; sufficient
   b. lowest; sufficient
   c. lowest; insufficient
   d. highest insufficient
   e. average; sufficient

6. Economies of scale and diseconomies of scale explain
   a. cost behavior in the short run.
   b. profit maximization in the long run.
   c. the U-shape of the long-run cost curve.
   d. the U-shape of the short-run cost curves.
   e. the U-shape of the marginal cost curves.

■ FIGURE 10.4

Average total cost (dollars per unit)

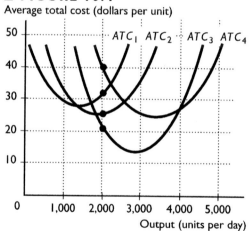

7. Figure 10.4 shows four of a firm's *ATC* curves. If the firms produces 2,000 units per day, it will use the plant size that corresponds to
   a. *ATC*₁.
   b. *ATC*₂.
   c. *ATC*₃.
   d. *ATC*₄.
   e. either *ATC*₁ or *ATC*₄.

Complete the graph

■ FIGURE 10.5

Average total cost (dollars per unit)

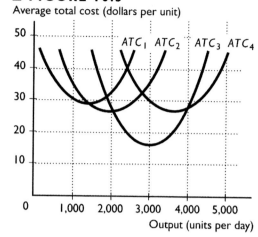

1. In Figure 10.5, darken the firm's long-run average total cost curve. Show over which range of output the firm has economies of scale and over which range of output the firm has diseconomies of scale.

Short answer and numeric questions

1. Describe how a long-run average cost curve is constructed.

2. What are economies of scale? What leads to economies of scale?

SELF TEST ANSWERS

■ CHECKPOINT 10.1

Fill in the blanks

The firm's goal is to maximize <u>profit</u>. A cost paid in money is an <u>explicit</u> cost; a cost incurred when a firm uses a factor of production for which it does not make a direct money payment is an <u>implicit</u> cost. The return to entrepreneurship is <u>normal</u> profit and <u>is</u> part of the firm's opportunity cost. A firm's total revenue minus total opportunity cost is <u>economic</u> profit.

True or false

1. True; page 248
2. False; page 248
3. False; page 249
4. True; pages 249-250

Multiple choice

1. a; page 248
2. c; page 248
3. c; page 249
4. c; page 249
5. a; page 249
6. c; page 249

Short answer and numeric questions

1. A firm that does not seek to maximize profit is either driven out of business or bought by firms that do seek that goal; page 248.
2. a. An accountant calculates profit as total revenue minus explicit costs. Bobby's explicit costs are $26,000 + $24,000 + $10,000 + $200,000, which equals $260,000. The accountant calculates profit as $300,000 − $260,000, which is $40,000; page 248.
   b. Bobby's opportunity cost is the sum of his explicit costs and his implicit costs. Bobby's explicit costs are $260,000. His implicit costs are the sum of his income forgone as a veterinarian, $80,000, and normal profit, $30,000. So Bobby's implicit costs are $110,000. His total opportunity cost is $260,000 + $110,000, which is $370,000. Bobby's economic profit is his total revenue minus his opportunity cost,

which is $300,000 − $370,000 = −$70,000. Bobby incurs an economic loss; pages 319-250.

3. Wages are a cost because they are paid to hire a factor of production, labor. A normal profit is a cost because it is paid to obtain the use of another factor of production, entrepreneurship; page 249.

■ CHECKPOINT 10.2

Fill in the blanks

The time frame in which the quantities of some resources are fixed is the <u>short</u> run and the time frame in which the quantities of *all* resources can be varied is the <u>long</u> run. Marginal product equals <u>the change in total product</u> divided by the <u>increase in the quantity of labor</u>. Average product equals the <u>total product</u> divided by the <u>quantity of labor</u>. When the marginal product of an additional worker is less than the marginal product of the previous worker, the firm has experienced decreasing <u>marginal</u> returns. The law of decreasing returns states that as a firm uses more of a <u>variable</u> input, with a given quantity of <u>fixed</u> inputs, the marginal product of the <u>variable</u> input eventually decreases. If the marginal product exceeds the average product, the average product curve slopes <u>upward</u>.

True or false

1. True; page 252
2. False; page 254
3. False; page 254
4. False; pages 256-257

Multiple choice

1. a; page 252
2. c; page 252
3. c; page 252
4. b; pages 254-255
5. e; pages 254-255
6. b; page 254
7. d; page 256

Complete the graph

1. a. The completed table is below; pages 253-256.

Quantity of labor	Total product (turkeys per day)	Average product (turkeys per worker)	Marginal product (turkeys per worker)
0	0	xx	
			100
1	100	100	
			200
2	300	150	
			150
3	450	150	
			30
4	480	120	
			20
5	500	100	

■ FIGURE 10.6

Total product (turkeys per day)

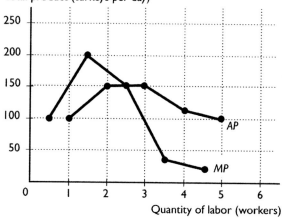

b. Figure 10.6 plots the *MP* and *AP* curves. The curves intersect where the *AP* curve is at its maximum; page 256.

c. When the *MP* curve is above the *AP* curve, the *AP* curve is rising. When the *MP* curve is below the *AP* curve, the *AP* curve is falling; pages 256-257.

Short answer and numeric questions

1. The short run is the time frame in which the quantities of some resources (the plant) are fixed. The long run is the time frame in which the quantities of *all* resources can be changed; page 252.

2. As Pizza Hut initially adds workers, the marginal product of each additional worker exceeds the marginal product of the previous worker. The marginal product increases because the workers can specialize. Some workers can make the pizzas and others can deliver them. As more workers are added, eventually the marginal product of each additional worker is less than the marginal product of the previous worker. The marginal product decreases because more workers are using the same equipment, so there is less productive work for each new worker; page 254.

3. The law of decreasing returns states that as a firm uses more of a variable input, with a given quantity of fixed inputs, the marginal product of the variable input eventually decreases; page 256.

4. If the marginal product of a worker exceeds the average product, then hiring the worker will increase the average product; page 257.

■ CHECKPOINT 10.3

Fill in the blanks

Total cost equals total fixed cost plus total variable cost. Marginal cost is the change in total cost that results from a one-unit increase in output. Average total cost equals average fixed cost plus average variable cost. The average total cost curve is U-shaped. When the firm hires the quantity of labor so that the marginal product is at its maximum, marginal cost is at its minimum.

True or false

1. True; page 259
2. False; page 262
3. True; page 262
4. True; page 265

Multiple choice

1. c; page 259
2. c; page 259
3. c; page 259
4. d; page 260

5. e; page 260
6. b; page 261
7 b; page 261
8. b; page 263

Complete the graph

Labor	Output	TC	ATC	MC
0	0	30	xx	
				1.00
1	10	40	4.00	
				0.67
2	25	50	2.00	
				1.00
3	35	60	1.71	
				2.00
4	40	70	1.75	
				3.33
5	43	80	1.86	
				5.00
6	45	90	2.00	

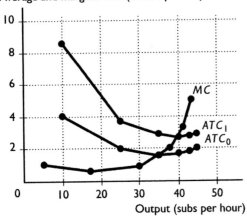

■ FIGURE 10.7
Average and marginal cost (dollars per sub)

Output (subs per hour)

1. a. The completed table is above; page 261.
   b. Figure 10.7 plots the curves as ATC_0 and MC.
   c. The completed table after the change in costs is at the top of the next column and Figure 10.7 plots the new curves as ATC_1 and MC; page 261.
   d. The average cost curve shifts upward; the marginal cost curve does not change; page 264.

Labor	Output	TC	ATC	MC
0	0	75	xx	
				1.00
1	10	85	8.50	
				0.67
2	25	95	3.80	
				1.00
3	35	105	3.00	
				2.00
4	40	115	2.88	
				3.33
5	43	125	2.91	
				5.00
6	45	135	3.00	

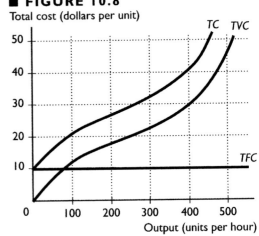

■ FIGURE 10.8
Total cost (dollars per unit)

Output (units per hour)

2. The labeled figure, Figure 10.8, is above; page 260.

Short answer and numeric questions

1. Yes, even a closed firm might still have fixed costs. So even if zero output is produced, the firm might have (fixed) costs such as interest payments on a loan or rent on a lease that has not expired; page 259

2. Marginal cost is the change in total cost that results from a one-unit increase in output. Average total cost is total cost per unit of output, which equals average fixed cost plus average variable cost; pages 260-261.

3. When output increases, the firm spreads its total fixed cost over a larger output and its average fixed cost decreases—its average fixed cost curve slopes downward.

Decreasing marginal returns means that as output increases, ever larger amounts of labor are needed to produce an additional unit of output. So average variable cost eventually increases, and the *AVC* curve eventually slopes upward.

Initially as output increases, both average fixed cost and average variable cost decrease, so average total cost decreases and the *ATC* curve slopes downward. But as output increases further and decreasing marginal returns set in, average variable cost begins to increase. Eventually, average variable cost increases more quickly than average fixed cost decreases, so average total cost increases and the *ATC* curve slopes upward; page 263.

4. The marginal cost curve intersects the average variable cost curve and the average total cost curve at the point where they are the minimum; page 262.

5. Cost curves shift if there is a change in technology or a change in the price of a factor of production; pages 264-265.

■ CHECKPOINT 10.4

Fill in the blanks

In the long run, a firm <u>can</u> vary its quantity of labor and <u>can</u> vary its quantity of capital. Economies of scale occur if, when a firm increases its plant size and labor employed by the same percentage, the firm's average total cost <u>decreases</u>. When the firm has <u>diseconomies</u> of scale, its long-run average cost curve slopes upward.

True or false

1. False; page 267
2. True; page 267
3. True; page 268
4. False; page 268

Multiple choice

1. d; page 267
2. c; page 267
3. c; page 268
4. d; page 268

5. b page 268
6. c; page 268
7. c; page 269

Complete the graph

■ FIGURE 10.9

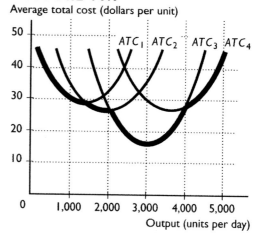
Average total cost (dollars per unit)

1. Figure 10.9 darkens the firm's long-run average total cost curve. As indicated by the dotted line, the firm has economies of scale at all output levels less than 3,000 and has diseconomies of scale at all output levels greater than 3,000; page 269.

Short answer and numeric questions

1. A long-run average cost curve is a curve that shows the lowest average total cost at which it is possible to produce each output when the firm has had sufficient time to change both its plant size and labor employed. Suppose a newspaper publisher can operate with four different plant sizes. The segment of each of the four average total cost curves for which that plant has the lowest average total cost is the scallop-shaped curve that is the long-run average cost curve; page 267.

2. Economies of scale is a condition in which, when a firm increases its plant size and labor force by the same percentage, its output increases by a larger percentage and its long-run average cost decreases. The main source of economies of scale is greater specialization of both labor and capital; page 267.

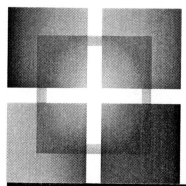

Perfect Competition

Chapter
11

In Chapter 11 we study perfect competition, the market that arises when the demand for a product is large relative to the output of a single producer.

1 Explain a perfectly competitive firm's profit-maximizing choices and derive its supply curve.

Perfect competition exists when: many firms sell an identical product to many buyers; there are no restrictions on entry into (or exit from) the market; established firms have no advantage over new firms; and sellers and buyers are well informed about prices. A firm in perfect competition is a price taker—it cannot influence the price of its product. The market demand curve is downward sloping. A perfectly competitive firm faces a perfectly elastic demand so its demand curve is horizontal. Marginal revenue is the change in total revenue that results from a one-unit increase in the quantity sold. In perfect competition, marginal revenue equals price. A firm maximizes its profit at the output level at which total revenue exceeds total cost by the largest amount. Another way to find the profit-maximizing output is to use marginal analysis. A firm maximizes its profit at the output level at which marginal revenue equals marginal cost. The shutdown point is the output and price at which the firm just covers its total variable cost. If a firm shuts down, it incurs a loss equal to its total fixed cost. A firm's supply curve is its marginal cost curve above minimum average variable cost.

2 Explain how output, price, and profit are determined in the short run.

The market supply curve in the short run shows the quantity supplied at each price by a fixed number of firms. Market demand and market supply determine the price and quantity bought and sold. Each firm takes the price as given and produces its profit-maximizing output. When price equals the average total cost, a perfectly competitive firm earns a normal profit. The firm earns an economic profit when price exceeds average total cost and incurs economic loss when price is less than average total cost.

3 Explain how output, price, and profit are determined in the long run and explain why perfect competition is efficient.

Economic profit is an incentive for new firms to enter a market, but as they do so, the price falls and the economic profit of each existing firm decreases. Economic loss is an incentive for firms to exit a market, and as they do so the price rises and the economic loss of each remaining firm decreases. In the long run, a firm earns a normal profit and there is no entry or exit. A In a market undergoing technological change, firms that adopt the new technology make an economic profit. Firms that stick with the old technology incur economic losses. They either exit the market or switch to the new technology. Competition eliminates economic profit in the long run. Perfect competition is efficient because in a perfectly competitive market the market demand curve is the same as the marginal benefit curve and the market supply curve is the same as the entire market's marginal cost curve.

CHECKPOINT 11.1

■ **Explain a perfectly competitive firm's profit-maximizing choices and derive its supply curve.**

Quick Review

- *MC = MR* Profit is maximized when production is such that marginal cost equals marginal revenue.
- *A firm's short-run supply curve* At prices less than its minimum average variable cost, the firm shuts down. At prices above the minimum average variable cost, the supply curve is the marginal cost curve.
- *Shutdown point* The output and price at which price equals the minimum average variable cost.

Additional Practice Problem 11.1

1. Patricia is a perfectly competitive wheat farmer. Her average variable cost curve and her marginal cost are shown in the figure.

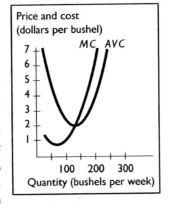

Price and cost (dollars per bushel)

MC AVC

Quantity (bushels per week)

   a. If the price of a bushel of wheat is $6 per bushel, how much wheat will Patricia produce?
   b. If the price of a bushel of wheat falls to $4 per bushel, how much wheat will Patricia produce?
   c. What are two points on Patricia's supply curve?
   d. What is the lowest price for which Patricia will produce wheat rather than shut down?
   e. Suppose that when the price of a bushel of wheat is $6, Patricia produces a quantity of wheat such that her marginal revenue is greater than marginal cost. Explain why she is not maximizing her profit.

Solution to Additional Practice Problem 11.1

1a. When the price of a bushel of wheat is $6 per bushel, Patricia's marginal revenue curve is shown in the figure as MR_1. To maximize her profit, Patricia produces 200 bushels of wheat, the quantity at which marginal revenue equals marginal cost.

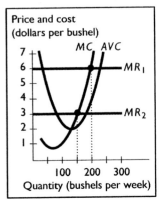

Price and cost (dollars per bushel)

MC AVC

MR_1

MR_2

Quantity (bushels per week)

1b. If the price of wheat falls to $3 per bushel, Patricia's marginal revenue curve is shown in the figure as MR_2. She decreases the quantity of wheat she produces to 150 bushels per week because that is the quantity at which marginal revenue equals marginal cost.

1c. One point on Patricia's supply curve is a price of $6 and 200 bushels. Another point is a price of $3 and a quantity of 150 bushels.

1d. The lowest price for which Patricia produces rather than shuts down is the price equal to her minimum average variable cost. The figure shows that this price is equal to $2 per bushel.

1e. If marginal revenue exceeds marginal cost, then the extra revenue from selling one more bushel of wheat exceeds the extra cost incurred to produce it. So if Patricia produces one more bushel of wheat, the marginal revenue that she receives from selling that bushel is greater than the cost to produce that bushel and this bushel increases her profit. To maximize profit, Patricia must increase her output until she reaches the point where the marginal revenue equals the marginal cost.

■ **Self Test 11.1**

Fill in the blanks

The conditions that define perfect competition arise when the market demand for the product is ____ (large; small) relative to the output of a single producer. A perfectly competitive firm faces a perfectly ____ (elastic; inelastic) demand. The change in total revenue that results from a one-unit increase in the quantity sold is the marginal ____ (cost; price; revenue). When a perfectly competitive firm maximizes profit, marginal revenue equals ____ (average variable; marginal) cost. When a firm shuts down, it incurs a loss equal to its total ____ (variable; fixed) cost. A firm will shut down if price is less than minimum ____ (marginal; average total; average variable) cost. A perfectly competitive firm's supply curve is its marginal ____ (cost; revenue) curve above the minimum ____ (average total; average variable) cost.

True or false

1. A perfectly competitive market has many firms.

2. A firm in perfect competition is a price taker.

3. When a perfectly competitive firm is maximizing its profit, the vertical difference between the firm's marginal revenue curve and its marginal cost curve is as large as possible.

4. Stan's U-Pick blueberry farm, a perfectly competitive firm, will shut down if its total revenue is less than its total cost.

5. A perfectly competitive firm's short-run supply curve is its average total cost above minimum average variable cost.

Multiple choice

1. The four market types are
   a. perfect competition, imperfect competition, monopoly, and oligopoly.
   b. oligopoly, monopsony, monopoly, and imperfect competition.
   c. perfect competition, monopoly, monopolistic competition, and oligopoly.
   d. oligopoly, oligopolistic competition, monopoly, and perfect competition.
   e. perfect competition, imperfect competition, monopoly, and duopoly.

2. A requirement of perfect competition is that
   i. many firms sell an identical product to many buyers.
   ii. there are no restrictions on entry into (or exit from) the market, and established firms have no advantage over new firms.
   iii. sellers and buyers are well informed about prices.
   a. i only.
   b. i and ii.
   c. iii only.
   d. i and iii.
   e. i, ii, and iii.

3. A perfectly competitive firm is a price taker because
   a. many other firms produce the same product.
   b. only one firm produces the product.
   c. many firms produce a slightly differentiated product.
   d. a few firms compete.
   e. it faces a vertical demand curve.

4. The demand curve faced by a perfectly competitive firm is
   a. horizontal.
   b. vertical.
   c. downward sloping.
   d. upward sloping.
   e. U-shaped.

5. For a perfectly competitive corn grower in Nebraska, the marginal revenue curve is
   a. downward sloping.
   b. the same as the demand curve.
   c. upward sloping.
   d. U-shaped.
   e. vertical at the profit maximizing quantity of production.

6. A perfectly competitive firm maximizes its profit by producing at the point where
   a. total revenue equals total cost.
   b. marginal revenue is equal to marginal cost.
   c. total revenue is equal to marginal revenue.
   d. total cost is at its minimum.
   e. total revenue is at its maximum.

■ **FIGURE 11.1**

Price and cost (dollars per shirt)

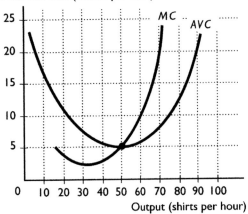

Output (shirts per hour)

7. Figure 11.1 shows cost curves for Wring Around the Collar, a perfectly competitive dry cleaner. If the price of dry cleaning a shirt is $20 per shirt, the firm will dry clear ____ shirts per hour.
   a. 0
   b. between 1 and 49
   c. 50
   d. 60
   e. 61 or more.

8. In Figure 11.1, if the price of dry cleaning a shirt is $10 per shirt, the firm will dry clear ____ shirts per hour.
   a. 0
   b. between 1 and 49
   c. 50
   d. 60
   e. 61 or more.

9. Based on Figure 11.1, the lowest price for which the company might remain open is
   a. $25 per shirt.
   b. $20 per shirt.
   c. $15 per shirt.
   d. $10 per shirt.
   e. $5 per shirt.

10. If the market price is lower than a perfectly competitive firm's average total cost, the firm will
    a. immediately shut down.
    b. continue to produce if the price exceeds the average fixed cost.
    c. continue to produce if the price exceeds the average variable cost.
    d. shut down if the price exceeds the average fixed cost.
    e. shut down if the price is less than the average fixed cost.

11. One part of a perfectly competitive trout farm's supply curve is its
    a. marginal cost curve below the shutdown point.
    b. entire marginal cost curve.
    c. marginal cost curve above the shutdown point.
    d. average variable cost curve above the shutdown point.
    e. marginal revenue curve above the demand curve.

Complete the graph

■ **FIGURE 11.2**

Price and cost (dollars per unit)

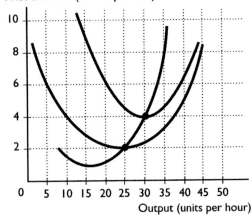

Output (units per hour)

1. Figure 11.2 shows a perfectly competitive firm's cost curves.
   a. Label the curves.
   b. If the market price is $8, what is the firm's equilibrium output and price?

c. If the market price is $4, what is the firm's equilibrium output and price?

d. What is the firm's shutdown price?

e. Darken the firm's supply curve.

Short answer and numeric questions

1. What are the conditions that define perfect competition?

2. What is a "price taker?" Why are perfectly competitive firms price takers?

3. What is the difference between a perfectly competitive firm's demand curve and the market demand curve?

4. Willy, a perfectly competitive wheat farmer, can sell 999 bushels of wheat for $3 per bushel or 1,000 bushels for $3 per bushel. What is Willy's marginal revenue and total revenue if he sells 1,000 bushels of wheat?

Quantity (hogs)	Total cost (dollars)	Total revenue (dollars)	Economic profit (dollars)
0	300	——	——
1	350	——	——
2	425	——	——
3	575	——	——
4	825	——	——
5	1,200	——	——

5. Peter owns Peter's Porkers, a small hog farm. The above table gives Peter's total cost schedule. Peter is in a perfectly competitive market and can sell each hog for $200.

a. Complete the table.

b. What is Peter's profit-maximizing number of hogs and what price will Peter set?

c. When Peter increases his production from 2 hogs to 3 hogs, what is the marginal cost? Is the third hog profitable for Peter?

d. When Peter increases his production from 3 hogs to 4 hogs, what is the marginal cost? Is the fourth hog profitable for Peter?

e. What is the marginal cost of the third hog?

6. When will a firm temporarily shut down?

CHECKPOINT 11.2

■ **Explain how output, price, and profit are determined in the short run.**

Quick Review

- *Economic profit* If the price exceeds the average total cost, the firm earns an economic profit.

- *Economic loss* If the price is less than the average total cost, the firm incurs an economic loss.

Additional Practice Problem 11.2

Quantity (roses per week)	Average total cost	Marginal cost
	(dollars per rose)	
100	2.00	1.50
200	1.50	1.50
300	1.67	2.50
400	2.00	5.00

1. Growing roses is a perfectly competitive industry. There are 100 rose growers and all have the same cost curves. The above table gives the costs of one of the growers, Rosita's Roses. The market demand schedule for roses is in the table to the right.

Price (dollars per rose)	Quantity (roses per week)
1.00	50,000
1.50	45,000
2.00	40,000
2.50	30,000
3.00	20,000

a. Plot the market supply curve and the market demand curve in the figure.

b. What is the equilibrium price of a rose?

c. How many roses does Rosita produce? What is her economic profit or loss?

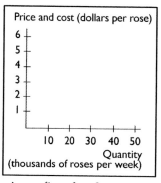

Price and cost (dollars per rose)

Quantity (thousands of roses per week)

Solution to Additional Practice Problem 11.2

1a. The market demand curve and market supply curve are plotted in the figure. The quantity supplied in the market at any price is the sum of the

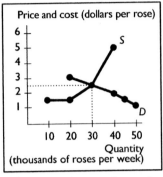

quantities supplied by each firm at that price. Because each firm is identical, the market quantity supplied is 100 times the quantity supplied by any one firm. The firm's supply curve is its marginal cost curve above the minimum average variable cost. For instance, when the price is $2.50 a rose, Rosita's marginal cost schedule shows she will supply 300 roses a week. So the quantity supplied in the market equals 100 × (300 roses a week), which is 30,000 roses a week.

1b. The figure shows that the equilibrium price of a rose is $2.50.

1c. In the short run, a firm can make an economic profit or incur an economic loss. A firm earns an economic profit when price exceeds average total cost and incurs an economic loss when price is less than average total cost. In the case at hand, Rosita produces 300 roses. Rosita earns an economic profit. Rosita's economic profit per rose equals the price of a rose minus the average total cost, which is $2.50 − $1.67 = $0.83. She produces 300 roses, a week so her total economic profit is (300 roses a week) × ($0.83) = $249 a week.

■ Self Test 11.2

Fill in the blanks

In a perfectly competitive industry, the quantity supplied in the market at any price is ____ (determined by the market demand curve; equal to the sum of the quantities supplied by all firms at that price). A firm earns an economic profit when price exceeds ____ (marginal revenue; average total cost). A firm ____ (can; cannot) incur an economic loss in the short run.

True or false

1. The market supply curve in the short run shows the quantity supplied at each price by a fixed number of firms.

2. Market supply in a perfectly competitive market is perfectly elastic at all prices.

3. A perfectly competitive firm earns an economic profit if price equals average total cost.

4. In a perfectly competitive industry, a firm's economic profit is equal to price minus marginal revenue multiplied by quantity.

5. A perfectly competitive firm has an economic loss if price is less than the marginal cost.

Multiple choice

1. If the market supply curve and market demand curve for a good intersect at 600,000 units and there are 10,000 identical firms in the market, then each firm is producing
   a. 600,000 units.
   b. 60,000,000,000 units.
   c. 60,000 units.
   d. 60 units.
   e. 10,000 units.

2. A perfectly competitive firm definitely earns an economic profit in the short run if price is
   a. equal to marginal cost.
   b. equal to average total cost.
   c. greater than average total cost.
   d. greater than marginal cost.
   e. greater than average variable cost.

3. If a perfectly competitive firm is maximizing its profit and earning an economic profit, which of the following is correct?
   i. price equals marginal revenue
   ii. marginal revenue equals marginal cost
   iii. price is greater than average total cost
   a. i only.
   b. i and ii only.
   c. ii and iii only.
   d. i and iii only.
   e. i, ii, and iii.

■ **FIGURE 11.3**
Price and cost (dollars per unit)

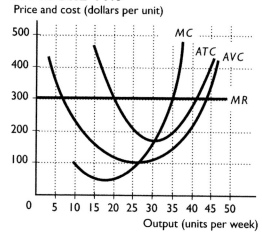

Output (units per week)

4. Figure 11.3 shows the marginal revenue and cost curves for a perfectly competitive firm. The firm
   a. is incurring an economic loss.
   b. will shut down and will incur an economic loss.
   c. will shut down and will earn zero economic profit.
   d. is earning zero economic profit.
   e. is earning an economic profit.

5. The market for watermelons in Alabama is perfectly competitive. A watermelon producer earning a normal profit could earn an economic profit if the
   a. average total cost of selling watermelons does not change.
   b. average total cost of selling watermelons increases.
   c. average total cost of selling watermelons decreases.
   d. marginal cost of selling watermelons does not change.
   e. marginal cost of selling watermelons does not change.

6. Juan's Software Service Company is in a perfectly competitive market. Juan has total fixed cost of $25,000, average variable cost for 1,000 service calls is $45, and marginal revenue is $75. Juan's makes 1,000 service calls a month. What is his economic profit?
   a. $5,000
   b. $25,000
   c. $45,000
   d. $75,000.
   e. $50,000

7. If a perfectly competitive firm finds that price is less than its *ATC*, then the firm
   a. will raise its price to increase its economic profit.
   b. will lower its price to increase its economic profit.
   c. is earning an economic profit.
   d. is incurring an economic loss.
   e. is earning zero economic profit.

8. A perfectly competitive video-rental firm in Phoenix incurs an economic loss if the average total cost of each video rental is
   a. greater than the marginal revenue of each rental.
   b. less than the marginal revenue of each rental.
   c. equal to the marginal revenue of each rental.
   d. equal to zero.
   e. less than the price of each video.

9. In the short run, a perfectly competitive firm
   a. must make an economic profit.
   b. must suffer an economic loss.
   c. must earn a normal profit.
   d. might make an economic profit, incur an economic loss, or make a normal profit.
   e. must earn an economic profit.

Complete the graph

■ **FIGURE 11.4**

Price and cost (dollars per lawn)

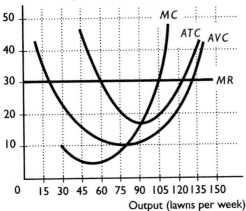

Output (lawns per week)

1. Moe's Mowers is a perfectly competitive lawn mowing company. Moe's costs and marginal revenue are illustrated in Figure 11.4.

    a. How many lawns does Moe mow?

    b. Is Moe earning an economic profit or incurring an economic loss? Darken the area that shows the economic profit or loss. What is the amount of economic profit or loss?

■ **FIGURE 11.5**

Price and cost (dollars per lawn)

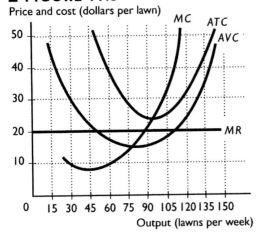

Output (lawns per week)

2. Larry's Lawns is (another) perfectly competitive lawn mowing company in another city. Larry's costs and marginal revenue are illustrated in Figure 11.5.

    a. How many lawns does Larry mow?

    b. Is Larry earning an economic profit or incurring an economic loss? Darken the area that shows the economic profit or loss. In the short run, will Larry remain open or shut down?

Short answer and numeric questions

1. In a perfectly competitive market, how is the market supply calculated?

2. If price is less than average total cost, is the firm earning an economic profit or incurring an economic loss?

CHECKPOINT 11.3

■ **Explain how output, price, and profit are determined in the long run and explain why perfect competition is efficient.**

Quick Review

• *Entry* Economic profit is an incentive for new firms to enter a market, but as they do so, the price falls and the economic profit of each existing firm decreases.

• *Exit* Economic loss is an incentive for firms to exit a market, but as they do so, the price rises and the economic loss of each remaining firm decreases.

Additional Practice Problem 11.3

Quantity (roses per week)	Average total cost (dollars)	Marginal cost (dollars)
100	2.00	1.50
200	1.50	1.50
300	1.67	2.50
400	2.00	5.00

1. Growing roses is a perfectly competitive industry. Initially there are 100 rose growers and all have the same cost curves. The above table gives the costs of one of the growers, Rosita's Roses. The table to the right has the market demand schedule for roses.

Price (dollars per rose)	Quantity (roses per week)
1.00	50,000
1.50	45,000
2.00	40,000
2.50	30,000
3.00	20,000

The equilibrium price for a rose initially is $2.50.

a. Plot Rosita's marginal cost curve and her marginal revenue curve in the figure to the right. Is Rosita earning an economic profit or is Rosita incurring an economic loss?

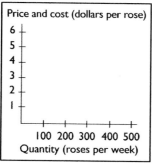

b. As time passes, what takes place in the market?

c. What will be the long-run price of a rose? What will be Rosita's profit in the long run? In the long run, how many growers will be in the market?

Solution to Additional Practice Problem 11.3

1a. The figure shows Rosita's marginal cost curve and marginal revenue curve. The figure shows that she is producing 300 roses a week. Rosita is earning an economic profit because the price of a rose, $2.50, exceeds her average total cost of producing 300 roses, $1.67.

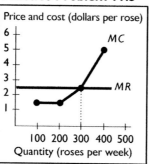

1b. A perfectly competitive firm earns a normal profit in the long run. A firm will not incur an economic loss in the long run because it will shut down. And a perfectly competitive firm cannot earn an economic profit in the long run because the presence of an economic profit attracts entry, which drives down the price and eliminates economic profit. Competitive firms cannot prevent entry into their market and so they cannot protect any economic profit.

In the case of the rose growers, rose growers are earning an economic profit, so more rose growers enter the market. The supply of roses increases and the market supply curve shifts rightward. The equilibrium price of a rose falls and the market equilibrium quantity increases.

1c. The long-run price of a rose will be $1.50 because that is the minimum average total cost. At that price, all rose growers, including Rosita, earn a normal profit. Indeed, the fact that they are earning only a normal profit is what removes the incentive for further firms to enter the industry. When the price of a rose is $1.50, the demand schedule shows that the quantity demanded is 45,000 roses. At a price of $1.50, each grower produces 200 roses. There will be 225 growers, each producing 200 roses.

■ Self Test 11.3

Fill in the blanks

In the long run, a perfectly competitive firm ____ (can; cannot) earn an economic profit, ____ (can; cannot) incur an economic loss, and ____ (can; cannot) earn a normal profit. In the long run, a perfectly competitive firm ____ (produces; does not produce) at minimum average total cost. Entry into an industry shifts the market ____ (demand; supply) curve ____ (rightward; leftward). Firms exit an industry when they are ____ (making a normal profit; incurring an economic loss). A technological change results in perfectly competitive firms ____ (temporarily; permanently) earning an economic profit.

True or false

1. When price equals average total cost, the firm earns a normal profit.

2. Entry into a perfectly competitive market lowers the price.

3. In the long run, firms respond to an economic loss by exiting a perfectly competitive market.

4. New technology shifts a firm's cost curves upward and the market supply curve leftward.

5. Perfect competition is efficient because it results in the efficient quantity being produced.

Multiple choice

1. In the long run, new firms enter a perfectly competitive market when
   a. normal profits are greater than zero.
   b. economic profits are equal to zero.
   c. normal profits are equal to zero.
   d. economic profits are greater than zero.
   e. the existing firms are weak because they are incurring economic losses.

2. In a perfectly competitive market, if firms are earning an economic profit, the economic profit
   a. attracts entry by more firms, which lowers the price.
   b. can be earned both in the short run and the long run.
   c. is less than the normal profit.
   d. leads to a decrease in market demand.
   e. generally leads to firms exiting as they seek higher profit in other markets.

3. If firms in a perfectly competitive market are earning an economic profit, then
   a. the market is in its long-run equilibrium.
   b. new firms enter the market and the equilibrium profit of the initial firms decreases.
   c. new firms enter the market and the equilibrium profit of the initial firms increases.
   d. firms exit the market and the equilibrium profit of the remaining firms decreases.
   e. firms exit the market and the equilibrium profit of the remaining firms increases.

4. Firms exit a competitive market when they incur an economic loss. In the long run, this exit means that the economic losses of the surviving firms
   a. increase.
   b. decrease until they equal zero.
   c. decrease until economic profits are earned.
   d. do not change.
   e. might change but more information is needed about what happens to the price of the good as the firms exit.

5. If firms in a perfectly competitive market have economic losses, then as time passes firms ____ and the market ____.
   a. enter; demand curve shifts leftward
   b. enter; supply curve shifts rightward
   c. exit; demand curve shifts leftward
   d. exit; supply curve shifts rightward
   e. exit; supply curve shifts leftward

6. As a result of firms leaving the perfectly competitive frozen yogurt market in the 1990s, the market
   a. supply curve shifted leftward.
   b. supply curve did not change.
   c. demand curve shifted rightward.
   d. supply curve shifted rightward.
   e. demand curve shifted rightward.

7. In the long run, a firm in a perfectly competitive market will
   a. earn zero economic profit, that is, it will earn a normal profit.
   b. earn zero normal profit but it will earn an economic profit.
   c. remove all competitors and become a monopolistically competitive firm.
   d. incur an economic normal loss but not earn a positive economic profit.
   e. remove all competitors and become a monopoly.

8. Technological change brings a ____ to firms that adopt the new technology.
   a. permanent economic profit
   b. temporary economic profit
   c. permanent economic loss
   d. temporary economic loss
   e. temporary normal profit

Complete the graph

■ FIGURE 11.6

Price and cost (dollars per unit)

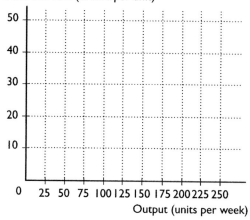

1. In Figure 11.6, suppose that the price of the good is $20. Show the long-run equilibrium for a perfectly competitive firm that produces 150 units per week.

■ FIGURE 11.7

Price and cost (dollars per unit)

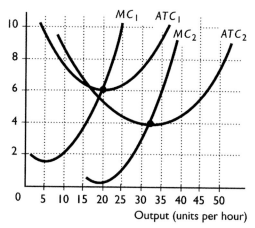

2. Figure 11.7 shows cost curves for two firms in an industry undergoing technological change. Firm 1 uses the old technology and has an average total cost curve ATC_1 and marginal cost curve MC_1. Firm 2 uses the new technology and has an average total cost curve ATC_2 and marginal cost curve MC_2. Initially the price of the product was $6.
   a. At the price of $6, do firm 1 and firm 2 earn an economic profit, normal profit, or incur economic loss?
   b. As more firms adopt the new technology, what happens to market supply and price? Do firms 1 and 2 earn an economic profit, normal profit, or incur an economic loss?
   c. In the long run, what will be the new price? Will firm 1 earn an economic profit, a normal profit, or incur an economic loss? Will firm 2 earn an economic profit, a normal profit, or incur an economic loss?

Short answer and numeric questions

1. Why are perfectly competitive firms unable to earn an economic profit in the long run? Why won't they incur an economic loss in the long run?

2. Is perfect competition efficient?

3. The Eye on Your Life discusses how competition benefits you by leading to the production of the vast array of goods and services you consume. Competition also benefits you by affecting the prices you pay for goods and services. The market for home delivered pizza is extremely competitive. How does this competition affect the price you pay for home delivered pizza?

SELF TEST ANSWERS

■ CHECKPOINT 11.1

Fill in the blanks

The conditions that define perfect competition arise when the market demand for the product is <u>large</u> relative to the output of a single producer. A perfectly competitive firm faces a perfectly <u>elastic</u> demand. The change in total revenue that results from a one-unit increase in the quantity sold is the marginal <u>revenue</u>. When a perfectly competitive firm maximizes profit, marginal revenue equals <u>marginal</u> cost. When a firm shuts down, it incurs a loss equal to its total <u>fixed</u> cost. A firm will shut down if price is less than minimum <u>average variable</u> cost. A perfectly competitive firm's supply curve is its marginal <u>cost</u> curve above the minimum <u>average variable</u> cost.

True or false

1. True; page 276
2. True; page 277
3. False; page 280
4. False; page 281
5. False; pages 282-283

Multiple choice

1. c; page 276
2. e; page 276
3. a; page 277
4. a; page 278
5. b; page 278
6. b; page 280
7. e; page 280
8. d; page 280
9. e; pages 281-282
10. c; pages 281-282
11. c; pages 282-283

Complete the graph

1. a. Figure 11.8 labels the curves; page 282.
   b. Output is 35 units and the price is $8; page 280.
   c. Output is 30 units and the price is $4; page 280.

■ FIGURE 11.8

Price and cost (dollars per unit)

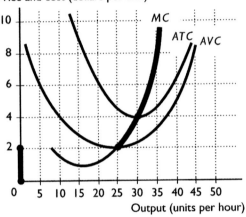

d. The shutdown price is $2; pages 281-282.
e. The firm's supply curve is darkened in Figure 11.8; page 283.

Short answer and numeric questions

1. Perfect competition exists when many firms sell an identical product to many buyers; there are no restrictions on entry into (or exit from) the market; established firms have no advantage over new firms; and sellers and buyers are well informed about prices; page 276.

2. A price taker is a firm that cannot influence the price of the good or service it produces. Perfectly competitive firms are price takers because there are many competing firms selling an identical product. Any individual firm is such a small part of the market that its actions cannot affect the price; page 277.

3. A perfectly competitive firm's demand is perfectly elastic because all sellers produce goods that are perfect substitutes. So the firm's demand curve is horizontal. The market demand curve is downward sloping; page 278.

4. Willy's marginal revenue equals the price of a bushel of wheat, which is $3. His total revenue equals price multiplied by quantity, which is $3,000; page 279.

Quantity (hogs)	Total cost (dollars)	Total revenue (dollars)	Economic profit (dollars)
0	300	0	−300
1	350	200	−150
2	425	400	−25
3	575	600	25
4	825	800	−25
5	1,200	1,000	−200

5. a. The completed table is above; page 279.

b. The profit-maximizing number of hogs is 3. Peter charges $200 a hog; page 279.

c. The marginal cost is the change in total cost that results from producing the third hog. So marginal cost is $150. This is a profitable hog because the marginal revenue from the hog exceeds its marginal cost; page 280.

d. The marginal cost is $250. This hog is not profitable; page 280.

e. The marginal cost of the third hog is $200, which is the average of the marginal cost of increasing production from 2 to 3 hogs and of increasing production from 3 to 4 hogs. The marginal cost of the third hog equals the marginal revenue so 3 hogs is the profit-maximizing output; page 280.

6. If a firm shuts down, it incurs an economic loss equal to total fixed cost. If the firm produces some output, it incurs an economic loss equal to total fixed cost plus total variable cost minus total revenue. If total revenue exceeds total variable cost, the firm's economic loss is less than total fixed cost. It pays the firm to produce. But if total revenue is less than total variable cost, the firm's economic loss exceeds total fixed cost. The firm shuts down; pages 281-282.

■ CHECKPOINT 11.2

Fill in the blanks

In a perfectly competitive industry, the market supply at any price is <u>equal to the sum of the quantities supplied by all firms at that price</u>. A perfectly competitive firm earns an economic profit if the price exceeds <u>average total cost</u>. A firm <u>can</u> incur an economic loss in the short run.

True or false

1. True; page 285
2. False; page 285
3. False; page 286
4. False; page 287
5. False; page 288

Multiple choice

1. d; page 285
2. c; page 287
3. e; page 287
4. e; page 287
5. c; page 287
6. a; page 287
7. d; page 288
8. a; page 288
9. d; pages 286-288

Complete the graph

■ **FIGURE 11.9**

Price and cost (dollars per lawn)

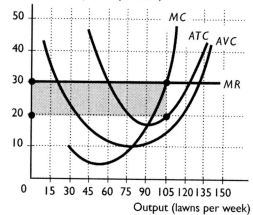

1. a. Moe mows 105 lawns per week because that is the quantity at which marginal revenue equals marginal cost; page 280.

b. Moe is earning an economic profit. Figure 11.9 illustrates the economic profit. The economic profit per lawn equals price minus average total cost, which is $30 − $20 = $10 per lawn. The quantity is 105 lawns, so the total economic profit equals ($10 per lawn) × (105 lawns), which is $1,050 a week; page 287.

■ FIGURE 11.10

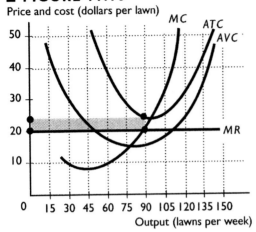

Price and cost (dollars per lawn)

2. a. Larry mows 90 lawns per day because that is the quantity at which marginal revenue equals marginal cost; page 280.

   b. Larry has an economic loss. Figure 11.10 illustrates the economic loss as the darkened rectangle. Even though he has an economic loss, Larry remains open in the short run because the price exceeds his average variable cost; page 288.

Short answer and numeric questions

1. The market supply in the short run is the quantity supplied at each price by a fixed number of firms. The quantity supplied at a given price is the sum of the quantities supplied by all firms at that price. For example, if there are 100 firms in the geranium market and each produces 50 geraniums when the price is $3, then the quantity supplied in the market at $3 is 5,000 geraniums; page 285.

2. The firm is suffering an economic loss. If the price is less than average total cost, the firm is incurring an economic loss on each unit produced and has an overall economic loss; page 288.

■ CHECKPOINT 11.3

Fill in the blanks

In the long run, a perfectly competitive firm <u>cannot</u> earn an economic profit, <u>cannot</u> incur an economic loss, and <u>can</u> earn a normal profit. In the long run, a perfectly competitive firm <u>produces</u> at minimum average total cost. Entry into an industry shifts the market <u>supply</u> curve <u>rightward</u>. Firms exit an industry when they are <u>incurring an economic loss</u>. A technological change results in perfectly competitive firms <u>temporarily</u> earning an economic profit.

True or false

1. True; page 290
2. True; pages 291-292
3. True; pages 291-292
4. False; pages 294-295
5. True; page 296

Multiple choice

1. d; page 291
2. a; pages 291-292
3. b; pages 291-292
4. b; page 293
5. e; pages 292-293
6. a; page 292
7. a; pages 291-293
8. b; pages 294-295

Complete the graph

1. Figure 11.11 (on the next page) shows a perfectly competitive firm in long-run equilibrium. The marginal revenue curve is horizontal at the price of $20. The firm produces 150 units because that is the quantity at which marginal revenue equals marginal cost. The firm has zero economic profit because the price, $20 per unit, equals the average total cost, also $20 per unit; page 290.

■ **FIGURE 11.11**

Price and cost (dollars per unit)

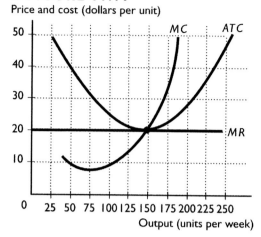

Output (units per week)

■ **FIGURE 11.12**

Price and cost (dollars per unit)

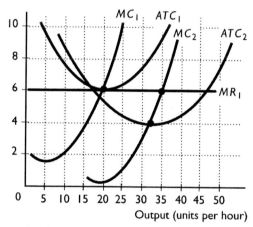

Output (units per hour)

2. a. At the price of $6, the marginal revenue curve is MR_1 in Figure 11.12. Firm 1 produces 20 units and earns a normal profit because the $6 price equals average total cost. Firm 2 produces 35 units and earns an economic profit because the $6 price exceeds average total cost; pages 294-295.

   b. Market supply increases and the price falls. Firm 1 now incurs an economic loss

and Firm 2 earns a smaller economic profit; pages 294-295.

   c. In the long run, the new price will $4 because that is the minimum of the new average total cost. Firm 1 will either have adopted the new technology and be earning a normal profit or will have exited the industry. Firm 2 will earn a normal profit; pages 294-295.

Short answer and numeric questions

1. Perfectly competitive firms cannot earn an economic profit in the long run because the existence of an economic profit invites entry by new firms. As these new firms enter, the market supply increases, driving down the price and eventually eliminating the economic profit. No firm will incur an economic loss in the long run because it will close; pages 291-293.

2. Perfect competition is efficient. In a perfectly competitive market, equilibrium occurs at the intersection of the supply and demand curves. Key, however, the facts that the supply curve also is the marginal cost curve and the demand curve also is the marginal benefit curve. So the equilibrium quantity also is the quantity at which the marginal cost equals the marginal benefit, which is the efficient quantity; pages 296-297.

3. Competition in the market for home delivered pizza keeps the price of home delivered pizza low. The producers of pizza would like to charge the highest price they can. However their price is limited by competition and it is this competition that protects you by keeping the price of home delivered pizza low.

Chapter 12

Monopoly

In Chapter 12 we study how a monopoly chooses its price and quantity, discuss whether a monopoly is efficient or fair, and investigate how monopolies can be regulated.

1 Explain how monopoly arises and distinguish between single-price monopoly and price-discriminating monopoly.

A monopoly is a market with a single supplier of a good or service that has no close substitutes and in which natural, ownership, or legal barriers to entry prevent competition. A single-price monopoly is a monopoly that sells each unit of its output for the same price to all its customers. A price-discriminating monopoly is a monopoly that is able to sell different units of a good or service for different prices.

2 Explain how a single-price monopoly determines its output and price.

The demand curve for a monopoly is the downward sloping market demand curve. For a single-price monopoly, marginal revenue is less than price, so the marginal revenue curve lies below the demand curve. A monopoly maximizes profit by producing the quantity at which marginal revenue equals marginal cost and finding the highest price at which it can sell this output on the demand curve.

3 Compare the performance of a single-price monopoly with that of perfect competition.

Compared to perfect competition, a single-price monopoly produces a smaller output and charges a higher price. A monopoly is inefficient because it creates a deadweight loss. A monopoly redistributes consumer surplus so that the producer gains and the consumers lose. Rent seeking is the act of obtaining special treatment by the government to create an economic profit or divert consumer surplus or producer surplus away from others. Rent seeking restricts competition and can create a monopoly.

4 Explain how price discrimination increases profit.

To be able to price discriminate, a firm must be able to identify and separate different types of buyers and sell a product that cannot be resold. Price discrimination converts consumer surplus into economic profit so price discrimination increases the firm's profit. Perfect price discrimination leaves no consumer surplus but is efficient.

5 Explain why natural monopoly is regulated and the effects of regulation.

Regulation generally sets the prices a regulated firm can charge. The social interest theory of regulation is that regulation seeks an efficient use of resources; the capture theory is that regulation helps producers maximize economic profit. Natural monopolies are usually regulated. A marginal cost pricing rule sets price equal to marginal cost and achieves an efficient level of output but the regulated firm incurs an economic loss. An average cost pricing rule sets price equal to average total cost. The firm earns a normal profit but there is a deadweight loss. Rate of return regulation sets the price so that the firm can earn a target rate of return on its capital. Price cap regulation specifies the highest price the firm can set.

CHECKPOINT 12.1

■ **Explain how monopoly arises and distinguish between single-price monopoly and price-discriminating monopoly.**

- *Barrier to entry* Any constraint that protects a firm from competitors.

Additional Practice Problem 12.1

1. What is the source of the monopoly for each of the following situations? What sort of barrier to entry protects these producers?
   a. The U.S. Postal Service has a monopoly on first class mail delivery.
   b. DeBeer's, while not truly a monopoly, nonetheless controls about 80 percent of the world's diamond sales.
   c. Tampa Electric is the only electric utility company supplying power to Tampa, Florida.

Solution to Additional Practice Problem 12.1

1a. The U.S. Postal Service derives its monopoly status by a government franchise to deliver first class mail. So the U.S. Postal Service is protected by a legal barrier to entry. Though it retains its franchise on first class mail delivery, it faces competition from the overnight services provided by FedEx, United Parcel Service, and others.

1b. DeBeers gained its monopoly power in diamond sales by buying up supplies of diamonds from sources throughout the world. So DeBeers is protected by an ownership barrier to entry.

1c. Tampa Electric has been granted a public franchise to be the only distributor of electricity in Tampa. Although Tampa Electric might be a natural monopoly, the public franchise, a legal barrier to entry, is perhaps the most immediate source of monopoly.

■ Self Test 12.1

Fill in the blanks

One of the requirements for monopoly is that there ____ (are; are no) close substitutes for the good. A ____ (legal; natural) monopoly exists when one firm can meet the entire market demand at a lower average total cost than two or more firms could. A monopoly that is able to sell different units of a good or service for different prices is a ____ (legal-price; natural-price; price-discriminating) monopoly.

True or false

1. A legal barrier creates a natural monopoly.
2. A firm experiences economies of scale along a downward-sloping long-run average total cost curve.
3. A monopoly always charges all customers the same price.

Multiple choice

1. A monopoly market has
   a. a few firms.
   b. a single firm.
   c. two dominating firms in the market.
   d. only two firms in it.
   e. some unspecified number of firms in it.

2. Two of the three types of barriers to entry that can protect a firm from competition are
   a. legal and illegal.
   b. natural and legal.
   c. natural and illegal.
   d. natural and rent seeking.
   e. ownership and rent seeking.

3. A natural monopoly is one that arises from
   a. patent law.
   b. copyright law.
   c. a firm buying up all of a natural resource.
   d. economies of scale.
   e. ownership of a natural resource.

4. A legal barrier is created when a firm
   a. has economies of scale, which allow it to produce at a lower cost than two or more firms.
   b. is granted a public franchise, government license, patent, or copyright.
   c. produces a unique product or service.
   d. produces a standardized product or service.
   e. has an ownership barrier to entry.

5. Pizza producers charge one price for a single pizza and almost give away a second one. This is an example of
   a. monopoly.
   b. a barrier to entry.
   c. behavior that is not profit-maximizing.
   d. price discrimination.
   e. rent seeking.

Short answer and numeric questions

1. What conditions define monopoly?
2. What are the two types of barriers to entry?
3. What are the two pricing strategies a monopoly can use? Why don't perfectly competitive firms have these same strategies?

CHECKPOINT 12.2

■ **Explain how a single-price monopoly determines its output and price.**

Quick Review

- *Marginal revenue* The change in total revenue resulting from a one-unit increase in the quantity sold.
- *Maximize profit* A single-price monopoly maximizes its profit by producing where $MR = MC$ and then using the demand curve to determine the price for this quantity of output.

Additional Practice Problems 12.2

Quantity (pizzas per hour)	Total cost (dollars per pizza)	Average total cost (dollars per pizza)	Marginal cost (dollars per pizza)
0	1.00		
			____
1	6.00	____	
			____
2	13.00	____	
			____
3	22.00	____	
			____
4	33.00	____	

1. In a small town, Leonardo's Pizza is the sole restaurant. The table above gives Leonardo's total cost schedule. Complete the table.

Quantity demanded (pizzas per hour)	Price (dollars per pizza)	Marginal revenue (dollars per pizza)
0	16.00	
		____
1	14.00	
		____
2	12.00	
		____
3	10.00	
		____
4	8.00	

2. The table above gives the demand schedule for Leonardo's pizzas. Complete the table.
3. In a figure, plot Leonardo's demand curve, average total cost curve, marginal cost curve, and marginal revenue curve.
   a. What is Leonardo's equilibrium quantity and price?
   b. What is Leonardo's economic profit or loss? In the figure show the economic profit or loss.

Solutions to Additional Practice Problems 12.2

Quantity (pizzas per hour)	Total cost (dollars per pizza)	Average total cost (dollars per pizza)	Marginal cost (dollars per pizza)
0	1.00		
			5.00
1	6.00	6.00	
			7.00
2	13.00	6.50	
			9.00
3	22.00	7.33	
			11.00
4	33.00	8.25	

1. The completed table is above.

Quantity demanded (pizzas per hour)	Price (dollars per pizza)	Marginal revenue (dollars per pizza)
0	16.00	
		14.00
1	14.00	
		10.00
2	12.00	
		6.00
3	10.00	
		2.00
4	8.00	

2. The completed table is above.

3. The figure shows Leonardo's demand curve, average total cost curve, marginal cost curve, and marginal revenue curve.

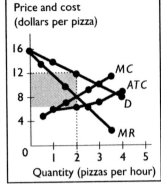

Price and cost (dollars per pizza)

Quantity (pizzas per hour)

3a. Both a monopoly and a perfectly competitive firm maximize their profit by producing the quantity at which marginal revenue equals marginal cost. So Leonardo's maximizes its profit by producing 2 pizzas per hour. The price, from the demand curve, is $12 per pizza.

3b. Leonardo's sells each pizza for $12.00. The average total cost for 2 pizzas is $6.50. So for each pizza Leonardo's earns an economic profit of $5.50 for a total economic profit of $5.50 per pizza × 2 pizzas, or $11.00. This economic profit is equal to the area of the darkened rectangle in the figure.

■ Self Test 12.2

Fill in the blanks

For each level of output, marginal revenue for a single-price monopoly is _____ (greater than; equal to; less than) price. When demand is inelastic, marginal revenue is _____ (positive; negative). A single-price monopoly maximizes profit by producing the quantity at which marginal revenue _____ (is greater than; equals; is less than) marginal cost and then finds the highest price for which it can sell that output by using the _____ (demand; marginal revenue; average total cost) curve.

True or false

1. For a single-price monopoly, marginal revenue exceeds price.

2. Marginal revenue is always positive for a monopoly.

3. A single-price monopoly maximizes profit by producing the quantity at which marginal revenue equals marginal cost.

Multiple choice

1. For a single-price monopoly, price is
   a. greater than
   b. one half of marginal revenue
   c. equal to
   d. unrelated to marginal revenue.
   e. always less than average total cost when the firm maximizes its profit.

2. A single-price monopoly can sell 1 unit for $9.00. To sell 2 units, the price must be $8.50 per unit. The marginal revenue from selling the second unit is
   a. $17.50.
   b. $17.00.
   c. $8.50.
   d. $8.00.
   e. $9.00.

3. When demand is elastic, marginal revenue is
   a. positive.
   b. negative.
   c. zero.
   d. increasing as output increases.
   e. undefined.

4. To maximize profit, a single-price monopoly produces the quantity at which
   a. the difference between marginal revenue and marginal cost is as large as possible.
   b. marginal revenue is equal to marginal cost.
   c. average total cost is at its minimum.
   d. the marginal cost curve intersects the demand curve.
   e. the marginal revenue curve intersects the horizontal axis.

5. Once a monopoly has determined how much it produces, it will charge a price that
   a. is determined by the intersection of the marginal revenue and marginal cost curves.
   b. minimizes marginal cost.
   c. is determined by its demand curve.
   d. is independent of the amount produced.
   e. is equal to its average total cost.

Complete the graph

Quantity (hamburgers per hour)	Price (dollars)	Marginal revenue (dollars)
1	8.00	
2	7.00	___
3	6.00	___
4	5.00	___
5	4.00	___

1. The table above gives the demand schedule for Bud's Burgers, a monopoly seller of hamburgers in a small town. Complete the table by calculating the marginal revenue.

■ FIGURE 12.1
Price and marginal revenue (dollars per hamburger)

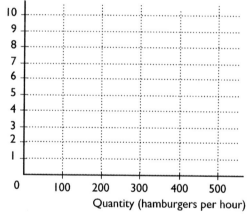

a. In Figure 12.1 draw the demand curve and marginal revenue curve.

b. Suppose the marginal cost is $3 no matter how many hamburgers Bud's produces. Draw the marginal cost curve in the figure. To maximize his profit, how many burgers will Bud grill in an hour and what will be their price?

■ FIGURE 12.2
Price and cost (dollars per unit)

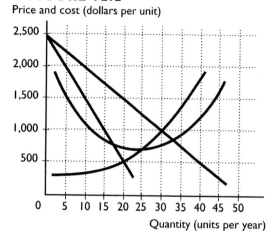

2. Figure 12.2 shows a monopoly's cost curves and demand and marginal revenue curves. Label the curves. Identify the profit-maximizing quantity price. Is the monopoly earning an economic profit or incurring an economic loss? Darken the area that shows the economic profit or economic loss.

Short answer and numeric questions

1. What is the relationship between the elasticity of demand and marginal revenue?

2. Both perfectly competitive and monopoly firms maximize their profit by producing where $MR = MC$. Why do both use the same rule?

3. Why can a monopoly earn an economic profit in the long run?

CHECKPOINT 12.3

■ Compare the performance of a single-price monopoly with that of perfect competition.

Quick Review

- *Monopoly and competition compared* Compared to perfect competition, a single-price monopoly produces a smaller output and charges a higher price.

Additional Practice Problems 12.3

1. In River Bend, Mississippi, suppose that the owners of the Acme cab company have convinced the city government to grant it a public franchise so it is the only cab company in town. Prior to this, the cab market in River Bend was perfectly competitive. The figure shows the market demand and marginal revenue curves for cab rides as well as the marginal cost curve.

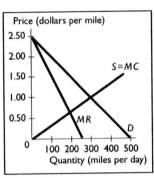

a. Before the government granted Acme its monopoly, how many miles of taxi rides were driven and what was the price?

b. As a monopoly, how many miles of taxi rides will Acme drive? What is the price Acme sets?

c. What is the efficient number of miles?

d. On the graph, show the deadweight loss that results from Acme's monopoly.

2. Suppose that Acme is put up for sale. Looking at the entire future, say Acme's total economic profit is $2 million. If the bidding for Acme is a competitive process, what do you expect will be the price for which the company is sold? What result are you illustrating?

Solutions to Additional Practice Problems 12.3

1a. Before the monopoly was granted, the equilibrium number of miles and price were determined by the demand and supply curves. As the figure shows, the equilibrium number of miles was 300 miles per day and the price was $1.00 per mile.

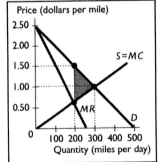

1b. To maximize its profit, the figure shows that Acme drives 200 miles per day because that is the quantity at which marginal revenue equals marginal cost. The price is set from the demand curve and is $1.50 per mile.

1c. The efficient quantity is the quantity at which marginal benefit equals marginal cost. The demand curve is the marginal benefit curve, so the figure shows that the efficient quantity is 300 miles a day.

1d. Single-price monopolies create a deadweight loss because a monopoly produces where $MR = MC$ but efficiency requires production where $MB = MC$. The figure illustrates the deadweight loss as the darkened triangle.

2. Bidders are willing to pay up to $2 million for Acme because if they can buy it for any price less than $2 million, they receive an economic profit. Because the bidding is competitive, the price of Acme will be bid up to $2 million, so that the winning bidder earns a normal profit. This result demonstrates rent-seeking equilibrium in which the rent-seeking costs exhaust the economic profit.

■ Self Test 12.3

Fill in the blanks

Compared to perfect competition, a single-price monopoly produces a _____ (larger; smaller) output and charges a _____ (higher; lower) price. A single-price monopoly _____ (creates; does not create) a deadweight loss. The act of obtaining special treatment by the government to create an economic profit is called _____ (government surplus; rent seeking). Rent seeking _____ (decreases; increases) the amount of deadweight loss.

True or false

1. A monopoly charges a higher price than a perfectly competitive industry would charge.

2. A monopoly redistributes consumer surplus so that the consumers gain and the producer loses.

3. The buyer of a monopoly always makes an economic profit.

Multiple choice

1. If a perfectly competitive industry is taken over by a single firm that operates as a single-price monopoly, the price will ____ and the quantity will ____.
   a. fall; decrease
   b. fall; increase
   c. rise; decrease
   d. rise; increase
   e. not change; decrease

■ **FIGURE 12.3**

Price and costs (dollars per gallon)

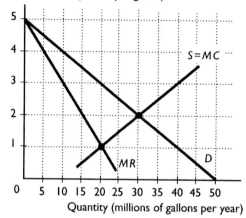

Quantity (millions of gallons per year)

2. Figure 12.3 shows the market for gasoline in a town. If the market is perfectly competitive, the price is ____ per gallon and if the market is taken over by a firm that operates as a single-price monopoly, the price is ____.
   a. $1; $2
   b. $1; $3
   c. $1; $1
   d. $2; $1
   e. $2; $3

3. Figure 12.3 shows the market for gasoline in a town. If the market is perfectly competitive, the quantity is ____ million gallons a year and if the market is taken over by a firm that operates as a single-price monopoly, the quantity is ____ million gallons a year.
   a. 50; 20
   b. 50; 30
   c. 30; 20
   d. 50; 10
   e. 20; 30

4. Comparing single-price monopoly to perfect competition, monopoly
   a. increases the amount of consumer surplus.
   b. has the same amount of consumer surplus.
   c. has no consumer surplus.
   d. decreases the amount of consumer surplus.
   e. decreases the amount of economic profit.

5. Is a single-price monopoly efficient?
   a. Yes, because it creates a deadweight loss.
   b. No, because it creates a deadweight loss.
   c. Yes, because consumers gain and producers lose some of their surpluses.
   d. Yes, because consumers lose and producers gain some of their surpluses.
   e. Yes, because it produces the quantity at which $MR=MC$.

6. Monopolies
   a. are always fair but are not efficient.
   b. might or might not be fair and are always efficient.
   c. might or might not be fair and are generally inefficient.
   d. are always fair and are always efficient.
   e. are never fair and are always efficient.

7. In equilibrium, rent seeking eliminates the
   a. deadweight loss.
   b. economic profit.
   c. consumer surplus.
   d. demand for the product.
   e. opportunity to price discriminate.

Complete the graph

■ **FIGURE 12.4**

Price and costs (dollars per ostrich)

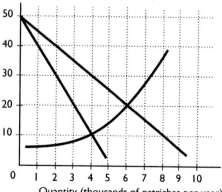

Quantity (thousands of ostriches per year)

1. Figure 12.4 shows the market for ostrich

farming, an industry that is initially perfectly competitive. Then one farmer buys all the other farms and operates as a single-price monopoly. In the figure, label the curves. What was the competitive price and quantity? What is the monopoly price and quantity? Darken the deadweight loss area.

Short answer and numeric questions

1. How does the quantity produced and the price set by a single-price monopoly compare to those in a perfectly competitive market?

2. What happens to consumer surplus with a single-price monopoly?

3. What is rent seeking? How does rent seeking affect society?

CHECKPOINT 12.4

■ Explain how price discrimination increases profit.

Quick Review

- *Price discrimination* Price discrimination is selling a good at a number of different prices.

- *Consumer surplus* The consumer surplus of a good is its marginal benefit, which equals the maximum price the consumer is willing to pay, minus the price paid for it summed over the quantity consumed.

Additional Practice Problems 12.4

1. Frequently the price of the first scoop of ice cream in a cone is less than the price of the second scoop. Why is this the case?

2. Why is the price to attend a movie less on a weekday afternoon than on a weekend evening?

3. How does price discrimination affect the amount of consumer surplus? The amount of the firm's economic profit?

Solutions to Additional Practice Problems 12.4

1. The ice cream store is price discriminating among units of the good by charging different prices for different scoops of ice cream. The store knows that consumers' marginal benefits from ice cream decrease, so that the consumer is willing to pay less for the second scoop than for the first scoop. By charging less for the second scoop, the store will sell more scoops and increase its profit.

2. When the price to attend a movie is less on a weekday afternoon than on a weekend evening, the movie theater is practicing price discrimination among two groups of buyers. Each group has a different average willingness to pay to see a movie. By having two different prices, the movie theater maximizes profit by converting consumer surplus into economic profit.

3. Price discrimination decreases consumer surplus because it allows the business to set a price that is closer to the maximum the consumer is willing to pay. Price discrimination increases the firm's profit, which is why firms price discriminate.

■ Self Test 12.4

Fill in the blanks

It is _____ (sometimes; never) possible for a monopoly to charge different customers different prices. The key idea behind price discrimination is to convert _____ (consumer surplus; producer surplus) into economic profit. Price discrimination results in consumers with a higher willingness paying a _____ (higher; lower) price than consumers with a lower willingness to pay. Perfect price discrimination results in _____ (the maximum; zero) consumer surplus and _____ (creates; does not create) a deadweight loss.

True or false

1. Price discrimination lowers a firm's profit.

2. Price discrimination converts producer surplus into consumer surplus.

3. With perfect price discrimination, the firm produces the efficient quantity of output and has a larger profit than it would if it did not price discriminate.

Multiple choice

1. Which of the following must a firm be able to do to successfully price discriminate?
   i. divide buyers into different groups according to their willingness to pay
   ii. prevent resale of the good or service
   iii. identify into which group (high willingness to pay or low willingness to pay) a buyer falls
   a. ii only.
   b. i and ii.
   c. i and iii.
   d. iii only.
   e. i, ii, and iii.

2. Which of the following is (are) price discrimination?
   i. charging different prices based on differences in production cost
   ii. charging business flyers a higher airfare than tourists
   iii. charging more for the first pizza than the second
   a. i only.
   b. ii only.
   c. ii and iii.
   d. i and iii.
   e. i, ii, and iii.

3. When a monopoly price discriminates, it
   a. increases the amount of consumer surplus.
   b. decreases its economic profit.
   c. converts consumer surplus into economic profit.
   d. converts economic profit into consumer surplus.
   e. has no effect on the deadweight loss.

4. If a monopoly is able to perfectly price discriminate, then consumer surplus is
   a. equal to zero.
   b. maximized.
   c. unchanged from what it is with a single-price monopoly.
   d. unchanged from what it is in a perfectly competitive industry.
   e. not zero but is less than with a single-price monopoly.

5. With perfect price discrimination, the quantity of output produced by the monopoly is _____ the quantity produced by a perfectly competitive industry.
   a. greater than but not equal to
   b. less than
   c. equal to but not greater than
   d. not comparable to
   e. either greater than or equal to

Complete the graph

■ FIGURE 12.5

Price and cost (dollars per article of clothing)

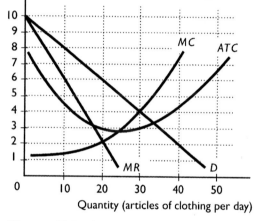

1. Figure 12.5 shows the cost and demand curves for a dry-cleaner that has a monopoly in a small town.
   a. In the figure, lightly darken the area of the economic profit for a single-price monopoly. What is the amount of economic profit this firm earns?
   b. Suppose the firm can price discriminate and set one price for the first 10 articles of clothing and another price for the second 10 articles of clothing. What prices would it set? Darken the additional economic profit the firm earns. What is the amount of the firms economic profit now?
   c. Suppose the firm is able to perfectly price discriminate. More heavily darken the additional economic profit the firm now earns. What is the amount of the firm's economic profit now?

Short answer and numeric questions

1. Explain the effect of price discrimination on consumer surplus and economic profit.

2. When does a price discriminating monopoly produce the efficient quantity of output?

CHECKPOINT 12.5

■ **Explain why natural monopoly is regulated and the effects of regulation.**

- *Marginal cost pricing rule* A price rule for a natural monopoly that sets price equal to marginal cost.
- *Average cost pricing rule* A price rule for a natural monopoly that sets price equal to average cost.

Additional Practice Problems 12.5

1. The figure shows the demand and cost curves for the local water distributing company. The company is a natural monopoly.

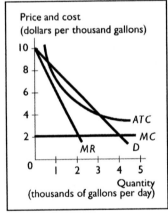

a. If the company is unregulated, what price does it charge for water and how much is distributed? Does the firm earn an economic profit, a normal profit, or an economic loss?

b. If the company is regulated using an average cost pricing rule, what price does it charge for water and how much is distributed? Does the firm earn an economic profit, a normal profit, or an economic loss?

c. If the company is regulated using a marginal cost pricing rule, what price does it charge for water and how much is dis-

tributed? Does the firm earn an economic profit, a normal profit, or an economic loss?

2. The Airmail Act of 1934 awarded airline routes on the basis of competitive bidding. The airlines bid for routes (the bids were the fares the airline would charge) and the low bidder won. The Interstate Commerce Commission regulated the fares. Frequently, after having won a route, an airline was allowed to raise its fare to a profitable level.

The Civil Aeronautics Act was passed in 1938 and served to regulate airlines for the next four decades. There was complete control over entry and exit, as well as fare and route structure. Over this period of time, virtually no new airlines were allowed to enter the market. For two decades after World War II, utilization continued to decline until less than half of seating capacity was being utilized.

In 1978, the airlines opposed deregulation but nonetheless deregulation occurred. Airlines were free to enter or exit and were also free to determine the fare they would charge. Since deregulation in 1978, passenger airline miles have more than doubled, prices have fallen, and mergers have occurred.

Which theory, the social interest or capture theory, best describes each of these three periods of the airline industry history?

Solutions to Additional Practice Problems 12.5

1a. An unregulated monopoly produces the quantity where marginal revenue equals marginal cost and the price is determined by the demand curve. In the figure, marginal revenue equals marginal cost when 2 thousand

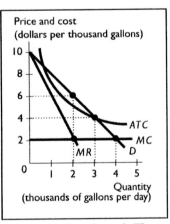

gallons of water per day are distributed. The price is $6 per thousand gallons. The firm earns an economic profit.

1b. If an average cost pricing rule is used, price and quantity are determined by where the average total cost curve intersects the demand curve. From the figure, the price is $4 per thousand gallons and the quantity is 3 thousand gallons per day. The firm earns a normal profit.

1c. If a marginal cost pricing rule is used, price and quantity are determined by where the marginal cost curve intersects the demand curve. From the figure, the price is $2 per thousand gallons and the quantity is 4 thousand gallons per day. The firm incurs an economic loss.

2. From 1934 to 1938, the competitive bidding suggests that social interest might have been more important than in the 1938 to 1978 period. But during the early four-year period, airlines were learning to expect a handout from government regulators.

During the four-decade era of the Civil Aeronautics Act, the industry is best described by the capture theory. Airlines were protected from competition by new entrants. They also faced little competition from existing airlines because fares were fixed. Competition took the form of frills, such as fancy dinners, champagne, and attractive accommodations and services.

Since 1978 airline behavior more typically resembles social interest theory and has as its legacy lower prices, higher capacity utilization, new low-fare entrants, bankruptcies, and mergers.

■ Self Test 12.5

Fill in the blanks

The theory that regulation seeks an efficient use of resources is the ____ (capture; social interest) theory, and the theory that regulation helps producers maximize economic profit is the ____ (capture; social interest) theory. With ____ (an average; a marginal) cost pricing rule, a natural monopoly incurs an economic loss. Regulated firms have an incentive to inflate their costs under ____ (rate of return; price cap) regulation.

True or false

1. Social interest theory assumes that the political process introduces regulation that eliminates deadweight loss.

2. A regulated natural monopoly produces the efficient quantity of output when it is regulated to use a marginal cost pricing rule.

3. Price cap regulation is designed to give firms the incentive to raise the price of their output, provided competition in the market increases.

Multiple choice

1. The theory that regulation seeks an efficient use of resources is the
   a. social interest theory.
   b. producer surplus theory.
   c. consumer surplus theory.
   d. capture theory.
   e. deadweight loss theory.

2. Which of the following best describes the capture theory of regulation?
   i. Regulation seeks an efficient use of resources
   ii. Regulation is aimed at keeping prices as low as possible
   iii. Regulation helps firms maximize economic profit
   a. i only.
   b. ii only.
   c. iii only.
   d. i and ii.
   e. i, ii, and iii.

3. At a level of output when regulators require a natural monopoly to set a price that is equal to marginal cost, the firm
   a. earns a normal profit.
   b. earns an economic profit.
   c. incurs an economic loss.
   d. earns a normal-economic profit.
   e. earns either a normal profit or an economic profit, depending on whether the firm's average total cost equals or is less than the marginal cost.

4. If a natural monopoly is told to set price equal to average cost, then the firm
   a. is not able to set marginal revenue equal to marginal cost.
   b. automatically also sets price equal to marginal cost.
   c. will earn a substantial economic profit.
   d. will incur an economic loss
   e. sets a price that is lower than its marginal cost.

■ **FIGURE 12.6**

Price and cost (dollars per month)

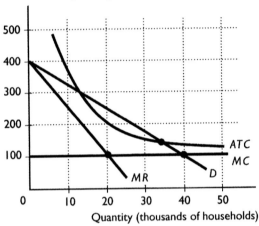

5. If the natural monopoly illustrated in Figure 12.6 was regulated using a marginal cost pricing rule, the price would be _____.
   a. $100
   b. between $100.01 and $200.00
   c. between $200.01 and $300.00
   d. between $300.01 and $400.00
   e. more than $400.01

6. If the natural monopoly illustrated in Figure 12.6 was regulated using an average total cost pricing rule, the price would be _____.
   a. $100
   b. between $100.01 and $200.00
   c. between $200.01 and $300.00
   d. between $300.01 and $400.00
   e. more than $400.01

7. If the natural monopoly illustrated in Figure 12.6 was unregulated, the price would be

   _____.
   a. $100
   b. between $100.01 and $200.00
   c. between $200.01 and $300.00
   d. between $300.01 and $400.00
   e. more than $400.01

Complete the graph

■ **FIGURE 12.7**

Price and cost (dollars per month)

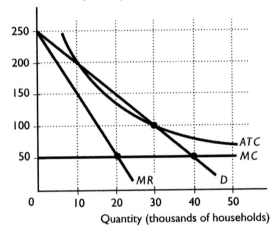

Quantity (thousands of households)

1. Figure 12.7 shows both the average total cost curves of a cable TV company that is a regulated monopoly. Also given are the demand curve and marginal revenue curve.
   a. What price would the regulator set using the marginal cost pricing rule?
   b. What price would the regulator set using the average cost pricing rule?
   c. What price would the firm set if it was unregulated?

Short answer and numeric questions

1. Why doesn't the government regulate all industries?
2. What is the social interest theory of regulation? The capture theory?
3. What is the advantage of using a marginal cost pricing rule to regulate a natural monopoly? The disadvantage?
5. What is the goal of price cap regulation?

SELF TEST ANSWERS

■ CHECKPOINT 12.1

Fill in the blanks

One of the requirements for monopoly is that there are no close substitutes for the good. A natural monopoly exists when one firm can meet the entire market demand at a lower average total cost than two or more firms could. A monopoly that is able to sell different units of a good or service for different prices is a price-discriminating monopoly.

True or false

1. False; pages 304-305
2. True; page 305
3. False; page 306

Multiple choice

1. b; page 304
2. b; page 304
3. d; page 304
4. b; page 305
5. d; page 306

Short answer and numeric questions

1. Monopoly occurs when there is a market with a single firm selling a good or service that has no close substitutes and in which the firm is protected by either a natural, ownership, or a legal barrier to entry; page 304.

2. Barriers to entry are anything that protects a firm from the entry of new competitors. Barriers to entry are either natural barriers, ownership barriers, or legal barriers; pages 304-305.

3. A monopoly can sell each unit of its output for the same price to all its customers or it can price discriminate by selling different units of its good or service at different prices. A perfectly competitive firm cannot affect the price so it must charge a single price determined by market demand and market supply; page 306.

■ CHECKPOINT 12.2

Fill in the blanks

For each level of output, marginal revenue for a single-price monopoly is less than price. When demand is inelastic, marginal revenue is negative. A single-price monopoly maximizes profit by producing the quantity at which marginal revenue equals marginal cost and then finds the highest price for which it can sell that output by using the demand curve.

True or false

1. False; page 308
2. False; page 309
3. True; page 311

Multiple choice

1. a; page 308
2. d; page 308
3. a; page 309
4. b; page 311
5. c; page 311

Complete the graph

Quantity (hamburgers per hour)	Price (dollars)	Marginal revenue (dollars)
1	8.00	
		6.00
2	7.00	
		4.00
3	6.00	
		2.00
4	5.00	
		0.00
5	4.00	

1. The completed table is above
   a. Figure 12.8 (on the next page) plots the demand and marginal revenue curves; page 311.
   b. Figure 12.8 shows the marginal cost curve. To maximize his profit, Bud produces the quantity at which marginal revenue equals marginal cost. So Bud prepares 300 hamburgers per hour. From the demand curve, the price of a hamburger is $6; pages 310-311.

■ **FIGURE 12.8**

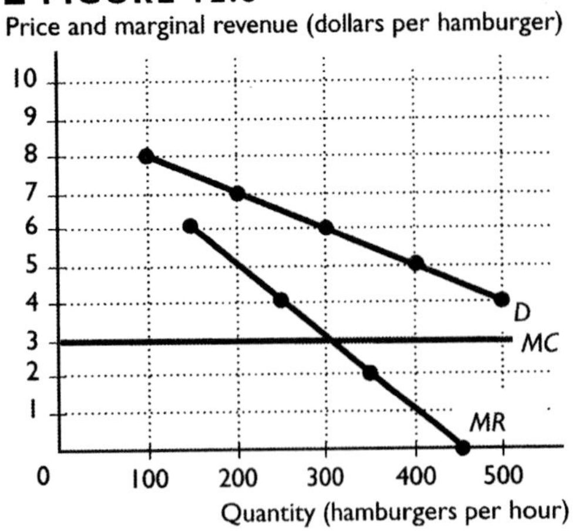

Price and marginal revenue (dollars per hamburger)

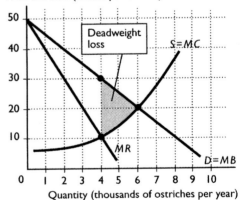

■ **FIGURE 12.9**

Price and cost (dollars per unit)

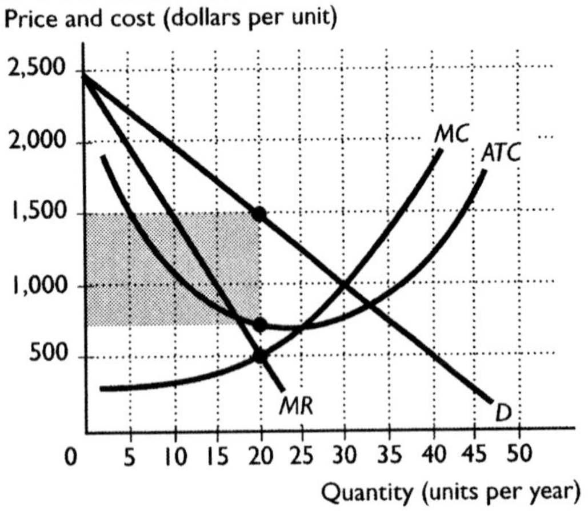

2. The curves are labeled in Figure 12.9. The profit-maximizing quantity is 20 units and the price is $1,500. The economic profit equals the area of the dark rectangle; page 311.

Short answer and numeric questions

1. If demand is elastic, marginal revenue is positive; if demand is unit elastic, marginal revenue is zero; and if demand is inelastic, marginal revenue is negative; page 309.

2. Both perfectly competitive and monopoly firms maximize profit by producing where $MR = MC$ because for *any* firm, a unit of output is produced if $MR > MC$ and is not produced if $MR < MC$. As long as $MR > MC$, *any* firm increases its total profit by continuing to produce additional output until it reaches

the point at which $MR = MC$; pages 310-311.

3. A monopoly can earn an economic profit in the long run because it is protected by a barrier to entry. Other firms want to enter the market in order also to earn some economic profit, but they cannot do so; page 311.

■ **CHECKPOINT 12.3**

Fill in the blanks

Compared to perfect competition, a single-price monopoly produces a <u>smaller</u> output and charges a <u>higher</u> price. A single-price monopoly <u>creates</u> a deadweight loss. The act of obtaining special treatment by the government to create an economic profit is called <u>rent seeking</u>. Rent seeking <u>increases</u> the amount of deadweight loss.

True or false

1. True; page 313
2. False; page 314
3. False; page 315

Multiple choice

1. c; page 313
2. e; page 313
3. c; page 313
4. d; page 314
5. b; page 314
6. c; page 315
7. b; page 316

Complete the graph

■ **FIGURE 12.10**

Price and cost (dollars per ostrich)

1. Figure 12.10 shows that the perfectly com-

petitive price is $20 an ostrich and the quantity is 3,000 ostriches. The monopoly price is $30 an ostrich and the quantity is 2,000 ostriches a year. The deadweight loss is the dark triangular area; page 314.

Short answer and numeric questions

1. The price set by a monopoly exceeds the price in a competitive market and the quantity produced by a monopoly is less than the quantity produced in a competitive market; page 314.

2. Consumer surplus decreases with a single-price monopoly. Consumer surplus decreases because the monopoly produces less output and charges a higher price; page 314.

3. Rent seeking is the act of obtaining special treatment by the government to create economic profit or to divert consumer surplus or producer surplus away from others. Rent seeking harms society because in a competitive rent-seeking equilibrium, the amount of the deadweight loss increases; page 315.

■ CHECKPOINT 12.4

Fill in the blanks

It is <u>sometimes</u> possible for a monopoly to charge different customers different prices. The key idea behind price discrimination is to convert <u>consumer surplus</u> into economic profit. Price discrimination results in consumers with a higher willingness paying a <u>higher</u> price than consumers with a lower willingness to pay. Perfect price discrimination results in <u>zero</u> consumer surplus and <u>does not create</u> a deadweight loss.

True or false

1. False; pages 318-320
2. False; page 318
3. True; page 321

Multiple choice

1. e; page 318
2. c; page 318
3. c; pages 318-320
4. a; pages 321
5. c; page 321

Complete the graph

■ **FIGURE 12.11**

Price and cost (dollars per article of clothing)

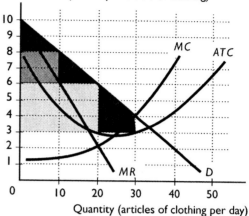

1. a. The economic profit is the light gray rectangle in Figure 12.11. The economic profit equals the area of the rectangle, which is $60 a day; page 319.

   b. The firm will set a price of $8 for each of the first 10 articles and $6 for each of the second 10 articles. The added profit is the darker gray rectangle for the first 10 articles. The total economic profit the firm now earns is $80 a day; page 320.

   c. The economic profit is increased by the addition of the three very dark gray areas. The economic profit is now $120 a day; page 321.

Short answer and numeric questions

1. Price discrimination decreases consumer surplus and increases economic profit. Price discrimination allows the firm to charge a price closer to the maximum the consumer is willing to pay, which is the marginal benefit of the good. Consumer surplus is converted into economic profit; page 318.

2. With perfect price discrimination, the monopoly increases output to the point at which price equals marginal cost. This output is identical to that of perfect competition. Deadweight loss with perfect price discrimination is zero. So perfect price discrimination produces the efficient quantity; page 321.

■ CHECKPOINT 12.5

Fill in the blanks

The theory that regulation seeks an efficient use of resources is the <u>social interest</u> theory, and the theory that regulation helps producers maximize economic profit is the <u>capture</u> theory. With <u>a marginal</u> cost pricing rule, a natural monopoly incurs an economic loss. Regulated firms have an incentive to inflate their costs under <u>rate of return</u> regulation.

True or false

1. True; page 325
2. True; page 326
3. False; page 329

Multiple choice

1. a; page 325
2. c; page 325
3. c; page 326
4. a; page 327
5. a; page 326
6. b; page 327
7. c; page 311

Complete the graph

1. a. Using marginal cost pricing, the regulator sets a price of $50 a month; pages 325.
   b. Using average cost pricing, the regulator sets a price of $100 a month; page 327.
   c. The firm serves 20,000 household, where marginal revenue equals marginal cost, and sets the price at $150 a month.

Short answer and numeric questions

1. The government does not regulate all industries because not all industries need to be regulated. Competitive industries do not need regulation because competition produces an efficient outcome. But a natural monopoly is not a competitive industry and so government regulation might help move the monopoly toward efficiency; pages 324-329.

2. The social interest theory of regulation is that the regulators pursue the public's interest by devising regulation that achieves an efficient use of resources. The capture theory of regulation is that the producers have "captured the regulators" and, as a result, the regulation helps producers maximize their economic profit; page 325.

3. The advantage of using a marginal cost pricing rule is that the firm produces the efficient quantity of output. The disadvantage is that the firm incurs an economic loss; page 326.

4. Price cap regulation gives regulated firms the incentive to cut their costs and produce efficiently, without exaggerating their costs or wasting resources; page 329.

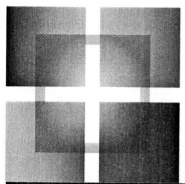

Monopolistic Competition and Oligopoly

Chapter 13

CHAPTER CHECKLIST

Chapter 13 studies the two market structures that lie between the extremes of perfect competition and monopoly: monopolistic competition and oligopoly.

1 Explain how price and quantity are determined in monopolistic competition.

Monopolistic competition is a market structure in which a large number of firms compete; each firm produces a differentiated product; firms compete on product quality, price, and marketing; and firms are free to enter and exit. The four-firm concentration ratio and the Herfindahl-Hirschman Index are indexes that measure the extent to which a market is dominated by a small number of firms. A firm in monopolistic competition maximizes profit by producing the output at which marginal revenue equals marginal cost. The price is determined by the demand. Entry and exit result in zero economic profit in the long run. Monopolistically competitive firms have excess capacity in long-run equilibrium because they produce less than the efficient scale. In monopolistic competition price exceeds marginal cost—which indicates inefficiency—but the inefficiency arises from product variety—a gain for consumers.

2 Explain why selling costs are high in monopolistic competition.

To maintain economic profit, firms in monopolistic competition innovate and develop new products, and incur huge costs to ensure that buyers appreciate the differences between their own products and those of their competitors. Selling costs, such as advertising, are a fixed cost and increase the total cost, but they might lower average total cost if they increase the quantity sold by a large enough amount.

3 Explain the dilemma faced by firms in oligopoly.

An oligopoly is a market structure in which a small number of firms compete and natural or legal barriers prevent the entry of new firms. Firms in oligopoly would make the same economic profit as a monopoly if they could act together to restrict output to the monopoly level. Each firm can make a larger economic profit by increasing production, but this action decreases the economic profits of the other firms. A cartel is a group of firms acting together to limit output, raise price, and thereby increase economic profit. The duopolists' dilemma is that each firm, taking actions to maximize its profit, could wind up with a lower profit because of the self-interest of the other firms, taking similar profit-maximizing actions to expand their productions.

4 Use game theory to explain how price and quantity are determined in oligopoly.

Game theory is the tool economists use to analyze strategic behavior. Games have rules, strategies, and payoffs. The prisoners' dilemma is a game between two prisoners that shows why it is hard to cooperate, even when it would be beneficial to both players to do so. The Nash equilibrium of a game occurs when each player takes the best possible action given the action of the other player. The equilibrium of the prisoners' dilemma game is not the best outcome for the prisoners. The duopolist's dilemma is like the prisoners' dilemma because the equilibrium is not the best outcome for the firms. In a repeated game, a "tit-for-tat" strategy can produce a monopoly output, price, and economic profit.

CHECKPOINT 13.1

■ **Explain how price and quantity are determined in monopolistic competition.**

Quick Review

- *Four-firm concentration ratio* The four-firm concentration ratio is the percentage of the value of sales accounted for by the four largest firms in an industry.
- *Herfindahl-Hirschman Index (HHI)* The HHI is the square of the percentage market share of each firm summed over the largest 50 firms (or summed over all the firms if there are fewer than 50) in a market.
- *Profit maximization* A firm in monopolistic competition produces where marginal revenue equals marginal cost. The price is determined from the demand curve.

Additional Practice Problems 13.1

Firm	Total revenue (millions of dollars)	Percent of total revenue (percent)
McDonald's	1,200	___
Burger King	600	___
Wendy's	600	___
Hardee's	300	___
Checker's	180	___
Other 20 smaller firms	720	___

1. The table gives some hypothetical data on sales in the fast-food hamburger market. Suppose that the sales of each of the 20 smallest firms is the same and each has total revenue of $36 million.
   a. Complete the table.
   b. Calculate the four-firm concentration ratio.
   c. Calculate the Herfindahl-Hirschman Index.
   d. Based on the hypothetical concentration ratios, in what market structure would you classify the fast-food hamburger market?

2. The figure shows the demand and costs for Bernie's Burger barn, a firm in monopolistic competition.

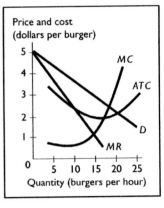

   a. To maximize its profit, how many burgers does Bernie produce in an hour? What is the price of a hamburger?
   b. Is the firm earning an economic profit or loss and, if so, how much?
   c. Does this figure show the firm in the short run or the long run? Explain your answer.

3. The Piece A' Pie company is a pizza restaurant in competition with many other pizza restaurants. Piece A' Pie produces 50 pizzas an hour.
   a. If Piece A' Pie's average total cost is $10 a pizza and its price is $12 a pizza, what is its economic profit?
   b. If Piece A' Pie's average total cost is $12 a pizza and its price is $12 a pizza, what is its economic profit?
   c. If Piece A' Pie's average total cost is $15 a pizza and its price is $12 a pizza, what is its economic profit?
   d. Which of the three situations outlined in parts (a), (b), and (c) can represent a short-run equilibrium? A long-run equilibrium? Why?

Solutions to Additional Practice Problems 13.1

Firm	Total revenue (millions of dollars)	Percent of total revenue (percent)
McDonald's	1,200	33.3
Burger King	600	16.7
Wendy's	600	16.7
Hardee's	300	8.3
Checker's	180	5.0
Other 20 smaller firms	720	20.0

1a. The sales shares are in the table above. To calculate the shares, first determine the total sales within the market, which is $3,600 million. A firm's total sales share equals its total revenue divided by $3,600 million and then multiplied by 100.

1b. The four-firm concentration ratio is the percentage of the total sales accounted for by the four largest firms in the industry, which is 33.3 percent + 16.7 percent + 16.7 percent + 8.3 percent = 75.0 percent.

1c. To calculate the Herfindahl-Hirschman Index (HHI), we need to square and then sum the market shares of the firms. The market shares are equal to each firm's percentage of total sales. Each of the 20 smaller firms has total revenue of $36 million, so each has a 1 percentage point market share. So the HHI = $(33.3)^2 + (16.7)^2 + (16.7)^2 + (8.3)^2 + (5.0)^2 + (1.0)^2 \times 20 = 1,108.89 + 278.89 + 278.89 + 68.89 + 25.00 + 20.00$, which is 1,780.56.

1d. Based on concentration ratios, the fast-food hamburger market is just on the borderline between monopolistic competition and oligopoly. To make a decision whether this industry is monopolistically competitive or an oligopoly, information about the presence or absence of barriers to entry is needed.

2a. To maximize its profit, Bernie's will produce where $MR = MC$. So Bernie's produces 15 burgers per hour. Bernie's demand curve shows that Bernie will set a price of $3 for a burger.

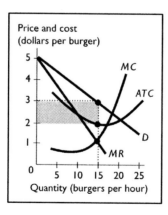

2b. Bernie's is earning an economic profit, because its price is greater than its average total cost. Its economic profit equals the area of the darkened rectangle in the figure. Bernie's earns an economic profit of $1 (its price, $3, minus its average total cost, $2) on each burger, so its total economic profit is $1 × 15 = $15.

2c. Bernie's is in its short-run equilibrium. It is not in its long-run equilibrium because the firm is earning an economic profit. Firms in monopolistic competition cannot earn an economic profit in the long run; they can earn an economic profit only in the short run.

3a. Piece A' Pie's economic profit on a pizza is equal to price minus average total cost. So Piece A' Pie earns an economic profit of $12 a pizza minus $10 a pizza, which is $2 a pizza. Piece A' Pie produces 50 pizzas an hour, so its total economic profit is $2 a pizza × 50 pizzas an hour, which is $100 an hour.

3b. Piece A' Pie's economic profit on a pizza is equal to price minus average total cost. So Piece A' Pie earns an economic profit of $12 a pizza minus $12 a pizza, which is zero dollars a pizza. Piece A' Pie earns zero economic profit so it earns a normal profit.

3c. Piece A' Pie's economic profit on a pizza is equal to price minus average total cost. So Piece A' Pie earns an economic profit of $12 a pizza minus $15 a pizza, which is –$3 a pizza. Piece A' Pie produces 50 pizzas an hour, so its total economic profit is –$3 a pizza × 50 pizzas an hour, which is –$150 an hour. So Piece A' Pie incurs an economic loss of $150 an hour.

3d. In the short run, depending on market conditions, a firm in monopolistic competition can earn an economic profit, can earn zero economic profit, or can incur an economic loss. Only the situation in part (b) can represent a long-run equilibrium. In the long run, the absence of barriers to entry means that firms in monopolistic competition earn zero economic profit.

■ Self Test 13.1

Fill in the blanks

In monopolistic competition there are a ____ (large; small) number of firms producing ____ (identical; differentiated) products. A firm in monopolistic competition has a ____ (downward-sloping; horizontal) demand curve. The square of the percentage market share of each firm summed over the 50 largest firms is the _____ (50-firm concentration ratio; Herfindahl-Hirschman Index). A firm in monopolistic competition produces the quantity where marginal revenue _____ (is greater than; equals; is less than) marginal cost. In the long run, a firm in monopolistic competition _____ (can; cannot) earn an economic profit. A firm in monopolistic competition _____ (does not have; has) excess capacity in the long run.

True or false

1. A firm in monopolistic competition faces a downward-sloping demand curve.

2. The larger the four-firm concentration ratio, the more competitive the industry.

3. A firm in monopolistic competition can make an economic profit in the short run.

4. In a broader view of efficiency, monopolistic competition brings gains for consumers.

Multiple choice

1. In monopolistic competition there
   a. are a large number of firms.
   b. are several large firms.
   c. is one large firm.
   d. might be many, several, or one firm.
   e. are many firms but only a few buyers.

2. Product differentiation means
   a. making a product that has perfect substitutes.
   b. making a product that is entirely unique.
   c. the inability to set your own price.
   d. making a product that is slightly different from products of competing firms.
   e. making your demand curve horizontal.

3. If the four-firm concentration ratio for the market for pizza is 28 percent, then this industry is best characterized as
   a. a monopoly.
   b. monopolistic competition.
   c. an oligopoly.
   d. perfect competition.
   e. oligoplistic competition.

4. Each of the four firms in an industry has a market share of 25 percent. The Herfindahl-Hirschman Index equals
   a. 3,600.
   b. 100.
   c. 625.
   d. 25.
   e. 2,500.

5. The larger the four-firm concentration, the _____ competition within an industry; the larger the Herfindahl-Hirschman Index, the _____ competition within an industry.
   a. more; more
   b. more; less
   c. less; more
   d. less; less
   e. The premise of the question is wrong because the four-firm concentration ratio applies only to markets with four firms in it and these markets are, by definition, not competitive.

6. A firm in monopolistic competition has _____ demand curve.
   a. a downward-sloping
   b. an upward-sloping
   c. a vertical
   d. a horizontal
   e. a U-shaped

7. A firm in monopolistic competition maximizes profit by producing so that
   a. price equals marginal revenue.
   b. price equals marginal cost.
   c. demand equals marginal cost.
   d. marginal revenue equals marginal cost.
   e. price equals average total cost.

8. Monopolistic competition is efficient when compared to
   a. perfect competition.
   b. complete product uniformity.
   c. the short run.
   d. the long run.
   e. None of the above answers is correct.

■ **FIGURE 13.1**

Price and cost (dollars per lunch)

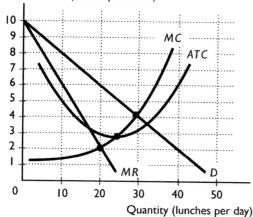

9. Figure 13.1 shows Louie's Lunches, a lunch counter in competition with many other restaurants. To maximize its profit, Louie's produces ___ lunches per day.
   a. 10
   b. 20
   c. 30
   d. between 31 and 40
   e. more than 40

10. Figure 13.1 shows the costs and demand curves for Louie's Lunches. To maximize its profit, Louie's sets a price of ___ per lunch.
    a. $2
    b. $4
    c. between $5.00 and $5.99
    d. $6
    e. more than $6.01

11. Figure 13.1 shows the costs and demand curves for Louie's Lunches. Louie's is in the ___ and is ___.
    a. short run; earning an economic profit
    b. short run; earning a normal profit
    c. short run; incurring an economic loss
    d. long run; earning an economic profit
    e. long run; earning a normal profit

12. The absence of barriers to entry in monopolistic competition means that in the long run firms
    a. earn an economic profit.
    b. earn zero economic profit.
    c. incur an economic loss.
    d. earn either an economic profit or a normal profit.
    e. earn either a normal profit or suffer an economic loss.

Complete the graph

■ **FIGURE 13.2**

Price and cost (dollars per pizza)

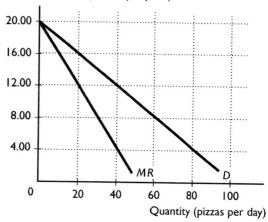

1. Figure 13.2 shows the demand and marginal revenue curves for Seaside Pizza, a firm in monopolistic competition. Draw the average total cost curve and marginal cost curve so that Seaside's output is 40 pizzas a day and its economic profit is $160. Is this a short-run or long-run equilibrium?

2. Figure 13.3 (on the next page) shows the demand and the marginal revenue curves for Surf Pizza, a firm in monopolistic competition. Draw the average total cost curve and marginal cost curve so that Surf's output is 20 pizzas a day and Surf's earns zero economic profit. Is this a short-run or long-run equilibrium?

■ **FIGURE 13.3**
Price and cost (dollars per pizza)

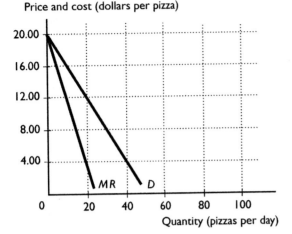

Quantity (pizzas per day)

Short answer and numeric questions

1. What conditions define monopolistic competition?

Firm	Total revenue (millions of dollars)	Percent of total revenue (percent)
Dell	1,000	____
HP	800	____
IBM	500	____
Toshiba	400	____
Other 46 smaller firms	2,300	____

2. The table gives some hypothetical data on sales in the desktop computer market. Suppose that the total revenue of each of the 46 smallest firms is the same and each has total revenue of $50 million.
   a. Complete the table.
   b. Calculate the four-firm concentration ratio.
   c. Calculate the Herfindahl-Hirschman Index.

3. Industry A has 1 firm with a market share of 57 percent and 43 other firms, each with a market share of 1 percent. Industry B has 4 firms, each with a market share of 15 percent, and 40 other firms, each with a market share of 1 percent.
   a. Calculate the four-firm concentration ratio for the two industries.
   b. Calculate the Herfindahl-Hirschman Index for the two industries.

4. Why do firms in monopolistic competition earn zero economic profit in the long run?
5. Is monopolistic competition efficient?

CHECKPOINT 13.2

■ Explain why selling costs are high in monopolistic competition.

Quick Review

- *Selling costs* Selling costs such as advertising expenditures might lower average total cost if they increase the quantity sold by a large enough amount.

Additional Practice Problem 13.2

1. Selling costs are high in monopolistic competition. The table gives the costs of producing a pair of Nikes.

   a. The cost of producing the shoe in Asia is $20. The remaining costs are selling costs. What percentage of the retail price is selling costs?

   b. When the shoes reach America, selling costs are the result of activity at Nike Headquarters and local retailing activity. What proportion of the $70 price is attributable to Nike and what proportion to local retailers?

Item	Cost (dollars)
Asia	
Materials	9.00
Labor	2.75
Capital	3.00
Profit	1.75
Shipping	0.50
Import duty	3.00
Nike	
Distribution	5.00
Advertising	4.00
R and D	0.25
Profit	6.25
Local	
Labor	9.50
Shop rent	9.00
Other costs	7.00
Profit	9.00

Solution to Additional Practice Problem 13.2

1a. Selling costs account for ($50 ÷ $70) × 100, which is 71.4 percent of the price.

1b. Nike accounts for ($15.50 ÷ $70) × 100, which is 22.1 percent of the price. Local retailers account for ($34.50 ÷ $70) × 100, which is 49.3 percent of the price.

■ Self Test 13.2

Fill in the blanks

Firms in monopolistic competition ____ (are; are not) continuously developing new products. In monopolistic competition, product improvement ____ (does; does not) equal its efficient level. Advertising costs ____ (are; are not) large in monopolistic competition. Advertising costs are a ____ (fixed; variable) cost and shift the average total cost curve ____ (downward; upward). Monopolistic competition ____ (definitely is; might be; definitely is not) efficient.

True or false

1. Firms in monopolistic competition innovate without regard to cost.
2. Firms in monopolistic competition often undertake extensive advertising.
3. Because advertising increases the demand for a firm's product, increasing the amount of advertising shifts the firm's cost curves downward.
4. Whether monopolistic competition is efficient depends on the value people place on product variety.

Multiple choice

1. Because economic profits are eliminated in the long run in monopolistic competition, to earn an economic profit firms continuously
   a. shut down.
   b. exit the industry.
   c. innovate and develop new products.
   d. declare bankruptcy.
   e. decrease their costs by decreasing their selling costs.

2. A firm in monopolistic competition that introduces a new and differentiated product will temporarily have a ____ demand for its product and is able to charge ____.
   a. less elastic, a lower price than before
   b. less elastic, a higher price than before
   c. more elastic, a lower price than before
   d. more elastic, a higher price than before
   e. less elastic, the same price as before

3. The decision to innovate
   a. depends on the marketing department's needs.
   b. depends on whether the firm wants to benefit its customers.
   c. is based on the marginal cost and the marginal revenue of innovation.
   d. is unnecessary in a monopolistically competitive market.
   e. None of the above answers is correct.

4. Advertising costs and other selling costs are
   a. efficient.
   b. fixed costs.
   c. variable costs.
   d. marginal costs.
   e. considered as part of demand because they affect the demand for the good.

5. For a firm in monopolistic competition, selling costs
   a. increase costs and reduce profits.
   b. always increase demand.
   c. can change the quantity produced and lower the average total cost.
   d. can lower total cost.
   e. has no effect on the quantity sold.

6. The efficiency of monopolistic competition
   a. is as clear-cut as the efficiency of perfect competition.
   b. depends on whether the gain from extra product variety offsets the selling costs and the extra cost that arises from excess capacity.
   c. comes from its excess capacity.
   d. is eliminated in the long run.
   e. is equal to that of monopoly.

Short answer and numeric questions

1. Why do firms in monopolistic competition engage in innovation and product development?

2. How might advertising lower average total cost?

3. Are advertising, brand names, and product differentiation efficient?

CHECKPOINT 13.3

■ **Explain the dilemma faced by firms in oligopoly.**

Quick Review

- *Oligopoly* An oligopoly is characterized by having a small number of firms competing with natural or legal barriers preventing the entry of new firms.
- *Duopoly* A market in which there are only two producers.
- *Duopolists' dilemma* When each firm follows its self-interest to increase its profit, *both* firms earn a lower profit.

Additional Practice Problems 13.3

1. What is the key difference between oligopoly and monopolistic competition?

2. Just as in the textbook, Isolated Island has two natural gas wells, one owned by Tom and the other owned by Jerry. Each well has a valve that controls the rate of flow of gas, and the marginal cost of producing gas is zero. The table gives the demand schedule for gas on this island. Suppose Tom and Jerry agree to operate as a monopoly. A monopoly produces 6 units and charges $6 a unit. Tom and Jerry agree that each will produce 3 units and charge $6. There are no fixed costs

Price (dollars per unit)	Quantity demanded (units per day)
12	0
11	1
10	2
9	3
8	4
7	5
6	6
5	7
4	8
3	9
2	10
1	11
0	12

 a. If neither Tom nor Jerry cheat on the agreement what is Tom's profit? Jerry's profit? The combined profit?

 b. Suppose Tom decides to cheat on the agreement by producing 4 units. Jerry sticks to the agreement. If 7 units are produced, what is the price? What is Tom's profit? Jerry's profit? The combined profit?

 c. Why would Tom ever consider cheating on the agreement he made with Jerry?

Solution to Additional Practice Problem 13.3

1. The key difference between oligopoly and monopolistic competition is that oligopoly is characterized by having only a small number of firms. Monopolistic competition has a large number of competing firms. Because there are only a few firms in oligopoly, the firms in oligopoly face the temptation to collude, which is an incentive missing from monopolistic competition.

2a. Profit is equal to total revenue because total cost is zero. Tom's profit is $18, Jerry's profit is $18, and the combined profit is $36.

2b. If 7 units are produced, the price is $5 a unit. Tom's profit on his 4 units is $20 and Jerry's profit on his 3 units is $15. Combined profit is $35.

2c. Tom considers cheating because cheating increases his profit. Tom realizes that if he alone cheats, his profit will be more, $20 versus $18. Jerry's profit falls more than Tom's rises but Tom is concerned only about his own profit.

■ Self Test 13.3

Fill in the blanks

In an oligopoly a ____ (large; small) number of firms compete. A ____ (cartel; duopoly) is a group of firms acting together to limit output, raise price, and increase economic profit. When a duopoly charges the perfectly competitive price, each firm receives ____ (no; positive) economic profit. When a duopoly charges the monopoly price, economic profit is ____ (maximized; minimized).

True or false

1. Oligopoly is a market in which a small number of firms compete.

2. The aim of a cartel is to lower price, increase output, and increase economic profit.

3. In a duopoly, the highest price that the firms might set is the perfectly competitive price.

4. A duopoly is currently making, in total, the same economic profit as a monopoly. If one firm increases its output, the economic profit of the other firm increases.

5. A duopoly's total profit is the largest when it produces more than the monopoly level of output.

Multiple choice

1. Oligopoly is a market structure in which
   a. many firms each produce a slightly differentiated product.
   b. one firm produces a unique product.
   c. a small number of firms compete.
   d. many firms produce an identical product.
   e. the number of firms is so small that they do not compete with each other.

2. Collusion results when a group of firms
   i. act separately to limit output, lower price, and decrease economic profit.
   ii. act together to limit output, raise price, and increase economic profit.
   iii. in the United States legally fix prices.
   a. i only.
   b. ii only.
   c. iii only.
   d. i and iii.
   e. ii and iii.

3. A cartel is a group of firms
   a. acting separately to limit output, lower price, and decrease economic profit.
   b. acting together to limit output, raise price, and increase economic profit.
   c. legally fixing prices.
   d. acting together to erect barriers to entry.
   e. that compete primarily with each other rather than the other firms in the market.

4. A market with only two firms is called a
   a. duopoly.
   b. two-firm monopolistic competition.
   c. two-firm monopoly.
   d. cartel.
   e. two-firm quasi-monopoly.

■ **FIGURE 13.4**

Price and cost (dollars per bottle of shampoo)

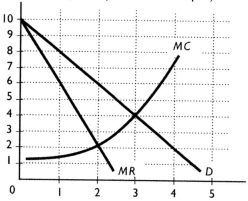

Quantity (millions of bottles of shampoo per day)

5. Suppose only two companies make shampoo. Figure 13.4 shows the market demand curve and associated marginal revenue curve. It also shows the combined marginal cost curve of the two companies. If these companies formed a cartel that operated as a monopoly, production would be ____ million bottles of shampoo and the price would be ____ per bottle of shampoo.
   a. 5; $4
   b. 2; $6
   c. 3; $6
   d. 2; $2
   e. 3; $4

6. Suppose the two companies that make shampoo illustrated in Figure 13.4 operate as perfect competitors. In this case, production would be ____ million bottles of shampoo and the price would be ____ per bottle of shampoo.
   a. 5; $4
   b. 2; $6
   c. 3; $6
   d. 2; $2
   e. 3; $4

7. For a duopoly, the maximum total profit is reached when the duopoly produces
   a. the same amount of output as the competitive outcome.
   b. the same amount of output as the monopoly outcome.
   c. an amount of output that lies between the competitive outcome and the monopoly outcome.
   d. more output than the competitive outcome.
   e. less output than the monopoly outcome.

8. If a duopoly has reached the monopoly outcome, a firm can increase its profit if it and it alone ____ its price and ____ its production.
   a. raises; increases
   b. raises; decreases
   c. lowers; increases
   d. lowers; decreases
   e. raises; does not change

9. If a duopoly has reached the monopoly outcome and only one firm increases its production, that firm's profit ____ and the other firm's profit ____.
   a. increases; increases
   b. increases; decreases
   c. decreases; increases
   d. decreases; decreases
   e. increases; does not change

10. Suppose a duopoly had reached the monopoly outcome and then the first firm increased its production. If the second firm next increases its production, the second firm's profit ____ and the first firm's profit ____.
    a. increases; increases
    b. increases; decreases
    c. decreases; increases
    d. decreases; decreases
    e. increases; does not change

Complete the graph

Quantity (thousands of newspapers per day)	Price (cents)	Marginal revenue (cents)
0	60	60
2	50	40
4	40	20
6	30	0
8	20	−20

1. Anytown, USA has two newspapers that have a duopoly in the local market. The table contains information on the market demand and marginal revenue for newspapers. Marginal cost of a newspaper is 20 cents.
   a. Graph the demand curve, marginal revenue curve, and marginal cost curve in Figure 13.5.

■ **FIGURE 13.5**

Price and marginal revenue (cents per newspaper)

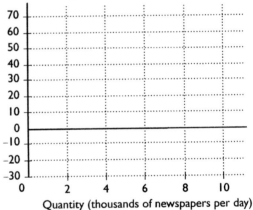

Quantity (thousands of newspapers per day)

   b. What price and quantity represent the competitive outcome?
   c. What price and quantity represent the monopoly outcome?
   d. What range of price and quantity represent the potential duopoly outcomes?

Short answer and numeric questions

1. What conditions define oligopoly?
2. What is a cartel?
3. In oligopoly, one firm's profit-maximizing actions might decrease its competitors' prof-

its. Why is this fact a problem for firms in oligopoly?

4. Why do firms in an oligopoly have an incentive to form a cartel that boosts the price and decreases the output?

5. Why does a firm have the incentive to cheat on a collusive agreement to limit production and raise the price?

CHECKPOINT 13.4

■ **Use game theory to explain how price and quantity are determined in oligopoly.**

Quick Review

- *Game theory* The tool that economists use to analyze strategic behavior—behavior that recognizes mutual interdependence and takes account of the expected behavior of others.

- *Nash equilibrium* An equilibrium in which each player takes the best possible action given the action of the other player.

Additional Practice Problem13.4

1. Coke and Pepsi are engaged in an advertising game. They each know that if they both limit their advertising, they will make the maximum attainable joint economic profit of $400 million, divided so that each has an economic profit of $200 million. They also know that if either of them advertises while the other does not, the one advertising makes an economic profit of $300 million and the one that does not advertise incurs an economic loss of $100 million dollars. And they also know that if they both advertise, they both earn zero economic profit.

   a. Construct a payoff matrix for the game that Coke and Pepsi must play.
   b. Find the Nash equilibrium.
   c. What is the equilibrium if this game is played repeatedly?
   d. Suppose that Coke and Pepsi are both playing a tit-for-tat strategy and that last time both did not advertise. Today, however, Coke really needs some extra income. So Coke advertises. What takes place today and in the future?

Solution to Additional Practice Problem 13.4

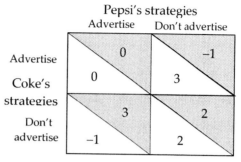

1a. A payoff matrix is a table that shows payoffs for every possible action by each player, Coke and Pepsi, given every possible action by the other player. The payoff matrix is above. The number in each square is the economic profit in millions of dollars.

1b. To find the Nash equilibrium of a game, place yourself in the position of the first player. Ask yourself "what if" your opponent takes one action: What will you do? Then ask "what if" the opponent takes the other action: now what will you do? This analysis allows you to determine the first player's action. Then place yourself in the position of the second player and repeat the "what if" analysis to determine the second player's action. So, to find Coke's strategy, ask what Coke will do for each of Pepsi's choices. If Pepsi advertises (the first column of the payoff matrix), Coke advertises because that gives Coke a larger profit ($0 versus a loss of $1 million). If Pepsi does not advertise (the second column of the payoff matrix), Coke advertises gallons because that gives Coke a larger profit ($3 million versus $2 million). Regardless of Pepsi's action, Coke advertises. Similar reasoning shows that Pepsi also advertises. So the Nash equilibrium is for each to advertise and earn zero economic profit.

1c. In a repeated game, Coke and Pepsi both do not advertise and earn the maximum joint economic profit. This outcome occurs if they use a tit-for-tat strategy.

1d. Today, Coke earns an economic profit of $3 million and Pepsi incurs an economic loss of $1 million. But in the second year, Pepsi will advertise. Coke might go back to not advertising to induce Pepsi to not advertise in the third year. So in the second year, Pepsi earns an economic profit of $3 million and Coke incurs an economic loss of $1 million. Over the two years, Coke earns a total economic profit of $2 million (and Pepsi also earns a total economic profit of $2 million.) But if Coke had not "cheated" on the agreement and advertised in the first year, then over the two years Coke's total economic profit would have been $4 million, not just $2 million. So, by cheating on the agreement Coke earns more profit immediately but over the longer haul earns less profit.

■ Self Test 13.4

Fill in the blanks

Game theory is the main tool that economists use to analyze ____ (irrational; strategic) behavior. Games feature ____, ____, and ____. The Nash equilibrium is ____ (always; not always) the best possible equilibrium for the players. Game theory shows that duopolists ____ (can; cannot) always reach the best possible equilibrium. In a ____ (repeated; single-play) game, a tit-for-tit strategy can be used. The ____ (larger; smaller) the number of firms, the harder it is for an oligopoly to maintain the monopoly output.

True or false

1. Game theory is used to analyze strategic behavior.

2. A prisoners' dilemma has no equilibrium.

3. A Nash equilibrium is the best outcome for all players in a prisoners' dilemma game.

4. The monopoly outcome is more likely in a repeated game than in a one-play game.

5. If firms in oligopoly play a repeated game and end up restricting their output, then oligopoly is efficient.

Multiple choice

1. One of the main tools economists use to analyze strategic behavior is
   a. the Herfindahl-Hirschman Index.
   b. game theory.
   c. cartel theory.
   d. the collusion index.
   e. dual theory, which is used to study duopolies.

2. A Nash equilibrium occurs
   a. when each player acts without considering the actions of the other player.
   b. when each player takes the best possible action given the action of the other player.
   c. only when players use the tit-for-tat strategy.
   d. only if the game is played in Nashville, TN.
   e. when each player takes the action that makes the combined payoff for all players as large as possible.

3. Game theory reveals that
   a. the equilibrium might not be the best solution for the parties involved.
   b. firms in oligopoly are not interdependent.
   c. each player looks after what is best for the industry.
   d. if all firms in an oligopoly take the action that maximizes their profit, then the equilibrium will have the largest possible combined profit of all the firms.
   e. firms in an oligopoly choose their actions without regard for what the other firms might do.

4. The prisoners' dilemma game
   a. shows that prisoners are better off if they cooperate.
   b. shows it is easy to cooperate.
   c. has an equilibrium in which both prisoners are made as well off as possible.
   d. would have the same outcome even if the prisoners can communicate and cooperate.
   e. has an equilibrium in which one prisoner is made as well off as possible and the other prisoner is made as worse off as possible.

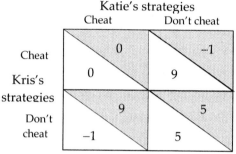

Katie's strategies

5. Katie and Kris are duopolists who formed a collusive agreement to boost prices and decrease production. Their payoff matrix is above and the entries are millions of dollars of economic profit. They now have the choice of cheating on the agreement or not cheating. If Kris cheats, then
   a. Kris definitely earns an economic profit of $9 million.
   b. Kris definitely earns $0.
   c. Kris definitely incurs an economic loss of $1 million.
   d. Kris definitely earns an economic profit of $5 million.
   e. Kris might earn an economic profit of $9 million or might earn $0 depending on what Katie does.

6. Based on the payoff matrix above, the Nash equilibrium is for
   a. Kris to cheat and Katie to cheat.
   b. Kris to not cheat and Katie to not cheat.
   c. Kris to cheat and Katie to not cheat.
   d. Kris to not cheat and Katie to cheat.
   e. Kris and Katie to invite a third person to determine what each of them should do.

7. Based on the payoff matrix above, in the Nash equilibrium the total profit that Katie and Kris earn together is ____ million.
   a. $8
   b. $9
   c. $10
   d. $0
   e. −$1

8. Firms in oligopoly can achieve an economic profit
   a. always in the long run.
   b. if they cooperate.
   c. only if the demand for their products is inelastic.
   d. only if the demand for their products is elastic.
   e. if they reach the non-cooperative equilibrium.

9. When duopoly games are repeated and a "tit-for-tat" strategy is used,
   a. the competitive outcome is more likely to be reached than when the game is played once.
   b. the monopoly outcome is more likely to be reached than when the game is played once.
   c. both firms begin to incur economic losses.
   d. one firm goes out of business.
   e. because the game is repeated it is impossible to predict whether the competitive or the monopoly outcome is more likely.

10. Oligopoly is
    a. always efficient.
    b. efficient only if the firms cooperate.
    c. efficient only if they play non-repeated games.
    d. generally not efficient.
    e. efficient only if the firms innovate.

Complete the graph

Cameron's strategies

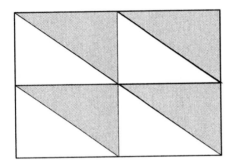

Art's strategies

1. Art and Cameron own the only two movie theaters in a small, isolated town. They have recently agreed to an illegal cartel agreement in which they will boost their ticket prices. If they both comply with the agreement, both will make $1 million of economic profit. If one cheats by lowering his price, the cheater will make $1.5 million of economic profit and the other will suffer an economic loss if $0.5 million. If they both cheat by lowering their prices, each makes zero economic profit.
   a. Complete the payoff matrix above.
   b. What is the Nash equilibrium of this game?

Intel's strategies

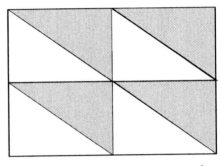

AMD's strategies

2. Intel and AMD are involved in a game to determine the amount they will spend on research and development. If they each spend $2 billion, their economic profit is zero. If they each spend $1 billion, their economic profit is $500 million. And if one spends $2 billion and the other spends $1 billion, the one spending $2 billion has an economic profit of $1,500 million and the other has an economic loss of $100 million.
   a. Complete the payoff matrix above.
   b. What is the Nash equilibrium of this game?

Short answer and numeric questions
1. What are "strategies" in game theory?
2. In a prisoners' dilemma, why don't the players cooperate?
3. In the duopolists' dilemma, why don't the players cooperate?
4. How does the number of players in a game affect its outcome?

■ CHECKPOINT 13.1

Fill in the blanks

In monopolistic competition there are a <u>large</u> number of firms producing <u>differentiated</u> products. A firm in monopolistic competition has a <u>downward-sloping</u> demand curve. The square of the percentage market share of each firm summed over the 50 largest firms is the <u>Herfindahl-Hirschman Index</u>. A firm in monopolistic competition produces the quantity where marginal revenue <u>equals</u> marginal cost. In the long run, a firm in monopolistic competition <u>cannot</u> earn an economic profit. A firm in monopolistic competition <u>has</u> excess capacity in the long run.

True or false

1. True; page 337
2. False; page 338
3. True; page 339
4. True; page 341

Multiple choice

1. a; page 336
2. d; page 336
3. b; page 338
4. e; page 338
5. d; page 338
6. a; pages 337, 339
7. d; page 339
8. b; page 341
9. b; page 339
10. d; page 339
11. a; page 339
12. b; page 340

Complete the graph

1. Figure 13.6 shows the average total cost curve and marginal cost curve so that Seaside Pizza's output is 40 pizzas a day and economic profit is $160. The figure shows a short-run equilibrium because Seaside is earning an economic profit; page 339.

■ FIGURE 13.6

Price and cost (dollars per pizza)

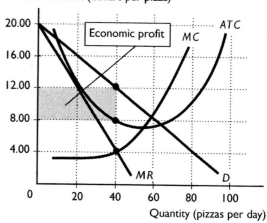

■ FIGURE 13.7

Price and cost (dollars per pizza)

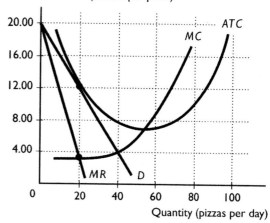

2. Figure 13.7 shows the average total cost curve and marginal cost curve so that Surf Pizza's output is 20 pizzas a day and it earns zero economic profit. The figure shows a long-run equilibrium because Surf is earning zero economic profit; page 340.

Short answer and numeric questions

1. Monopolistic competition occurs when a large number of firms compete; each firm produces a differentiated product, the firms compete on product quality; price, and

marketing; and firms are free to enter and exit; page 336.

Firm	Total revenue (millions of dollars)	Percent of total revenue (percent)
Dell	1,000	<u>20</u>
HP	800	<u>16</u>
IBM	500	<u>10</u>
Toshiba	400	<u>8</u>
Other 46 smaller firms	2,300	<u>46</u>

2 a. The total revenue shares are in the table above. The total revenue within the market is $5,000 million. A firm's share equals its total revenue divided by $5,000 million and then multiplied by 100.

b. The four-firm concentration ratio is the percentage of the total revenue, or sales, accounted for by the four largest firms in the industry, which is 20 percent + 16 percent + 10 percent + 8 percent = 54 percent; page 338.

c. To calculate the Herfindahl-Hirschman Index (HHI), square and then sum the market shares of the firms. The market shares are equal to each firm's percentage of total revenue. Each of the 20 smaller firms has total revenue of $50 million, so each has a 1 percentage point market share. So the HHI = $(20)^2 + (16)^2 + (10)^2 + (8)^2 + (1.0)^2 \times 46 = 400 + 256 + 100 + 64 + 46$, which is 866; page 338.

3. a. The four-firm concentration ratios are the same for both industries, 60 percent; page 338.

b. The Herfindahl-Hirschman Index is 3,292 for Industry A and 940 for Industry B; page 338.

4. There is no restriction on entry in monopolistic competition, so if firms in an industry are making an economic profit, other firms have an incentive to enter the industry. The entry of new firms decreases the demand for each firm's product. The demand curve and marginal revenue curve shift leftward. When all firms in the industry are earning zero economic profit, there is no new incentive for new firms to enter and the industry is in long-run equilibrium. Similarly, if firms in an industry are incurring an economic loss, firms have an incentive to exit the industry and in the long run the remaining firms make zero economic profit; page 340.

5. In monopolistic competition, price exceeds marginal revenue and marginal revenue equals marginal cost, so price exceeds marginal cost—a sign of inefficiency. But this inefficiency arises from product differentiation that consumers value and for which they are willing to pay. So the loss that arises because marginal benefit exceeds marginal cost must be weighed against the gain that arises from greater product variety; page 341.

■ CHECKPOINT 13.2

Firms in monopolistic competition <u>are</u> continuously developing new products. In monopolistic competition, product improvement <u>does not</u> equal its efficient level. Advertising costs <u>are</u> large in monopolistic competition. Advertising costs are a <u>fixed</u> cost and shift the average total cost curve <u>upward</u>. Monopolistic competition <u>might be</u> efficient.

True or false
1. False; page 343
2. True; page 344
3. False; page 345
4. True; page 346

Multiple choice
1. c; page 343
2. b; page 343
3. c; page 343
4. b; page 345
5. c; page 345
6. b; page 346

Short answer and numeric questions
1. Firms innovate and develop new products to increase the demand for their product and earn an economic profit; page 343.

2. Although advertising increases a firm's total costs, it also might increase sales. If the quantity sold increases by a large enough amount, it can lower *average* total cost of the quantity produced because the greater fixed cost is spread over an even greater amount of output; page 345.

3. The bottom line on the question of whether advertising, brand names, and product differentiation are efficient is ambiguous. Advertising and product differentiation provide consumers with variety, which is a benefit. Brand names provide a signal to consumers, which also benefits consumers because they know the product's quality. But these benefits need to be weighed against the costs of advertising and product differentiation as well as the possibility that the actual differences between products might be very small; page 346.

■ CHECKPOINT 13.3

Fill in the blanks

In an oligopoly a <u>small</u> number of firms compete. A <u>cartel</u> is a group of firms acting together to limit output, raise price, and increase economic profit. When a duopoly charges the perfectly competitive price, each firm receives <u>no</u> economic profit. When a duopoly charges the monopoly price, economic profit is <u>maximized</u>.

True or false

1. True; page 348
2. False; page 348
3. False; page 349
4. False; page 350
5. False; page 350

Multiple choice

1. c; page 348
2. b; page 348
3. b; page 348
4. a; page 348
5. b; page 349
6. e; page 349
7. b; page 350

8. c; page 350
9. b; pages 350-351
10. b; page 351

Complete the graph

■ FIGURE 13.8

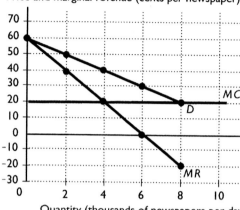

Price and marginal revenue (cents per newspaper)

Quantity (thousands of newspapers per day)

1. a. The curves are graphed in Figure 13.8.
   b. The competitive equilibrium is 8,000 newspapers a day and a price of 20¢ a newspaper; page 349.
   c. The monopoly equilibrium is 4,000 newspapers a day and a price of 40¢ a newspaper; page 349.
   d. The exact price and quantity can't be predicted, but it will be somewhere between the competitive and monopoly outcomes. The price will be between 40¢ and 20¢ a newspaper and the output will be between 4,000 and 8,000 newspapers a day; pages 349-351.

Short answer and numeric questions

1. Oligopoly occurs when a small number of firms compete and natural or legal barriers prevent the entry of new firms; page 348.

2. A cartel is a group of firms acting together to limit output, raise price, and increase economic profit; page 348.

3. The point that one firm's actions can decrease another firm's profits is what makes competition difficult in an oligopoly. While the firms might be better off cooperating, each firm trying to increase its profit takes

actions that lead the profits of its competitors to decrease, so that all the firms wind up worse off; pages 349-351.

4. If the firms can form and maintain a cartel that boosts the price and decreases the output, all the firms' profits can increase; page 349.

5. Every firm has the incentive to cheat on an output-limiting agreement because if it and it alone cheats by boosting its output and cutting its price, its economic profit will increase; page 349-350.

■ CHECKPOINT 13.4

Fill in the blanks

Game theory is the main tool that economists use to analyze <u>strategic</u> behavior. Games feature <u>rules</u>, <u>strategies</u>, and <u>payoffs</u>. The Nash equilibrium is <u>not always</u> the best possible equilibrium for the players. Game theory shows that duopolists <u>cannot</u> always reach the best possible equilibrium. In a <u>repeated</u> game, a tit-for-tat strategy can be used. The <u>larger</u> the number of firms, the harder it is for an oligopoly to maintain the monopoly output.

True or false

1. True; page 353
2. False; pages 353-354
3. False; page 355
4. True; page 358
5. False; page 358

Multiple choice

1. b; page 353
2. b; page 354
3. a; page 355
4. a; page 355
5. e; page 355
6. a; page 356
7. d; page 356
8. b; page 356
9. b; page 358
10. d; page 359

Complete the graph

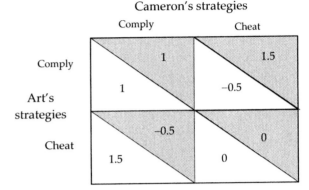

Cameron's strategies

1. a. The completed payoff matrix is above. The payoffs are in millions of dollars; page 355.

   b. The Nash equilibrium is for both Cameron and Art to cheat on the collusive agreement and each earn zero economic profit; pages 356.

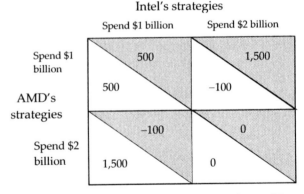

Intel's strategies

1. a. The completed payoff matrix is above. The payoffs are in millions of dollars; page 355.

   b. The Nash equilibrium is for both Intel and AMD to spend $2 billion on research and development and each earn zero economic profit; page 357.

Short answer and numeric questions

1. Strategies are all the possible actions of each player. In the prisoners' dilemma game, strategies are "to confess" or "to deny;" in the Airbus/Boeing duopoly game, strategies

are "to produce 4 airplanes a week" or "to produce 3 airplanes a week;" page 354.

2. In the prisoners' dilemma game, the players do not cooperate because they do not see cooperation as being in their best interest. Regardless of what the second player does, the first player is better off confessing. Regardless of what the first player does, the second player is better off confessing. Because it is in each player's separate best interest to confess rather than cooperate by denying, both players confess; pages 354-355.

3. In the duopolists' dilemma game, the players do not cooperate for precisely the same reason they do not cooperate in the prisoners' dilemma game: The players do not see cooperation as being in their best interest. As a result, because each player's profit-maximizing actions harm the other player, the equilibrium can be the worst outcome for both; page 356.

4. The more players in a game, the harder it is to maintain the monopoly outcome; page 356.

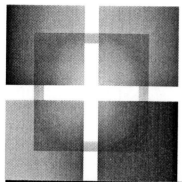

GDP and the Standard of Living

Chapter 14

1 **Define GDP and explain why the value of production, income, and expenditure are the same for an economy.**

The standard of living is the level of the consumption of the goods and services that people enjoy, on the average. It is measured by the average income per person. Gross Domestic Product, GDP, is the market value of all the final goods and services produced within a country in a given time period. Only final goods and services are included in GDP; intermediate goods and services are not included. Expenditures are consumption expenditure (C), investment (I), government expenditure on goods and services (G), and net exports of goods and services (NX). Investment is the purchase of new capital goods and additions to inventories. Total expenditure equals $C + I + G + NX$. Firms pay out the revenue they receive to households as payment for labor, capital, land, and entrepreneurship. These payments are households' income. We call total income Y. The circular flow shows that total expenditure equals total income so that $Y = C + I + G + NX$.

2 **Describe how economic statisticians measure GDP and distinguish between nominal GDP and real GDP.**

GDP is measured using the expenditure approach and the income approach. The expenditure approach adds the four sources of expenditure: consumption expenditure, investment, government expenditure on goods and services, and net exports of goods and services. Expenditures on used goods and financial assets are not in GDP. The income approach adds two categories of income (wages plus interest, rent, and profit). This sum is net domestic product at factor cost. To get to GDP from this, subsidies are subtracted, and indirect taxes and depreciation are added. A statistical discrepancy is added or subtracted so that GDP using the income approach equals GDP using the expenditure approach. Disposable personal income is the income received by households minus the personal income taxes paid. Real GDP is the value of final goods and services produced in a given year expressed in the prices of a base year; nominal GDP is the value of final goods and services produced in a given year using prices of that year.

3 **Describe and explain the limitations of real GDP as a measure of the standard of living.**

Real GDP per person can be used to compare the standard of living over time or across nations. Real GDP fluctuates in a business cycle, going from an expansion to a peak to a recession to a trough. Real GDP per person is not a perfect measure of the standard of living because it does not measure household production, underground production, the value of leisure time, the environmental quality, health and life expectancy, or political freedom and justice.

CHECKPOINT 14.1

■ **Define GDP and explain why the value of production, income, and expenditure are the same for an economy.**

Quick Review

- *Total expenditure* Total expenditure is the total amount received by producers of final goods and services and equals $C + I + G + NX$.
- *Total income* Total income is the income paid to all factors of production and equals total expenditure.

Additional Practice Problems 14.1

1. Last year consumption expenditure was $70 billion, investment was $16 billion, government purchases of goods and services were $12 billion, exports were $4 billion, and imports were $3 billion.
   a. What did GDP last year equal?
   b. This year imports increased to $5 billion. If all the other types of expenditure stay the same, what does GDP this year equal?

2. Suppose that GDP equals $12 trillion, consumption expenditure equals $7 trillion, investment equals $3.5 trillion, and government expenditure on goods and services equals $2.5 trillion. What does net exports equal?

3. One of the four expenditure categories is net exports. How can net exports be negative?

Solutions to Additional Practice Problems 14.1

1a. To solve this problem use the equality between GDP and expenditure, $GDP = C + I + G + NX$. Last year's GDP = $70 billion + $16 billion + $12 billion + ($4 billion – $3 billion) = $99 billion.

1b. This year, imports increased from $3 billion to $5 billion, so replace the $3 billion in the calculation with $5 billion and GDP for this year is $97 billion. The $2 billion increase in imports results in a $2 billion decrease in GDP.

2. $GDP = C + I + G + NX$. So $NX = GDP – C – I – G$. In this case, $NX = 12 trillion – $7 trillion – $3.5 trillion – $2.5 trillion, which equals –$1 trillion.

3. Net exports equals the value of exports of goods and services minus the value of imports of goods and services. If, as is the case in the United States, the value of imports exceeds the value of exports, net exports will be negative.

■ **Self Test 14.1**

Fill in the blanks

The market value of all the final goods and services produced within a country in a given time period is _____ (GDP; investment). _____ (Two; Three; Four) groups buy the final goods and services produced. Net exports of goods and services equals the value of _____ (imports; exports) minus the value of _____ (imports; exports). $C + I + G + NX$ equals _____ and _____.

True or false

1. The computer chip that Dell Corp. buys from Intel Corp. is a final good.

2. Expenditure on a bulldozer is consumption expenditure.

3. The value of net exports of goods and services can be negative.

4. The value of production equals income, which equals expenditure.

Multiple choice

1. The abbreviation "GDP" stands for
   a. Gross Domestic Product.
   b. Gross Domestic Prices.
   c. General Domestic Prices.
   d. Great Domestic Prices.
   e. Government's Domestic Politics.

2. GDP is equal to the _____ value of all the final goods and services produced within a country in a given period of time.
   a. production
   b. market
   c. wholesale
   d. retail
   e. typical

3. The following are all *final* goods except
   a. flour used by the baker to make cup cakes.
   b. bread eaten by a family for lunch.
   c. pencils used by a 6th grader in class.
   d. Nike shoes used by a basketball player.
   e. a computer used by Intel to design new computer chips.

4. Investment is defined as
   a. the purchase of a stock or bond.
   b. financial capital.
   c. what consumers do with their savings.
   d. the purchase of new capital goods by firms.
   e. spending on capital goods by governments.

5. In one year, a firm increases its production by $9 million and increases sales by $8 million. All other things in the economy remaining the same, which of the following is true?
   a. GDP increases by $8 million and inventory investment decreases by $1 million.
   b. GDP increases by $9 million and inventory investment increases by $1 million.
   c. Inventory investment decreases by $1 million.
   d. GDP increases by $8 million and investment increases by $1 million.
   e. GDP increases by $17 million.

6. Total expenditure equals
   a. $C + I + G + NX$.
   b. $C + I + G - NX$.
   c. $C + I - G + NX$.
   d. $C - I + G + NX$.
   e. $C - I - G - NX$.

Short answer and numeric questions

1. Why aren't intermediate goods or services counted in GDP?

2. Classify each of the following into the components of U.S. GDP: consumption expenditure, investment, government purchases of goods and services, exports, or imports.
   a. The purchase of a Sony DVD player made in Japan.

   b. A family's purchase of a birthday cake at the local Safeway grocery store.
   c. Microsoft's purchase of 100 Dell servers.
   d. The purchase of a new pizza oven by Pizza Hut.
   e. The government's purchase of 15 stealth fighters.

3. Why does total expenditure equal total income?

CHECKPOINT 14.2

■ **Describe how economic statisticians measure GDP and distinguish between nominal GDP and real GDP.**

Quick Review

- *Expenditure approach* GDP equals the sum of consumption expenditure, investment, government expenditure on goods and services and net exports of goods and services.
- *Income approach* GDP equals the sum of wages plus interest, rent, and profit minus subsidies plus indirect taxes and depreciation plus or minus any statistical discrepancy.

Additional Practice Problem 14.2

Item	Amount (billions of dollars)
Wages	5,875
Consumption expenditure	6,987
Indirect taxes less subsidies	630
Interest, rent, and profit	2,248
Depreciation	1,329
Investment	1,586
Statistical discrepancy	0
Net exports	−349

1. The table above gives some of the items in the U.S. National Income and Product Accounts in 2001.
   a. Calculate U.S. GDP in 2001.

b. Did you use the expenditure approach or the income approach to make this calculation?

c. What was the government's expenditure on goods and services in 2001?

Solution to Additional Practice Problem 14.2

1a. This question focuses on calculating GDP. To solve problems such as this, you need to know how to use the expenditure approach and the income approach. The expenditure approach adds four categories of expenditure while the income approach adds the two income categories and then makes a few additional adjustments.

To calculate GDP using the expenditure approach the four categories of expenditure you need to know are: consumption, investment, government expenditure, and net exports. The table does not give the value of government expenditures on goods and services, so you cannot find GDP using the expenditure approach.

To calculate GDP using the income approach you need to know the values of wages and of interest, rent, and profit. Adding these two together yields net domestic income at factor cost. To adjust to GDP, you need also indirect taxes less subsidies, depreciation, and any statistical discrepancy. All these items are listed in the table, so GDP can be calculated using the income approach. In this case, GDP = $5,875 billion + $2,248 + $630 billion + $1,329 billion + $0, which is $10,082 billion.

1b The only way GDP can be calculated in part (a) is by the income approach, which is the approach used.

1c. GDP was calculated in part (a) using the income approach. The expenditure approach notes that GDP = $C + I + G + NX$. Subtract C, I, and NX from both sides of the equation to show that $G = GDP - C - I - NX$. Using the values of GDP, C, I, and NX yields G = $10,082 billion − $6,987 billion − $1,586 billion + $349 billion = $1,858 billion. (The net exports were negative, so −(−$349 billion) equals + $349 billion).

■ Self Test 14.2

Fill in the blanks

The _____ approach and the _____ approach are two methods used to calculate GDP. Expenditure on used goods _____ (is; is not) included in GDP. Wages is part of the _____ (expenditure; income) approach to calculating GDP. To calculate GDP, depreciation is _____ (added to; subtracted from) net domestic product at factor cost. GNP equals GDP _____ (plus; minus) net factor income from abroad. For the United States, the difference between GDP and GNP is _____ (large; small). _____ (Real; Nominal) GDP values production during the year using constant prices; _____ (real; nominal) GDP values production using prices that prevailed during the year.

True or false

1. The expenditure approach measures GDP by using data on consumption expenditure, investment, government expenditures on goods and services, and net exports of goods and services.

2. In the United States, expenditure on used goods is becoming an increasingly large fraction of GDP.

3. The income approach uses data on consumption expenditure, investment, government purchases of goods and services, and net exports of goods and services to calculate GDP.

4. Personal disposable income is usually larger than GDP.

Multiple choice

1. In calculating GDP, economists
   a. measure total expenditure as the only true measure.
   b. can measure either total expenditure or total income.
   c. measure total income as the only true measure.
   d. measure total income minus total expenditure.
   e. measure total income plus total expenditure.

2. The expenditure approach to measuring GDP is based on summing
   a. wages, interest, rent, and profit.
   b. each industry's production.
   c. the total values of final goods, intermediate goods, used goods, and financial assets.
   d. consumption expenditure, investment, government expenditure on goods and services, and net exports of goods and services.
   e. consumption expenditure, investment, government expenditure on goods and services, and net exports of goods and services minus wages, interest, rent, and profit.

3. Suppose GDP is $10 billion, consumption expenditure is $7 billion, investment is $2 billion, and government expenditure on goods and services is $2 billion. Net exports of goods and services must be
   a. $1 billion.
   b. −$1 billion.
   c. $2 billion.
   d. −$2 billion.
   e. $10 billion.

4. According to the expenditure approach to measuring GDP, in the United States the largest component of GDP is
   a. consumption expenditure.
   b. investment.
   c. government expenditure on goods and services.
   d. net exports of goods and services.
   e. wages.

5. Which of the following is NOT one of the income categories used in the income approach to measuring GDP?
   a. wages
   b. rent
   c. interest
   d. taxes paid by persons
   e. profit

6. Nominal GDP can change
   a. only if prices change.
   b. only if the quantities of goods and services change.
   c. only if prices increase.
   d. if either prices or the quantities of goods and services change.
   e. only if prices *and* the quantities of the goods and services change.

7. The difference between nominal GDP and real GDP is
   a. the indirect taxes used in their calculations.
   b. the prices used in their calculations.
   c. that nominal GDP includes the depreciation of capital and real GDP does not.
   d. that nominal GDP includes net exports of goods and services and real GDP includes net imports.
   e. that real GDP includes the depreciation of capital and nominal GDP does not.

Short answer and numeric questions

Item	Amount (dollars)
Wages	3,900
Consumption expenditure	4,000
Indirect taxes minus subsidies	400
Interest, rent, and profit	1,400
Government expenditure	1,000
Investment	1,100
Net exports	300
Statistical discrepancy	300

1. The table above gives data for a small nation:
   a. What is the nation's GDP? Did you use the expenditure or income approach to calculate GDP?
   b. What is the net domestic product at factor cost?
   c. What does depreciation equal?

2. What adjustments must be made to net domestic product at factor cost to convert it to GDP? Why must these adjustments be made?

3. What adjustments must be made to GDP to calculate GNP? To calculate disposable personal income?

4. What is the difference between real GDP and

nominal GDP? Are the two ever equal?

5. To measure changes in production, why do we use real GDP rather than nominal GDP?

CHECKPOINT 14.3

■ **Describe and explain the limitations of real GDP as a measure of the standard of living.**

Quick Review

- *Standard of living* The standard of living among different nations or over a period of time can be compared using real GDP per person.

- *Goods and services omitted from GDP* Household production, underground production, leisure time, and environmental quality are omitted from GDP.

Additional Practice Problems 14.3

1. How has real GDP per person changed in the United States since 1967?

2. How do you think the standard of living in the United States today compares with the standard of living 150 years ago?

Solutions to Additional Practice Problems 14.3

1. Real GDP per person has increased substantially since 1967. In fact, real GDP per person has more than doubled since 1967. Historically, in the United States for the past 100 years real GDP per person has doubled about every 30 years.

2. The standard of living now is dramatically higher than it was 150 years ago. First, even though no totally accurate data on real GDP per person is available from 150 years ago, it is certain that real GDP per person is much higher today even after taking account of the fact that household production was more common 150 years ago. The underground economy is larger today, which boosts today's standard of living, and people today enjoy significantly more leisure time, which also boosts today's standard of living. Per-

haps the edge on environment quality goes to the past. Considering health and life expectancy, and political freedom and social justice, people today are much better off than people 150 years ago.

■ Self Test 14.3

Fill in the blanks

The value of household production ____ (is; is not) included in GDP. The value of people's leisure time ____ (is; is not) included in GDP. As it is calculated, GDP ____ (does; does not) subtract the value of environmental degradation resulting from production. Real GDP ____ (takes; does not take) into account the extent of a country's political freedom.

True or false

1. As currently measured, real GDP does not include the value of home production.

2. Production in the underground economy is part of the "investment" component of GDP.

3. The production of anti-pollution devices installed by electric utilities is not counted in GDP because the devices are designed only to eliminate pollution.

4. The measure of a country's real GDP does not take into account the extent of political freedom in the country.

Multiple choice

1. Which of the following is <u>NOT</u> part of the business cycle?
   a. recession
   b. peak
   c. inflation
   d. trough
   e. expansion

2. In the business cycle, what immediately precedes the time when real GDP is falling?
   a. recession
   b. peak
   c. depression
   d. trough
   e. expansion

3. The measurement of GDP handles household production by
   a. estimating a dollar value of the goods purchased to do housework.
   b. estimating a dollar value of the services provided.
   c. ignoring it.
   d. including it in exactly the same way that all other production is included.
   e. including it in real GDP but not in nominal GDP because there are no prices paid for the work.

4. You hire some of your friends to help you move to a new house and pay them a total of $200 and buy them dinner at Pizza Hut. Which of the following is true?
   a. The $200 should be counted as part of GDP but not the dinner at Pizza Hut.
   b. If your friends do not report the $200 on their tax forms, it becomes part of the underground economy.
   c. The dinner at Pizza Hut should be counted as part of GDP but not the $200.
   d. Hiring your friends is an illegal activity and should not be counted in GDP.
   e. Neither the $200 nor the dinner should be counted in GDP because both are household production.

5. The value of leisure time is
   a. directly included in GDP and, in recent years, has become an increasing large part of GDP.
   b. excluded from GDP.
   c. zero.
   d. directly included in GDP but, in recent years, has become a decreasing large part of GDP.
   e. directly included in GDP and, in recent years, has not changed much as a fraction of GDP.

6. A new technology is discovered that results in all new cars producing 50 percent less pollution. The technology costs nothing to produce and cars do not change in price. As a result of the technology, there is a reduction in the number of visits people make to the doctor to complain of breathing difficulties. Which of the following is true?
   a. real GDP decreases as a result of fewer doctor services being provided.
   b. real GDP is not affected.
   c. nominal GDP increases to reflect the improvement in the health of the population.
   d. real GDP will decrease to reflect the decrease in pollution.
   e. nominal GDP does not change and real GDP increases because people's health increases.

7. The calculation of GDP using the income approach EXCLUDES
   a. rent.
   b. interest.
   c. environmental quality.
   d. wages.
   e. profit.

8. Good health and life expectancy are
   a. included in GDP but not in our standard of living.
   b. included in both GDP and in our standard of living.
   c. included in our standard of living but not in GDP.
   d. not included in either our standard of living or in GDP.
   e. sometimes included in GDP if they are large enough changes but are never included in our standard of living.

Short answer and numeric questions

1. What are the parts of a business cycle? What is their order?

2. What general categories of goods and services are omitted from GDP? Why is each omitted?

3. If you cook a hamburger at home, what happens to GDP? If you go to Burger King and purchase a hamburger, what happens to GDP?

SELF TEST ANSWERS

■ CHECKPOINT 14.1

Fill in the blanks

The market value of all the final goods and services produced within a country in a given time period is <u>GDP</u>. <u>Four</u> groups buy the final goods and services produced. Net exports equals the value of <u>exports</u> minus the value of <u>imports</u>. $C + I + G + NX$ equals <u>total expenditure</u> and <u>total income</u>.

True or false

1. False; page 366
2. False; page 367
3. True; page 368
4. True; page 339

Multiple choice

1. a; page 366
2. b; page 366
3. a; page 366
4. d; page 367
5. b; page 367
6. a; page 368

Short answer and numeric questions

1. Intermediate goods or services are not counted in GDP because if they were, they would be double counted. A computer produced by Dell Corp. is included in GDP. But if the Intel chip that is part of the computer is also included in GDP, then the Intel chip is counted twice: once when it is produced by Intel, and again when it is included in the computer produced by Dell; page 366.

2. a. Import; page 367.
   b. Consumption expenditure; page 366.
   c. Investment; page 366.
   d. Investment; page 366.
   e. Government expenditure on goods and services; page 366.

3. Total expenditure is the amount received by producers of final goods and services from the sales of these goods and services

Because firms pay all the revenue they receive to households in payment for the factors of production, total expenditure equals total income. From the viewpoint of firms, the value of production is the cost of production, and the cost of production is equal to income. From the viewpoint of consumers of goods and services, the value of production is the cost of buying the production, which equals expenditure; pages 368-369.

■ CHECKPOINT 14.2

Fill in the blanks

The <u>expenditure</u> approach and the <u>income</u> approach are two methods used to calculate GDP. Expenditure on used goods <u>is not</u> included in GDP. Wages is part of the <u>income</u> approach to calculating GDP. To calculate GDP, depreciation is <u>added to</u> net domestic product at factor cost. GNP equals GDP <u>plus</u> net factor income from abroad. For the United States, the difference between GDP and GNP is <u>small</u>. <u>Real</u> GDP values production during the year using constant prices; <u>nominal</u> GDP values production using prices that prevailed during the year.

True or false

1. True; page 371
2. False; page 372
3. False; page 373
4. False; page 375

Multiple choice

1. b; page 371
2. d; page 371
3. b; page 371
4. a; page 371
5. d; page 373
6. d; page 376
7. b; page 376

Short answer and numeric questions

1. a. GDP = $6,400, which is the sum of consumption expenditure, investment, gov-

ernment expenditures on goods and services, and net exports of goods and services. The expenditure approach was used; page 371.

b. Net domestic product at factor cost equals $5,300, the sum of wages plus interest, rent, and profit; page 373.

c. The difference between GDP and net domestic product at factor cost, which is $1,100, equals indirect taxes minus subsidies plus depreciation plus any statistical discrepancy. The statistical discrepancy equals zero. Indirect taxes minus subsidies equals $400, so depreciation equals $700; pages 373-374.

2. To change net domestic product at factor cost to GDP, three sets of adjustments must be made. First, net domestic product at factor cost is measured at firms' costs; to convert costs to equal the market prices paid, taxes must be added and subsidies subtracted. Second, net domestic product does not include depreciation but GDP does. So, depreciation must be added. Finally, any statistical discrepancy must be added or subtracted; pages 373-374.

3. To calculate GNP, net factor income from abroad must be added (or subtracted, if it is negative) from GDP. Then, to calculate disposable personal income, from GNP depreciation and retained profits must be subtracted, transfer payments must be added, and then any statistical discrepancy must be either added or subtracted; page 375.

4. The difference between real GDP and nominal GDP lies in the prices used to value the final goods and services. Real GDP uses prices from a fixed base year. Nominal GDP uses prices from the current year for which GDP is being calculated. Real GDP equals nominal GDP in the base year; page 376.

5. Nominal GDP is computed using prices and quantities from the given year. From one year to the next, both prices and quantities can change, so nominal GDP will change if either the prices change or the quantities—

production—change. Real GDP uses prices from a base year. So from one year to the next changes in real GDP reflect changes in the quantities, that is, changes in production; page 376.

■ CHECKPOINT 14.3

Fill in the blanks

The value of household production is not included in GDP. The value of people's leisure time is not included in GDP. As it is calculated, GDP does not subtract the value of environmental degradation resulting from production. Real GDP does not take into account the extent of a country's political freedom.

True or false

1. True; page 380
2. False; page 380
3. False; page 382
4. True; page 383

Multiple choice

1. c; page 379
2. b; pages 379-380
3. c; page 381
4. b; page 381
5. b; page 381
6. a; page 382
7. c; page 382
8. c; page 383

Short answer and numeric questions

1. The business cycle is made up of the expansion phase, when real GDP is growing; the peak, when real GDP reaches its highest level; the recession phase, when real GDP is falling for at least 6 months; and the trough, when real GDP is at its lowest level. The order of the business cycle is from expansion to peak to recession to trough, and then back to expansion; pages 379-380.

2. Goods and services omitted from GDP are household production, underground production, leisure time, and environmental

quality. GDP measures the value of goods and services that are bought in markets. Because household production, leisure time, and environmental quality are not purchased in markets, they are excluded from GDP. Even though underground production frequently is bought in markets, the activity is unreported and is not included in GDP; pages 381-382.

3. If you cook a hamburger at home, the meat you purchased is included in GDP but the production of the hamburger is not included in GDP because it is household production. If you buy a hamburger at Burger King, the production of the hamburger is included in GDP; page 381.

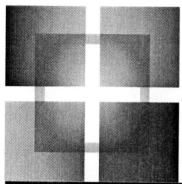

Chapter

Appendix: Measuring Real GDP

14

APPENDIX CHECKLIST

The appendix shows how the Bureau of Economic Analysis calculates real GDP.

1. Measuring Real GDP

Real GDP depends on the prices used to value the production of goods and services. The Bureau of Economic Analysis (BEA) uses prices from adjacent years to value the production and thereby creates a chained-dollar real GDP. For instance, between 2007 and 2008, first, prices from 2007 are used to value the production in 2007 and the production in 2008. Then the growth rate between these two years is calculated. Second, prices from 2008 are used to value the production in 2007 and the production in 2008. Then the (second) growth rate between these two years is calculated. These two growth rates are averaged to give the final growth rate between these two years. This growth rate is applied to real GDP for 2007 to calculate real GDP for 2008. The real GDPs for all the years are chained back to the base year real GDP by the growth rates between years.

CHECKPOINT 1

■ Measuring Real GDP

Quick Review

- *Real GDP* The value of the final goods and services produced in a given year valued at the prices of a base year.

- *Nominal GDP* The value of the final goods and services produced in a given year valued at the prices that prevailed in that year.

Additional Practice Problem 1

1. In a small, tropical nation suppose real GDP in 2007 was $5 billion and nominal GDP in 2007 was $10 billion. In 2008, nominal GDP was $12 billion. If GDP in 2008, measured using 2007 prices was $11.5 billion and GDP in 2007, measured using 2008 prices was $11 billion, what does real GDP in 2008 equal?

Solution to Additional Practice Problem 1

1. This question gives you practice in how real GDP is calculated. Take each part step-by-step:

First we need the growth rate of GDP from 2007 to 2008 measured using 2007 prices. Nominal GDP in 2007 (which is GDP in 2007 measured using 2007 prices) was $10 billion and GDP in 2008 measured using 2007 prices was $11.5 billion. So the growth in GDP using 2004 prices was [($11.5 billion − $10.0 billion) ÷ $10 billion] × 100, which is 11.5 percent.

Next we need the growth rate of GDP from 2007 to 2008 measured using 2008 prices. GDP in 2007 measured with 2008 prices was $11 billion and nominal GDP in 2008 (which is GDP in 2008 measured using 2008 prices) was $12 billion. So the growth in GDP using 2005 prices was [($12 billion − $11 billion) ÷ $11 billion] × 100, which is 9.1 percent.

Finally, we average the two growth rates to give a growth rate of 10.3 percent between 2007 and 2008. This percentage change is applied to real GDP in 2007, $5 billion, to give real GDP in 2008, so that real GDP in 2008 equals ($5 billion × 1.103) which is $5.52 billion.

■ Self Test I

Fill in the blanks

The BEA calculates real GDP in a given year using prices from ____ (that year only; that year and the previous year). Real GDP in any given year ____ (is; is not) chained back to the base year.

True or false

1. Real GDP is just a more precise name for GDP.
2. Real GDP equals nominal GDP in the base year.
3. The base year for real GDP changes each year.

Multiple choice

1. Real GDP measures the value of goods and services produced in a given year valued using
   a. base year prices.
   b. prices of that same year.
   c. no prices.
   d. future prices.
   e. government approved prices.

2. In a small country, using prices of 2007, GDP in 2007 was $100 and GDP in 2008 was $110. Using prices of 2008, GDP in 2007 was $200 and GDP in 2008 was $210. The country's

BEA will calculate ____ percent as the growth in real GDP between those years.
   a. 10
   b. 5
   c. 15
   d. 7.5
   e. None of the above answers is correct.

3. Using prices from 2006, GDP grew 10 percent between 2006 and 2007; using prices from 2007, GDP grew 8 percent between 2006 and 2007. For its link back to the base year, the BEA will use ____ percent as the growth in real GDP between 2006 and 2007.
   a. 10
   b. 8
   c. 2
   d. 18
   e. 9

Short answer and numeric questions

Item	Data for 2008 Quantity	Data for 2008 Price	Data for 2009 Quantity	Data for 2009 Price
Pizza	100	$10.00	150	$20.00
Soda	50	$2.00	75	$4.00

1. An economy produces only pizza and soda. The table above gives the quantities produced and prices in 2008 and 2009. The base year is 2008.
   a. What is nominal GDP in 2008?
   b. What is real GDP in 2008?
   c. What is nominal GDP in 2009?
   d. What is real GDP in 2009?

2. How does the chained-dollar method of calculating real GDP link the current year's real GDP to the base year's real GDP?

SELF TEST ANSWERS

■ CHECKPOINT I

Fill in the blanks

The BEA calculates real GDP in a given year using prices from <u>that year and the previous year</u>. Real GDP in any given year <u>is</u> chained back to the base year.

True or false

1. False; page 389
2. True; page 389
3. False; page 391

Multiple choice

1. a; page 389
2. d; pages 390-391
3. e; page 391

Short answer and numeric questions

1. a. Nominal GDP = (100 pizzas × $10 per pizza) + (50 sodas × $2 per soda) = $1,100, the sum of expenditure on pizza and expenditure on soda; pages 389-390.

   b. Because 2008 is the base year, real GDP = nominal GDP, so real GDP = $1,100; pages 389-391.

   c. Nominal GDP = (150 pizzas × $20 per pizza) + (75 sodas × $4 per soda) = $3,300, the sum of expenditure on pizza and expenditure on soda; pages 389-390.

   d. Using 2008 prices, GDP grew from $1,100 in 2008 to $1,650 in 2009, a percentage increase of 50 percent. Using 2009 prices, GDP grew 50 percent between 2008 and 2009. The average growth is 50 percent, so real GDP in 2009 is 50 percent higher than in 2008, so that real GDP in 2009 is $1,650; pages 390-391.

2. From one year to the next, real GDP is scaled by the percentage change from the first year to the next. For instance, real GDP in 2008 is linked to real GDP in 2007 by the percentage change from 2007, and real GDP in 2009 in turn is linked to real GDP in 2008 by the percentage change from 2008, and so on. These links are like the links in a chain. They link real GDP in the current year back to the base year and the base year prices; page 391.

The CPI and the Cost of Living

Chapter

15

Chapter 15 explores how the CPI and other price level indices are measured.

1 Explain what the Consumer Price Index (CPI) is and how it is calculated.

The Consumer Price Index (CPI) measures the average of the prices paid by urban consumers for a fixed market basket of consumer goods and services. The CPI compares the cost of the fixed market basket of goods and services at one time with the cost of the fixed market basket in the reference base period, currently 1982–1984. The CPI in the base period is 100. If the CPI is now 150, it costs 50 percent more to buy the same goods and services than it cost in the base period. To construct the CPI market basket, households are surveyed on what they buy. Then, each month the Bureau of Labor Statistics checks the prices of the 80,000 goods and services in the basket. To calculate the CPI, the cost of the market basket using current prices is divided by the cost of the basket using base period prices and the result is multiplied by 100. The inflation rate is the percentage change in the price level from one year to the next and is equal to [(CPI in current year − CPI in previous year) ÷ (CPI in previous year)] × 100.

2 Explain the limitations of the CPI and describe other measures of the price level.

The CPI has four sources of bias that lead to an inaccurate measure of the cost of living. These biases are the new goods bias (new goods replace old goods), the quality change bias (goods and services increase in quality), the commodity substitution bias (changes in relative prices lead consumers to change the items they buy), and the outlet substitution bias (consumers switch to shopping more often in discount stores). The overall CPI bias has been estimated to overstate inflation by 1.1 percentage points per year. The CPI bias distorts private contracts, increases government outlays, and decreases government tax revenues. The GDP deflator is an average of current prices of all the goods and services included in GDP expressed as a percentage of base-year prices. It equals (nominal GDP ÷ real GDP) × 100. The GDP deflator is constructed using, in part, the CPI, and so the GDP deflator inherits the same biases as the CPI. The PCE (personal consumption expenditure) deflator an average of the current prices of the goods and services included in the consumption expenditure component of GDP expressed as a percentage of base year prices.

3 Adjust money values for inflation and calculate real wage rates and real interest rates.

Comparing values measured in dollars in different years is misleading if the value of money changes. To make the comparison, the nominal values must be converted to real values. Real GDP equals nominal GDP divided by the price level and multiplied by 100. The real wage rate measures the quantity of goods and services that an hour's work can buy. It equals the nominal wage rate divided by the CPI and multiplied by 100. The real interest rate equals the nominal interest rate minus the inflation rate.

CHECKPOINT 15.1

■ **Explain what the Consumer Price Index (CPI) is and how it is calculated.**

Quick Review

- *CPI market basket* The goods and services in the CPI and the relative importance attached to each of them.
- *CPI formula* The CPI equals:

$$\frac{\text{Cost of CPI basket at current period prices}}{\text{Cost of CPI basket at base period prices}} \times 100.$$

- *Inflation rate* The inflation rate equals:

$$\frac{(\text{CPI in current year} - \text{CPI in previous year})}{\text{CPI in previous year}} \times 100.$$

Additional Practice Problem 15.1

Item	Quantity (2008)	Price (2008)	Quantity (2009)	Price (2009)
Limes	20	$1.00	15	$1.00
Biscuits	30	$1.00	45	$0.75
Rum	10	$10.00	8	$11.00

1. A Consumer Expenditure Survey in Scurvy shows that people consume only limes, biscuits, and rum. The Consumer Expenditure Survey for both 2008 and 2009 are in the table above. The reference base year is 2008.
   a. What and how much is in the CPI market basket?
   b. What did the CPI market basket cost in 2008? What was the CPI in 2008?
   c. What did the CPI market basket cost in 2009? What was the CPI in 2009?
   d. What was the inflation rate between 2008 and 2009?

Solution to Additional Practice Problem 15.1

1a. The market basket is 20 limes, 30 biscuits, and 10 rums, the quantities consumed in the base year of 2008.

1b. In 2008 the market basket cost (20 × $1.00) + (30 × $1.00) + (10 × $10.00) = $150. Because 2008 is the reference base year, the CPI = 100.0.

1c. In 2009 the market basket cost (20 × $1.00) + (30 × $0.75) + (10 × $11.00) = $152.50. The CPI in 2009 is equal to ($152.50) ÷ ($150.00) × 100, which is 101.7.

1d. The inflation rate equals [(101.7 − 100.0) ÷ 100] × 100 = 1.7 percent.

■ **Self Test 15.1**

Fill in the blanks

The _____, also called the CPI, is a measure of the average of the prices paid by urban consumers for a fixed market basket of consumer goods and services. In the base reference period, the CPI equals _____. Each _____ (month; year) the Bureau of Labor Statistics checks the prices of the goods and services in the CPI basket. The CPI equals the cost of the CPI basket at current prices _____ (plus; minus; divided by) the cost of the CPI basket at base period prices, all multiplied by 100. To measure changes in the cost of living, the _____ (inflation rate; CPI in the base reference period) is used.

True or false

1. In the reference base period, the CPI equals 1.0.
2. The CPI market basket is changed from one month to the next.
3. If the cost of the CPI basket at current period prices equals $320, then the CPI equals 320.
4. If the cost of the CPI basket at current period prices exceeds the cost of the CPI basket at base period prices, the inflation rate between these two periods is positive.
5. If the CPI increases from 110 to 121, the inflation rate is 11 percent.

Multiple choice

1. The CPI is reported once every
   a. year.
   b. quarter.
   c. month.
   d. week.
   e. other year.

2. The Consumer Price Index (CPI) measures
   a. the prices of a few consumer goods and services.
   b. the prices of those consumer goods and services that increased in price.
   c. the average of the prices paid by urban consumers for a fixed market basket of goods and services.
   d. consumer confidence in the economy.
   e. the average of the costs paid by businesses to produce a fixed market basket of consumer goods and services.

3. If a country has a CPI of 105.0 last year and a CPI of 102.0 this year, then
   a. the average prices of goods and services increased between last year and this year.
   b. the average prices of goods and services decreased between last year and this year.
   c. the average quality of goods and services decreased between last year and this year.
   d. there was an error when calculating the CPI this year.
   e. the quantity of consumer goods and services produced decreased between last year and this year.

4. The period for which the Consumer Price Index is defined to equal 100 is called the
   a. reference base period.
   b. base year.
   c. starting point.
   d. zero period.
   e. beginning period.

5. The good or service given the most weight in the CPI basket when calculating the CPI is
   a. food and beverages.
   b. taxes.
   c. housing.
   d. medical care.
   e. recreation.

6. Suppose a basket of consumer goods and services costs $180 using the base period prices, and the same basket of goods and services costs $300 using the current period prices. The CPI for the current year period equals
   a. 166.7.
   b. 66.7.
   c. 160.0.
   d. 60.0.
   e. 300.0.

7. Suppose the CPI last year was 82.3 and this year is 90.9. Based on this information, we can calculate that the inflation rate between these years is
   a. 10.4 percent.
   b. 8.6 percent.
   c. 90.9 percent.
   d. 82.3 percent.
   e. 9.09 percent.

8. In the United States since 1977, on average the inflation rate in the last ten years was
   a. higher than between 1977 to 1981.
   b. higher than in the 1980s.
   c. lower than between 1977 to 1981.
   d. much higher than between 1985 to 1995.
   e. negative.

Short answer and numeric questions

Item	Quantity (2008)	Price (2008)	Quantity (2009)	Price (2009)
Pizza	10	$10.00	15	$10.00
Burritos	20	$1.00	25	$0.75
Rice	30	$0.50	20	$1.00

1. The table above gives the expenditures of households in the small nation of Studenvia. In Studenvia, 2008 is the reference base period.
   a. What is the cost of the CPI basket in 2008?
   b. What is the cost of the CPI basket in 2009?
   c. What is the CPI in 2008?
   d. What is the CPI in 2009?
   e. What is the inflation rate in 2009?

2. Suppose the CPI was 100.0 in 2005, 110.0 in 2006, 121.0 in 2007, and 133.1 in 2008. What is the inflation rate in 2006, 2007, and 2008?

3. If the price level rises slowly, is the inflation rate positive or negative? Why?

CHECKPOINT 15.2

■ **Explain the limitations of the CPI and describe other measures of the price level.**

Quick Review

- *Commodity substitution bias* People cut back on their purchases of items that become relatively more costly and increase their consumption of items that become relatively less costly.

Additional Practice Problem 15.2

1. Nowadays when households buy broccoli, they discard some of it because it is bruised. Suppose 20 percent is discarded. Now new, genetically engineered broccoli is developed that does not bruise so that all the broccoli that is purchased can be used. People prefer the new broccoli, so they switch to buying the new broccoli. If the price of the new broccoli is 10 percent higher than the old, what actually happens to the CPI and what should happen to the CPI?

2. When the price of textbook is $95 a book, Anthony buys his books at the bookstore closest to him. When textbooks rise in price to $125 a book at that store, Anthony drives several miles away to a store where the books are sold for only $110. How does Anthony's decision affect the CPI?

3. Nominal GDP = $10 trillion, real GDP = $9 trillion. What is the GDP deflator?

Solution to Additional Practice Problem 15.2

1. With the introduction of the new broccoli, the CPI rises because the new broccoli's price is higher (10 percent) than the old broccoli. But, the CPI should actually decrease because people pay only 10 percent more for 20 percent more (useable) broccoli. This problem illustrates how the quality change bias can bias the CPI upwards.

2. Anthony's decision reflects outlet substitution. When the price of a good rises, consumers, such as Anthony, switch the stores from which they buy goods and services to less expensive outlets. But the CPI, as constructed, does not take into account this point. The CPI will record that the price of textbooks rose by $30, from $95 to $125. This outlet substitution bias means that the CPI overstates the true rise in the cost of living.

3. GDP deflator = (Nominal GDP ÷ Real GDP) × 100 = ($10 trillion ÷ $9 trillion) × 100 = 111.1.

■ Self Test 15.2

Fill in the blanks

The sources of bias in the CPI as a measure of the cost of living are the ____, ____, ____, and ____. The Boskin Commission concluded that the CPI ____ (overstates; understates) inflation by ____ (1.1; 2.2; 3.3) percentage points a year. The CPI bias leads to ____ (an increase; a decrease) in government outlays. The GDP deflator equals 100 times ____ (real nominal) GDP divided by ____ (real; nominal) GDP.

True or false

1. The CPI is a biased measure of the cost of living.

2. Commodity substitution bias refers to the ongoing replacement of old goods by new goods.

3. The bias in the CPI is estimated to overstate inflation by approximately 1.1 percentage points a year.

4. The CPI bias can distort private contracts.

5. If real GDP is $600 billion and nominal GDP is $750 billion, then the GDP deflator is 125.

6. Inflation measured using the GDP deflator is generally lower than inflation measured using the CPI.

Multiple choice

1. All of the following are a bias in the CPI EX-CEPT the
   a. new goods bias.
   b. outlet substitution bias.
   c. commodity substitution bias.
   d. GDP deflator bias.
   e. quality change bias.

2. An example of the new goods bias in the calculation of the CPI is a price increase in
   a. butter relative to margarine.
   b. an MP3 player relative to a Walkman.
   c. a 2009 Honda Civic LX relative to a 2005 Honda Civic LX.
   d. textbooks bought through the campus bookstore relative to textbooks bought through Amazon.com.
   e. a Caribbean cruise for a couple who has never been on a cruise before.

3. The price of dishwashers has remained constant while the quality of dishwashers has improved. The CPI
   a. is adjusted monthly to reflect the improvement in quality.
   b. is increased monthly to reflect the increased quality of dishwashers.
   c. has an upward bias if it is not adjusted to take account of the higher quality.
   d. has an upward bias because it does not reflect the increased production of dishwashers.
   e. does not take account of any quality changes because it is a price index not a quality index.

4. Joe buys chicken and beef. If the price of beef rises and the price of chicken does not change, Joe will buy ____ for the CPI.
   a. more beef and create a new goods bias
   b. more chicken and create a commodity substitution bias
   c. the same quantity of beef and chicken and create a commodity substitution bias
   d. less chicken and beef and create a quality change bias
   e. more chicken and eliminate the commodity substitution bias

5. The CPI bias was estimated by the Congressional Advisory Commission on the Consumer Price Index as
   a. understating the actual inflation rate by about 5 percentage points a year.
   b. understating the actual inflation rate by more than 5 percentage points a year.
   c. overstating the actual inflation rate by about 1 percentage point a year.
   d. overstating the actual inflation rate by more than 5 percentage points a year.
   e. understating the actual inflation rate by about 1 percentage point a year.

6. A consequence of the CPI bias is that it
   a. decreases government outlays.
   b. increases international trade.
   c. reduces outlet substitution bias.
   d. distorts private contracts.
   e. means that it is impossible to measure the inflation rate.

7. The fact that the CPI is a biased measure of the inflation rate means government outlays will
   a. increase at a faster rate than the actual inflation rate.
   b. increase at the same rate as the actual inflation rate.
   c. increase at a slower rate than the actual inflation rate.
   d. sometimes increase faster and sometimes increase slower than the actual inflation rate depending on whether the actual inflation rate exceeds 1.1 percent per year or is less than 1.1 percent per year.
   e. None of the above because the bias in inflation measured using the CPI has nothing to do with government outlays.

8. The GDP deflator is a measure of
   a. taxes and subsidies.
   b. changes in quantities.
   c. prices.
   d. depreciation.
   e. changes in nominal GDP.

9. The GDP deflator is calculated as
   a. (nominal GDP ÷ real GDP) × 100.
   b. (real GDP ÷ nominal GDP) × 100.
   c. (nominal GDP + real GDP) ÷ 100.
   d. (nominal GDP − real GDP) ÷ 100.
   e. (real GDP − nominal GDP) ÷ 100.

10. Nominal GDP is $12.1 trillion and real GDP is $11.0 trillion. The GDP deflator is
    a. 90.1.
    b. 121.
    c. 1.10.
    d. 91.0.
    e. 110.

Short answer and numeric questions

1. What are the sources of bias in the CPI? Briefly explain each.

2. Once you graduate, you move to a new town and sign a long-term lease on a townhouse. You agree to pay $1,000 a month rent and to change the monthly rent annually by the percentage change in the CPI. For the next 4 years, the CPI increases 5 percent each year. What will you pay in monthly rent for the second, third, and fourth years of your lease? Suppose the CPI overstates the inflation rate by 1 percentage point a year. If the CPI bias was eliminated, what would you pay in rent for the second, third, and fourth years?

3. Calculate the price level.
   a. Nominal GDP = $12 trillion, real GDP = $10 trillion.
   b. Nominal GDP = $12 trillion, real GDP $16 trillion.
   c. Nominal GDP = $8 trillion, real GDP = $4 trillion.

CHECKPOINT 15.3

■ **Adjust money values for inflation and calculate real wage rates and real interest rates.**

Quick Review

- *Real wage rate* The real wage rate equals the nominal wage rate divided by the CPI and multiplied by 100.

- *Real interest rate* The real interest rate equals the nominal interest rate minus the inflation rate.

Additional Practice Problems 15.3

Year	Minimum wage (dollars per hour)	CPI
1955	0.75	26.7
1965	1.25	31.6
1975	2.10	56.7
1985	3.35	107.5
1995	4.25	152.4
2005	5.15	194.1

1. The table above shows the minimum wage and the CPI for six different years. The reference base period is 1982–1984.
   a. Calculate the real minimum wage in each year in 1982–1984 dollars.
   b. In which year was the minimum wage the highest in real terms?
   c. In which year was the minimum wage the lowest in real terms?

2. Suppose Sally has saved $1,000 dollars. Sally wants a 3 percent real interest rate on her savings. What nominal interest rate would she need to receive if the inflation rate is 7 percent?

Solutions to Additional Practice Problems 15.3

Year	Real minimum wage (1982-1984 dollars per hour)
1955	2.81
1965	3.96
1975	3.70
1985	3.12
1995	2.79
2005	2.65

1a. Using the CPI to adjust nominal values to real values is a key use of the CPI. Keep in mind that to convert a nominal price (such as the nominal wage rate) into a real price (such as the real wage rate), you divide by the CPI and multiply by 100, but to convert the nominal interest rate into the real interest rate, you subtract the inflation rate. To convert the nominal minimum wages in the table to real prices, divide the price by the CPI in that year and then multiply by 100. In 1955, the nominal minimum wage gas was $0.75 an hour and the CPI was 26.7, so the real minimum wage is ($0.75 ÷ 26.7) × 100 = $2.81. The rest of the real minimum wages in the table above are calculated similarly.

1b. In real terms, the minimum wage was highest in 1965 when it equaled $3.96.

1c. In real terms, the minimum wage was the lowest in 2005 when it equaled $2.65.

2. The real interest rate equals the nominal interest rate minus the inflation rate. Rearranging this formula shows that the nominal interest rate equals the real interest rate plus the inflation rate. To get a 3 percent real interest rate with a 7 percent inflation rate, Sally needs the nominal interest rate to be equal to 3 percent plus 7 percent, or 10 percent.

■ Self Test 15.3

Fill in the blanks

The nominal wage rate is the average hourly wage rate measured in ____ (current; reference base year) dollars. The real wage rate is the average hourly wage rate measured in dollars of the ____ (current; given base) year. The real wage rate equals the nominal wage rate (plus; times; divided by) the CPI multiplied by 100. The real interest rate equals the nominal interest rate ____ (plus; minus; divided by) the ____ (CPI; inflation rate).

True or false

1. The CPI was 171 in 2000 and 24.4 in 1950, so the price level in 2000 was 7 times higher than what it was in 1950.

2. Real GDP equals nominal GDP divided by the CPI, multiplied by 100.

3. A change in the real wage rate measures the change in the goods and services that an hour's work can buy.

4. The nominal interest rate is the percentage return on a loan expressed in dollars; the real interest rate is the percentage return on a loan expressed in purchasing power.

5. If the nominal interest rate is 8 percent a year and the inflation rate is 5 percent a year, then the real interest rate is 3 percent a year.

Multiple choice

1. In 2007, in New York, apples cost $1.49 a pound. Suppose the CPI was 120 in 2007 and 140 in 2008. If there is no change in the real value of an apple in the year 2008, how much would a pound of apples sell for in 2008?
   a. $2.74
   b. $1.69
   c. $1.66
   d. $1.74
   e. $1.28

2. In 1970, the CPI was 39 and in 2000 it was 172. A local phone call cost $0.10 in 1970. What is the price of this phone call in 2000 dollars?
   a. $1.42
   b. $0.39
   c. $1.72
   d. $0.44
   e. $0.23

3. The nominal wage rate is the
   a. minimum hourly wage that a company can legally pay a worker.
   b. average hourly wage rate measured in the dollars of a given reference base year.
   c. minimum hourly wage rate measured in the dollars of a given reference base year.
   d. average hourly wage rate measured in current dollars.
   e. wage rate after inflation has been adjusted out of it.

4. In 2006, the average starting salary for an economics major was $29,500. If the CPI was 147.5, the real salary was
   a. $200.00 an hour.
   b. $20,000.
   c. $35,000.
   d. $43,513.
   e. $14,750.

5. If we compare the nominal wage versus the real wage in the United States since 1983, we see that the
   a. real wage rate increased steadily.
   b. nominal wage rate increased and the real wage rate did not change by very much.
   c. real wage rate increased more than the nominal wage rate.
   d. nominal wage rate increased at an uneven pace whereas the increase in the real wage rate was steady and constant.
   e. nominal wage rate and real wage rate both decreased.

6. The real interest rate is equal to the
   a. nominal interest rate plus the inflation rate.
   b. nominal interest rate minus the inflation rate.
   c. nominal interest rate times the inflation rate.
   d. nominal interest rate divided by the inflation rate.
   e. inflation rate minus the nominal interest rate.

7. You borrow at a nominal interest rate of 10 percent. If the inflation rate is 4 percent, then the real interest rate is
   a. the $10 in interest you have to pay.
   b. 16 percent.
   c. 2.5 percent.
   d. 6 percent.
   e. 14 percent.

8. In the United States for the last 40 years, the
   a. nominal and real interest rates both decreased in almost every year.
   b. nominal and real interest rates were both constant in almost every year.
   c. real interest rate was constant in most years and the nominal interest rate fluctuated.
   d. nominal interest rate was greater than the real interest rate in all years.
   e. nominal interest rate was greater than the real interest rate in about one half of the years and the real interest rate was greater than the nominal interest rate in the other half of the years.

Short answer and numeric questions

Job	Salary (dollars per year)	CPI
Job A	20,000	105
Job B	25,000	120
Job C	34,000	170

1. Often the cost of living varies from state to state or from large city to small city. After you graduate, suppose you have job offers in 3 locales. The nominal salary and the CPI for each job is given in the table above.
   a. Which job offers the highest real salary?
   b. Which job offers the lowest real salary?
   c. In determining which job to accept, what is more important: the real salary or the nominal salary? Why?

Year	Real interest rate (percent per year)	Nominal interest rate (percent per year)	Inflation rate (percent per year)
2004	___	10	5
2005	___	6	1
2006	4	6	___
2007	5	___	3

2. The table above gives the real interest rate, nominal interest rate, and inflation rate for various years in a foreign country. Complete the table.

3. In 1980, the nominal interest rate was 12 percent. In 2007, the nominal interest rate was 7 percent. From this information, can you determine if you would rather have saved $1,000 in 1980 or 2007? Explain your answer.

SELF TEST ANSWERS

■ CHECKPOINT 15.1

Fill in the blanks

The <u>Consumer Price Index</u>, also called the CPI, is a measure of the average of the prices paid by urban consumers for a fixed market basket of consumer goods and services. In the base reference period, the CPI equals <u>100</u>. Each <u>month</u> the Bureau of Labor Statistics checks the prices of the goods and services in the CPI basket. The CPI equals the cost of the CPI basket at current prices <u>divided by</u> the cost of the CPI basket at base period prices, all multiplied by 100. To measure changes in the cost of living, the <u>inflation rate</u> is used.

True or false

1. False; page 394
2. False; page 394
3. False; page 397
4. True; page 397
5. False; page 398

Multiple choice

1. c; page 394
2. c; page 394
3. b; page 394
4. a; page 394
5. c; page 395
6. a; page 397
7. a; page 397
8. c; pages 398

Short answer and numeric questions

1. a. The cost is $135; page 396.
   b. The cost is $145. The quantities used to calculate this cost are the base period, 2008, quantities; page 396.
   c. The CPI is 100; page 397.
   d. The CPI is 107.4; page 397.
   e. The inflation rate is 7.4 percent; page 397.
2. The inflation rate for each year is 10 percent; page 397.
3. Whenever the price level rises, the infla-

tion rate is positive. If the price level rises slowly, the inflation rate is small; if the price level rises rapidly, the inflation rate is large; page 398.

■ CHECKPOINT 15.2

Fill in the blanks

The sources of bias in the CPI as a measure of the cost of living are the <u>new goods bias</u>, <u>quality change bias</u>, <u>commodity substitution bias</u>, and <u>outlet substitution bias</u>. The Boskin Commission concluded that the CPI <u>overstates</u> inflation by <u>1.1</u> percentage points a year. The CPI bias leads to <u>an increase</u> in government outlays. The GDP deflator equals 100 times <u>nominal</u> GDP divided by <u>real</u>.

True or false

1. True; page 400
2. False; page 401
3. True; page 401
4. True; page 403
5. True; pages 404

Multiple choice

1. d; page 400
2. b; page 400
3. c; pages 400-401
4. b; page 401
5. c; page 401
6. d; page 402
7. a; page 402
8. c; page 403
9. c page 403
10. e page 403

Short answer and numeric questions

1. There are four sources of bias in the CPI: the new goods bias, the quality change bias, the commodity substitution bias, and the outlet substitution bias. The new goods bias refers to the fact that new goods replace old goods. The quality change bias occurs because at times price

increases in existing goods are the result of increased quality. The commodity substitution bias occurs because consumers buy fewer goods and services when their prices rise compared to other, comparable products. The fixed market basket approach taken in the CPI's calculation cannot take account of this method by which households offset higher prices. Finally, the outlet substitution bias refers to the fact that when prices rise, people shop more frequently at discount stores to take advantage of the lower prices in these stores; pages 400-401.

2. The monthly rent increases by 5 percent each year. For the second year the monthly rent equals $1,000 × 1.05, which is $1,050. For the third year the monthly rent equals $1,050 × 1.05, which is $1,102.50. And for the fourth year the monthly rent equals $1,102.50 × 1.05, which is $1,157.63. If the CPI bias was eliminated, the monthly rent would increase by 4 percent each year. The monthly rent would be $1,040 for the second year, $1,081.60 for the third year, and $1,124.86 for the third year; page 401.

3. a. GDP deflator = ($12 trillion ÷ $10 trillion) × 100 = 120; page 403.

   b. GDP deflator = ($12 trillion ÷ $16 trillion) × 100 = 75; page 403.

   c. GDP deflator = ($8 trillion ÷ $4 trillion) × 100 = 200; page 403.

■ CHECKPOINT 15.3

Fill in the blanks

The nominal wage rate is the average hourly wage rate measured in <u>current</u> dollars. The real wage rate is the average wage rate measured in dollars of the <u>given base</u> year. The real wage rate equals the nominal wage rate <u>divided by</u> the CPI multiplied by 100. The real interest rate equals the nominal interest rate <u>minus</u> the <u>inflation rate</u>.

True or false

1. True; page 406
2. False; page 407
3. True; page 409
4. True; page 410
5. True; page 410

Multiple choice

1. d; page 404
2. d; page 406
3. d; page 408
4. b; page 408
5. b; page 409
6. b; page 410
7. d; page 410
8. d; page 411

Short answer and numeric questions

1. a. The real salary equals (nominal salary ÷ CPI) × 100. The real salary is $19,048 for Job A, $20,833 for Job B, and $20,000 for Job C. The real salary is highest for Job B; page 408.

   b. The real salary is lowest for Job A; page 408.

   c. The real salary is more important than the nominal salary because the real salary measures the quantity of goods and services you will be able to buy; page 409.

Year	Real interest rate (percent per year)	Nominal interest rate (percent per year)	Inflation rate (percent per year)
2004	<u>5</u>	10	5
2005	<u>5</u>	6	1
2006	4	6	<u>2</u>
2007	5	<u>8</u>	3

2. The completed table is above; page 411.

3. You cannot determine when you would rather have been a saver. Savers are interested in the real interest rate because the real interest rate is the percentage return expressed in purchasing power. Without knowing the inflation rate, there is not enough data given to compute the real interest rate; page 411.

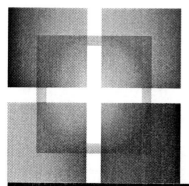

Jobs and Unemployment

Chapter 16

Chapter 16 explores one of the economy's important markets, the labor market, by defining indicators of its performance and explaining how these indicators have changed over time. Chapter 16 also discusses unemployment and its relationship to real GDP.

1 Define the unemployment rate and other labor market indicators.

The Current Population Survey is a monthly survey of 60,000 households across the country that is the basis for the nation's labor market statistics. The working-age population is non-institutionalized people aged 16 and over who are not in the U.S. Armed Forces. The labor force is the sum of the employed and unemployed. To be unemployed, a person must have no employment, be available for work, and either have made an effort to find a job during the previous four weeks or be waiting to be recalled to a job from which he or she was laid off. The unemployment rate is the percentage of people in the labor force who are unemployed. The labor force participation rate is the percentage of the working-age population who are members of the labor force. A discouraged worker is a person who is available and willing to work but has not made specific efforts to find a job within the previous four weeks. Full-time workers are those who usually work 35 hours or more a week. Part-time workers are those who usually work less than 35 hours per week. Involuntary part-time workers and part-time workers who are looking for full-time work. Aggregate hours are the total number of hours worked by all the people employed.

2 Describe the trends and fluctuations in the indicators of labor market performance in the United States.

From 1967 to 2007, the average unemployment rate was 5.9 percent. The lowest unemployment rates were achieved in the late 1960s and in the late 1990s. In the Great Depression of the 1930s, the U.S. unemployment rate reached 25 percent. From 1967 to 2007, the labor force participation rate had generally an upward trend and is a bit less than 67 percent. The labor force participation rate for men decreased and for women increased. Generally about 16 to 17 percent of workers have part-time jobs. The involuntary part-time rate rises during recessions and falls during expansions. Aggregate hours have an upward trend. The average workweek has fallen from 38 hours in 1967 to 34 hours in 2007.

3 Describe the sources and types of unemployment, define full employment, and explain the link between unemployment and real GDP.

People who become unemployed are job losers, job leavers, entrants, or reentrants. People who leave unemployment are hires, recalls, or withdrawals. Unemployment is either frictional (normal labor turnover), structural (changes in necessary job skills or job locations), seasonal (changes in the seasons), or cyclical (changes in the business cycle). The duration of unemployment increases in recessions. Full employment occurs when there is no cyclical unemployment. At full employment, the unemployment rate is the natural unemployment rate. The unemployment rate rises in recessions.

CHECKPOINT 16.1

■ **Define the unemployment rate and other labor market indicators.**

Quick Review

- *Unemployment rate* The unemployment rate is the percentage of the people in the labor force who are unemployed. That is,

$$\text{Unemployment rate} = \frac{(\text{Unemployed people})}{(\text{Labor force})} \times 100$$

- *Labor force participation rate* The labor force participation rate is the percentage of the working-age population who are members of the labor force. It equals

$$\text{Participation rate} = \frac{(\text{Labor force})}{(\text{Working - age people})} \times 100$$

- *Aggregate hours* The aggregate hours are the total number of hours worked by all the people employed, both full time and part time, during a year.

Additional Practice Problems 16.1

1. Determine the labor market status of each of the following people:
   a. Don is 21 and a full-time college student.
   b. Shirley works for 20 hours a week as an administrative assistant and is looking for a full-time job.
   c. Clarence was laid off from his job selling keyboards to computer manufacturers and is actively seeking a new job.
   d. Pat quit her job as an account executive 6 months ago but, unable to find a new position, has stopped actively searching.

2. The Bureau of Labor Statistics reported that in June 2005, the labor force was 149.1 million, employment was 141.6 million, and the working-age population was 225.9 million. Average weekly hours for that month were 33.7. Calculate for that month the:
   a. Unemployment rate.
   b. Labor force participation rate.
   c. Aggregate hours worked in a week.

Solutions to Additional Practice Problems 16.1

1a. Don is neither working nor looking for work, so he is not in the labor force.

1b. Shirley is working for pay for more than 1 hour a week, so she is employed and part of the labor force. She is working less than 35 hours a week, so she is a part-time worker. Because she is looking for a full-time job, Shirley is an involuntary part-time worker.

1c. Clarence is actively seeking a new job, so he is unemployed. Clarence is part of the labor force.

1d. Pat is neither working nor actively looking for work, so she is not in the labor force. Pat is a discouraged worker.

2a. The labor force equals the sum of the number of people employed and the number of people unemployed. Subtracting the number employed from the labor force gives the number of unemployed. The labor force is 149.1 million and the number of employed is 141.6 million, so the number unemployed is 149.1 million − 141.6 million, which is 7.5 million. To calculate the unemployment rate, divide the number of unemployed by the labor force and multiply by 100. The unemployment rate equals (7.5 million ÷ 149.1 million) × 100, which is 5.0 percent.

2b. The labor force participation rate is the percentage of the working-age population who are members of the labor force. The labor force participation rate equals the labor force divided by the working-age population all multiplied by 100, which is (149.1 million ÷ 225.9 million) × 100 = 66.0 percent.

2c. In June, 2005, 141.6 million people worked an average of 33.7 hours a week, so the aggregate hours worked in a week is 141.6 million × 33.7 hours, which is 4,771.9 million hours.

■ **Self Test 16.1**

Fill in the blanks

The ____ (working-age population; labor force) is the total number of people aged 16 years and over and who are not in jail, hospital, or some other form of institutional care. The unemployment rate equals the _____ divided by the _____, all multiplied by 100. The labor force participation rate equals the _____ divided by the _____, all multiplied by 100. Involuntary part-time workers _____ (are; are not) counted as employed. The total number of hours worked in a year by all the people employed are _____.

True or false

1. When contacted by the Bureau of Labor Statistics, Bob states that he has been laid off by Ford Motor Corporation, but expects to be recalled within the next three weeks. Bob is considered part of the labor force.

2. People are counted as unemployed as long as they are working less than 40 hours per week.

3. The unemployment rate decreases when unemployed workers find jobs.

4. The labor force participation rate measures the percentage of the labor force that is employed.

5. If the number of discouraged workers increases, the unemployment rate will increase.

Multiple choice

1. Assume the U.S. population is 300 million. If the working age population is 240 million, 150 million are employed, and 6 million are unemployed, what is the size of the labor force?
   a. 300 million
   b. 240 million
   c. 156 million
   d. 150 million
   e. 144 million

2. To be counted as employed by the BLS, you must have worked for pay _____ in the week before the survey.
   a. at least 1 hour
   b. at least 5 hours
   c. more than 20 hours
   d. 40 hours
   e. None of the above are right because the BLS counts anyone who works volunteer hours at a non-profit institution or school as employed.

3. Which of the following statements about the United States is (are) correct?
   i.   The size of the labor force is greater than the number of employed people.
   ii. The size of the labor force is greater than the number of unemployed people.
   iii. The number of unemployed people is greater than the number of employed people.
   a. ii only.
   b. iii only.
   c. ii and iii.
   d. i and ii.
   e. i, ii, and iii.

4. If you are available and willing to work but have not actively looked for work in the past month then you are _____ of the labor force and are _____.
   a. part; counted as unemployed
   b. part; not counted as unemployed
   c. not part; not counted as unemployed
   d. not part; counted as unemployed only if you have had a job within the last 12 months
   e. not part; counted as unemployed regardless of whether or not you have held a job within the last 12 months

5. The unemployment rate equals
   a. (number of people without a job ÷ population) × 100.
   b. (number of people unemployed ÷ labor force) × 100.
   c. (number of people without a job ÷ working-age population) × 100.
   d. (number of people unemployed ÷ population) × 100.
   e. [(working-age population – number of people employed) ÷ labor force] × 100.

6. If the working age population is 200 million, 150 million are employed, and 6 million are unemployed, the unemployment rate is _____.
   a. 3.0 percent
   b. 25.0 percent
   c. 4.0 percent
   d. 12.0 percent
   e. 3.8 percent

7. A discouraged worker is
   a. counted as employed by the BLS but is not part of the labor force.
   b. counted as employed by the BLS and is part of the labor force.
   c. counted as unemployed by the BLS and is part of the labor force.
   d. not part of the labor force.
   e. counted as unemployed by the BLS but is not part of the labor force.

8. While in school, Kiki spends 20 hours a week as a computer programmer for Microsoft and studies 30 hours a week.
   a. Kiki is classified as a full-time worker, working 50 hours a week.
   b. Kiki is classified as a part-time worker, working 30 hours a week.
   c. Kiki is classified as a part-time worker, working 20 hours a week.
   d. Because Kiki is a student, she is not classified as working.
   e. Because Kiki is a student, she is classified as a full-time worker, working 20 hours a week at a paid job.

9. Part-time workers for noneconomic reasons are people who
   a. work less than 35 hours a week but would like to work more than 35 hours a week.
   b. work more than 35 hours a week but would like to work less than 35 hours a week.
   c. have lost their jobs within the last four weeks and are seeking another job.
   d. do not want to work full time.
   e. are discouraged workers.

Short answer and numeric questions

Category	Number of people
Total population	2,600
Working-age population	2,000
Not in the labor force	500
Employed	1,300

1. The table above gives the status of the population of a (small!) nation.
   a. What is the size of the labor force?
   b. What is the number of unemployed workers?
   c. What is the unemployment rate?
   d. What is the labor force participation rate?

Category	Number of people
Working-age population	3,000
Unemployed	100
Employed	1,900

2. The table above gives the status of the population of another (small!) nation.
   a. What is the size of the labor force?
   b. What is the unemployment rate?
   c. What is the labor force participation rate?

3. What criteria must a person meet to be counted as unemployed?

4. What is a discouraged worker? Explain why a discouraged worker is not counted as part of the labor force.

5. Are involuntarily part-time workers counted as employed or unemployed?

CHECKPOINT 16.2

■ **Describe the trends and fluctuations in the indicators of labor market performance in the United States.**

Quick Review
- *Labor force participation rate* The percentage of the working-age population who are members of the labor force.
- *Aggregate hours* The total number of hours worked by all the people employed, both full time and part time, during a year.

Additional Practice Problems 16.2
1. How does the unemployment rate change in a recession? Since 1967, when was the unemployment rate the highest and what did it equal?
2. How do aggregate hours change in a recession?

3. Are involuntary part-time workers counted as unemployed when calculating the unemployment rate? If they are, how do they affect the unemployment rate; if they are not, how would their inclusion affect the unemployment rate?

Solutions to Additional Practice Problems 16.2

1. The unemployment rate rises during recessions. Since 1967, the unemployment rate reached its peak of almost 10 percent during the 1982 recession.

2. Aggregate hours fall during a recession.

3. Involuntary part-time workers are *not* counted as unemployed. Indeed, they are counted as employed when computing the unemployment rate. If they were counted as, say, "partially" unemployed, the unemployment rate would increase. And, as Figure 16.4 in the textbook shows, the increase would be larger during recessions when the number of involuntary part-time workers increases.

■ Self Test 16.2

Fill in the blanks

The unemployment rate in 2007 was slightly _____ (higher; lower) than the average between 1967 and 2007. Since 1967, the male labor force participation rate _____ and the female participation rate _____. Since 1977, the percentage of workers who have part-time jobs _____ (rose; fell; barely changed). Since 1967, the total number of labor hours _____ and the length of the average workweek _____.

True or false

1. The average unemployment rate in the United States during the 1970s and 1980s was above the average unemployment rate during the 1960s and 1990s.

2. Since 1995 the U.S. unemployment rate has consistently been above its 40-year average because of layoffs brought about by the technology that has created the "new economy."

3. Although the female labor force participation rate increased over the last 40 years, it is still less than the male labor force participation rate.

4. The percentage of involuntary part-time workers rises during a recession.

5. Aggregate hours worked in the United States have not grown as quickly as the number of people employed.

Multiple choice

1. From 1967 to 2007, the average unemployment rate in the United States was approximately
   a. 3 percent.
   b. 6 percent.
   c. 12 percent.
   d. 24 percent.
   d. 9 percent.

2. From 1992 to 2007, the unemployment rate in the United States
   a. was always lower than the unemployment rate in Japan.
   b. almost always equaled the unemployment rate in Canada.
   c. generally rose while the unemployment rate in the Eurozone fell.
   d. was lower than the unemployment rate in the Eurozone.
   e. was usually higher than the unemployment rate in Canada.

3. Which of the following statements is correct for the United States? Between 1967 and 2007,
   a. both the male and female labor force participation rates increased.
   b. the male labor force participation rate decreased rapidly, the female labor force participation rate decreased slowly, and the two rates are now equal.
   c. the male labor force participation rate decreased and the female labor force participation rate increased.
   d. both the male and female labor force participation rates decreased slowly.
   e. the male labor force participation rate did not change and the female labor force participation rate increased.

4. The total U.S. labor force participation rate increased since 1967 because
   a. the female labor force participation rate increased.
   b. more men are retiring early.
   c. fewer women are attending college.
   d. many blue-collar jobs with rigid work hours have been created in the last decade.
   e. the male labor force participation rate increased.

5. The women's labor force participation rate is
   a. higher in Japan than in the United States.
   b. higher in the United States than in France.
   c. higher in Italy than in the United States.
   d. higher in Spain than in Iceland.
   e. higher in the United States than in Iceland or Norway.

6. Part-time workers were about ____ of all workers in 1977 and were about ____ in 2007.
   a. 17 percent; 50 percent
   b. 17 percent; 17 percent
   c. 2 percent; 4 percent
   d. 10 percent; 40 percent
   e. 35 percent; 22 percent

7. In the United States in 2007, involuntary part-time workers
   a. account for more than 66 percent of all part-time workers.
   b. account for between 36 percent and 65 percent of all part-time workers.
   c. account for between 5 percent and 10 percent of all part-time workers.
   d. account for between 11 percent and 20 percent of all part-time workers.
   e. account for between 21 percent and 35 percent of all part-time workers.

8. In the United States since 1967, aggregate hours have ____ and average weekly hours per worker have ____.
   a. risen; risen
   b. risen; fallen
   c. fallen; risen
   d. fallen; fallen
   e. risen; not changed

Short answer and numeric questions

1. During a recession, what happens to:
   a. the unemployment rate?
   b. aggregate hours?
   c. average weekly hours?

2. Compare the U.S. unemployment rate between 1990 to 2007 to the unemployment rate in
   a. Japan.
   b. Canada.

3. How does the unemployment rate during the Great Depression compare with more recent unemployment rates?

CHECKPOINT 16.3

■ **Describe the sources and types of unemployment, define full employment, and explain the link between unemployment and real GDP.**

Quick Review

- *Frictional unemployment* Unemployment that arises from normal labor market turnover.
- *Structural unemployment* Unemployment that arises when changes in technology or international competition change the skills needed to perform jobs or change the location of jobs.
- *Seasonal unemployment* Unemployment that arises because of seasonal weather patterns.
- *Cyclical unemployment* Unemployment that fluctuates over the business cycle, rising during a recession and falling during an expansion.

Additional Practice Problem 16.3

1. Each of the following people is actively seeking work. Classify each as either frictionally, structurally, seasonally, or cyclically unemployed:
   a. Perry lost his job because his company went bankrupt when faced with increased foreign competition.

b. Sam did not like his boss and so he quit his job.

c. Sherry just graduated from college.

d. Hanna lost her job selling cotton candy on the boardwalk when winter arrived and the tourists left.

e. Jose was fired when his company downsized in response to a recession.

f. Pat was laid off from her job at the Gap because customers decided they liked the fashions at JCPenney better.

Solution to Additional Practice Problem 16.3

1a. Perry is structurally unemployed.

1b. Sam is frictionally unemployed.

1c. Sherry is frictionally unemployed.

1d. Hanna is seasonally unemployed.

1e. Jose is cyclically unemployed.

1f. Pat is frictionally unemployed.

■ Self Test 16.3

Fill in the blanks

People who become unemployed are ____, ____, or ____. Unemployed people who stop looking for jobs are ____ (recalls; job losers; withdrawals). The normal unemployment from labor market turnover is called ____ unemployment, and the unemployment that fluctuates over the business cycle is called ____ unemployment. When ____ (frictional; structural; cyclical) unemployment equals zero, the economy is experiencing ____ employment. When potential GDP exceeds real GDP, the unemployment rate ____ (is higher than; is lower than) the natural unemployment rate.

True or false

1. If Amazon.Com Inc. must lay off 20 percent of its workers, the laid-off workers would be considered job leavers.

2. The only way to end a spell of unemployment is by finding a job.

3. The unemployment that arises when technology changes is termed technological unemployment.

4. When the U.S. economy is at full employment, the unemployment rate is zero.

5. Potential GDP is the level of real GDP produced when the economy is at full employment.

Multiple choice

1. Generally, most unemployed workers are ____; the fewest number of unemployed workers are ____.
   a. job losers; job leavers
   b. job leavers; reentrants and entrants
   c. job losers; reentrants and entrants
   d. reentrants and entrants; job leavers
   e. job leavers; job losers

2. Reentrants are people who
   a. are laid off.
   b. leave the labor force voluntarily.
   c. recently left school.
   d. have returned to the labor force.
   e. voluntarily leave their job.

3. Tommy graduates from college and starts to look for a job. Tommy is
   a. frictionally unemployed.
   b. structurally unemployed.
   c. cyclically unemployed.
   d. seasonally unemployed.
   e. not unemployed because he is looking for work.

4. If an entire industry relocates to a foreign country, the relocation leads to a higher rate of ____ unemployment.
   a. frictional
   b. structural
   c. seasonal
   d. cyclical
   e. structural and cyclical

5. Of the following, who is cyclically unemployed?
   a. Casey, who lost his job because the technology changed so that he was no longer needed.
   b. Katrina, an assistant manager who quit her job to search for a better job closer to home.
   c. Kathy, a steelworker who was laid off but has stopped looking for a new job because she can't find a new job.
   d. David, a new car salesman who lost his job because the economy went into a recession.
   e. Samantha, who worked part-time in JCPenney to help with the Christmas rush but was laid off in January.

6. In the United States, the highest unemployment rates occur among
   a. white teenagers.
   b. black teenagers.
   c. white females aged 20 and over.
   d. black males aged 20 and over.
   e. white males aged 20 and over.

7. When the economy is at full employment,
   a. the natural unemployment rate equals zero.
   b. the amount of cyclical unemployment equals zero.
   c. the amount of structural unemployment equals zero.
   d. there is no unemployment.
   e. the amount of frictional unemployment equals zero.

8. When the unemployment rate is less than the natural unemployment rate, real GDP is _____ potential GDP.
   a. greater than
   b. less than
   c. unrelated to
   d. equal to
   e. not comparable to

Short answer and numeric questions

1. What are sources of unemployment? How does unemployment end?
2. What are the four types of unemployment?
3. How does the average duration of unemployment change during a recession?
4. What is the relationship between full employment, the natural unemployment rate, and potential GDP?
5. If the unemployment rate exceeds the natural unemployment rate, what is the relationship between real GDP and potential GDP?

SELF TEST ANSWERS

■ CHECKPOINT 16.1

Fill in the blanks

The <u>working-age population</u> is the total number of people aged 16 years and over and who are not in jail, hospital, or some other form of institutional care. The unemployment rate equals the <u>number of people unemployed</u> divided by the <u>labor force</u>, all multiplied by 100. The labor force participation rate equals the <u>labor force</u> divided by the <u>working-age population</u>, all multiplied by 100. Involuntary part-time workers <u>are</u> counted as employed. The total number of hours worked in a year by all the people employed are <u>aggregate hours</u>.

True or false

1. True; page 418
2. False; page 418
3. True; page 419
4. False; page 420
5. False; page 420

Multiple choice

1. c; page 418
2. a; page 418
3. d; page 418
4. c; page 418
5. b; page 419
6. e; page 419
7. d; page 420
8. c; page 420
9. d; page 420

Short answer and numeric questions

1. a. 1,500; page 418.
   b. 200; page 418.
   c. 13.3 percent; page 419.
   d. 75.0 percent; page 420.
2. a. 2,000; page 418.
   b. 5.0 percent; page 419.
   c. 66.7 percent; page 420.
3. The person must be without employment, available for work, and actively searching or waiting to be recalled to a job from which he or she was laid off; page 418.
4. A discouraged worker is an unemployed worker who is not actively looking for a job. A discouraged worker is not unemployed because the worker is not actively seeking a job; page 420.
5. Employed; page 420.

■ CHECKPOINT 16.2

Fill in the blanks

The unemployment rate in 2007 was slightly <u>lower</u> than the average between 1967 and 2007. Since 1967, the male labor force participation rate <u>fell</u> and the female participation rate <u>rose</u>. Since 1977, the percentage of workers who have part-time jobs <u>barely changed</u>. Since 1967, the total number of labor hours <u>rose</u> and the length of the average workweek <u>fell</u>.

True or false

1. True; page 423
2. False; page 423
3. True; page 424
4. True; page 426
5. True; pages 426-427

Multiple choice

1. b; page 423
2. d; page 425
3. c; pages 424-425
4. a; pages 424-425
5. b; page 427
6. b; page 426
7. d; page 426
8. b; pages 426-427

Short answer and numeric questions

1. a. The unemployment rate rises; page 423.
   b. Aggregate hours fall; page 427.
   c. Average weekly hours falls; page 427.
2. a. The Japanese unemployment rate between 1999 and 2001 was slightly greater than the U.S. unemployment rate. During the

other years, the Japanese unemployment rate was slightly lower; page 425.

   b. The Canadian unemployment rate has mirrored changes in the U.S. unemployment rate but has been about 4 percentage points higher; page 425.

3. The unemployment rate during the Great Depression was *much* higher, reaching near 25 percent, than the recent unemployment rate, which reached its peak of approximately 10 percent in 1982; page 424.

■ CHECKPOINT 16.3

Fill in the blanks

People who become unemployed are job losers, job leavers, or entrants and reentrants. Unemployed people who stop looking for jobs are withdrawals. The normal unemployment from labor market turnover is called frictional unemployment, and the unemployment that fluctuates over the business cycle is called cyclical unemployment. When cyclical unemployment equals zero, the economy is experiencing full employment. When potential GDP exceeds real GDP, the unemployment rate is higher than the natural unemployment rate.

True or false

1. False; page 429
2. False; page 430
3. False; page 431
4. False; page 433
5. True; pages 434-435

Multiple choice

1. a; pages 429-430
2. d; page 429
3. a; page 431
4. b; page 431
5. d; page 432
6. b; page 433
7. b; page 433
8. a; page 435

Short answer and numeric questions

1. Sources of unemployment are job losers, job leavers, entrants, and reentrants. People who end a period of unemployment rate are hires, recalls, or withdrawals; pages 429-430.

2. Unemployment is either frictional, structural, seasonal, or cyclical; pages 430-433.

3. The average duration of unemployment (the length of time a person is unemployed) rises in a recession; page 432.

4. When the economy is at full employment, the unemployment rate is the natural unemployment rate. When the economy is at full employment, the amount of GDP produced is potential GDP; pages 433-435.

5. If the unemployment rate exceeds the natural unemployment rate, real GDP is less than potential GDP; page 435.

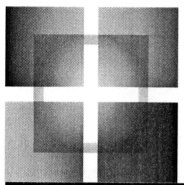

Potential GDP and Economic Growth

Chapter 17

Classical macroeconomics asserts that markets work well and no government intervention is needed. Keynesian economics asserts that recessions are the result of too little spending and calls for government intervention to assist the economy. The new macroeconomics is a newer approach that focuses on how macroeconomic outcomes are the result of microeconomic choices.

1 Explain the forces that determine potential GDP and the real wage rate and employment at full employment.

Potential GDP is the amount of GDP that would be produced if the economy were at full employment. The production function shows the maximum quantity of real GDP that can be produced as the quantity of labor employed changes and all other influences on production remain the same. Its shape reflects diminishing returns: each additional hour of labor employed produces smaller increases in real GDP. The quantity of labor employed is determined in the labor market. The quantity of labor demanded increases (decreases) as the real wage rate falls (rises). The quantity of labor supplied increases (decreases) as the real wage rate rises (falls). Labor market equilibrium occurs at the intersection of the labor supply and the labor demand curves. When the labor market is in equilibrium, the economy is at full employment and real GDP, determined using the production function, is potential GDP.

2 Define and calculate the economic growth rate, and explain the implications of sustained growth.

Economic growth is a sustained expansion of production possibilities measured as the increase in real GDP over a given time period. The economic growth rate is the annual percentage change of real GDP. The standard of living depends on real GDP per person, which equals real GDP divided by the population. The Rule of 70 points out that the number of years it takes a variable to double approximately equals 70 divided by the annual growth rate of the variable.

3 Identify the sources of economic growth and explain the growth process.

Real GDP grows when the quantities of the factors of production grow or when technology advances. Labor productivity is the quantity of real GDP produced by one hour of labor. When labor productivity grows, real GDP per person grows. Growth of labor productivity depends on saving and investment in more physical capital, acquisition of more human capital, and discovery of better technologies. Our unlimited wants will lead us to ever greater productivity and perpetual economic growth.

4 Describe policies that might speed economic growth.

The preconditions for economic growth are economic freedom, property rights, and markets. Governments can increase economic growth by creating incentives to save, invest, and innovate; by encouraging saving; by encouraging research and development; by encouraging international trade; and by improving the quality of education.

CHECKPOINT 17.1

■ **Explain the forces that determine potential GDP and the real wage rate and employment at full employment.**

Quick Review

- *Production function* The production function shows the relationship between the maximum quantity of real GDP that can be produced as the quantity of labor employed changes when all other influences on production remain constant.
- *Equilibrium in a market* The equilibrium in a market occurs at the intersection of the demand and supply curves.

Additional Practice Problem 17.1

Quantity of labor demanded (billions of hours per year)	Real GDP (hundreds of billions of 2000 dollars)	Real wage rate (2000 dollars per hour)
0	0	50
10	5	40
20	9	30
30	12	20
40	14	10

1. The table above describes an economy's production function and its demand for labor. The table below describes the supply of labor in this economy.

Quantity of labor supplied (billions of hours per year)	Real wage rate (2000 dollars per hour)
0	10
10	20
20	30
30	40
40	50

a. Make graphs of the production function and the labor market.
b. Does the production function show diminishing returns?
c. What is the equilibrium employment, real wage rate, and potential GDP?

d. Suppose that the population grows so that the quantity of labor supplied increases by 20 billion hours at every real wage rate. What is the effect on the real wage rate and on potential GDP?

Solution to Additional Practice Problem 17.1

1a. The production function is a graph of the first two columns of the first table. The figure to the right shows the relationship between labor and real GDP.

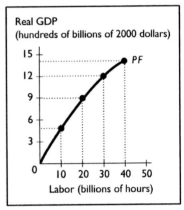

The second figure to the right shows the labor market. The labor demand curve is the first and third columns in the first table. It shows the relationship

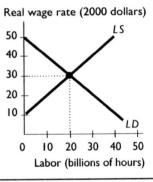

between the real wage rate and the quantity of labor demanded. The labor supply curve is from the second table and shows the relationship between the real wage rate and the quantity of labor supplied.

1b. The production function shows diminishing returns because every additional 10 billion hours of labor employed increases real GDP by less.

1c. Find the equilibrium in the labor market. Then use the production function to determine how much GDP this full-employment quantity of labor produces, which is the potential GDP. Equilibrium employment is where the labor demand curve and the labor supply curve intersect. The second figure in part (a) shows that the equilibrium real wage rate is $30 an hour and the equilibrium employment is 20 billion hours per year. The production function, in the first figure in part (a), shows that when 20 billion hours of labor are employed, GDP is $900 billion, so potential GDP equals $900 billion.

Quantity of labor supplied (billions of hours per year)	Real wage rate (2000 dollars per hour)
20	10
30	20
40	30
50	40
60	50

1d. The new labor supply schedule is given in the table above and shown in the figure. In the figure, the labor supply curve shifts rightward from LS_1 to LS_2. The equilibrium quantity of labor increases to 30 billion hours and the equilibrium real wage rate falls to $20. The production function in the first table in the practice problem shows that when employment is 30 billion hours, real GDP is $1,200 billion. So, the increase in the population increases potential GDP to $1,200 billion.

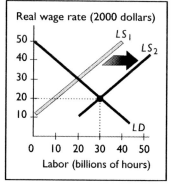

■ Self Test 17.1

Fill in the blanks

____ (Classical; Keynesian) macroeconomics asserts that government intervention is needed to achieve full employment. The new macroeconomics says that macro outcomes depend on ____ (macro; micro) choices. The relationship that shows the maximum quantity of real GDP that can be produced as the quantity of labor employed changes is ____ (the production func-

tion; potential GDP). The quantity of labor demanded ____ (increases; decreases) as the real wage rate falls and the quantity of labor supplied ____ (increases; decreases) as the real wage rate falls. If the real wage rate exceeds the equilibrium real wage rate, there is a ____ (shortage; surplus) of labor. When the labor market is in equilibrium, there is ____ and real GDP equals ____.

True or false

1. Classical macroeconomics says that markets work well and government intervention cannot improve on the performance of markets.

2. New macroeconomists agree that the problem of business cycle fluctuations is much more important than the problem of sustaining economic growth.

3. Real GDP can exceed potential GDP permanently.

4. The production function shows how the quantity of labor hired depends on the real wage rate.

5. The nominal wage rate influences the quantity of labor demanded because what matters to firms is the number of dollars they pay for an hour of labor.

6. At the labor market equilibrium the real wage rate is such that the quantity of labor demanded equals the quantity of labor supplied.

7. When the labor market is in equilibrium, the economy is at full employment and real GDP equals potential GDP.

Multiple choice

1. ____ adopts the view that how the economy works depends on the micro choices people make.
   a. Classical macroeconomics
   b. Keynesian economics
   c. The new macroeconomics
   d. The Lucas wedge
   e. The Okun gap

2. Potential GDP
   a. is the quantity of GDP produced when the economy is at full employment.
   b. can never be exceeded.
   c. can never be attained.
   d. is another name for real GDP.
   e. is another name for nominal GDP.

3. With fixed quantities of capital, land, and entrepreneurship and fixed technology, the amount of real GDP produced increases when _____ increases.
   i.   the quantity of labor employed
   ii. the inflation rate
   iii. the price level
   a. i only.
   b. ii only.
   c. iii only.
   d. ii and iii.
   e. i, ii, and iii.

4. The production function graphs the relationship between
   a. nominal GDP and real GDP.
   b. real GDP and the quantity of labor employed.
   c. real GDP and capital.
   d. nominal GDP and the quantity of labor employed.
   e. real GDP and the supply of labor.

5. The quantity of labor demanded definitely increases if the
   a. real wage rate rises.
   b. real wage rate falls.
   c. nominal wage rate rises.
   d. nominal wage rate falls.
   e. supply of labor decreases.

6. The supply of labor curve has a _____ slope because as the real wage rate rises, _____.
   a. negative; firms hire fewer workers
   b. positive; the opportunity cost of leisure rises
   c. positive; the opportunity cost of leisure falls
   d. negative; households work more hours
   e. positive; firms offer more jobs

7. The real wage rate is $35 an hour. At this wage rate there are 100 billion labor hours supplied and 200 billion labor hours demanded. There is a
   a. shortage of 300 billion hours of labor.
   b. shortage of 100 billion hours of labor.
   c. surplus of 100 billion hours of labor.
   d. surplus of 300 billion hours of labor.
   e. shortage of 200 billion hours of labor.

■ **FIGURE 17.1**

Real wage rate (2000 dollars per hour)

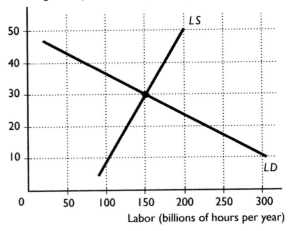

8. In Figure 17.1, the equilibrium real wage rate is _____ and equilibrium employment is _____ billions of hours per year.
   a. $50; 200
   b. $10; 100
   c. $30; more than 300
   d. $20; 125
   e. $30; 150

9. In Figure 17.1, full employment is reached when employment is _____ billions of hours a year.
   a. 150
   b. 200
   c. 250
   d. more than 300
   e. More information is needed about the nation's production function to answer the question.

10. When the labor market is in equilibrium, real GDP ____ potential GDP.
    a. is greater than
    b. is equal to
    c. is less than
    d. might be greater than, less than, or equal to
    e. is not comparable to

11. Compared to the U.S. production function, the European production function is
    a. higher.
    b. lower.
    c. the same.
    d. lower than the U.S. production function at low levels of employment and higher than the U.S. production function at high levels of employment.
    e. higher than the U.S. production function at low levels of employment and lower than the U.S. production function at high levels of employment.

Complete the graph

Quantity of labor (billions of hours per year)	Real GDP (billions of 2000 dollars)
0	0
10	400
20	725
30	900
40	960
50	1,000

1. The above table gives data for a nation's production function. In Figure 17.2, draw the production function. Label the axes. How are diminishing returns reflected?

2. Figure 17.3 illustrates the labor market for the nation with the production function given in the previous problem. In the figure, identify the equilibrium real wage rate and employment. Using the production function in Figure 17.2, what is the nation's potential GDP?

3. Using the data in Problems 1 and 2, suppose that both the labor supply and labor demand curves shift rightward by 10 billion labor hours and the production function does not change. What is the nation's potential GDP?

■ **FIGURE 17.2**

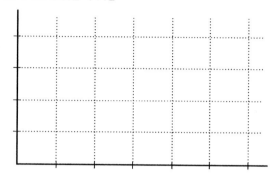

■ **FIGURE 17.3**

Real wage rate (2000 dollars per hour)

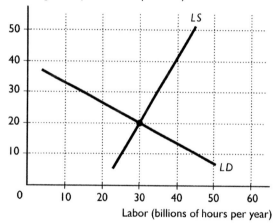

Labor (billions of hours per year)

Short answer and numeric questions

1. What are the differences between classical macroeconomics and Keynesian macroeconomics?

2. What is the relationship between equilibrium in the labor market and potential GDP? Be sure to explain the role played by the production function.

3. Suppose a nation's production function shifts upward. If the equilibrium quantity of labor does not change, what is the effect on the nation's potential GDP?

4. Suppose a nation's production function shifts upward and the equilibrium quantity of labor increases. What is the effect on the nation's potential GDP?

CHECKPOINT 17.2

■ **Define and calculate the economic growth rate, and explain the implications of sustained growth.**

Quick Review

- *Growth rate* The growth rate of real GDP equals

$$\frac{\left(\begin{array}{c}\text{Real GDP in} \\ \text{current year}\end{array}\right) - \left(\begin{array}{c}\text{Real GDP in} \\ \text{previous year}\end{array}\right)}{\left(\text{Real GDP in previous year}\right)} \times 100$$

- *Growth rate of real GDP per person* The growth rate of real GDP per person equals (growth rate of real GDP)–(growth rate of population).

- *Rule of 70* The number of years it takes for the level of any variable to double is approximately 70 divided by the annual percentage growth rate of the variable.

Additional Practice Problem 17.2

1. In the nation of Transylvania in 2010, real GDP was $3.0 million and the population was 1,000. In 2011, real GDP was $3.3 million and the population was 1,050.
    a. What is Transylvania's economic growth in 2011?
    b. What is the population growth rate?
    c. What is Transylvania's growth rate of real GDP per person?
    d. Did Transylvania's standard of living rise?
    e. Approximately how long will it take for real GDP per person to double?

Solution to Additional Practice Problem 17.2

1. This question uses three growth rate formulas. The first is the formula that calculates the economic growth rate; the second is the formula that calculates the growth rate of real GDP per person; the third is the Rule of 70.
1a. The economic growth rate is the growth rate of real GDP. Transylvania's economic growth rate equals [($3.3 million – $3.0 million) ÷ $3.0 million] × 100 = 10 percent.

1b. Transylvania's population growth rate equals [(1,050 – 1,000) ÷ 1,000] × 100 = 5 percent.

1c. Transylvania's real GDP per person growth rate equals the growth rate of real GDP minus the growth rate of the population, or 10 percent – 5 percent = 5 percent.

1d. Transylvania's real GDP per person rose, so Transylvania's standard of living increased.

1e. The number of years it takes for real GDP per person to double is given by the Rule of 70. Transylvania's real GDP per person is growing at 5 percent per year, so it will take approximately 70 ÷ 5 or 14 years for Transylvania's real GDP per person to double.

■ Self Test 17.2

Fill in the blanks

The growth rate of real GDP equals real GDP in the current year minus real GDP in the previous year divided by real GDP _____ in the (current; previous) year, all multiplied by 100. The growth rate of real GDP per person equals the growth rate of real GDP _____ (minus; plus) the growth rate of the population. The number of years it takes for the level of any variable to double is approximately _____ divided by the annual percentage growth rate of the variable.

True or false

1. If real GDP last year was $1.00 trillion and real GDP this year is $1.05 trillion, the growth rate of real GDP this year is 5 percent.

2. Real GDP per person equals real GDP divided by the population.

3. If a nation's population grows at 2 percent and its real GDP grows at 4 percent, then the growth rate of real GDP per person is 2 percent.

4. If real GDP is growing at 2 percent a year, it will take 70 years for real GDP to double.

Multiple choice

1. The economic growth rate is measured as the
   a. annual percentage change of real GDP.
   b. annual percentage change of employment.
   c. level of real GDP.
   d. annual percentage change of the population.
   e. amount of population.

2. Real GDP is $9 trillion in the current year and $8.6 trillion in the previous year. The economic growth rate between these years has been
   a. 10.31 percent.
   b. 4.65 percent.
   c. 5.67 percent.
   d. 7.67 percent.
   e. $0.4 trillion.

3. The standard of living is measured by
   a. real GDP.
   b. employment.
   c. employment per person.
   d. real GDP per person.
   e. the population.

4. If the growth rate of population is greater than a nation's growth rate of real GDP, then its real GDP per person
   a. falls.
   b. rises.
   c. does not change.
   d. might rise or fall.
   e. cannot be measured.

5. If real GDP increases by 6 percent and at the same time the population increases by 2 percent, then real GDP per person grows by
   a. 6 percent.
   b. 4 percent.
   c. 2 percent.
   d. 8 percent.
   e. 3 percent.

6. If a country experiences a real GDP growth rate of 4 percent a year, real GDP will double in
   a. 14 years.
   b. 17.5 years.
   c. 23.3 years.
   d. 35 years.
   e. 25 years.

Short answer and numeric questions

Year	Real GDP (billions of 2000 dollars)
2005	100.0
2006	110.0
2007	121.0
2008	133.1

1. The above table gives a nation's real GDP. What is the growth rate of real GDP in 2006? In 2007? In 2008?

Year	Real GDP growth rate (percent)	Population growth rate (percent)
2005	3	2
2006	4	2
2007	1	2
2008	4	4

2. The table above gives the growth rate of real GDP and the growth rate of population for a nation.
   a. What is the growth rate of real GDP per person for each year?
   b. In what years did the standard of living improve?

3. If a nation's real GDP grows at 3 percent a year, how long does it take for real GDP to double? If the growth rate is 4 percent, how long does it take for real GDP to double? If the growth rate is 5 percent, how long does it take real GDP to double?

CHECKPOINT 17.3

■ **Identify the sources of economic growth and explain the growth process.**

Quick Review

- *Labor productivity* Labor productivity equals real GDP divided by aggregate hours. When labor productivity grows, real GDP per person grows.

Additional Practice Problem 17.3

Item	2003	2004
Aggregate hours (billions)	232.2	234.5
Real GDP (trillions of 2000 dollars)	10.32	10.76

1. The table above provides some data on the U.S. economy in 2003 and 2004.

    a. Calculate the growth rate of real GDP in 2004.

    b. Calculate labor productivity in 2003 and 2004.

    c. Calculate the growth rate of labor productivity in 2004.

    d. How does the growth rate of labor productivity you calculated compare with the typical growth in the United States since 1960?

Solution to Additional Practice Problem 17.3

1a. The growth rate of real GDP in 2004 is [($10.76 trillion – $10.32 trillion) ÷ $10.32 trillion] × 100, which is 4.3 percent.

1b. Labor productivity is real GDP divided by aggregate hours. So labor productivity in 2003 is $10.32 trillion ÷ 232.2 billion hours, which is $44.44 per hour of labor. In 2004 labor productivity is $10.76 trillion ÷ 234.5 billion hours, which is $45.88 per hour of labor.

1c. The growth rate of labor productivity is labor productivity in 2004 minus the labor productivity in 2003, divided by labor productivity in 2003, all multiplied by 100. The growth rate of labor productivity equals [($45.88 per hour – $44.44 per hour) ÷ $44.44 per hour] × 100, which is 3.24 percent.

1d. The increase in labor productivity in 2004 was slower than in the early 1960s but was larger than has been the average since then.

■ Self Test 17.3

Fill in the blanks

All influences on real GDP growth can be divided into those that increase aggregate hours and ____ (labor productivity; population). Labor productivity equals real GDP ____ (multiplied by; divided by) aggregate hours. Saving and investment in physical capital ____ (increases; decreases) labor productivity. Education, training, and job experience increase ____ (investment in physical capital; human capital). To reap the benefits of technological change, capital must ____ (increase; decrease).

True or false

1. Real GDP increases if aggregate hours increase or labor productivity increases.

2. If labor productivity increases and aggregate hours do not change, then real GDP per person increases.

3. Higher wages are a source of growth in labor productivity.

4. The discovery and applications of new technology has increased labor productivity.

Multiple choice

1. The only source of growth in aggregate labor hours that is sustainable over long periods of time is

    a. an increase in the labor force participation rate.

    b. population growth.

    c. a decrease in labor productivity.

    d. a decrease in the unemployment rate.

    e. an increase in labor productivity.

2. Real GDP equals aggregate hours

    a. divided by labor productivity.

    b. minus labor productivity.

    c. plus labor productivity.

    d. multiplied by labor productivity.

    e. multiplied by human capital.

3. If real GDP is $1,200 billion, the population is 60 million, and aggregate hours are 80 billion, labor productivity is
   a. $5.00 an hour.
   b. $6.67 an hour.
   c. $15.00 an hour.
   d. $20,000.
   e. $150 an hour.

4. If aggregate hours are 100 billion hours and labor productivity is $40 an hour, than real GDP equals
   a. $100 billion.
   b. $40 billion.
   c. $100 trillion.
   d. $2.5 trillion.
   e. $4 trillion.

5. Which of the following lists gives factors that increase labor productivity?
   a. saving and investment in physical capital, and wage increases
   b. expansion of human capital, labor force increases, and discovery of new technologies
   c. expansion of human capital, population growth, and discovery of new technologies
   d. saving and investment in physical capital, expansion of human capital, and discovery of new technologies
   e. labor force increases and wage increases

6. Growth in physical capital depends most directly upon the amount of
   a. saving and investment.
   b. years the firm has been in existence.
   c. population growth.
   d. government expenditures.
   e. human capital.

7. Human capital is
   a. the same as labor productivity.
   b. a measure of the number of labor hours available.
   c. the accumulated skills and knowledge of workers.
   d. the average number of years of schooling of the labor force.
   e. is what people are born with and cannot be changed.

Short answer and numeric questions

Year	Real GDP (trillion of 2000 dollars)	Aggregate hours (billions)
1964	3.00	133.6
1974	4.32	158.7
1984	5.81	185.3
1994	7.84	211.5
2004	10.76	234.5

1. The table above has data from the United States. For each year, calculate labor productivity.

2. Real GDP is $9 trillion and aggregate hours are 200 billion. What is labor productivity?

3. Aggregate hours are 200 billion and labor productivity is $45 an hour. What is real GDP?

4. What three factors increase labor productivity?

CHECKPOINT 17.4

■ **Describe policies that might speed economic growth.**

Quick Review

- *Preconditions for economic growth* The three preconditions are economic freedom, property rights, and markets.
- *Policies to achieve growth* Five policies are to create incentive mechanisms, encourage saving, encourage research and development, encourage international trade, and improve the quality of education.

Additional Practice Problem 17.4

1. In 1949 East and West Germany had about the same real GDP per person. By 1989 West Germany had a real GDP per person more than twice the level of East Germany's. Why did East Germany grow so much more slowly than West Germany over those 40 years?

Solution to Additional Practice Problem 17.4

1. In 1949, East Germany was formed with state ownership of capital and land, and virtually no economic freedom. West Germany was formed

with private ownership of most capital and land, and significant economic freedom.

West Germany had the preconditions for economic growth; East Germany did not. When East Germany collapsed in 1989, West Germany had more human capital, more capital per hour of labor, and better technology. The different incentives had given West German workers the incentive to acquire human capital, West German investors the incentive to acquire physical capital, and West German entrepreneurs the incentive to innovate new and better technology.

■ Self Test 17.4

Fill in the blanks

____, ____, and ____ are preconditions for economic growth. Policies the government can take to encourage faster economic growth are to ____ (create; discourage) incentive mechanisms; ____ (encourage; discourage) saving; ____ (encourage; discourage) research and development; ____ (encourage; discourage) international trade; and improve the quality of ____ (education; pollution control).

True or false

1. To achieve economic growth, economic freedom must be coupled with a democratic political system.
2. Markets slow specialization and hence slow economic growth.
3. Encouraging saving can increase the growth of capital and stimulate economic growth.
4. Limiting international trade will increase economic growth.

Multiple choice

1. Economic freedom means that
   a. firms are regulated by the government.
   b. some goods and services are free.
   c. people are able to make personal choices and their property is protected.
   d. the rule of law does not apply.
   e. the nation's government is a democracy.

2. Property rights protect
   a. the rights participate in markets.
   b. only the rights to financial property.
   c. only the rights to intellectual property.
   d. rights to physical property, financial property, and intellectual property.
   e. the government's right to impose taxes.

3. Which of the following statements is FALSE?
   a. Saving helps create economic growth.
   b. Improvements in the quality of education are important for economic growth.
   c. Free international trade helps create economic growth.
   d. Faster population growth is the key to growth in real GDP per person.
   e. Economic freedom requires property rights.

4. Saving
   a. slows growth because it decreases consumption.
   b. finances investment which brings capital accumulation.
   c. has no impact on economic growth.
   d. is very low in most East Asian nations.
   e. is important for a country to gain the benefits of international trade.

5. The fastest growing nations today are those with
   a. barriers that significantly limit international trade.
   b. the fastest growing exports and imports.
   c. government intervention in markets to ensure high prices.
   d. few funds spent on research and development.
   e. the least saving.

6. Economic growth is enhanced by
   a. free international trade.
   b. limiting international trade so that the domestic economy can prosper.
   c. discouraging saving, because increased saving means less spending.
   d. ignoring incentive systems.
   e. increasing welfare payments to the poor so they can afford to buy goods.

Short answer and numeric questions

1. Does persistent economic growth necessarily occur when a nation meets all the preconditions for growth?

2. What role do specialization and trade play in determining economic growth?

3. Is it possible for the government to create a large increase in the economic growth rate, say from 3 percent to 10 percent in a year?

4. The Eye on Your Life discussed the roles played by economic growth in your life. How important do you think the technological advances that have lead to economic growth are in determining the quality of your life?

SELF TEST ANSWERS

■ CHECKPOINT 17.1

Fill in the blanks

<u>Keynesian</u> macroeconomics asserts that government intervention is needed to achieve full employment. The new macroeconomics says that macro outcomes depend on <u>micro</u> choices. The relationship that shows the maximum quantity of real GDP that can be produced as the quantity of labor employed changes is <u>the production function</u>. The quantity of labor demanded <u>increases</u> as the real wage rate falls and the quantity of labor supplied <u>decreases</u> as the real wage rate falls. If the real wage rate exceeds the equilibrium real wage rate, there is a <u>surplus</u> of labor. When the labor market is in equilibrium, there is <u>full employment of labor</u> and real GDP equals <u>potential GDP</u>.

True or false

1. True; page 442
2. False; page 443
3. False; page 445
4. False; page 446
5. False; page 447
6. True; pages 450-451
7. True; page 451

Multiple choice

1. c; page 443
2. a; page 445
3. a; page 445
4. b; page 446
5. b; page 448
6. b; pages 449-450
7. b; pages 450-451
8. e; page 451
9. a; page 451
10. b; page 451
11. b; page 452

Complete the graph

1. Figure 17.4 illustrates the production function. In the table, diminishing returns are demonstrated by the fact that each additional

■ FIGURE 17.4

Real GDP (billions of 2000 dollars)

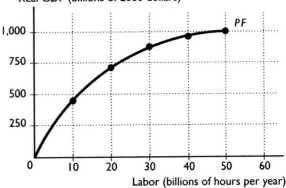

10 billion hours of labor increases real GDP by a smaller amount. In the figure, diminishing returns are illustrated by the slope of the production function, which becomes less steep as the quantity of labor increases; pages 446-447.

2. The equilibrium real wage rate is $20 an hour and the equilibrium employment is 30 billion hours. Potential GDP is $900 billion; page 451.

3. If both the labor demand and labor supply curves shift rightward by 10 billion labor hours, then equilibrium employment increases by 10 billion hours to 40 billion hours. Potential GDP increases to $960 billion; page 451.

Short answer and numeric questions

1. Classical macroeconomics believes that markets work well and government intervention cannot improve the economy. Keynesian economics believes that a market economy is unstable and needs government intervention to help it reach full employment and sustained economic growth; page 442.

2. The equilibrium quantity of labor is the amount of full employment. The production function shows how much GDP this full-employment quantity of labor produces and this quantity of GDP is potential GDP; page 451.

3. If the production function shifts upward, the amount of real GDP produced by every quantity of labor increases. The nation's potential GDP increases; pages 446, 451.

4. On both counts, the upward shift of the production function and the increase in employment, potential GDP increases; pages 446, 451.

■ CHECKPOINT 17.2

Fill in the blanks

The growth rate of real GDP equals real GDP in the current year minus real GDP in the previous year divided by real GDP in the <u>previous</u> year, all multiplied by 100. The growth rate of real GDP per person equals the growth rate of real GDP <u>minus</u> the growth rate of the population. The number of years it takes for the level of any variable to double is approximately <u>70</u> divided by the annual percentage growth rate of the variable.

True or false

1. True; page 454
2. True; page 454
3. True; page 455
4. False; page 455

Multiple choice

1. a; page 454
2. b; page 454
3. d; page 454
4. a; page 455
5. b; page 455
6. b; page 455

Short answer and numeric questions

1. 10 percent; 10 percent; 10 percent; page 454.

2. a. 1 percent; 2 percent; –1 percent; 0 percent; page 455.

   b. 2005 and 2006; page 454.

3. Use the Rule of 70. So, 70 ÷ 3 = 23.3 years; 70 ÷ 4 = 17.5 years; 70 ÷ 5 = 14 years; page 455.

■ CHECKPOINT 17.3

Fill in the blanks

All influences on real GDP growth can be divided into those that increase aggregate hours and <u>labor productivity</u>. Labor productivity equals real GDP <u>divided by</u> aggregate hours. Saving and investment in physical capital <u>increases</u> labor productivity. Education, training, and job experience increase <u>human capital</u>. To reap the benefits of technological change, capital must <u>increase</u>.

True or false

1. True; page 458
2. True; page 459
3. False; page 459
4. True; page 460

Multiple choice

1. b; page 458
2. d; page 458
3. c; page 458
4. e; page 458
5. d; page 459
6. a; page 459
7. c; page 459

Short answer and numeric questions

1. Labor productivity equals real GDP ÷ aggregate hours. So labor productivity in 1964 was $22.45 an hour; in 1974 was $27.22 an hour; in 1984 was $31.35 an hour; in 1994 was $37.07 an hour; and in 2004 was $45.88 an hour; page 458.

2. Labor productivity is $45 an hour; page 458.

3. Real GDP is $9 trillion; page 458.

4. Labor productivity is increased by three factors. First, increasing saving and investment in physical capital gives workers more capital with which to work. Second, increasing the amount of human capital makes workers more productive and increases labor productivity. Finally, discovering new technologies makes workers more productive and increases labor productivity; by pages 459-460.

■ CHECKPOINT 17.4

Fill in the blanks

Economic freedom, property rights, and markets are preconditions for economic growth. Policies the government can take to encourage faster economic growth are to create incentive mechanisms; encourage saving; encourage research and development; encourage international trade; and improve the quality of education.

True or false

1. False; page 463
2. False; pages 463-464
3. True; page 464
4. False; page 465

Multiple choice

1. c; page 463
2. d; page 463
3. d; page 463-464
4. b; page 464
5. b; page 465
6. a; page 465

Short answer and numeric questions

1. No. The preconditions for growth are necessary for growth to occur. But for growth to be persistent, people must face incentives that encourage saving and investment, expansion of human capital, and the discovery and application of new technologies; pages 463-464.

2. Growth begins when people can specialize in the activities in which they have a comparative advantage and trade with each other. As an economy reaps the benefits from specialization and trade, production and consumption grow, real GDP per person increases, and the standard of living rises; page 464.

3. No, the government cannot create a huge increase in the economic growth rate. The government can pursue policies that will nudge the growth rate upward. And, over time, policies that create even small increases in the economic growth rate will have large benefits; page 465.

4. The importance of these technological advances are hard to overstate. For instance, the next time you watch a movie from the 1930s, the 1940s, the 1950s, the 1960s, or even the 1970s look carefully at what is *not* present. Do you see personal computers? Cell phones? MP3 players? Elaborate life-saving equipment in hospitals? Cars with enhanced safety features and incredible durability? The answers are, of course, no. All of these technological advances came in response to people's insatiable desire for a higher standard of living and other people's equally insatiable pursuit of profit.

Chapter 18

Money and the Monetary System

1 Define money and describe its functions.

Money is any commodity or token that is generally accepted as a means of payment. Money serves as a medium of exchange, a unit of account, and a store of value. Money consists of currency (dollar bills and coins) and deposits at banks and other financial institutions. Currency in a bank, credit cards, debit cards, and electronic checks are not money. M1 (currency held by individuals and businesses and traveler's checks plus checkable deposits owned by individuals and businesses) and M2 (M1 plus savings and time deposits, and money market funds and other deposits) are two measures of money.

2 Describe the functions of banks.

Banks (and other financial institutions) accept deposits and provide the services that enable people and businesses to make and receive payments. Banks make loans at a higher interest rate than the interest rate paid on deposits. A bank's cash assets consist of its reserves and funds that are due from other banks as payments for checks that are being cleared.

3 Describe the functions of the Federal Reserve System (the Fed).

The Federal Reserve System is the U.S. central bank. The Federal Open Market Committee is the Fed's main policy-making committee. The Fed has three policy tools: required reserve ratios (the minimum percentage of deposits banks must hold as reserves), discount rate (the interest rate at which the Fed stands ready to lend reserves to commercial banks), and open market operations (purchase or sale of government securities by the Fed in the open market). The monetary base is the sum of coins, Federal Reserve notes, and banks' reserves held at the Fed.

4 Explain how banks create money and how the Fed controls the quantity of money.

When a bank makes a loan, it deposits the amount loaned in the checkable deposit of the borrower, thereby creating money. To spend the loan, the borrower writes a check. The bank loses deposits and reserves when the check clears. The bank in which the check is deposited gains the reserves and deposits. It now has excess reserves, which it lends. The process is limited and eventually concludes because at each round the change in excess reserves shrinks. Open market operations are the major tool the Fed uses to change the quantity of money. If the Fed buys government securities, banks' excess reserves increase, banks lend the excess reserves, new deposits are created, and the quantity of money increases. If the Fed sells government securities, banks' excess reserves decrease, banks decrease their lending, deposits are destroyed, and the quantity of money decreases. The monetary base changes by the amount of the open market operation but the quantity of money changes by more than the amount of the open market operation. The money multiplier is the number by which a change in the monetary base is multiplied to find the resulting change in the quantity of money. It equals $(1 + C) \div (R + C)$ where C, the currency drain ratio, is the ratio of currency to deposits and R is the required reserve ratio.

CHECKPOINT 18.1

■ **Define money and describe its functions.**

Quick Review

- *M1* M1 consists of currency held by individuals and businesses, and traveler's checks plus checkable deposits owned by individuals and businesses. Currency inside banks is not counted.

- *M2* M2 consists of M1 plus savings deposits and small time deposits, money market funds, and other deposits.

Additional Practice Problems 18.1

1. You go to the bank and withdraw $200 from your checking account. You keep $100 in cash and deposit the other $100 in your savings account. What is the change in M1? What is the change in M2?

2. Janice goes to her bank's website and transfers $300 from her checking account to her savings account. What is the change in M1? What is the change in M2

3. In January 2001, currency held by individuals and businesses was $534.9 billion; traveler's checks were $8.1 billion; checkable deposits owned by individuals and businesses were $559.3 billion; savings deposits were $1,889.7 billion; small time deposits were $1,052.6 billion; and money market funds and other deposits were $952 billion.
   a. What was M1 in January 2001?
   b. What was M2 in January 2001?

Solutions to Additional Practice Problems 18.1

1. Your checking account decreased by $200, your currency increased by $100, and your savings account increased by $100. M1, which includes your currency and your checkable deposit, is changed by the decrease in the checking account and the increase in currency. The net effect on M1 is –$200 + $100 = –$100, that is, M1 decreases by $100. M2, which includes your currency, your checkable deposits, and your savings account, does not change. The change

in your checkable deposits, –$200, is balanced by the change in your currency, +$100, and the change in your savings account, +100. There was no change in M2.

2. M1 decreases by $300. While the funds were in Janice's checking account, they were part of M1. But once they are transferred to her savings account, they are no longer part of M1. M2 does not change. The $300 was part of M2 when it was in Janice's checking account because funds in checking accounts are part of M1 and all of M1 is in M2. And, funds in savings accounts are also part of M2. So switching funds from a checking account to a savings account does not change M2.

3a. M1 is the sum of currency, traveler's checks, and checkable deposits owned by individuals and businesses. So, M1 equals $534.9 billion + $8.1 billion + $559.3 billion, which is $1,102.3 billion.

3b. M2 equals M1 plus savings deposits, small time deposits, and money market funds and other deposits. So M2 equals $1,102.3 billion + $1,889.7 billion + $1,052.6 billion + $952 billion, which is $4,996.6 billion.

■ Self Test 18.1

Fill in the blanks

Any commodity or token that is generally accepted as a means of payment is ____. A ____ (unit of account; store of value; medium of exchange) is an object that is generally accepted in return for goods and services. A ____ (unit of account; store of value; medium of exchange) is an agreed-upon measure for stating prices of goods and services. A ____ (unit of account; store of value; medium of exchange) is any commodity or token that can be held and exchanged later for goods and services. Currency inside the banks ____ (is; is not) money and currency outside the banks ____ (is; is not) money. A credit card ____ (is; is not) money. M1 is ____ (more; less) than M2. Checkable deposits ____ (are; are not) part of M1 and savings deposits ____ (are; are not) part of M1.

True or false

1. Using money as a medium of exchange is called barter.
2. Prices in terms of money reflect money's role as a unit of account.
3. Currency is money but checkable deposits at banks are not money.
4. M1 and M2 are official measures of money.
5. A debit card is not money.

Multiple choice

1. Which of the following best defines what money is now and what it has been in the past?
   a. currency
   b. currency plus checking deposits
   c. currency plus credit cards
   d. anything accepted as a means of payment
   d. anything used as a store of value

2. Which of the following is not a function of money?
   i.   unit of account
   ii. store of value
   iii. unit of debt
   a. i only.
   b. ii only.
   c. iii only.
   d. Both ii and iii.
   e. Both i and ii.

3. Barter is
   a. the exchange of goods and services for money.
   b. the pricing of goods and services with one agreed upon standard.
   c. the exchange of goods and services directly for other goods and services.
   d. a generally accepted means of payment.
   e. storing money for use at a later date.

4. If someone buries money in a tin can beneath a tree, the money is functioning as a
   a. medium of exchange.
   b. unit of account.
   c. means of payment.
   d. store of value.
   e. bartering tool.

5. Which of the following counts as part of M1?
   a. $5,000 worth of gold
   b. $5,000 worth of government bonds
   c. $5,000 in a checking account
   d. $5,000 credit line on a credit card
   e. $5,000 of real estate

6. M2 equals
   a. M1 and is just another name for currency outside of banks.
   b. M1 plus savings deposits, small time deposits, and money market fund deposits.
   c. M1 minus traveler's checks because they are not really money.
   d. currency plus savings deposits, all time deposits, and money market funds and other deposits.
   e. M1 plus savings deposits and small time deposits minus money market fund deposits.

7. If currency held by individuals and businesses is $800 billion; traveler's checks are $10 billion; checkable deposits owned by individuals and businesses are $700 billion; savings deposits are $4,000 billion; small time deposits are $1,000 billion; and money market funds and other deposits are $800 billion, then M1 equals ____ billion.
   a. $7,310
   b. $5,800
   c. $2,510
   d. $1,510
   e. $710

8. Credit cards, debit cards, and e-checks are
   a. always counted as money.
   b. not money.
   c. sometimes counted as money, depending on how they are used.
   d. sometimes counted as money, depending on what is purchased.
   e. sometimes counted as money, depending on what measure of money is being used.

Short answer and numeric questions

1. Why was it possible at one time to use whale's teeth as money?

2. What are the functions of money?

3. Why is currency money?

4. In January 2005, currency held by individuals and businesses was $699.6 billion; traveler's checks were $7.5 billion; checkable deposits owned by individuals and businesses were $649.2 billion; savings deposits were $3,544.7 billion; small time deposits were $824.5 billion; and money market funds and other deposits were $711.4 billion.
   a. What was M1 in January 2005?
   b. What was M2 in January 2005?

5. Some parts of M2 are not money. Why are these parts included in M2?

6. Why are e-checks not money?

CHECKPOINT 18.2

■ Describe the functions of banks.

Quick Review

- *Reserves* A bank's reserves consist of the currency in its vault plus the balance on its reserve account at a Federal Reserve Bank.

Additional Practice Problems 18.2

1. The Acme Bank just sold $100 in securities in exchange for a $100 bill. It made a $50 loan, and the borrower left with the cash. It also accepted a $60 cash deposit.
   a. How have the bank's reserves changed as a result of all these actions?
   b. How have its deposits changed?

2. A bank has the following deposits and assets: $300 in checkable deposits, $800 in savings deposits, $900 in small time deposits, $1,000 in loans to businesses, $950 in government securities, $20 in currency, and $30 in its reserve account at the Fed. Calculate the bank's:
   a. Total deposits
   b. Deposits that are part of M1
   c. Deposits that are part of M2
   d. Reserves
   e. What is the ratio of the bank's reserves to its deposits?

Solutions to Additional Practice Problems 18.2

1a. The $100 sale of securities adds $100 to reserves. The $50 loan which the borrower then withdrew as cash removes $50 from the bank and out of its reserves, and the $60 deposit adds to reserves. The net result is +$100 − $50 + $60, which is +$110. Acme has $110 more in reserves.

1b. The $60 deposit is the only transaction that affects its deposits, so deposits rise by $60.

2a. Total deposits are the sum of checkable deposits, $300, savings deposits, $800, and small time deposits, $900, which equals a total of $2,000.

2b. The only deposits that are part of M1 are checkable deposits, $300.

2c. All of the bank's deposits are part of M2, so deposits that are part of M2 are $2,000.

2d. Reserves are the currency in the bank's vault plus the balance on its reserve account at a Federal Reserve Bank. Reserves are $20 + $30, which equals $50.

2e. The ratio of reserves to deposits is $50 ÷ $2,000, which equals 2.5 percent.

■ Self Test 18.2

Fill in the blanks

The currency in a bank's vault is part of the bank's ____ (reserves; loans). Banks can borrow or lend reserves in the ____ (reserves; federal funds) market. At commercial banks in the United States, the majority of deposits ____ (are; are not) checkable deposits.

True or false

1. A commercial bank accepts checkable deposits, savings deposits, and time deposits.

2. A commercial bank maximizes its stockholders' long-term wealth by refusing to make any risky loans.

3. When a credit union has excess reserves, it makes loans to its members at an interest rate called the federal funds rate.

Multiple choice

1. A commercial bank's main goal is to
   a. provide loans to its customers.
   b. maximize the long-term wealth of its stockholders.
   c. help the government when it needs money.
   d. lend money to the Federal Reserve banks.
   e. open checking accounts.

2. Which of the flowing lists includes only banks' assets?
   a. cash assets, interbank loans, securities, and loans.
   b. reserves, savings deposits, bonds, and loans.
   c. reserves, bonds, cash securities, and savings deposits
   d. securities, reserves, debts, and interbank cash.
   e. reserves, checkable deposits, securities, and loans.

3. A commercial bank's reserves are
   a. bonds issued by the U.S. government that are very safe.
   b. the provision of funds to businesses and individuals.
   c. currency in its vault plus the balance on its reserve account at a Federal Reserve Bank.
   d. savings and time deposits.
   e. its loans.

4. A bank has $400 in checking deposits, $800 in savings deposits, $700 in time deposits, $900 in loans to businesses, $300 in outstanding credit card balances, $500 in government securities, $10 in currency in its vault, and $20 in deposits at the Fed. The bank's deposits that are part of M1 are equal to
   a. $1,900.
   b. $400.
   c. $1,210.
   d. $530.
   e. $410.

5. Which of the following accepts deposits from or sell shares to the general public?
   i. money market funds.
   ii. thrift institutions.
   iii. commercial banks.
   a. i only.
   b. ii only.
   c. iii only.
   d. ii and iii.
   e. i, ii, and iii.

6. Which of the following is a thrift institution?
   a. a savings and loan association
   b. a money market fund
   c. a commercial bank
   d. a loan institution
   e. the Federal Reserve

Short answer and numeric questions

1. What are a bank's reserves? How does a bank use its account at the Federal Reserve Bank?

CHECKPOINT 18.3

■ **Describe the functions of the Federal Reserve System (the Fed).**

Quick Review

- *Federal Reserve System* The Federal Reserve System is the central bank of the United States.

Additional Practice Problems 18.3

1. What are required reserve ratios?
2. What is the discount rate?
3. In August, 2005 Federal Reserve notes and coins were $785 billion, and banks' reserves at the Fed are $9 billion, the gold stock was $11 billion, and the Fed owned $742 billion of government securities. What did the monetary base equal?

Solutions to Additional Practice Problems 18.3

1. Banks are required by law to hold a certain fraction of their deposits as reserves. The Federal Reserve determines what fraction banks

must hold as reserves. These fractions are called the banks' required reserve ratios.

2. Banks can borrow reserves from the Federal Reserve. The interest rate they pay on these loans is the discount rate.

3. The monetary base is the sum of the coins and Federal Reserve notes plus banks' reserves at the Fed. In this case the monetary base equals $785 billion + $9 billion, which is $794 billion.

■ Self Test 18.3

Fill in the blanks

There are ____ (2; 6; 12) Federal Reserve Banks. The Fed's main policy-making committee is the ____ (Board of Governors; Federal Open Market Committee). The Fed sets the minimum percentage of deposits that must be held as reserves, which is called the ____ (discount rate; required reserve ratio). The interest rate at which the Fed stands ready to lend reserves to commercial banks is the ____ (discount; open market operation) rate. The purchase or sale of government securities by the Federal Reserve is an ____.

True or false

1. The Federal Reserve System is the central bank of the United States.

2. An open market operation is the purchase or sale of government securities by the Federal Reserve from the U.S. government.

3. If banks use $1 million of reserves to buy $1 million worth of newly printed bank notes from the Fed, the monetary base does not change.

Multiple choice

1. Regulating the amount of money in the United States is one of the most important responsibilities of the
   a. State Department.
   b. state governments.
   c. Treasury Department.
   d. Federal Reserve.
   e. U.S. Mint.

2. The Board of Governors of the Federal Reserve System has
   a. 12 members appointed by the president of the United States.
   b. 12 members elected by the public.
   c. seven members appointed by the president of the United States.
   d. seven members elected by the public.
   e. seven members appointed to life terms.

3. The Fed's policy is determined by the
   a. Federal Open Market Committee.
   b. Executive Council to the Governor.
   c. Regional Federal Reserve Banks.
   d. Board of Governors.
   e. Federal Monetary Policy Committee.

4. The Fed's policy tools include
   a. required reserve ratios, the discount rate, and open market operations.
   b. holding deposits for the U.S. government, reserve requirements, and the discount rate.
   c. setting regulations for lending standards and approving or rejecting loans banks make to large corporations.
   d. supervision of the banking system and buying and selling commercial banks.
   e. required reserve ratios, income tax rates, and open market operations.

5. The minimum percent of deposits that banks must hold and cannot loan is determined by the
   a. interest rate.
   b. discount rate.
   c. required reserve ratio.
   d. federal funds rate.
   e. ratio of M2 to M1.

6. The discount rate is the interest rate that
   a. commercial banks charge their customers.
   b. commercial banks charge each other for the loan of reserves.
   c. the Fed charges the government.
   d. the Fed charges commercial banks for the loan of reserves.
   e. the Fed pays commercial banks on their reserves held at the Fed.

7. The monetary base is the
   a. minimum reserves banks must hold to cover any losses from unpaid loans.
   b. sum of coins, Federal Reserve notes, and banks' reserves at the Fed.
   c. sum of gold and foreign exchange held by the Fed.
   d. sum of government securities and loans to banks held by the Fed.
   e. sum of coins, required reserves, and bank loans.

8. If Federal Reserve notes and coins are $765 billion, and banks' reserves at the Fed are $8 billion, the gold stock is $11 billion, and the Fed owns $725 billion of government securities, what does the monetary base equal?
   a. $765 billion.
   b. $773 billion.
   c. $776 billion.
   d. $744 billion.
   e. $1,509 billion.

9. If the Federal Reserve _____ the required reserve ratio, the interest rate _____.
   a. lowers; rises
   b. lowers; falls
   c. raises; does not change
   d. raises; falls
   e. Not enough information is given because the effect depends also on the size of the monetary base.

Short answer and numeric questions

1. How many people are on the Board of Governors of the Federal Reserve System? How are they selected?

2. What is the FOMC and who are its members?

3. Suppose that banks' deposits are $600 billion and that the required reserve ratio is 10 percent.
   a. What is the minimum amount of reserves banks must hold?
   b. Suppose the Federal Reserve lowers the required reserve ratio to 8 percent. Now what is the minimum amount of reserves banks must hold?

c. Suppose the Federal Reserve raises the required reserve ratio to 12 percent. Now what is the minimum amount of reserves banks must hold?

4. What is the monetary base?

CHECKPOINT 18.4

■ **Explain how banks create money and how the Fed controls the quantity of money.**

Quick Review

- *Excess reserves* Excess reserves equal actual reserves minus required reserves.

- *Money multiplier* The number by which a change in the monetary base is multiplied to find the resulting change in the quantity of money.

Additional Practice Problems 18.4

1. The required reserve ratio is 0.05 and banks have no excess reserves. Katie deposits $500 in currency in her bank. Calculate:
   a. The change in the bank's reserves as soon as Katie makes the deposit.
   b. The bank's excess reserves as soon as Katie makes the deposit.
   c. The maximum amount that Katie's bank can loan.

2. If the required reserve ratio is 10 percent and the currency drain ratio is 30 percent, what is the size of the money multiplier? By how much will a $10 billion increase in the monetary base change the quantity of money?

3. If the required reserve ratio is 20 percent and the currency drain ratio is 30 percent, what is the size of the money multiplier? By how much will a $10 billion increase in the monetary base change the quantity of money?

4. Using problems 2 and 3, what is the effect of a rise in the required reserve ratio on the increase in the quantity of money?

Solution to Additional Practice Problems 18.4

1a. The new deposit of $500 increases the bank's actual reserves by $500.

1b. The bank is required to keep 5 percent of deposits as reserves. So required reserves increase by 5 percent of the deposit, or ($500) × (0.05), which is $25. As a result, excess reserves, which are actual reserves minus required reserves, increase by $500 − $25, which is $475.

1c. The crucial point to keep in mind is that banks can loan their excess reserves in order to boost their revenue and profit. So Katie's bank can loan a maximum of $475.

2. The money multiplier equals $(1 + C) \div (R + C)$ where C is the currency drain ratio and R is the required reserve ratio, both expressed as decimals. So the money multiplier equals $(1 + 0.3) \div (0.1 + 0.3)$, which is 3.25. So a $10 billion increase in the monetary base increases the quantity of money by 3.25 × $10 billion, or $32.5 billion.

3. The money multiplier equals $(1 + C) \div (R + C)$ where C is the currency drain ratio and R is the required reserve ratio, both expressed as decimals. So the money multiplier equals $(1 + 0.3) \div (0.2 + 0.3)$, which is 2.6. So a $10 billion increase in the monetary base increases the quantity of money by 2.6 × $10 billion, or $26 billion.

4. An increase in the required reserve ratio shrinks the amount by which the quantity of money increases.

■ Self Test 18.4

Fill in the blanks

When the Fed purchases government securities, it ____ (decreases; increases) the quantity of money. An open market sale of government securities by the Fed ____ (decreases; increases) the monetary base and ____ (decreases; increases) banks' excess reserves. An increase in currency held outside the banks is called ____ (an excess currency removal; a currency drain; a multiplier reserve). If the money multiplier is 2.0, a $4 million increase in the monetary base will create an increase of ____ ($2; $8) million in the quantity of money. The larger the required reserve ratio, the ____ (larger; smaller) is the ____ (currency drain; money multiplier).

True or false

1. When a bank increases its loans, it creates money.

2. The required reserve ratio has no effect on the amount of money banks can create.

3. When the Fed buys securities in an open market operation, it pays for them with newly created bank reserves.

4. When the Fed sells government securities, it decreases the quantity of banks' reserves.

5. When the Fed buys government securities, the effect on the money supply depends on whether the Fed buys the securities from a bank or the general public.

6. If the Fed increases the monetary base by $1 billion, the ultimate increase in the quantity of money will be less than $1 billion.

7. The larger the currency drain ratio, the larger the money multiplier.

8. If the currency drain ratio is 20 percent and the required reserve ratio is 10 percent, the money multiplier is 1.675.

Multiple choice

1. Excess reserves are the
   a. same as the required reserves.
   b. amount of reserves the Fed requires banks to hold.
   c. amount of reserves held above what is desired.
   d. amount of reserves a bank holds at the Fed.
   e. amount of reserves banks keep in their vaults.

2. Banks can make loans up to an amount equal to their
   a. total deposits.
   b. total reserves.
   c. required reserves.
   d. excess reserves.
   e. total government securities.

3. When the Fed sells securities in an open market operation
   a. the monetary base increases and the quantity of money increases.
   b. the monetary base does not change.
   c. only commercial banks can be buyers.
   d. the monetary base does not change.
   e. buyers pay for the securities with money and bank reserves.

4. If the Fed buys government securities, then
   a. the quantity of money is not changed, just its composition.
   b. new bank reserves are created.
   c. the quantity of money decreases.
   d. bank reserves are destroyed.
   e. banks' excess reserves decrease.

5. The Citizens First Bank sells $100,000 of government securities to the Fed. This sale immediately
   a. decreases the quantity of money.
   b. decreases the bank's checkable deposits.
   c. increases the bank's reserves.
   d. decreases the bank's assets.
   e. increases the bank's required reserves.

6. When the Fed conducts an open market purchase, the first round changes in the money creation process are that excess reserves ____, bank deposits ____, and the quantity of money ____.
   a. decreases; decreases; decrease
   b. increases; do not change; increase
   c. decreases; increases; does not change
   d. do not change; increases; increase
   e. increase; increase; increases

7. A currency drain is cash ____ and has ____ effect on the money multiplier.
   a. draining into the banks; no
   b. draining into the banks; an
   c. held outside the banks; an
   d. held at the Fed; an
   e. held as reserves; no

8. The money multiplier is used to determine how much the
   a. monetary base increases when the Fed purchases government securities.
   b. quantity of money increases when the monetary base increases.
   c. monetary base increases when the quantity of money increases.
   d. quantity of money increases when the required reserve ratio increases.
   e. monetary base increases when the Fed sells government securities.

9. The Fed makes an open market operation purchase of $200,000. The currency drain ratio is 33 percent and the required reserve ratio is 10 percent. By how much does the quantity of money increase?
   a. $800,000
   b. $333,333
   c. $2,000,000
   d. $618,604
   e. $465,116

Short answer and numeric questions

Round	Increase in deposits (dollars)	Increase in currency (dollars)	Increase in reserves (dollars)	Increase in excess reserves (dollars)
A			1,000	1,000
B	___	___	___	___
C	___	___	___	___
D	___	___	___	___

1. Suppose the Fed buys $1,000 of government securities from Hayward National Bank. The required reserve ratio is 10 percent and the currency drain ratio is 25 percent. Suppose that all banks loan all of their excess reserves. Complete the above table. Calculate the total increase in deposits and currency following the first four rounds of the multiplier process.

Round	Increase in deposits (dollars)	Increase in currency (dollars)	Increase in reserves (dollars)	Increase in excess reserves (dollars)
A			1,000	1,000
B	____	____	____	____
C	____	____	____	____
D	____	____	____	____

2. Suppose the Fed buys $1,000 of government securities from Fremont National Bank. The required reserve ratio is 10 percent and the currency drain ratio is 100 percent. Suppose that all banks loan all of their excess reserves. Complete the above table. Calculate the total increase in deposits and currency following the first four rounds of the multiplier process.

3. In which question, 1 or 2, was the increase in the quantity of money largest after four rounds?

4. Calculate the money multiplier when the required reserve ratio is 10 percent and the currency drain ratio is 20 percent. Calculate the money multiplier when the required reserve ratio is 10 percent and the currency drain ratio is 60 percent. As the currency drain ratio increases, what happens to the magnitude of the money multiplier?

5. Calculate the money multiplier when the required reserve ratio is 10 percent and the currency drain ratio is 20 percent. Calculate the money multiplier when the required reserve ratio is 20 percent and the currency drain ratio is 20 percent. As the required reserve ratio increases, what happens to the magnitude of the money multiplier?

6. Why does an increase in the required reserve ratio or in the currency drain ratio decrease the magnitude of the money multiplier?

7. The Eye on Your Life talks about your role in creating money. Money also will play a role in your life if you travel because nations often have different moneys. But the U.S. dollar is often accepted, especially in less developed nations. If you take some dollars with you when you travel and then spend a U.S. dollar bill in another nation, how does that affect the amount of U.S. M1?

SELF TEST ANSWERS

■ CHECKPOINT 18.1

Fill in the blanks

Any commodity or token that is generally accepted as a means of payment is <u>money</u>. A <u>medium of exchange</u> is an object that is generally accepted in return for goods and services. A <u>unit of account</u> is an agreed-upon measure for stating prices of goods and services. A <u>store of value</u> is any commodity or token that can be held and exchanged later for goods and services. Currency inside the banks <u>is not</u> money and currency outside the banks <u>is</u> money. A credit card <u>is not</u> money. M1 is <u>less</u> than M2. Checkable deposits <u>are</u> part of M1 and savings deposits <u>are not</u> part of M1.

True or false

1. False; page 473
2. True; page 473
3. False; page 474
4. True; page 475
5. True; page 476

Multiple choice

1. d; page 472
2. c; pages 472-473
3. c; page 473
4. d; page 473
6. c; page 474
7. b; page 474
8. d; page 474
5. b; pages 475-476

Short answer and numeric questions

1. It was possible to use whale's teeth as money because whale's teeth were generally accepted as a means of payment. At one time, most people were willing to trade goods and services in exchange for whale's teeth; page 472.

2. Money has three functions. It is a medium of exchange, an object that is generally accepted in return for goods and services. It is a unit of account, an agreed-upon measure for stating the prices of goods and services. And it is a store of value, a commodity or token that can be held and exchanged at a later date for goods and services; pages 472-473.

3. Currency is money because it is generally accepted as a means of payment. It is generally accepted because the government has declared that currency is money, so that currency is fiat money; page 474.

4. a. M1 is the sum of currency, traveler's checks, and checkable deposits owned by individuals and businesses. So, M1 equals $699.6 billion + $7.5 billion + $649.2 billion, which is $1,356.3 billion; page 474.

   b. M2 equals M1 plus savings deposits, small time deposits, and money market funds and other deposits. So M2 equals $1,356.3 billion + $3,544.7 billion + $824.5 billion + $711.4 billion, which is $6,436.9 billion; page 474.

5. Time deposits, money market funds, and some of the savings deposits included in M2 are not money. They are not money because they are not a means of payment. They are included in M2 because they are very easily converted into money; page 475.

6. E-checks are not money because they are instructions to transfer money from one person's deposit account to another person's deposit account; page 476.

■ CHECKPOINT 18.2

Fill in the blanks

The currency in a bank's vault is part of the bank's <u>reserves</u>. Banks can borrow or lend reserves in the <u>federal funds</u> market. At commercial banks in the United States, the majority of deposits <u>are not</u> checkable deposits.

True or false

1. True; page 478
2. False; page 479
3. False; page 479

Multiple choice

1. b; page 479

2. a; page 479
3. c; page 479
4. b; page 479
5. e; pages 478, 480
6. a; page 480

Short answer and numeric questions
1. A bank's reserves are the currency in its vault plus the balance on its reserve account at a Federal Reserve bank. A bank uses its account at the Fed to receive and make payments to other banks and to obtain currency; page 479.

■ CHECKPOINT 18.3

Fill in the blanks
There are <u>12</u> Federal Reserve Banks. The Fed's main policy-making committee is the <u>Federal Open Market Committee</u>. The Fed sets the minimum percentage of deposits that must be held as reserves, which is called the <u>required reserve ratio</u>. The interest rate at which the Fed stands ready to lend reserves to commercial banks is the <u>discount</u> rate. The purchase or sale of government securities by the Federal Reserve is an <u>open market operation</u>.

True or false
1. True; page 483
2. False; page 485
3. True; page 485

Multiple choice
1. d; page 484
2. c; page 484
3. a; page 484
4. a; pages 484-485
5. c; page 484
6. d; page 485
7. b; page 485
8. b; page 485
9. b; page 485

Short answer and numeric questions
1. There are seven members on the Board of Governors of the Federal Reserve System. They are appointed by the president of the United States and confirmed by the U.S. Senate; page 484.

2. The FOMC is the Federal Open Market Committee and it is the main policy-making committee of the Federal Reserve. The members are the seven members of the Board of Governors, the president of the Federal Reserve Bank of New York, and, on an annual rotating basis, four presidents of the other regional Federal Reserve banks; page 484.

3. a. If the required reserve ratio is 10 percent, banks must keep ($600 billion × 0.10) = $60 billion as reserves; page 484.
   b. If the required reserve ratio is lowered to 8 percent, banks must keep ($600 billion × 0.08) = $48 billion as reserves. A decrease in the required reserve ratio decreases the total amount of reserves banks must keep; page 484.
   c. If the required reserve ratio is raised to 12 percent, banks must keep ($600 billion × 0.12) = $72 billion as reserves. An increase in the required reserve ratio increases the total amount of reserves banks must keep page 484.

4. The monetary base is the sum of coins, Federal Reserve notes, and banks' reserves at the Federal Reserve; page 485.

■ CHECKPOINT 18.4

Fill in the blanks
When the Fed purchases government securities, it <u>increases</u> the quantity of money. An open market sale of government securities by the Fed <u>decreases</u> the monetary base and <u>decreases</u> banks' excess reserves. An increase in currency held outside the banks is called <u>a currency drain</u>. If the money multiplier is 2.0, a $4 million increase in the monetary base will create an increase of <u>$8</u> million in the quantity of money. The larger the required reserve ratio, the <u>smaller</u> is the <u>money multiplier</u>.

True or false
1. True; page 487

2. False; pages 487-488, 494
3. True; pages 488-490
4. True; page 491
5. False; pages 490-491
6. False; pages 492-494
7. False; page 494
8. False; page 494

Multiple choice
1. c; page 488
2. d; pages 487-488
3. e; page 491
4. b; page 491
5. c; page 491
6. e; page 491
7. c; pages 488, 494
8. b; page 493
9. d; page 494

Short answer and numeric questions

Round	Increase in deposits (dollars)	Increase in currency (dollars)	Increase in reserves (dollars)	Increase in excess reserves (dollars)
A			1,000.00	1,000.00
B	800.00	200.00	800.00	720.00
C	576.00	144.00	576.00	518.40
D	414.72	103.68	414.72	373.25

1. The completed table is above. After four rounds, currency increases by $447.68, deposits increase by $1,790.72, and the quantity of money increases by the sum of the increase in currency and the increase in deposits, which is $2,238.40; page 493.

Round	Increase in deposits (dollars)	Increase in currency (dollars)	Increase in reserves (dollars)	Increase in excess reserves (dollars)
A			1,000	1,000
B	500.00	500.00	500.00	450.00
C	225.00	225.00	225.00	202.50
D	101.25	101.25	101.25	91.13

2. The completed table is above. After four rounds, currency increases by $826.25, deposits increase by $826.25, and the quantity of money increases by the sum of the in-

crease in currency and the increase in deposits, which is $1,652.50; page 493.

3. The increase in the quantity of money is greater when the currency drain is smaller, in question 1; page 493.

4. The money multiplier equals $(1 + C) \div (C + R)$ where C is the currency drain ratio and R is the required reserve ratio expressed as decimals. The money multiplier for the first part of the question equals $(1 + 0.20) \div (0.20 + 0.10)$, or $(1.20) \div (0.30)$ which is 4.00. The money multiplier for the second part of the question is $(1 + 0.60) \div (0.60 + 0.10)$, or $(1.60) \div (0.70)$, which is 2.29. As the currency drain ratio increases, the magnitude of the money multiplier decreases; pages 493-494.

5. The money multiplier equals $(1 + C) \div (C + R)$ where C is the currency drain ratio and R is the required reserve ratio expressed as decimals. The money multiplier for the first part of the question equals $(1 + 0.20) \div (0.20 + 0.10)$, or $(1.20) \div (0.30)$ which is 4.00. The money multiplier for the second part of the question is $(1 + 0.20) \div (0.20 + 0.20)$, or $(1.20) \div (0.40)$, which is 3.00. As the required reserve ratio increases, the magnitude of the money multiplier decreases; pages 493-494.

6. The money multiplier exists because of the repeating process of loaning, depositing the proceeds in another bank, and then making another loan. The more each bank loans, the greater the final increase in the quantity of money and the larger the money multiplier. If the required reserve ratio increases in size, banks will be able to loan less of any additional deposit they receive. And if the currency drain ratio increases, less is deposited in a bank and the bank will be able to loan less. Because an increase in the required reserve ratio and an increase in the currency drain ratio decrease the amount that can be loaned, both decrease the size of the money multiplier; pages 493-494.

7. If you spend a U.S. dollar bill in another country, there is no effect on the amount of U.S. M1. Indeed, there are estimates that

upwards of half of all U.S. currency is abroad, being used by foreign residents. But the precise amount of U.S. currency abroad is very difficult to measure because often the currency is used for illegal purposes, and hence the users are not terribly eager to line up to have their holdings counted by the government!

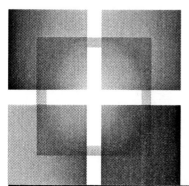

AS-AD, Cycles, and Inflation

Chapter 19

1 **Provide a technical definition of recession and describe the history of the U.S. business cycle and the global business cycle.**

A business cycle has two phases, expansion and recession, and two turning points, a peak and a trough. A standard definition of recession is a decrease in real GDP that lasts for at least two quarters. The United States has experienced 33 complete business cycles since 1854. Since World War II, the average recession has been 11 months and the average expansion has been 59 months.

2 **Define and explain the influences on aggregate supply.**

Aggregate supply is the output from all firms. Other things remaining the same, a rise in the price level increases the quantity of real GDP supplied. Moving along the aggregate supply curve, the only influence on production plans that changes is the price level. Along the potential GDP line, when the price level changes, the money wage rate and the money prices of other resources change by the same percentage as the change in the price level. Aggregate supply changes when potential GDP changes, the money wage rate changes, or the money prices of other resources change.

3 **Define and explain the influences on aggregate demand.**

The quantity of real GDP demanded is the total amount of final goods and services produced in the United States that people, businesses, governments, and foreigners plan to buy. A change in the price level changes the buying power of money, the real interest rate, and the real prices of exports and imports, which influence the quantity of real GDP demanded. An increase in the price level decreases the quantity of real GDP demanded and brings a movement along the aggregate demand curve. Factors that change aggregate demand are expectations about the future, fiscal policy and monetary policy, and the state of the world economy. The aggregate demand multiplier is an effect that magnifies changes in expenditure plans and brings potentially large fluctuations in aggregate demand.

4 **Explain how fluctuations in aggregate demand and aggregate supply create the business cycle.**

Macroeconomic equilibrium occurs at the intersection of the aggregate supply and aggregate demand curves. The macroeconomic equilibrium can be a full-employment equilibrium (real GDP equals potential GDP), an above full-employment equilibrium, or a below full-employment equilibrium. Fluctuations in aggregate demand and aggregate supply change real GDP and the price level. If real GDP exceeds potential GDP, an inflationary gap exists—the money wage rate rises, which decreases aggregate supply. The price level rises, real GDP decreases and a full-employment equilibrium is restored. If real GDP is less than potential GDP, a recessionary gap exists—the money wage rate falls, which increases aggregate supply and restores equilibrium. Persisting inflation is the result of persistent increases in aggregate demand brought about by persistent increases in the quantity of money.

CHECKPOINT 19.1

■ **Provide a technical definition of recession and describe the history of the U.S. business cycle and the global business cycle.**

Quick Review

- *Business cycle phases* The business cycle is the fluctuation in economic activity from an expansion to a peak to a recession to a trough and then to another expansion.

- *Recession* The conventional definition of a recession is a decrease in real GDP that lasts for at least six months.

Additional Practice Problems 19.1

Billions of 2000 dollars				
	Quarter			
Year	1	2	3	4
1973	4305	4355	4332	4373
1974	4335	4348	4306	4289
1975	4238	4269	4341	4398
1976	4497	4530	4552	4584
1977	4640	4731	4816	4817

1 The table shows real GDP in the United States from the first quarter of 1973 to the fourth quarter of 1977.

   a. Did the United States experience a recession during these years? If so, during which quarters?

   b. In which quarter was the United States at a business-cycle peak?

   c. In which quarter was the United States at a business-cycle trough?

   d. In what periods did the United States experience an expansion?

2. A country's real GDP grows at 5 percent a year for three quarters, slows to 0.5 percent a year for three quarters, and then increases back to 5 percent. Has the country experienced a recession?

Solutions to Additional Practice Problems 19.1

1a. Although GDP fell in the 3rd quarter of 1973 and the first quarter of 1974, it rebounded in each of the following quarters, so these do not qualify as recessions. The United States first experienced a recession from the 3rd quarter of 1974 until the 1st quarter of 1975, when real GDP decreased for three consecutive quarters.

1b. The United States was at a business cycle peak in the 2nd quarter of 1974. In the following quarters, real GDP decreased as the economy went into a recession.

1c. The United States was at a business cycle trough in the first quarter of 1975. In the quarters prior to this quarter, real GDP was decreasing. In the quarters following it, real GDP increased.

1d. The United States experienced an expansion from the 1st quarter of 1973 to the 2nd quarter of 1974 and then from the 2nd quarter of 1975 to the fourth quarter of 1977.

2. The standard definition of a recession is a decrease in real GDP that lasts for at least two quarters. The country has not experienced a decrease in real GDP so by the standard definition, a recession has not occurred.

■ Self Test 19.1

Fill in the blanks

A business cycle moves from an expansion to a ____ (peak; trough; recession), then to a ____ (peak; trough; recession), and then to a ____ (peak; trough; recession). A decrease in real GDP that lasts for at least two quarters is a ____. In the United States since 1854, the average length of an expansion is ____ (6; 35; 120) months and the average length of a recession is ____ (2; 18; 61) months. During the years since World War II the average expansion has ____ (shortened; lengthened) and the average recession has ____ (shortened; lengthened).

True or false

1. A recession begins at a trough and ends at a peak.

2. An expansion is a period during which real GDP decreases.

3. In the United States since 1854, there have been ten complete business cycles.

4. Potential GDP is not always equal to real GDP.

Multiple choice

1. The business cycle is
   a. a regular up and down movement in production and jobs.
   b. an irregular up and down movement in production and jobs.
   c. a regular movement in price changes.
   d. an irregular movement in price changes.
   e. an irregular up and down movement in the interest rate.

2. The turning point that reflects the end of an expansion is a
   a. peak.
   b. recession.
   c. trough.
   d. trend.
   e. stoppage.

3. A standard definition of recession is a decrease in real GDP that lasts for at least two
   a. years.
   b. quarters.
   c. months.
   d. weeks.
   e. reference periods.

4. Which organization or agency identifies and dates business-cycle phases and turning points in the United States?
   a. Bureau of Economic Analysis
   b. Department of Commerce
   c. National Bureau of Economic Research
   d. Federal Reserve System
   e. Bureau of the Treasury

5. Since 1854, the NBER has identified
   a. 82 complete business cycles.
   b. 33 expansions and 25 recessions.
   c. 33 complete business cycles.
   d. 25 expansions and 33 recessions.
   e. 17 complete business cycles.

6. During the twentieth century, recessions
   a. have shortened and expansions have lengthened.
   b. were as long as expansions.
   c. have lengthened and expansions have shortened.
   d. and expansions have shortened.
   e. and expansions have not changed in length.

Complete the graph

■ FIGURE 19.1

Real GDP (trillions of 2000 dollars)

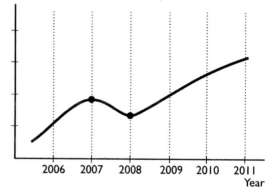

1. Figure 19.1 shows how GDP changes over time. In it, identify the different parts of the business cycle.

■ FIGURE 19.2

Real GDP (trillions of 2000 dollars)

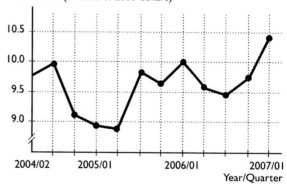

2. Identify when the economy in Figure 19.2 is experiencing recession.

Short answer and numeric questions

1. What is the standard definition of a recession?

2. Since World War II, how have the length of the average expansion and the average recession changed?

CHECKPOINT 19.2

■ **Define and explain the influences on aggregate supply.**

Quick Review

- *Aggregate supply* The relationship between the quantity of real GDP supplied and the price level when all other influences on production plans remain the same.

- *Factors that change aggregate supply* Aggregate supply decreases and the aggregate supply curve shifts leftward when potential GDP decreases, when the money wage rate rises, or when the money price of other resources rises.

Additional Practice Problem 19.2

1. The table shows the aggregate supply schedule for the United Kingdom.

a. Plot the aggregate supply curve in the figure.

b. If the money wage rate in the United Kingdom increases, show the effect on the aggregate supply curve. Is there a

Price level (GDP deflator)	Real GDP supplied (billions of 1995 pounds)
90	650
100	700
110	750
120	800
130	850

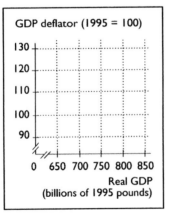

movement along the aggregate supply curve or a shift of the aggregate supply curve?

Solution to Additional Practice Problem 19.2

1a. The aggregate supply curve is plotted in the figure as AS_0. The aggregate supply curve has a positive slope, so as the price level rises, the quantity of real GDP supplied increases.

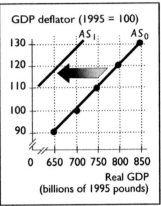

1b. To answer this Practice Problem remember that changes in the price level lead to changes in the aggregate quantity supplied and movements along the aggregate supply curve. Aggregate supply changes when any influence on production plans other than the price level changes. An increase in the money wage rate decreases aggregate supply and shifts the aggregate supply curve leftward, as illustrated by the shift to AS_1. A change in the money wage rate shifts the aggregate supply curve.

■ Self Test 19.2

Fill in the blanks

Moving along the aggregate supply curve, as the price level rises, the quantity of real GDP supplied ____ (decreases; does not change; increases) because the real wage rate ____ (falls; rises). Moving along the potential GDP line, the money wage rate ____ (changes; does not change) when the price level changes. When potential GDP increases, a ____ (movement along; shift of) the AS curve occurs. When the money wage rate changes, a ____ (movement along; shift of) the AS curve occurs.

True or false

1. Along the aggregate supply curve, a rise in the price level decreases the quantity of real GDP supplied.

2. A rise in the price level decreases potential GDP.

3. Anything that changes potential GDP shifts the aggregate supply curve.

4. An increase in potential GDP shifts the aggregate supply curve rightward.

Multiple choice

1. Moving along the potential GDP line, the money wage rate changes by the same percentage as the change in the price level so that the real wage rate
   a. increases.
   b. decreases.
   c. stays at the full-employment equilibrium level.
   d. might either increase or decrease.
   e. stays the same, though not necessarily at the full-employment equilibrium level.

2. The aggregate supply curve is
   a. upward sloping.
   b. downward sloping.
   c. a vertical line.
   d. a horizontal line.
   e. U-shaped.

3. When the price level falls,
   a. the *AS* curve shifts rightward but the potential GDP line does not shift.
   b. there is a movement upward along the *AS* curve.
   c. the *AS* curve shifts leftward but the potential GDP line does not shift.
   d. there is a movement downward along the *AS* curve.
   e. both the potential GDP line and the *AS* curve shift leftward.

4. As the price level rises relative to costs and the real wage rate falls, profits ____ and the number of firms in business ____.
   a. increase; increases
   b. increase; decreases
   c. decrease; increases
   d. decrease; decreases
   e. do not change; do not change

■ FIGURE 19.3

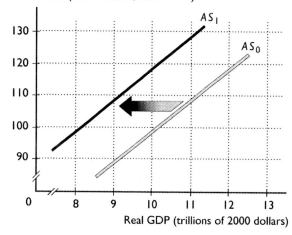

Price level (GDP deflator, 2000 = 100)

Real GDP (trillions of 2000 dollars)

5. In Figure 19.3, which of the following might be the reason for a shift of the aggregate supply curve from *AS₀* to *AS₁*?
   a. a fall in the money wage rate
   b. an increase in potential GDP
   c. an increase in investment
   d. a fall in the price of oil
   e. a rise in the money wage rate

6. When potential GDP increases,
   a. the *AS* curve shifts rightward.
   b. there is a movement up along the *AS* curve.
   c. the *AS* curve shifts leftward.
   d. there is a movement down along the *AS* curve.
   e. there is neither a movement along or a shift in the *AS* curve.

7. If the money wage rate rises,
   a. the *AS* curve shifts rightward.
   b. there is a movement up along the *AS* curve.
   c. the *AS* curve shifts leftward.
   d. there is a movement down along the *AS* curve.
   e. there is neither a movement along nor a shift in the *AS* curve.

Complete the graph

Price level (GDP deflator 2000 = 100)	Quantity of real GDP supplied (trillions of 2000 dollars)	Potential GDP (trillions of 2000 dollars)
140	17	13
130	15	13
120	13	13
110	11	13
100	9	13

■ FIGURE 19.4

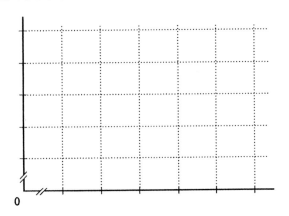

1. The table above gives the aggregate supply schedule and potential GDP schedule for a nation.
   a. Label the axes and then plot the *AS* curve and potential GDP line in Figure 19.4.
   b. Suppose the money wage rate falls. Show the effect of this change on aggregate supply and potential GDP in Figure 19.4.
   c. Use the data in the table to again plot the *AS* curve and potential GDP line in Figure 19.5. Be sure to label the axes.

■ FIGURE 19.5

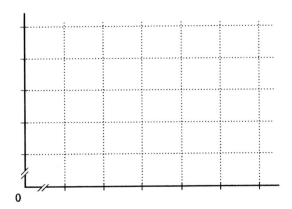

   d. Potential GDP increases by $2 trillion. Show the effect of this change on aggregate supply and potential GDP in Figure 19.5.

Short answer and numeric questions

1. Why does the *AS* curve slope upward?

2. Why does the aggregate supply curve shift when the money wage rate rises? Why doesn't the potential GDP line also shift?

3. What is the effect on aggregate supply if the money price of oil rises?

CHECKPOINT 19.3

■ Define and explain the influences on aggregate demand.

Quick Review
- *Aggregate demand* The relationship between the quantity of real GDP demanded and the price level when all other influences on expenditure plans remain the same.
- *Factors that change aggregate demand* Aggregate demand changes and the aggregate demand curve shifts if expected future income, inflation, or profit change; if the government or the Federal Reserve take steps that change expenditure plans, such as changes in taxes or in the quan-

tity of money; or the state of the world economy changes.

Additional Practice Problem 19.3

1. Draw aggregate demand curves and illustrate the effects of each event listed below either by a movement along the aggregate demand curve or a shift in the aggregate demand curve. These events are:
   a. The price level falls.
   b. Firms increase their investment because the expected future rate of profit increases.
   c. The government cuts its taxes.

Solution to Additional Practice Problem 19.3

1a. To answer this Practice Problem, remember that a change in any factor that influences expenditure plans other than the price level brings a change in aggregate demand and a shift in the *AD* curve. In this part, it *is* the price level that changes, so there is a change in the quantity of real GDP demanded and a movement along the aggregate demand curve. Because the price level falls, there is a downward movement along the aggregate demand curve, as illustrated.

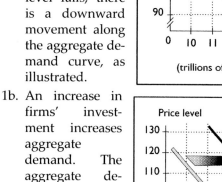

1b. An increase in firms' investment increases aggregate demand. The aggregate demand curve shifts rightward, as shown in the figure by the shift from *AD₀* to *AD₁*.

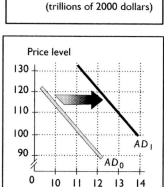

1c. When the government cuts its taxes, house-

holds' incomes rise and so they increase their consumption expenditure. Aggregate demand increases and the aggregate demand curve shifts rightward, as illustrated in the previous answer.

■ Self Test 19.3

Fill in the blanks

An increase in the price level ____ (decreases; increases) the quantity of real GDP demanded and a ____ (movement along; shift of) the aggregate demand curve occurs. An increase in expected future income shifts the *AD* curve ____ (leftward; rightward). A tax cut shifts the *AD* curve ____ (leftward; rightward). A decrease in foreign income shifts the *AD* curve ____ (leftward; rightward).

True or false

1. As the price level falls, other things remaining the same, the quantity of real GDP demanded increases.
2. An increase in expected future income will not increase aggregate demand until the income actually increases.
3. A decrease in government expenditure shifts the aggregate demand curve rightward.
4. An increase in income in Mexico decreases aggregate demand in the United States because Mexicans will buy more Mexican-produced goods.

Multiple choice

1. When the price level rises there is a ____ the aggregate demand curve.
   a. rightward shift of
   b. movement down along
   c. leftward shift of
   d. movement up along
   e. rotation of

2. A rise in the price level
   a. raises the buying power of money.
   b. decreases the prices of exports.
   c. lowers the buying power of money.
   d. increases aggregate demand.
   e. makes the aggregate demand curve steeper.

3. When the price level rises, the real interest rate ____ and the quantity of real GDP demanded ____.
   a. rises; increases
   b. rises; decreases
   c. falls; increases
   d. falls; decreases
   e. does not change; does not change

■ **FIGURE 19.6**

Price level (GDP deflator, 2000 = 100)

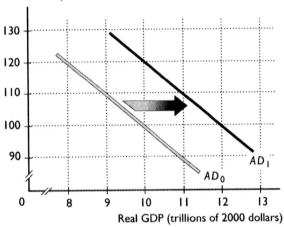

4. In Figure 19.6, the shift in the aggregate demand curve could be the result of
   a. an increase in the quantity of money
   b. a decrease in foreign incomes.
   c. a tax hike.
   d. a fall in the price level.
   e. a decrease in the expected future rate of profit.

5. A change in any of the following factors <u>EXCEPT</u> ____ shifts the aggregate demand curve.
   a. expectations about the future
   b. the money wage rate
   c. monetary and fiscal policy
   d. foreign income
   e. the foreign exchange rate

6. Which of the following shifts the aggregate demand curve leftward?
   a. a decrease in government expenditures on goods and services
   b. an increase in the price level
   c. a tax cut
   d. an increase in foreign income
   e. a decrease in the price level

7. When investment increases, the ____ in aggregate demand is ____ the change in investment.
   a. increase; greater than
   b. increase; smaller than
   c. increase; the same as
   d. decrease; the same as
   e. decrease; greater than

Complete the graph

■ **FIGURE 19.7**

Price level (GDP deflator, 2000 = 100)

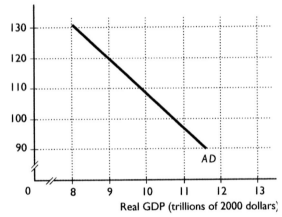

1. Figure 19.7 shows an aggregate demand curve.
   a. Suppose that government expenditure on goods and services increase. In Figure 19.7, illustrate the effect of this fiscal policy.
   b. Suppose the Federal Reserve decreases the quantity of money. In Figure 19.7, illustrate the effect of this monetary policy.

Short answer and numeric questions

1. Why does an increase in the price level decrease the quantity of real GDP demanded?

2. Expected future profit increases. Explain the effect on aggregate demand.

3. The government increases its taxes. What is the effect on aggregate demand?

4. What is the aggregate demand multiplier?

CHECKPOINT 19.4

■ **Explain how fluctuations in aggregate demand and aggregate supply create the business cycle.**

Quick Review

• *Effect of decrease in aggregate demand* A decrease in aggregate demand, everything else remaining the same, lowers the price level and decreases real GDP.

• *Effect of decrease in aggregate supply* A decrease in aggregate supply, everything else remaining the same, raises the price level and decreases real GDP.

Additional Practice Problem 19.4

1. The table shows aggregate demand and aggregate supply schedules for the United Kingdom.

Price level (GDP deflator)	Real GDP demanded	Real GDP supplied
	(billions of 1995 pounds)	
90	800	650
100	775	700
110	750	750
120	725	800
130	700	850

    a. Plot the aggregate demand curve.

    b. Plot the aggregate supply curve.

    c. What is the macroeconomic equilibrium?

    d. If potential GDP in the United Kingdom is £800 billion, what is the type of macroeconomic equilibrium?

    e. If the government increases its expenditures on goods and services, what is the effect on the British economy?

Solution to Additional Practice Problems 19.4

1a. The aggregate demand curve is plotted in the figure to the right. The aggregate demand curve has a negative slope, so as the price level falls, the quantity of real GDP demanded increases.

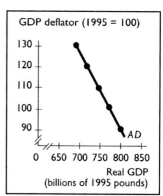

1b. The aggregate supply curve is plotted in the figure. The aggregate supply curve has a positive slope, so as the price level rises, the quantity of real GDP supplied increases.

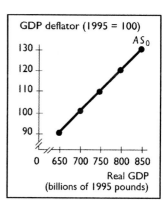

1c. The macroeconomic equilibrium is at a price level of 110 and real GDP of £750 billion. The macroeconomic equilibrium is at the intersection of the aggregate supply curve and the aggregate demand curve.

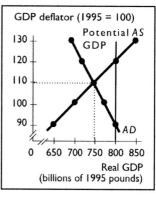

1d. Because potential GDP is £800 billion and the macroeconomic equilibrium is £750 billion, the economy is in a below full-employment equilibrium. Real GDP is less than potential GDP.

1e. If the government increases its expenditures on goods and services, the aggregate demand curve shifts rightward. As a result, the price level rises and real GDP increases, moving the nation closer to a full-employment equilibrium.

■ Self Test 19.4

Fill in the blanks

An increase in aggregate demand ____ (decreases; increases) real GDP. An increase in aggregate supply ____ (lowers; raises) the price level. Stagflation is a combination of ____ (expansion; recession) and a ____ (falling; rising) price level. When real GDP exceeds potential GDP, ____ (an inflationary; a recessionary) gap exists. When potential GDP exceeds real GDP, ____ (an inflationary; a recessionary) gap exists.

True or false

1. Starting from full employment, an increase in aggregate demand increases real GDP above potential GDP.

2. Starting from full employment, a decrease in aggregate demand shifts the aggregate demand curve leftward and creates an inflationary gap.

3. Starting from full employment, an increase in aggregate demand shifts the aggregate demand curve rightward and creates an inflationary gap.

4. A recessionary gap brings a rising price level to eliminate the gap.

Multiple choice

1. If the quantity of real GDP supplied equals the quantity of real GDP demanded, then
   a. nominal GDP must equal real GDP.
   b. real GDP must equal potential GDP.
   c. real GDP must be greater than potential GDP.
   d. real GDP might be greater than, equal to, or less than potential GDP.
   e. real GDP must be less than potential GDP.

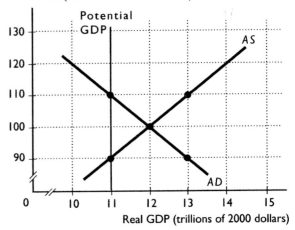

■ **FIGURE 19.8**

Price level (GDP deflator, 2000 = 100)

2. In Figure 19.8, the equilibrium price level is ____ and the equilibrium real GDP is ____ trillion.
   a. 110; $11
   b. 110; $13
   c. 100; $12
   d. 90; $11
   e. 90; $13

3. Figure 19.8 shows
   a. a full-employment equilibrium.
   b. an above full-employment equilibrium with an inflationary gap.
   c. an above full-employment equilibrium with a recessionary gap.
   d. a below full-employment equilibrium with an inflationary gap.
   e. a below full-employment equilibrium with a recessionary gap.

4. An increase in investment ____ aggregate demand, the aggregate demand curve shifts ____ and the economy is in the ____ phase of the business cycle.
   a. decreases; rightward; expansion
   b. increases; rightward; expansion
   c. decreases; leftward; recession
   d. increases; rightward; recession
   e. increases; leftward; recession

5. If the price of oil rises, the
   a. *AD* curve shifts rightward, real GDP increases, and the price level rises.
   b. *AS* curve shifts leftward, the price level rises, and real GDP decreases.
   c. *AD* curve and the *AS* curve shift leftward, real GDP decreases, and the price level rises.
   d. *AD* curve and the *AS* curve shift rightward, the price level rises, and real GDP decreases.
   e. *AS* curve shifts leftward, the price level rises, and real GDP increases.

6. Stagflation is a combination of ____ real GDP and a ____ price level.
   a. increasing; rising
   b. increasing; falling
   c. decreasing; rising
   d. decreasing; falling
   e. no change in; rising

7. An inflationary gap is created when
   a. real GDP is greater than potential GDP.
   b. real GDP equal to potential GDP.
   c. the inflation rate is less than potential inflation.
   d. the price level exceeds the equilibrium price level.
   e. potential GDP is greater than real GDP.

8. An economy is at full employment. If aggregate demand increases,
   a. an inflationary gap is created and the *AS* curve shifts leftward as the money wage rate rises.
   b. an inflationary gap is created and the *AD* curve shifts leftward.
   c. an inflationary gap is created and potential GDP increases to close the gap.
   d. a recessionary gap is created and the *AS* curve shifts leftward as the money wage rate falls.
   e. a recessionary gap is created and the *AS* curve shifts leftward as the money wage rate rises.

Complete the graph

■ **FIGURE 19.9**

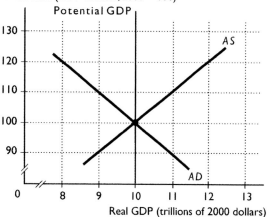

1. Figure 19.9 shows an economy. Suppose there is an increase in the future expected rate of profit.
   a. In Figure 19.9, show the effect of the change in expectations on the price level and real GDP.
   b. In Figure 19.9, show how the economy returns to potential GDP.

■ **FIGURE 19.10**

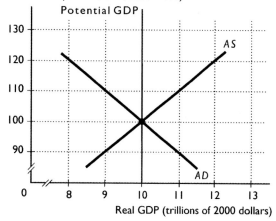

2. Figure 19.10 shows an economy. Show the effect a rise in the price of oil has on the price level and real GDP.

Short answer and numeric questions

1. What is stagflation? What can create stagflation?

2. What is an inflationary gap and how is it eliminated?

3. What factor leads to persisting inflation?

4. The Eye on Your Life on page 769 discussed some of the uses you can make of the *AS-AD* model. Another use lies in the political arena. For instance, if a politician is running a campaign in which he or she suggests raising taxes, using the *AS-AD* model, what do you expect will happen to real GDP if this campaign promise is carried out?

SELF TEST ANSWERS

■ CHECKPOINT 19.1

Fill in the blanks

A business cycle moves from an expansion to a <u>peak</u>, then to a <u>recession</u>, and then to a <u>trough</u>. A decrease in real GDP that lasts for at least two quarters is a <u>recession</u>. In the United States since 1854, the average length of an expansion is <u>35</u> months and the average length of a recession is <u>18</u> months. During the years since World War II the average expansion has <u>lengthened</u> and the average recession has <u>shortened</u>.

True or false

1. False; page 502
2. False; page 502
3. False; page 502
4. True; pages 504-505

Multiple choice

1. b; page 502
2. a; page 502
3. b; page 502
4. c; page 502
5. c; page 502
6. a; page 503

Complete the graph

■ FIGURE 19.11

Real GDP (trillions of 2000 dollars)

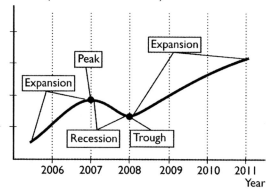

1. Figure 19.11 divides the data into the two phases and the two turning points of the business cycle; page 502.

2. A recession runs from the third quarter of 2004 to the second quarter of 2005 and from the first quarter of 2006 to the third quarter of 2006; page 502.

Short answer and numeric questions

1. The standard definition of a recession is a decrease in real GDP that lasts for at least two quarters (six months); page 502.
2. Since World War II, the average expansion has lengthened and the average recession has shortened; page 503.

■ CHECKPOINT 19.2

Fill in the blanks

Moving along the aggregate supply curve, as the price level rises, the quantity of real GDP supplied <u>increases</u> because the real wage rate <u>falls</u>. Moving along the potential GDP line, the money wage rate <u>does not change</u> when the price level changes. When potential GDP increases, a <u>shift of</u> the *AS* curve occurs. When the money wage rate changes, a <u>shift of</u> the *AS* curve occurs.

True or false

1. False; pages 508-509
2. False; pages 508-509
3. True; page 511
4. True; page 511

Multiple choice

1. c; pages 508-509
2. a; page 509
3. d; pages 508-509
4. a; page 510
5. e; page 512
6 a; page 511
7. c; page 512

Complete the graph

■ **FIGURE 19.12**

Price level (GDP deflator, 2000 = 100)

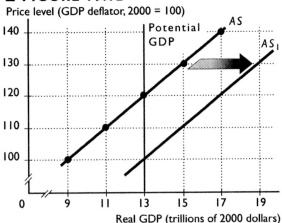

1. a. Figure 19.12 labels the axes. The aggregate supply curve is labeled *AS*; page 509.
   b. The fall in the money wage rate has no effect on potential GDP, so the potential GDP line does not change. Aggregate supply, however, increases so the *AS* curve shifts rightward, to an *AS* curve such as *AS₁*; page 512.

■ **FIGURE 19.13**

Price level (GDP deflator, 2000 = 100)

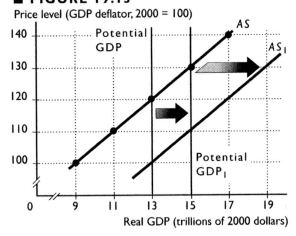

   c. Figure 19.13 labels the axes. The aggregate supply curve is labeled *AS*; page 509.
   d. The potential GDP line shifts rightward by $2 trillion, as indicated by the shift to Potential GDP₁. The aggregate supply curve also shifts rightward by $2 trillion, as shown by the shift to *AS₁*; page 511.

Short answer and numeric questions

1. The movement along the *AS* curve brings a change in the real wage rate (and changes in the real cost of other resources whose money prices are fixed). If the price level rises, the real wage rate falls.

   A fall in the real wage rate boosts a firm's profit. The number of firms in business increases.

   If the price level rises relative to costs, fewer firms will want to shut down, so more firms operate.

   If the price level rises and the money wage rate does not change, an extra hour of labor that was previously unprofitable becomes profitable. So, the quantity of labor demanded increases and production increases.

   For the economy as a whole, as the price level rises, the quantity of real GDP supplied increases; pages 509-511.

2. An increase in the money wage rate increases firms' costs. The higher are firms' costs, the smaller is the quantity that firms are willing to supply at each price level. Aggregate supply decreases and the *AS* curve shifts leftward. A change in the money wage rate does not change potential GDP. Potential GDP depends only on the economy's real ability to produce and on the full-employment quantity of labor, which occurs at the equilibrium real wage rate. The equilibrium real wage rate can occur at any money wage rate; page 512.

3. If the money price of oil rises, firm's costs increase. The higher are firms' costs, the smaller is the quantity that firms are willing to supply at each price level. Aggregate supply decreases and the aggregate supply curve shifts leftward; page 512.

■ **CHECKPOINT 19.3**

Fill in the blanks

An increase in the price level <u>decreases</u> the quantity of real GDP demanded and a <u>movement along</u> the aggregate demand curve occurs.

An increase in expected future income shifts the *AD* curve <u>rightward</u>. A tax cut shifts the *AD* curve <u>rightward</u>. A decrease in foreign income shifts the *AD* curve <u>leftward</u>.

True or false

1. True; page 514
2. False; page 516
3. False; page 517
4. False; pages 517-518

Multiple choice

1. d; page 515
2. c; pages 514-515
3. b; page 515
4. a; page 517
5. b; paged 516-518
6. a; pages 516-518
7. a; page 518

Complete the graph

■ FIGURE 19.14

Price level (GDP deflator, 2000 = 100)

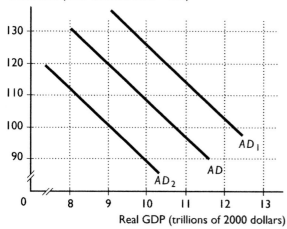

1. a. In Figure 19.14, an increase in government purchases increases aggregate demand and shifts the *AD* curve rightward, from *AD* to *AD₁*; page 517.

   b. In Figure 19.14, a decrease in the quantity of money decreases aggregate demand and shifts the *AD* curve leftward, from *AD* to *AD₂*; page 517.

Short answer and numeric questions

1. An increase in the price level decreases the quantity of real GDP demanded because an increase in the price level lowers the buying power of money, raises the real interest rate, raises the real prices of exports, and lowers the real price of imports; pages 514-516.

2. An increase in expected future profit increases the investment that firms plan to undertake and increases aggregate demand; page 516.

3. The government can influence aggregate demand by changing taxes. When the government increases taxes, aggregate demand decreases; page 517.

4. The aggregate demand multiplier is an effect that magnifies changes in expenditure and increases fluctuations in aggregate demand. For example, an increase in investment increases aggregate demand and increases income. The increase in income induces an increase in consumption expenditure so aggregate demand increases by more than the initial increase in investment; page 518.

■ CHECKPOINT 19.4

Fill in the blanks

An increase in aggregate demand <u>increases</u> real GDP. An increase in aggregate supply <u>lowers</u> the price level. Stagflation is a combination of <u>recession</u> and a <u>rising</u> price level. When real GDP exceeds potential GDP, <u>an inflationary</u> gap exists. When potential GDP exceeds real GDP, <u>a recessionary</u> gap exists.

True or false

1. True; pages 520-521
2. False; pages 520-521, 524
3. True; pages 520-521, 524
4. False; page 524

Multiple choice

1. d; page 520
2. c; page 520
3. b; pages 520-521, 524

4. b; pages 520-521
5. b; page 522-523
6. c; page 522
7. a; page 524
8. a; page 524

Complete the graph

■ **FIGURE 19.15**

Price level (GDP deflator, 2000 = 100)

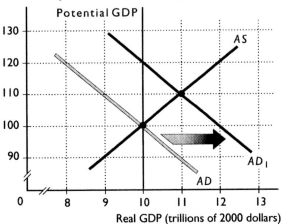

1. a. An increase in expected rate of profit increases firms' investment which increases aggregate demand. The aggregate demand curve shifts rightward from *AD* to *AD*1 in Figure 19.15. The equilibrium price level rises to 110 and equilibrium real GDP increases to $11 trillion; pages 520-522.

   b. An inflationary gap now exists. The money wage rate rises and aggregate supply decreases. In Figure 19.16 (at the top of the next column), the *AS* curve shifts leftward. Eventually the *AS* curve moves to *AS*1. Real GDP returns to potential GDP, $10 trillion, and the price level rises to 120; page 524.

■ **FIGURE 19.16**

Price level (GDP deflator, 2000 = 100)

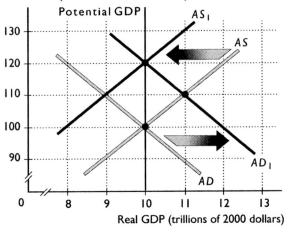

■ **FIGURE 19.17**

Price level (GDP deflator, 2000 = 100)

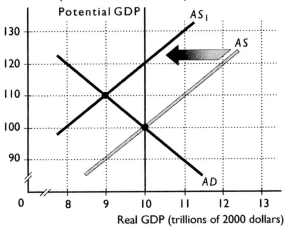

2. Figure 19.17 shows the effect of a rise in the price of oil. Aggregate supply decreases and the *AS* curve shifts leftward from *AS* to *AS*1. Real GDP decreases to $9 trillion and the price level rises to 110; page 522.

Short answer and numeric questions

1. Stagflation is a combination of recession (falling real GDP) and inflation (rising price level). Stagflation can be created by a decrease in aggregate supply; page 522.

2. An inflationary gap is a gap that exists when real GDP exceeds potential GDP. An inflationary gap brings a rising price level. Workers have experienced a fall in the buying power of their wages, and firms' profits have increased. Employment exceeds full employment. Workers demand higher wages. As the money wage rate rises, aggregate supply decreases and the aggregate supply curve shifts leftward. Eventually, real GDP will return to potential GDP and the inflationary gap is eliminated; page 524.

3. Persistent inflation is the result of persisting increases in aggregate demand that exceed increases in aggregate supply. The factor that creates persistent increases in aggregate is a growing quantity of money. So, ultimately persistent inflation is brought about by growth in the quantity of money; page 524.

4. If the politician is elected and, as a result, taxes are raised, then aggregate demand decreases and the *AD* curve shifts leftward. As a result, real GDP decreases.

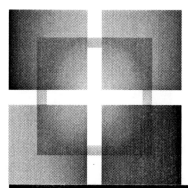

Fiscal Policy and Monetary Policy

Chapter 20

Chapter 20 provides a description of both fiscal and monetary processes and policies. On the fiscal side, fiscal policies are identified and illustrated using the *AD-AS* model. On the monetary side, how monetary policy affects the economy is discussed, and then the *AD-AS* model is used to illustrate monetary policy. The limits to both fiscal and monetary policy are examined.

■ Describe the federal budget process and explain the effects of fiscal policy.

The federal budget is an annual statement of the expenditures, tax receipts, and surplus or deficit of the U. S. government. If tax receipts exceed expenditures, the government has a budget surplus and if expenditures exceed tax receipts, the government has a budget deficit. Fiscal policy can be discretionary, which is policy initiated by an act of Congress, or automatic, which is policy that is triggered by the state of the economy. The government expenditure multiplier and the tax multiplier show that aggregate demand changes by more than an initiating change in government expenditures or taxes. With a recessionary gap, when real GDP is less than potential GDP, expansionary fiscal policy, an increase in government expenditures or a tax cut, can move the economy to potential GDP. If real GDP is greater than potential GDP, contractionary fiscal policy, a decrease in government expenditures or a tax hike, can move the economy to potential GDP. A cut in taxes or an increase in government expenditures on productive services also have supply-side effects that increase potential GDP and aggregate supply. The use of discretionary fiscal policy is hampered by law-making time lags, by estimating potential GDP, and by economic forecasting. Automatic stabilizers are features of fiscal policy, such as induced taxes and needs-tested spending, that stabilize real GDP without action by the government.

② Describe the Federal Reserve's monetary policy process and explain the effects of monetary policy.

Monetary policy is determined by the Federal Open Market Committee (FOMC) which sets its federal funds interest rate target. When the Fed raises the federal funds target, the Fed sells securities, which decreases commercial banks' reserves. As a result: other interest rates rise, the exchange rate rises, and the quantity of money decreases, so that consumption expenditure, investment, and net exports all decrease. In turn, aggregate demand decreases, which decreases real GDP and lowers the price level. The opposite effects occur if the Fed lowers its federal funds target. To fight inflation, the Fed sells securities. Aggregate demand decreases with a multiplied effect and the *AD* curve shifts leftward so that real GDP and the price level both decrease. If the Fed is worried about recession, it purchases securities, which lowers the interest rate. Aggregate demand increases, again with a multiplied effect, and real GDP and the price level both increase. Monetary policy has no law-making lag, but estimating potential GDP is hard and economic forecasting is error prone. Monetary policy also has the drawback that it depends on how private decision makers respond to a change in the interest rate.

CHECKPOINT 20.1

■ **Describe the federal budget process and explain the effects of fiscal policy.**

Quick Review

- *Discretionary fiscal policy* Fiscal policy action that is initiated by an act of Congress.
- *Automatic fiscal policy* Fiscal policy that is triggered by the state of the economy.
- *Government expenditure multiplier* The magnification effect of a change in government expenditures on aggregate demand.
- *Tax multiplier* The magnification effect of a change in taxes on aggregate demand.

Additional Practice Problems 20.1

1. The figure shows the U.S. economy in 2011.

   a. What is the equilibrium price level and real GDP?

   b. Is there an inflationary gap or a recessionary gap?

   GDP deflator (2000 = 100)

   Potential GDP   AS

   130
   120
   110
   100
   90

   0   14   15   16   17   18

   AD

   Real GDP
   (trillions of 2000 dollars)

   c. Should the government use an expansionary or contractionary fiscal policy to move the economy to potential GDP? What sorts of fiscal policies might be used?

   d. In the figure, show the effect of these policies after real GDP equals potential GDP. What is the new equilibrium price level and real GDP? (Ignore any supply-side effects from the policy.)

2. What is the balanced budget multiplier and why is it greater than zero?

Solutions to Additional Practice Problems 20.1

1a. The equilibrium price level and real GDP are determined by the intersection of the aggregate demand, *AD*, curve and the aggregate supply, *AS*, curve. The figure shows that the equilibrium price is 110 and the equilibrium quantity of real GDP is $16 trillion.

1b. Real GDP of $16 trillion exceeds potential GDP of $15 trillion, so there is an inflationary gap.

1c. In order to close the inflationary gap, the government must use contractionary fiscal policy. A contractionary fiscal policy will "contract" real GDP so that it equals potential GDP. Contractionary fiscal policy includes an increase in taxes and/or a decrease in government expenditures.

1d. The figure shows the effect of the contractionary fiscal policy. Both an increase in taxes or a decrease in government expenditure decrease aggregate demand. The aggregate demand curve shifts leftward, from AD_0 to AD_1 in the figure. As a result, the price level falls from 110 to 100 and real GDP decreases from $16 trillion back to potential GDP of $15 trillion. The inflationary gap is eliminated.

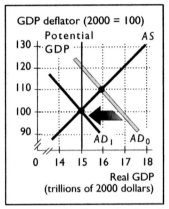

GDP deflator (2000 = 100)

Potential GDP   AS

130
120
110
100
90

0   14   15   16   17   18

AD_1 AD_0

Real GDP
(trillions of 2000 dollars)

2. The balanced budget multiplier is the magnification effect on aggregate demand of *simultaneous* changes in government expenditures and taxes that leave the budget balance unchanged. The balanced budget multiplier is not zero—it is positive—because the size of the government expenditure multiplier is larger than the size of the tax multiplier. That is, a $1 increase in government expenditures increases aggregate demand by more than a $1 increase in taxes decreases aggregate demand. So when both government expenditures and taxes increase by $1, aggregate demand still increases.

■ Self Test 20.1

Fill in the blanks

The national debt is ____ (tax receipts minus expenditures; the amount of debt outstanding that arises from past budget deficits). ____ (Automatic; Discretionary) fiscal policy is a fiscal policy action that is initiated by an act of Congress; ____ (automatic; discretionary) fiscal policy is a fiscal policy action triggered by the state of the economy. The government expenditures multiplier is the magnification of a change in government expenditures on aggregate ____ (demand; supply). A tax cut ____ (increases; decreases) aggregate supply and shifts the *AS* curve ____ (rightward; leftward). One limitation of discretionary fiscal policy is the ____ (needs-tested lag; law-making time lag).

True or false

1. Other things the same, a tax cut decreases the national debt.

2. The 2002 Bush tax cut package approved by Congress in 2002 is an example of discretionary fiscal policy.

3. The government expenditure multiplier is the magnification effect that a change in aggregate demand has on government expenditures on goods and services.

4. The magnitude of the tax multiplier is smaller than the government expenditure multiplier.

5. If government expenditures and taxes increase by the same amount, aggregate demand does not change.

6. To eliminate an inflationary gap, the government could decrease its expenditures on goods and services.

7. A tax cut increases aggregate supply but does not increase aggregate demand, so it increases real GDP and lowers the price level.

8. Automatic stabilizers are features of fiscal policy that work to stabilize real GDP without explicit action by the government.

Multiple choice

1. The annual statement of the expenditures, tax receipts, and surplus or deficit of the government of the United States is the federal
   a. surplus record.
   b. deficit record.
   c. budget.
   d. spending.
   e. debt to the public.

2. When government expenditures are less than tax receipts, the government has
   a. a budget with a positive balance.
   b. a budget deficit.
   c. a budget surplus.
   d. a budget with a negative debt.
   e. an illegal budget because expenditures must exceed tax receipts.

3. National debt decreases in a given year when a country has
   a. a budget deficit.
   b. a balanced budget.
   c. a budget supplement.
   d. a budget surplus.
   e. no discretionary fiscal policy.

4. Discretionary fiscal policy is a fiscal policy action, such as
   a. an interest rate cut, initiated by an act of Congress.
   b. an increase in payments to the unemployed, initiated by the state of the economy.
   c. a tax cut, initiated by an act of Congress.
   d. a decrease in tax receipts, initiated by the state of the economy.
   e. an increase in the quantity of money.

5. An example of automatic fiscal policy is
   a. an interest rate cut, initiated by an act of Congress.
   b. an increase in the quantity of money.
   c. a tax cut, initiated by an act of Congress.
   d. a decrease in tax receipts, triggered by the state of the economy.
   e. any change in the interest rate, regardless of its cause.

6. The government expenditure multiplier is the magnification effect of a change in government expenditures on
    a. aggregate demand.
    b. the budget deficit.
    c. tax receipts.
    d. aggregate supply.
    e. potential GDP.

7. The magnitude of the tax multiplier is ____ the magnitude of the government expenditure multiplier.
    a. equal to
    b. greater than
    c. smaller than
    d. the inverse of
    e. exactly one half

8. An example of expansionary fiscal policy is
    a. increasing the quantity of money.
    b. lowering the interest rate.
    c. decreasing government expenditure.
    d. decreasing needs-tested spending.
    e. cutting taxes.

9. Discretionary fiscal policy works to close a recessionary gap by shifting the
    a. *AD* curve leftward.
    b. *AS* curve leftward.
    c. *AD* curve leftward and the *AS* curve leftward.
    d. *AD* curve rightward.
    e. potential GDP line leftward.

10. If the economy is at an above full-employment equilibrium, ____ gap exists and discretionary fiscal policy that ____ will return real GDP to potential GDP.
    a. an inflationary; increases aggregate demand
    b. an inflationary; decreases aggregate demand
    c. a recessionary; increases aggregate supply
    d. a recessionary; decreases aggregate supply
    e. a recessionary; decreases aggregate demand

■ **FIGURE 20.1**

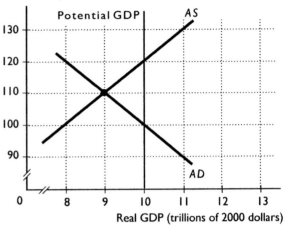

Price level (GDP deflator, 2000 = 100)

11. The figure above shows an economy with ____ gap and a fiscal policy that can eliminate this gap is ____.
    a. an inflationary; an increase in government expenditures
    b. an inflationary; a tax hike
    c. a recessionary; an increase in the quantity of money
    d. a recessionary; a tax hike
    e. a recessionary; an increase in government expenditures

12. The supply-side effects of a tax cut ____ potential GDP and ____ aggregate supply.
    a. increase; increase
    b. increase; decrease
    c. decrease; increase
    d. decrease; decrease
    e. increases; does not change

13. If a tax cut increases aggregate demand more than aggregate supply, real GDP ____ and the price level ____.
    a. increases; rises
    b. increases; falls
    c. decreases; rises
    d. decreases; falls
    e. increases; does not change

14. Discretionary fiscal policy is handicapped by
    a. law-making time lags, induced taxes, and automatic stabilizers.
    b. law-making time lags, estimation of potential GDP, and economic forecasting.
    c. economic forecasting, law-making time lags, and induced taxes.
    d. automatic stabilizers, law-making time lags, and potential GDP estimation.
    e. automatic stabilizers, the multipliers, and potential GDP estimation.

Complete the graph

■ FIGURE 20.2
Price level (GDP deflator, 2000 = 100)

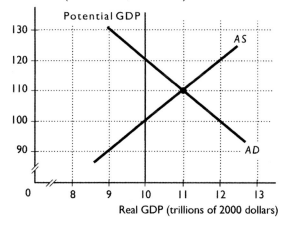

1. Figure 20.2 illustrates the economy.
   a. Is there an inflationary gap or a recessionary gap present?
   b. What type of fiscal policy might be used to restore the economy to full employment?
   c. Ignoring any supply-side effects, in Figure 20.2, illustrate the effect of the policy you suggested in your answer to part (b).

2. Figure 20.3 illustrates the economy. Potential GDP is $11 trillion. Suppose that the government cuts its taxes and that the supply-side effects are larger than the demand-side effects. If the economy moves back to potential GDP, in Figure 20.3, illustrate the effect of this government policy.

■ FIGURE 20.3
Price level (GDP deflator, 2000 = 100)

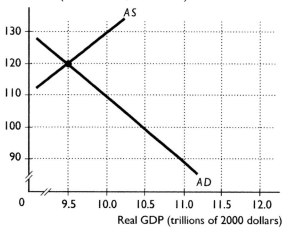

Short answer and numeric questions

1. What happens to the national debt if the government has a $100 billion budget deficit?

2. How can the government use fiscal policy to eliminate a recessionary gap?

3. What are the demand-side effects of a tax cut? What are the supply-side effects? Why does a tax cut have supply-side effects?

4. It is not easy to determine potential GDP. Why does this fact hamper the use of discretionary fiscal policy?

5. What are automatic stabilizers? Can they eliminate a recession?

CHECKPOINT 20.2

■ Describe the Federal Reserve's monetary policy process and explain the effects of monetary policy.

Quick Review
- *Ripple effects from monetary policy* When the Fed increases the federal funds rate, other events follow: the quantity of money and amount of loans decrease; other interest rates rise, which decreases the consumption expenditure and in-

vestment; the foreign exchange rate rises, which decreases net exports; aggregate demand decreases because of the initial decreases in consumption expenditure, investment, and net exports; a multiplier effect induces a further decrease in aggregate demand; the price level falls and real GDP rises.

Additional Practice Problems 20.2

1. If the Fed lowers the federal funds rate, explain how each of the following items changes:
   a. Businesses' investment
   b. Households' purchases of new cars and houses
   c. The price of the dollar on foreign exchange markets

2. The figure shows the U.S. economy in 2011.

   GDP deflator (2000 = 100)

   130 Potential GDP   AS
   120
   110
   100
   90
        AD
   0   14 15 16 17 18
           Real GDP
   (trillions of 2000 dollars)

   a. Will the Fed fear inflation or recession?
   b. What policy should the Fed undertake to avoid what it fears?
   c. In the figure, illustrate the effect of the Fed's policy.
   d. How does this set of answers compare to the answers of Additional Practice Problem 1 in Checkpoint 20.1?

3. What is an advantage that monetary policy has over fiscal policy?

Solutions to Additional Practice Problems 20.2

1a. A decrease in the federal funds rate lowers others interest rates. The interest rate is the opportunity cost of the funds used to finance investment. When the opportunity cost of investment decreases, businesses increase their purchases of new capital equipment or, in other words, investment increases.

1b. A decrease in the federal funds rate lowers others interest rates. The interest rate is the opportunity cost of the funds used to finance

the purchase of big-ticket consumer items. When the opportunity cost falls, households increase their purchases of new cars and houses.

1c. When the interest rate in the United States falls relative to the interest rate in other countries, people sell dollars and buy other currencies. With fewer dollars demanded and more dollars supplied, the price of the dollar falls on the foreign exchange market.

2a. There is an inflationary gap in the figure and so the Fed fears inflation.

2b. In order to eliminate the potential for inflation, the Fed should decrease the quantity of money. Decreasing the quantity of money decreases aggregate demand and thereby lowers the price level and decreases real GDP, which eliminates the possibility of inflation.

2c. The figure shows the effect of the monetary policy. A decrease in the quantity of money raises the interest rate, which, in turn, decreases consumption expenditure,

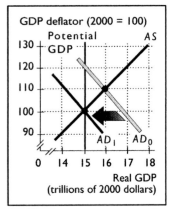

GDP deflator (2000 = 100)

130 Potential GDP   AS
120
110
100
90
        AD₁   AD₀
0   14 15 16 17 18
           Real GDP
   (trillions of 2000 dollars)

investment, and net exports. Aggregate demand decreases and the aggregate demand curve shifts leftward, from AD_0 to AD_1 in the figure. As a result, the price level falls from 110 to 100 and real GDP decreases from $16 trillion back to potential GDP of $15 trillion.

2d. The answers are very similar insofar as in both instances the correct policy was a contractionary policy. Both the contractionary fiscal policy in the earlier Practice Problem and the similarly contractionary monetary policy in this Practice Problem decrease aggregate demand and shift the AD cure leftward.

3. Monetary policy has an advantage over fiscal policy because it cuts out the law-making time lags. The FOMC meets eight times a year and can conduct telephone meetings between its scheduled meetings. And the actual actions that change the quantity of money are daily actions taken by the New York Fed operating under the guidelines decided by the FOMC. So monetary policy is a continuous policy process and is not subject to a long decision lag.

■ Self Test 20.2

Fill in the blanks

The Beige Book is a ____ (book that outlines the Fed's current monetary policy; report summarizing economic conditions). To raise the interest rate, the FOMC instructs the New York Fed to ____ (purchase; sell) securities in the open market. When the interest rate rises, investment and consumption expenditure ____ (increase; decrease) and net exports ____ (increase; decrease). When the Fed eases to fight recession, the aggregate ____ (demand; supply) curve shifts ____ (leftward; rightward).

True or false

1. The FOMC meets once a year in January to determine the nation's monetary policy.

2. A change in the federal funds rate changes net exports.

3. If the Fed's monetary policy raises the federal funds rate, aggregate demand decreases.

4. The Fed's monetary policy works by changing aggregate supply.

5. To combat a recession, the Fed lowers taxes, which increases aggregate demand and shifts the aggregate demand curve rightward.

6. If the Fed fears a recession, it lowers the federal funds rate.

7. Monetary policy is a perfect stabilization tool because it does not have law-making time lags.

Multiple choice

1. The FOMC is the
   a. report the Fed gives to Congress twice a year.
   b. group within the Fed that makes the monetary policy decisions.
   c. report that summarizes the economy across Fed districts.
   d. name of the meeting the Fed has with Congress twice a year.
   e. interest rate the Fed most directly influences.

2. The Fed affects aggregate demand through monetary policy by changing
   a. the federal funds rate and the quantity of reserves.
   b. tax rates and influencing disposable income.
   c. the quantity of reserves and determining government expenditure.
   d. government expenditures and so influencing the budget balance.
   e. tax rates on only interest income and so influencing disposable income.

3. If the Fed sells government securities, other interest rates ____ and the exchange rate ____.
   a. rise; rises
   b. do not change; rises
   c. fall; falls
   d. rise; does not change
   e. rise; falls

4. If the Fed decreases the federal funds rate, which of the following occurs?
   a. Investment increases.
   b. Consumption expenditure decreases.
   c. The price of the dollar on the foreign exchange market increases.
   d. Net exports decreases.
   e. Government expenditures on goods and services increases.

5. If the Fed increases the federal funds rate, which of the following occur?
   a. The price of the dollar on the foreign exchange market increases.
   b. Investment increases.
   c. Aggregate demand increases.
   d. Net exports increases.
   e. Consumption expenditure increases.

6. The Fed increases the federal funds rate when it
   a. fears recession.
   b. wants to increase the quantity of money.
   c. fears inflation.
   d. wants to encourage bank lending.
   e. cannot change the quantity of money.

7. Raising the federal funds rate shifts the aggregate demand curve ____, so that real GDP ____ and the price level ____.
   a. rightward; increases; rises
   b. leftward; decreases; rises
   c. rightward; increases; falls
   d. leftward; decreases; falls
   e. leftward; increases; rises

8. To fight a recession, the Fed can
   a. lower the federal funds rate by buying securities.
   b. lower the federal funds rate by selling securities.
   c. raise the federal funds rate by buying securities.
   d. raise the federal funds rate by selling securities.
   e. lower income taxes on interest income.

9. When the economy is in a recession, the Fed can ____ the federal funds interest rate, which ____ aggregate demand and ____ real GDP.
   a. lower; increases; decreases
   b. raise; decreases; increases
   c. lower; increases; increases
   d. raise; increases; decreases
   e. lower; decreases; decreases

10. An advantage monetary policy has over fiscal policy is that monetary policy
    a. can be quickly changed and implemented.
    b. is coordinated with fiscal policy.
    c. is approved by the president of the United States.
    d. affects consumption expenditure and investment without impacting international trade.
    e. has no multiplier effects.

Complete the graph

■ **FIGURE 20.4**

Price level (GDP deflator, 2000 = 100)

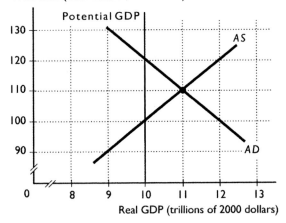

1. Figure 20.4 illustrates the economy.
   a. What type of monetary policy is used to restore the economy to full employment?
   b. In Figure 20.4, illustrate the effect of the policy you suggested in your answer to part (a).
   c. In the Complete the Graph question 1 from Checkpoint 20.1, you answered a similar question about fiscal policy. Compared to using fiscal policy, what is an advantage of using monetary policy to restore the economy to potential GDP? Compared to monetary policy, what is an advantage of using fiscal policy?

Short answer and numeric questions

1. How does the Fed keep the public informed about the state of the economy and its monetary policy decisions?

2. Suppose the Fed increases buys government securities. What is the effect on the federal funds rate? On investment? On aggregate demand?

3. How does monetary policy affect the price of the dollar on the foreign exchange market?

In your answer, explain the case in which the Fed raises the interest rate.

4. Suppose the Fed is concerned that the economy is entering a recession. What policy can the Fed pursue and what is the effect of the policy on real GDP and the price level?

SELF TEST ANSWERS

■ CHECKPOINT 20.1

Fill in the blanks

The national debt is <u>the total amount of debt outstanding that arises from past budget deficits</u>. <u>Discretionary</u> fiscal policy is a fiscal policy action that is initiated by an act of Congress; <u>automatic</u> fiscal policy is a fiscal policy action triggered by the state of the economy. The government expenditure multiplier is the magnification of a change in government expenditures on aggregate <u>demand</u>. A tax cut <u>increases</u> aggregate supply and shifts the *AS* curve <u>rightward</u>. One limitation of discretionary fiscal policy is the <u>law-making time lag</u>.

True or false
1. False; page 532
2. True; page 532
3. False; page 535
4. True; page 535
5. False; page 535
6. True; page 537
7. False; pages 538-540
8. True; page 542

Multiple choice
1. c; page 532
2. c; page 532
3. d; page 532
4. c; page 532
5. d; page 532
6. a; page 535
7. c; page 535
8. e; page 536
9. d; page 536
10. b; page 537
11. e; page 536
12. a; page 538
13. a; page 540
14. b; page 541

Complete the graph
1. a. There is an inflationary gap because real GDP exceeds potential GDP; page 537.

■ FIGURE 20.5
Price level (GDP deflator, 2000 = 100)

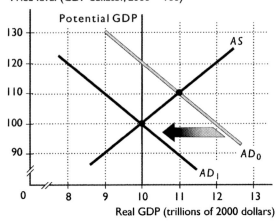

b. The economy will return to full employment with a tax hike or a decrease in government expenditures; page 537.

c. Figure 20.5 shows the results of the suggested policy. Aggregate demand decreases and the *AD* curve shifts leftward from AD_0 to AD_1. Real GDP decreases from $11 trillion to $10 trillion and the price level falls from 110 to 100; page 537.

■ FIGURE 20.6
Price level (GDP deflator, 2000 = 100)

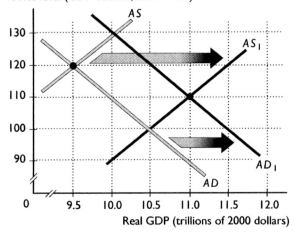

2. The tax cut increases both aggregate demand and aggregate supply, so in Figure 20.6, the aggregate demand curve shifts rightward

from *AD* to *AD*1 and the aggregate supply curve shifts rightward from *AS* to *AS*1. Because the effect on aggregate supply exceeds the effect on aggregate demand, the shift of the *AS* curve is larger than the shift of the *AD* curve. As a result, real GDP increases and the price level falls. The exact fall of the price level depends on the precise sizes of the shifts but in the figure it falls to 100; page 540.

Short answer and numeric questions

1. If the government has a $100 billion budget deficit, the national debt increases by $100 billion; page 532.

2. A recessionary gap exists when real GDP is less than potential GDP. The government can eliminate the recessionary gap by using expansionary fiscal policy to increase aggregate demand. The government can increase aggregate demand by increasing its expenditures on goods and services or by cutting taxes; page 536.

3. A tax cut increases disposable income, which increases consumption expenditure and aggregate demand. A tax cut creates an incentive to work and save. So a tax cut increases the supply of labor and the supply of saving. An increase in the supply of labor increases the equilibrium quantity of labor employed. An increase in the supply of saving increases the equilibrium quantity of investment and capital. With larger quantities of labor and capital, potential GDP increases and so does aggregate supply. So a decrease in taxes increases aggregate supply; pages 538-539.

4. It is not easy to tell whether real GDP is below, above, or at potential GDP. So a discretionary fiscal action can move real GDP *away* from potential GDP instead of toward it; page 542.

5. Automatic stabilizers are features of fiscal policy that stabilize real GDP without explicit action by the government. Automatic stabilizers include induced taxes and needstested spending. Induced taxes and needs-

tested spending decrease the multiplier effect of a change in expenditure. So they moderate both expansions and recessions and make real GDP more stable. But they cannot eliminate a recession; page 542.

■ CHECKPOINT 20.2

Fill in the blanks

The Beige Book is a <u>report summarizing economic conditions</u>. To raise the interest rate, the FOMC instructs the New York Fed to <u>sell</u> securities in the open market. When the interest rate rises, investment and consumption expenditure <u>decrease</u> and net exports <u>decrease</u>. When the Fed eases to fight recession, the aggregate <u>demand</u> curve shifts <u>rightward</u>.

True or false

1. False; page 544
2. True; pages 545-546, 548
3. True; pages 545, 548
4. False; pages 545, 548-550
5. False; page 550
6. True; page 550
7. False; page 551

Multiple choice

1. b; page 544
2. a; page 545
3. a; page 545-546
4. a; pages 545-548
5. a; pages 545-547
6. c; page 549
7. d; page 549
8. a; page 550
9. c; page 550
10. a; page 551

Complete the graph

■ FIGURE 20.7

Price level (GDP deflator, 2000 = 100)

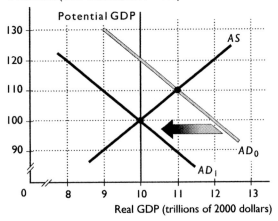

1. a. The economy will return to full employment with an open market sale of government securities that raises the federal funds rate and decreases the quantity of money; page 549.
   b. Figure 20.7 shows the results of the hike in the federal funds rate. Aggregate demand decreases and the AD curve shifts leftward from AD_0 to AD_1. Real GDP decreases from $11 trillion to potential GDP of $10 trillion and the price level falls from 110 to 100; page 549.
   c. The advantage of using monetary policy is that there is no law-making lag. The actions that change the quantity of money and the federal funds rate are taken each day. The advantage of using fiscal policy is that the impact on aggregate demand is direct. The effects of monetary policy are indirect and depend on how private decisions respond to a change in the federal funds rate. These responses are hard to forecast and vary from one situation to another in unpredictable ways; page 551.

Short answer and numeric questions

1. To keep the public informed about the state of the economy, the Fed makes available the Beige Book, which is a report that summarizes the current economic conditions in each Federal Reserve district and each sector of the economy. After each FOMC meeting the FOMC announces its decisions and describes its view of the likelihood that its goals of price stability and sustainable economic growth will be achieved. The minutes of the FOMC meeting are released only after the next meeting. The Fed is required to report twice a year to the House of Representatives Committee on Financial Services, at which time the Fed chairman testifies before the committee; page 544.

2. If the Fed buys government securities, it increases banks' reserves. The federal funds and other interest rates fall and investment increases. Aggregate demand increases because investment increases and because consumption expenditure and net exports also increase; pages 545-546.

3. If the U.S. interest rate rises relative to the interest rate in other countries, some people will want to move funds into the United States from other countries to take advantage of the higher interest rate they can now earn on U.S. bank deposits and bonds. To move money into the United States, people must buy dollars and sell other currencies. With more dollars demanded, the price of the dollar rises on the foreign exchange market; pages 545-547.

4. When the Fed is concerned that the economy is entering a recession, it makes an open market purchase of government securities. Banks' reserves increase and the federal funds rate and other interest rates fall. As a result, investment and consumption expenditure increase. Net exports also increases. Aggregate expenditure increases so the multiplier effect increases aggregate demand by even more than the initial changes. With the increase in aggregate demand, real GDP increases and the price level rises; page 550.